The Devotion of Collecting

Library of the Written Word

VOLUME 110

The Handpress World

Editor-in-Chief

Andrew Pettegree (*University of St. Andrews*)

Editorial Board

Ann Blair (*Harvard University*)
Falk Eisermann (*Staatsbibliothek zu Berlin – Preußischer Kulturbesitz*)
Shanti Graheli (*University of Glasgow*)
Earle Havens (*Johns Hopkins University*)
Ian Maclean (*All Souls College, Oxford*)
Alicia Montoya (*Radboud University*)
Angela Nuovo (*University of Milan*)
Helen Smith (*University of York*)
Mark Towsey (*University of Liverpool*)
Malcolm Walsby (*ENSSIB, Lyon*)
Arthur der Weduwen (*University of St. Andrews*)

VOLUME 89

The titles published in this series are listed at *brill.com/lww*

The Devotion of Collecting

*Dutch Ministers and the Culture of Print
in the Seventeenth Century*

By

Forrest C. Strickland

BRILL

LEIDEN | BOSTON

Cover illustration: Etching of Franciscus Ridderus with his library in the background. Courtesy Rijksmuseum Amsterdam (RP-P-OB-23.811).

Library of Congress Cataloging-in-Publication Data

Names: Strickland, Forrest C., author.
Title: The devotion of collecting : Dutch ministers and the culture of
   print in the seventeenth century / by Forrest C. Strickland.
Description: Leiden ; Boston : Brill, [2023] | Series: Library of the written word, 1874–4834 ; volume 110 |
   Includes bibliographical references and index. | Summary: "The history of the Netherlands in the
   seventeenth century cannot be adequately told without considering ministers' understanding of print,
   how they used print to encourage godliness and the nature of their personal libraries. This study is
   built upon an examination of 235 auction catalogues, nearly all that are known to survive, and the
   transcription of 55 of these catalogues. Libraries were possessions of central importance to the ministers
   who owned them. Knowing the kinds of print with which ministers interacted adds vital information
   into the daily life of a minister and the culture of the era. So, what books did these central theological
   figures own and how did they use them?"—Provided by publisher.
Identifiers: LCCN 2022051734 (print) | LCCN 2022051735 (ebook) |
   ISBN 9789004538184 (hardback ; acid-free paper) | ISBN 9789004538191 (ebook)
Subjects: LCSH: Private libraries—Netherlands—History—17th century. |
   Clergy—Books and reading—Netherlands—History—17th century. | Books
   and reading—Netherlands—History—17th century. | Books and reading—Religious
   aspects—Christianity. | Netherlands—Intellectual life—17th century.
Classification: LCC Z997.2.N4 S77 2023 (print) | LCC Z997.2.N4 (ebook) |
   DDC 027/.1492—dc23/eng/20221215
LC record available at https://lccn.loc.gov/2022051734
LC ebook record available at https://lccn.loc.gov/2022051735

Typeface for the Latin, Greek, and Cyrillic scripts: "Brill". See and download: brill.com/brill-typeface.

ISSN 1874-4834
ISBN 978-90-04-53818-4 (hardback)
ISBN 978-90-04-53819-1 (e-book)

Copyright 2023 by Koninklijke Brill NV, Leiden, The Netherlands.
Koninklijke Brill NV incorporates the imprints Brill, Brill Nijhoff, Brill Hotei, Brill Schöningh, Brill Fink,
Brill mentis, Vandenhoeck & Ruprecht, Böhlau, V&R unipress and Wageningen Academic.
All rights reserved. No part of this publication may be reproduced, translated, stored in a retrieval system,
or transmitted in any form or by any means, electronic, mechanical, photocopying, recording or otherwise,
without prior written permission from the publisher. Requests for re-use and/or translations must be
addressed to Koninklijke Brill NV via brill.com or copyright.com.

This book is printed on acid-free paper and produced in a sustainable manner.

When you come, bring the cloak that I left with Carpus at Troas, also the books, and above all the parchments.

2 Timothy 4:13

• • •

No one teaches well unless he has first learned well; no one learns well unless he learns in order to teach. And both learning and teaching are vain and unprofitable unless accompanied by practice.... It is when [the minister] goes forth from the sacred mount of contemplation, his soul manifestly replenished and radiant with the purest light, that he is best fitted to communicate that light of reflection to others.

HERMAN WITSIUS, *On the Character of a True Theologian*, ed. J. Ligon Duncan, III (reprint; Greenville, S.C.: Reformed Academic Press, 1994), pp. 29, 38

Contents

Acknowledgements   IX
List of Figures and Tables   XI
Abbreviations   XIV
Conventions   XV

1 **Ministers and Their Books in the Seventeenth-Century Dutch Republic**   1
   1   The Rise of the Book Auction Catalogue in the Netherlands   11
   2   The Dutch Context   14
   3   Available with the Booksellers   18
   4   Sold at Auction   25

2 **That All May Be Instructed**   28
   1   Print and Piety   33
   2   The Difficulty of the 'Reformed' Republic   38
   3   Vainglorious and Irreverent Books   44
   4   'I Must Have the New Tidings'   49
   5   Printers and the Dissemination of Piety   53
   6   The Book and Pen   60
   7   Creatures of the Book   63

3 **Buyers of Truth**   66
   1   Between Opulence and Poverty   68
   2   Dusty Attics   74
   3   The Home of the Muses   83
   4   The Legion of Books   87
   5   Learned Men   99
   6   Dwelling in Sparta   105

4 **Guardians of the Faith**   108
   1   The Academy of Academies   112
   2   The More Sound Schoolmen   122
   3   Our Doctors   129
   4   Learning from the Britons   140
   5   Trained in Righteousness   151

5 Learned Servants 153

1	Men of Letters	157
2	The Philosophers	162
3	Roads of the Sun	169
4	Amateur Physicians	175
5	They That Bear Silver	180
6	Reading the Stars	185
7	Learned Servants	192

Conclusion: The Ideal Ministerial Library 195

1	Timeless and Timely Libraries	198
2	Ministerial Libraries in a Golden Age	200
3	The Ideal Ministerial Library	202

Appendix: Analysed Ministerial Library Catalogues 205
Bibliography 218
Illustrations 253
Index 272

Acknowledgements

This book is the expansion of my doctoral thesis, submitted to the University of St. Andrews in October 2019. The research for this volume would not have been possible without the generous financial support of the Universal Short-Title Catalogue (USTC) and the Vera Gottschalk-Frank Foundation, to whom I am immensely grateful. Much of the research for this project took place in 2018 while I served as the Arminius Fellow at Universiteit Leiden, Scaliger Institute, a fellowship graciously funded by the Vera Gottschalk-Frank Foundation.

I owe a special debt of gratitude to Andrew Pettegree and Arthur der Weduwen. They have been a supervisor and a mentor of the best kind: encouraging when needed, critical when helpful and faithful readers of my writing since long before I had an idea about what the final product would be. I am tremendously grateful for their guidance through this process. If I am a better scholar and better writer now than I was when I started, it is largely because of their sharp editorial eye. I am pleased, now, to call them friends. Guidance from my thesis examiners, Bridget Heal at St. Andrews and August den Hollander at the Vrije Universiteit Amsterdam, helped me sharpened the text significantly.

Over the years this research took to come together, many friends were supportive through conversations, reading chapters as they were written, and suggesting sources. These friends include Hanna de Lange, Philippe Schmidt and Panagiotis Georgakakis. Hanna and Philippe kindly read through most of the chapters that now constitute this book. Conversations with Panos helped me clarify many of the ideas that now shape what I have written. Thanks are due to Graeme Kemp and Drew Thomas, who helped me the many times I had questions about Microsoft Access and Excel.

In addition to my fellowship in Leiden, I had the great pleasure of whiling away hours in several archives in the Netherlands, from the Zeeuws Archief in the west to Tresoar and Groningen in the east. Archives were essential to this pursuit, with tremendous resources on Dutch religious culture during the Golden Age, and innumerable archivists and librarians aided me in the research. My thanks especially to Anton van der Lem and Kasper van Ommen at Leiden and Jacob van Sluis at Tresoar for their help navigating their respective library collections.

Small portions of this work have appeared in previously published articles. My thanks to the editors of the following volumes, who have allowed me to reproduce that material: 'Building a library in early modern Europe: André Rivet and his Library', in Graeme Kemp, et al. (eds.), *Book Trade Catalogues in Early Modern Europe* (Brill, 2021); 'Learned Servants: Dutch Ministers, Their

Books and the Struggle for a Reformed Republic in the Golden Age', in Jamie Cumby, Helmer Helmers and Nina Lamal (eds.), *Print and Power* (Brill, 2021).

Finally, I cannot begin to thank adequately my wife, Laura. Her ceaseless encouragement through the course of this work has been incalculable. From start to finish she has been a steady source of motivation. I found myself regularly thinking of Solomon's words: "Many women have done excellently, but you surpass them all" (Proverbs 31:29). When this book began, we had been married for three years. Now, after eight years and welcoming two children to our family, she has been amazingly patient and encouraging while I researched and wrote. The three of you are constant reminders that there are more significant things in my life than academics. I pray this research shapes me into a better husband and father.

Figures and Tables

Figures

1.1 The fourth and fifth pages of the Demetrius library catalogue. Here, folios, quartos and octavos are intermixed, unlike almost all other catalogues. *AC Daniel Demetrius 1628* (Dordrecht: Peeter Verhagen, 1628), USTC 1122269   253

1.2 Isaac Lydius to Rivet, 11 April 1628, UB Leiden, ms. BPL 285 Bf199r. Bijzondere Collecties-Universiteit Leiden   254

1.3 The location of the auctions of ministerial book collections during the seventeenth century. Leiden, given its geographical and cultural contexts, far surpasses all other places in the number of auctions that took place within its city walls   255

1.4 The cities in which the libraries of Dutch ministers were auctioned during the seventeenth century   256

1.5 The cities, towns and villages where the ministers whose libraries were auctioned resided   257

1.6 The end of the medical section of Halsbergius' catalogue, and the start of the miscellaneous works. Elzevier separated the books into theology, jurisprudence, medical texts, a miscellaneous section called 'philosophy, history, oratory, and philology', music, another section of history, then vernacular texts, French, Italian and Spanish, German and Dutch, followed by unbound books, and an appendix. All of the books within these categories were then divided into size. *AC Johannes Halsbergius 1607* (Leiden: Louis Elzevier, 1607), USTC 1122231   258

1.7 The end of Wilhelm Merwy's historical books, and the start of his Dutch books. *AC Wilhelm Merwy 1636* (Leiden: Jan Pietersz. Waelpot, 1636), USTC 1027540   259

2.1 Print was seen as a necessary tool for the combat of Roman Catholic error. Here, the printed Bible stands alone one the scales of truth. *De Bijbel op de weegschaal*, anonymous, 1677–1693. Rijksmuseum RP-P-OB-78.823   259

2.2 In larger communities, godly reading was even central to taking communion. While reading, the believers wait patiently to take the supper. Frontispiece to *Het Rechte gebruyck van des Heeren H Avontmael* (Amsterdam: J. Spanseerder, [ca. 1730]). Universiteitsbibliotheek Utrecht – Bijzonder Collectie: EAG 21   260

2.3 The Rotterdam minister, Franciscus Ridderus set himself the task of helping the church struggle against error. Here, Ridderus includes a brief article on the early church heretic. Franciscus Ridderus, *Worstelende Kercke, ofte Historische Vertooninge van het bestreden geloove der ware Christenen* (Rotterdam: Weduwe van Aernoud Leers, 1679), USTC 1815771, p. 60   261

3.1 *Jacobus Arminius Oudewaterae natus.* Rijksmuseum RP-P-OB-55.251 262

3.2 *Portret van Balthasar Lydius*, 1656–1706. Rijksmuseum RP-P-1883-A-7068 263

3.3 *Portret van Guiljelmus Saldenus*, 1660–1693. Rijksmuseum RP-P-OB-17.521 264

3.4 *Portret van Tobias Govertsz. van den Wyngaert op 80-jarige leeftijd.* Rijksmuseum RP-P-BI-1837 265

3.5 *Portret van Franciscus Ridderus.* Rijksmuseum RP-P-OB-23.811 266

4.1 The title page for a 1626 edition of the Imitation of Christ likely printed in Amsterdam by Willem Jansz Blaeu, with a false Cologne imprint. A copy of it was owned by the Remonstrant minister and medical doctor Justinus van Assche. *Christus en een gevolg kruisdragers Titelpagina voor T. à Kempis, De imitatione Christi*, Pieter Serwouters, 1626. Rijksmuseum RP-P-1886-A-10523 267

4.2 The title page from the Dutch translation of Samuel Clark's *Annotation over 't N. Testament*, vol. 2 (Amsterdam: Johannes Boekholt, 1692), USTC 1822720 268

5.1 Leiden's two oldest churches, the Hooglandse Kerk and the Pieterskerk dominate the town's skyline. *Gezicht op Leiden*, Gaspar Bouttats, after Jan Peeters, 1675–1679. Rijksmuseum RP-P-BI-4251 269

5.2 Title page by Pieter Holsteyn from Ridderus' *Historisch Sterf-huys*, 1665. Rijksmuseum RP-P-1893-A-18048 270

6.1 Title-page of the second edition of Johannes Lomeier, *De bibliothecis* (Utrecht: Johannes Ribbius, 1680), USTC 1816644. Special Collections, University of Amsterdam, O 61-2850 271

Tables

1.1 Known auctions of ministerial libraries by city. These figures include those auctions whose catalogues do not survive, but whose occurrence is known through newspaper advertisements, city archives and so forth 19

3.1 Ten largest ministerial collections which sold at auction in the seventeenth century 88

3.2 Ten smallest ministerial collections which sold at auction in the seventeenth century 89

3.3 The size of ministerial book collections that sold at auction by decade 90

3.4 Ministerial collections which sold in the 1630s 91

3.5 Formats of books in ministerial book collections 92

3.6 Proportions of books by language in ministerial book collections 95

3.7 Median number of books by language listed in ministerial book auction catalogues. As these are not percentages or an average using the mean, the combination of the individual figures will not equal the total 100

FIGURES AND TABLES

3.8	Percentages of book formats in lawyers' book collections	100
3.9	Average proportions of lawyers' book collections by language	102
3.10	Average doctors' book collections by format	102
3.11	Average presence of languages in doctors' book auction catalogues	103
3.12–3.13	Average percentage formats and languages of books as listed in the auction catalogues of doctors, lawyers, and ministers	103
4.1	A selection of well-known Roman Catholic and Medieval authors listed in Dutch ministerial library catalogues	127
4.2	The twenty most popular theological authors as listed in ministerial library catalogues. All but Augustine worked in either the sixteenth or seventeenth century. Of the early modern authors, Erasmus and Bellarmine were the only non-Protestants	134
4.3	Collections with the most English books owned by Dutch ministers. The two Richard Madens are two different English ministers	145
4.4	Average proportion of English books by decade in Dutch ministerial library catalogues	146
4.5	Median proportion of English books by decade in Dutch ministerial library catalogues	147
4.6	Seventeen most common authors of English language books in Dutch ministerial library catalogues	149
5.1	A selection of popular authors from antiquity as listed in ministerial library catalogues, derived from the author's transcription of fifty-five ministerial library catalogues	165
5.2	The five most common places of publication for classical works listed in the auction catalogues of libraries owned by ministers	165
5.3	A selection of popular authors of geographical works, as listed in fifty-five ministerial library catalogues	172
5.4	Medical books in ministerial auction catalogues and their countries of imprint as derived from the 889 entries for which an imprint is known or inferred	178
5.5	A selection of the well-known medical authors as listed in ministerial book auction catalogues	179
5.6	The six most popular authors of astronomical and cosmographical works listed in ministerial auction catalogues	187
5.7	A selection of well-known and celebrated astronomical authors in fifty-five Dutch ministerial catalogues	188

Abbreviations

BSCO	*Book Sales Catalogues Online – Book Auctioning in the Dutch Republic, ca. 1500–ca. 1800.*, advisor: Brill, Leiden and Boston: Brill, 2015. <http://primarysources.brillonline.com/browse/book-sales-catalogues-online>
HUA	Het Utrechts Archief
HCO	Historisch Centrum Overijssel
NNBW	P. C. Molhuysen and P. J. Blok (eds.), *Nieuw Nederlandsch Biografisch Woordenboek* (10 vols; Leiden: A. W. Sijthoff, 1911–1937).
RAD	Regionaal Archief Dordrecht
RAN	Regionaal Archief Nijmegen
SAL	Stadsarchief Leiden
SAR	Stadsarchief Rotterdam
UB Amsterdam	Universiteit van Amsterdam, Bijzondere Collecties, Amsterdam
UB Groningen	Universiteit van Groningen, Bijzondere Collecties, Groningen
UB Leiden	Universiteit van Leiden, Bijzondere Collecties, Leiden
VU	Vrije Universiteit, Bijzondere Collecties, Amsterdam
WA	Westfries Archief, Hoorn
ZA	Zeeuws Archief, Middelburg

Conventions

This study uses the term 'Dutch Republic', or occasionally 'the Republic', to refer to the confederation of provinces which rebelled under King Philip II, forming an independent state in 1579. The 'United Provinces', as the Dutch Republic is also known, was a confederation of seven semi-autonomous regional principalities, 'provinces', Zeeland, Holland, Utrecht, Gelderland, Overijssel, Friesland and Groningen. The occupied territories of the Generality Lands and the province of Drenthe also formed part of the Republic. The dominant form of currency used in the Dutch Republic consisted of the *gulden* and *stuiver*. Twenty stuivers was one gulden. A day labourer in the seventeenth-century Dutch Republic earned about 250 gulden a year. A minister earned an annual salary of upwards of 500 gulden. For reference, an average book cost around one gulden, while short devotional books could be purchased for a few stuivers. Ten pounds of meat could be bought for about one gulden, and five stuivers bought three to four kilograms of rye bread.

In footnotes, I have shortened the titles of those book auction catalogues that are available at Book Sales Catalogues Online (BSCO) to *AC*, followed by the name of the owner whose library was to be auctioned, the date of publication and the bibliographic information. This method provides more immediately relevant information than citing the title in full. Only the names of places have been Anglicized. I endeavour to use the personal names by which figures from this period are best known. For example, the Utrecht theologian Gisbertus Voetius is better known for his Latinized name rather than the original Dutch, Gijsbert Voet. Whereas Willem Teellinck is known only by his Dutch name. All dates have been converted from Old Style (Julian) to New Style (Gregorian), unless noted in the text. In 1582, Holland and Zeeland were the first provinces to adopt the Gregorian calendar, while the remaining provinces did so throughout the course of the seventeenth century. There was roughly a ten-day difference between the two calendars, with the Julian ahead of the Gregorian. When transcribing quotations from foreign a language source, I adapt the spelling only if the printer had changed the spelling for printing convention (i.e., 'v' instead of 'u'). The early modern practice of using '/' has been replaced with a comma.

Unless quoting from a Dutch source, Scripture quotations are from the Holy Bible, English Standard Version (Wheaton: Crossway, 2001). All translations are my own unless otherwise indicated. I use the term 'minister' to refer to all those who served Protestant churches in pastoral capacities. This includes professors of theology, as they typically preached in a local church in addition to their academic duties, and also students of theology.

CHAPTER 1

Ministers and Their Books in the Seventeenth-Century Dutch Republic

To the Reader. For good consultation, the impartial reader may find the present catalogue with less order than that to which they are accustomed: indiscriminately, that is, the books are not ordered by genre. I preserve the series in which he, the deceased, assembled them. The collection is gathered in the interest of recognizing in his possession the home of the muses. To compensate for this disadvantage, I hope to record every single book, all of which the catalogue lists. Any learned buyers may request whatever is commodious to them and pleases their tastes. Farewell.[1]

⁙

With these words, Peeter Verhagen introduced the catalogue for the library formerly owned by Daniel Demetrius. Demetrius, a minister in Dordrecht's Reformed church, owned a respectable collection of books. The catalogue Verhagen composed to advertise the sale lists 901 books. The typography of the catalogue is strictly utilitarian. With a large, expressive title it announces its contents to any who glanced at it. Besides the printers' mark on the title page, little throughout the twenty-eight pages stands out in the mass of black. The books are not even divided by size, as was the custom. Only lot numbers and hanging indentation divide the text into recognizable, discrete entries (Fig. 1.1). Verhagen understood the market for a minister's collection of books. 'Learned buyers', he thought, would dominate the sale. For these educated readers, it

---

1 'Ad Lectorem. Boni consulat aequus lector hunc catalogum exhiberi ordine minus consueto: promiscuè scilicet, libris non figillatim in classes digestis. seruatâ interim serie quâ ipse defunctus bibliothecam collocare fuit coactus pro noui sui Musaei loco angustiore. Incommodum hoe, siquibus fortè obfuerit, affatim compensandum speramus insequendo numerum singulis libris inscriptum, qui catalogo respondet. quô doctis emptoribus commode suggeretur quodeunque palate cuiusvis adlibuerit. Vale'. Peeter Verhagen, *Ad Lectorem*, in AC *Daniel Demetrius 1628* (Dordrecht: Peeter Verhagen, 1628), USTC 1122269.

© KONINKLIJKE BRILL NV, LEIDEN, 2023 | DOI:10.1163/9789004538191_002

was an opportunity to acquire books by the Church Fathers, authors from Antiquity, popular devotional tracts, and grammars in Greek and Hebrew.

One such 'learned buyer' was André Rivet. As he settled into his role as professor of Hebrew and theology at the University of Leiden, André Rivet made use of a wildly popular phenomenon, the book auction. By 1628, after leaving his home in France seven years earlier, Rivet was sufficiently recognised in Dutch ministerial circles to ask his colleagues to purchase books on his behalf. On one such occasion, Rivet turned to a minister whose family was known for their own extravagant book buying. Balthazar Lydius and his sons were ministers in and around Dordrecht. Balthazar's collection sold at three auctions from 1629–1630, totalling 5,900 books.[2] Balthazar's brother a minister in Oudewater (near Utrecht) had a collection of 1,747 books.[3] Rivet knew that the Lydius family followed Dordrecht's book market closely. Before Demetrius' books were sold on 4 April, Rivet asked Isaac Lydius (Balthazar's oldest son) to buy a couple of books on his behalf.[4] Rivet had hoped that the auction would add several books to his collection, and it was a good occasion to buy (Fig. 1.2).

Though Rivet had a local agent, it does not appear that the auction contributed to his book collection. Embarrassed, Lydius wrote to him explaining why he had not fulfilled his responsibility. A friend's obligation or not, the books were surprisingly expensive. Béroald's *Chronicum* in quarto sold for 1 gulden 12 stuivers. David Chytraeus' commentary on the Pentateuch sold for three gulden. Several other commentaries sold for over a gulden and a half. Most egregious, Lydius thought, was Aeneas Sylvius' folio *Opera* selling for more than eleven gulden. A representative for the *Bibliothecae Zeelandia* bought many of the books, and Demetrius' sister held back a large proportion of the collection, presumably because they did not meet the reserve price. Lydius apologetically hoped he could be of use at another time.

Perhaps Isaac Lydius was being too cautious, or Rivet had been too greedy for bargains. The auction catalogue for the library Rivet built was composed after his death in 1651.[5] By then, Rivet had obtained most of the books Lydius listed, and almost all of them went for similar prices to what Lydius considered excessive. Matthieu Béroald's *Chronicum* (Frankfurt, 1606) sold for one gulden.[6] Chytraeus' commentary on the Pentateuch was not listed in Rivet's catalogue, but he had several of Chytraeus' other works, one of which raised

---

2 *AC Balthazar Lydius 1629 and 1630* (Dordrecht: widow of Peeter Verhagen, 1629–1630), USTC 1021755, 1021757, 1021756.
3 *AC Johannes Lydius* (Leiden: Franciscus Hackius, 1643), USTC 1122163.
4 Isaac Lydius to Rivet, 11 April 1628, UB Leiden, ms. BPL 285 Bf199r.
5 *AC André Rivet 1657* (Leiden: Pieter Leffen, 1657), USTC 1846296.
6 Ibid., p. 91. USTC 2079451.

three gulden.[7] Augustinus Torniellus' *Annales Veteris Testament* (Cologne, 1622) sold for seven gulden.[8] Rivet owned numerous French Bibles, and their prices ranged from two to twenty gulden. Though Rivet's catalogue does not list Sylvius' *Opera*, Rivet did eventually acquire his papal epistles, which sold for five gulden.[9] Bibliander's *De ratione linguarum* sold in a lot with two other books for five gulden sixteen stuivers.[10] Rivet's catalogue does not mention Pererius' commentary on Exodus. But price was again not the concern. Rivet's copy of his commentary on Genesis sold for seven gulden five stuivers.[11] Rivet owned several commentaries by Ferus, all of which sold for over a gulden and a half. By the end of his life, Rivet had acquired these books, whether at a different auction or in a bookshop.

Ministers like Demetrius, Rivet and Lydius were important public figures who exerted considerable influence on broader society. Ministers in the Netherlands subscribed to one of several Protestant confessions of faith and were charged with the spiritual health of their communities. Preachers, their assistants and professors of theology, all of whom were ordained, gave sermons, prayed for their neighbours and catechised church members. Students of theology, too, were often given some pastoral responsibilities prior to their formal ordination.

The Reformed Church of the Netherlands was the politically sanctioned church during this time. Other Christian congregations (Lutherans, Mennonites, and Roman Catholics) existed in great numbers throughout the Republic and faced regulations on their gatherings that were often capriciously enforced. A local sheriff might be paid to turn a blind eye to a gathering of Roman Catholics, for example.[12] Ministers and priests in these communities performed the same functions within their communities as the Reformed did in theirs, but the public nature of their work was, at least in the letter of the law, under more threat than that of their Reformed counterparts.

Ministers were often at the centre of a city's intellectual life, especially in smaller towns, and their profession was one built upon books. Bibles, commentaries, theological tracts, polemical works, lexicons and many others: ministers used books to fulfil their duties to the local congregation. Urs B. Leu and

---

7   Ibid., p. 86.
8   Ibid., p. 85. Likely, USTC 1021597.
9   Ibid., p. 86. USTC 435622.
10   Ibid., p. 93. USTC 631253.
11   Ibid., p. 16. USTC 2144262.
12   Christine Kooi, 'Paying off the sheriff: strategies of Catholic toleration in Golden Age Holland', R. Po-Chia Hsia and Henk van Nierop (eds.), *Calvinism and Religious Toleration in the Dutch Golden Age* (Cambridge: Cambridge University Press, 2010), pp. 86–111.

Sandra Weidmann noted that 'In addition to diaries and correspondence, a scholar's library provides valuable clues about his interests and his spiritual universe as well as revealing the texts which influenced him. Hence investigating someone's private library is just as crucial in tracing his spiritual and intellectual conflicts'.[13] The libraries owned by ministers in the Dutch Golden Age reflect part of the culture in which they served. To understand the history of the Netherlands during the seventeenth century, one must also understand the cultural hinterland of the ministers who preached in the Republic's churches and whose devotional works lined the shelves of its bookstores. For this, the printed catalogues of their libraries are invaluable.

Auction catalogues like that printed by Peeter Verhagen provide a fruitful source of inquiry into ministers and their book collecting habits, but to date they have remained largely unused as sources. Significantly more work has been done on the auction catalogue as an historical artefact, its emergence and development, than examining what the catalogue tells us about the culture of those who collected the libraries that were auctioned. Much English language work on auction catalogues can be traced to the ground-breaking study by Archer Taylor, *Book Catalogues: Their Variety and Uses*.[14] Taylor detailed the three main classes of catalogue (stock, publisher's, or personal library), and he suggested a general methodology for using catalogues to inform our understanding of the past. He concluded that catalogues were important sources for historical knowledge, though like all other sources they present their own unique difficulties, which I will discuss later in this introduction. In the Netherlands, however, the study of auction catalogues as an historical source had far earlier beginnings than Taylor. In 1845, a library was created by the Amsterdam antiquarian bookseller and auctioneer, Frederik Muller. Muller intended the library to help introduce new booksellers to their vocation. Central to the library was a collection of printed catalogues, either of a seller's stock or personal libraries. A century later, Wytze Hellinga built on this foundation a card index of known book catalogues. Hellinga was ground-breaking in his own right: in his index of known book catalogues he included advertisements and other sources that noted when a book auction took place, not only instances in which the catalogue survives.[15]

---

13   Urs B. Leu and Sandra Weidmann, *Huldrych Zwingli's Private Library* (Leiden: Brill, 2019), p. vii.

14   Archer Taylor, *Book Catalogues: Their Varieties and Uses* (Chicago: The Newberry Library, 1957).

15   Otto S. Lankhorst, 'Dutch Book Auctions in the Seventeenth and Eighteenth Century', in Robin Myers, et al. (eds.), *Under the Hammer: book auctions since the seventeenth century* (New Castle: Oak Knoll Press, 2001), pp. 77–78.

In 1971, Anthony Hobson published a paper entitled 'A Sale by Candle in 1608'.[16] In it, he presented what is now a standard history of the auction. The phenomenon of book auctions with a corresponding catalogue, beginning in earnest in the seventeenth century, emerged in a time and place in which it was already commonplace for a person's private library to be auctioned after their death. Hobson argued that auctions were frequent public events, beginning in ancient times, growing more popular through the medieval era, and continuing through the sixteenth century.

In the 1980s Bert van Selm took the narrative further, focussing on the Dutch Republic. Van Selm continued the work of his teacher, Hellinga, and traced the emergence and development of the Dutch book auction. Van Selm suggested possible factors that helped give rise to the phenomenon of the printed book auction catalogue. Van Selm argued that four factors influenced the rise of the book auction catalogue in the Netherlands: economic prosperity, ineffective regulations by the booksellers' guild, ease of trade so books could easily be shipped, and high levels of education. He further demonstrated one way in which catalogues were often incomplete: families of the deceased would sometimes withhold from auctions school books, vernacular devotional works and Bibles and Psalters that they valued for sentimental reasons or wanted to continue using.[17] Van Selm's *Een menighte treffelijcke Boeken* remains one of the few comprehensive studies of Dutch catalogues during the seventeenth century.

Similarly, Otto Lankhorst suggested four 'circumstances' that encouraged the rise of book auction catalogues in the Netherlands: a high literacy rate, insufficient public libraries, the fact that the Dutch did not feel particularly attached to family possessions and the copious number of books produced in the Netherlands.[18] The precepts proposed by Lankhorst and Van Selm are not mutually exclusive. They each touch on certain aspects of Dutch culture during the sixteenth and seventeenth centuries that led to the explosion of book auction catalogues, and I will return to these several factors throughout this work.

Four facsimiles of ministerial auction catalogues were reproduced between 1984 and 1996, but auction catalogues are rarely used as sources for understanding Dutch ministers and theologians during the seventeenth century.[19]

---

16   Anthony Hobson, 'A Sale by Candle in 1608', *The Library*, 26 (1971), pp. 215–233.

17   Bert van Selm, *Een menighte treffelijcke Boeken: Nederlandse boekhandelscatalogi in het begin van de zeventiende eeuw* (Utrecht: HES, 1987), p. 97.

18   Lankhorst, 'Dutch Book Auctions in the Seventeenth and Eighteenth Century', pp. 68–69.

19   J. D. Bangs (ed.), *The Auction Catalogue of the Library of Hugh Goodyear, English Reformed Minister at Leiden* (Leiden: Brill/Hes & De Graaf, 1984); C. O. Bangs (ed.), *The Auction Catalogue of the Library of J. Arminius* (Leiden: Brill/Hes & De Graaf, 1984); K. Sprunger

Occasionally, studies of specific ministers mention their auction catalogue in passing. Andreas Beck argued that the Utrecht theologian Gisbertus Voetius (1589–1676) sought to defend John Calvin from the charge that he made God the author of evil. For this, Beck first demonstrates how Voetius appreciated Calvin. In addition to recommending Calvin's written works to his students, 'It does not come as a surprise that Voetius owned an impressive collection of *Calviniana*', Beck wrote, 'as is evident from the auction catalogues of Voetius' private library'.[20] Beck made a similar point on Voetius' appropriation of Phillip Melanchthon.[21] In like manner, Aza Goudriaan examined the reception of Augustine by Jacob Arminius, and concluded such knowledge was dependent on 'first-hand reading'. This is confirmed, in part, by Arminius' auction catalogue listing several individual works by the Church Father and his *Opera*.[22] In only a few instances are Dutch ministerial libraries given focused attention.[23] Here again, these studies do not describe a general book culture beyond the individual in question. They do not place a ministerial catalogue in the broader context of libraries owned by other ministers and educated professionals. In these cases, little can be said about how the library compares to others and what distinctive information emerges from using that catalogue. For example, was Gisbertus Voetius' ownership of Calvin's books truly 'impressive'? Such a question can only be answered after a scholar understands the general readership of Calvin amongst ministers from their catalogues.

The study of private libraries owned by ministers has long been recognized as a fruitful source of inquiry, despite little work being done on ministerial auction catalogues. The book collections owned by many of the first Reformers have been recreated from archival sources (e.g., letters and inventories),

---

(ed.), *The Auction Catalogue of William Ames* (Leiden: Brill/Hes & De Graaf, 1987); E. Dekker, J. Knoop and C. M. L. Verdegaal (eds.), *The Auction Catalogue of the Library of F. Gomarus (Leiden, 1641)* (Leiden: Brill/Hes & De Graaf, 1996).

20   Andreas J. Beck, '"Expositio Reverentialis": Gisbertus Voetius's (1589–1676) Relationship with John Calvin', *Church History and Religious Culture*, 91 (2011), p. 124.

21   Andreas J. Beck, 'Melanchthonian Thought in Gisbertus Voetius' Scholastic Doctrine of God', in Maarten Wisse, et al., (eds.), *Scholasticism Reformed: Essays in Honour of Willem J. van Asselt* (Leiden: Brill, 2010), p. 111.

22   Aza Goudriaan, 'Jacob Arminius's Reception of Augustine', in Th. Marius van Leeuwen, Keith D. Stanglin and Marijke Tolsma (eds.), *Arminius, Arminianism, and Europe: Jacobus Arminius (1559/60–1609)* (Leiden: Brill, 2009), p. 71.

23   E.g., Arjan Nobel and Otto van der Meij, '"De Luijden sijn daer seer begeerich na": De veiling van de bibliotheek van André Rivet in 1657', in Maurits Ebben and Pieter Wagenaar (eds.), *De cirkel doorbroken* (Leiden: Instituut voor Geschiedenis, 2006), pp. 215–238; Marja Smolenaars and Ann Veenhoff, 'Hugh Goodyear and His Books' (Phd Thesis, Leiden University, 1993).

MINISTERS AND THEIR BOOKS IN THE 17TH-CENTURY DUTCH REPUBLIC

marginalia and ownership marks.[24] Libraries owned by less famous theologians have also been studied using archival material. Jüri Kivimäe examined the book collections owned by nine ministers in Livonian Reval (modern day Tallinn, Estonia), ranging from 1554 to 1616.[25] Kivimäe used probate inventories now in the Tallinn City Archives. A similar project based on probate inventories was recently completed on Danish ministers and their books in the seventeenth and eighteenth centuries.[26] These projects, in addition to my own, confirm that Protestant ministers were a substantial part of the early-modern book world. The nine collections Kivimäe studied were of ministers in a town of less than 10,000 inhabitants on the periphery of the book world, yet their inventories listed an average of about 200 works.[27] One substantial difference between auction catalogues and inventories is that auction catalogues tend to provide more bibliographic detail on the former owner's books than inventories. Therefore, auction catalogues provide an additional layer of information with which we can better understand the book world. Nevertheless, if it was normal for ministers in Livonian Reval to have collections of over one hundred books, how much more common would it have been for a minister in even rural parts of the Netherlands?

Bert van Selm traced the emergence and development of the Dutch book auction catalogue, and his work set the groundwork for all other studies of book auctions and their catalogues in the Netherlands. But he hoped his history of auction catalogues would open the way for a study of catalogues as purveyors of cultural truths. He stated:

---

24 Robert Stupperich, 'Martin Bucers Bücherverzeichnis von 1518', *Archiv für Kulturgeschiecte*, 57 (1975), pp. 162–185; Urs B. Leu and Sandra Weidmann, *Heinrich Bullingers Privatbibliothek*, in *Heinrich Bullinger Werke*, Abt. 1, Bd. 3 (Zurich: Theologischer Verlag, 2004); Alexandre Ganoczy, *La bibliothèque de l'académie de Calvin: le catalogue de 1572 es ses enseignments* (Geneva: Librarie Droz, 1969); Martin Brecht and Christian Peters, *Martin Luther. Annotierungen zu den Werken des Hieronymus, Archive zur Weimarer Ausgabe der Werke Martin Luthers, Texte und Untersuchungen*, vol. 8 (Cologne: Böhlau, 2000); Max Steinmetz, 'Thomas Müntzer und die Bücher', *Zeitschrift für Geschichtswissenschaft*, 32 (1984), 603–612; Leu and Weidmann, *Huldrych Zwingli's Private Library*.

25 Jüri Kivimäe, 'Books and Preachers: The Microcosm of Reval in the Age of the Reformation', in Heinrich Assel, et al. (eds.), *Reformatio Baltica: Kulturwirkungen der Reformation in den Metropolen des Osteeraums* (Berlin: De Gruyter, 2018), pp. 655–668.

26 Jonas Thorup Thomson, 'Gejstlig læsning i det tidligt moderne Danmark – Danske sognepræsters rolle i udbredelsen af nye tanker og strømninger 1660–1810', (PhD Thesis, Aarhus University, 2022).

27 Kivimäe, 'Books and Preachers: The Microcosm of Reval in the Age of the Reformation', p. 660.

8 CHAPTER 1

These sources can be used for the optimal study of the cultural climate and the 'sociology of knowledge', the knowledge of art, literature, and the history of ideas. Hopefully, these old auction catalogues will receive the attention they deserve as primary sources for the cultural history of the Republic.[28]

This project pursues part of the goal for which Van Selm envisioned his own research.

Ministers make up the most numerous professional group whose libraries were sold at auction in the seventeenth-century Dutch Republic, because ministers were fervent acquirers of books. Archer Taylor claimed that one of difficulties with using library catalogues as historical sources is 'they are rare and hard to find'.[29] Taylor especially focused on the number of lost catalogues. And yet, the surviving catalogues are neither rare nor hard to find. Of the known corpus of 2,092 library auctions, 457 contained books owned formerly by Dutch ministers. Approximately five and a half thousand Dutch ministers served Reformed congregations in the seventeenth century.[30] Several hundred ministers served other Protestant churches.

Of the corpus of ministerial collections, 261 printed auction catalogues survive. Most of the remaining 196 auctions can be identified from advertisements in newspapers. We know of others only from civic archives recording permission to hold an auction (for which a fee would be paid). The local magistrates required auctioneers to have a catalogue printed, so it is almost certain that a catalogue did exist for the auctions documented through archival sources.[31] Auction catalogues of a personal library were not intended to be collectors' items; they served a utilitarian purpose. This purpose contributed to their being lost or discarded, a point noted by Taylor.[32] Therefore, they tend

---

28 '... kunnen deze bronnen optimal benut worden bij de studie van het cultureel klimaat en de "sociology of knowledge", van de wetenschaps-, de kunst-, de literaturr- en de ideeëgeschiedenis. Hopelijk krijgen dan de oude veiligcatalogi de aandacht die ze als primaire bronnen voor de cultuurgeschiedenis van de Republic verdien'. Van Selm, *Een menighte treffelijcke Boeken*, p. 122.

29 Taylor, *Book Catalogues*, p. 93.

30 This figure is my own estimation derived from F. A. van Lieburg, *Profeten en hun vaderland: De geografische herkomst van de gereformeerde predikanten in Nederland van 1572 tot 1816* (Zoetermeer: Boekencentrum, 1996), p. 53.

31 Otto Lankhorst, 'Les ventes de livres en Hollande et leurs catalogues (XVIIe–XVIIIe siècles)', in Annie Charon and Élisabeth Parinet (eds.), *Les ventes de livres et leurs catalogues: XVIIe–XXe siècle. Actes des journées organisées par l'École nationale des chartes (Paris, 15 janvier 1998) et par l'ENSSIB (Villeurbanne, 22 janvier 1998)* (Paris: École nationale des chartes, 2000), p. 15.

32 Taylor, *Book Catalogues*, p. 93.

MINISTERS AND THEIR BOOKS IN THE 17TH-CENTURY DUTCH REPUBLIC 9

to survive in very poor numbers. About seventy per cent of all surviving catalogues survive in one copy. It would therefore not be unreasonable to conclude there were probably 750 or more auctions of ministers' book collections in the seventeenth century. The numbers of ministerial catalogues that actually circulated during the seventeenth century would have been be much higher than surviving catalogues would indicate.

Title pages to ministerial libraries often note if the confessional background of the owner was something other than Reformed. In my analysed corpus of 234 catalogues, seventeen Remonstrant ministers are present. Twenty-three are identified as Lutheran on the title page. Two libraries owned by Mennonite ministers have been analysed. One minister, Petrus Gribius is only identified as 'minister of the German congregation in Amsterdam'.[33] The church affiliation of the owners of the remaining 193 ministerial libraries are unrecorded. They would most likely have been ministers in the Reformed Church of the Netherlands: the exotic character of collections left by Mennonites and Lutherans ministers or Roman Catholic priests would certainly have been worth signalling.

Two kinds of sources serve as the basis upon which this thesis builds. First is the auction catalogues themselves. I have transcribed fifty-five auction catalogues of libraries owned formerly by ministers. These fifty-five auction catalogues are a cross-section of surviving ministerial catalogues. The process by which I chose these particular catalogues was based on three criteria. Certain catalogues were chosen because of the stature of their owner. André Rivet was professor of theology at Leiden, the personal tutor to William II and a prolific author. Jacob Arminius and Sibrandus Lubbertus were central actors in the Remonstrant controversy. Other catalogues were chosen because the printer included good descriptions for the books. Rather than only stating 'Augustine, *Opera*', these catalogues give a full bibliographic description such as Augustine's *Opera Omnia x tom 9 vol* (Basel, 1543). These two criteria were then filtered to provide geographic and chronologic diversity. I chose to transcribe catalogues whose owners resided in a wide range of places in the Netherlands throughout the century. All but one of the transcribed catalogues are available at Book Sales Catalogues Online (BSCO), the exception being the collection of Bernard Somer.[34] Envisioned in part by Bert van Selm, who served

---

33   *AC Petrus Gribius 1666* (Amsterdam: Johannes van Someren, 1666), USTC 1846470.

34   *Catalogus variorum ac insignium librorum instructissimae bibliothecae Bernardi Someri* (Amsterdam: Henricum & Viduam Theodori Boom, 1685) Wolfenbüttel, HAB: BC Sammelband 9:20, USTC 1825590. For all other catalogues I have transcribed, see *Book Sales Catalogues Online – Book Auctioning in the Dutch Republic, ca. 1500–ca. 1800.*, advisor: Brill, Leiden and Boston: Brill, 2015 <http://primarysources.brillonline.com/browse/book-sales-catalogues-online>.

as a founding editor, BSCO is the most comprehensive database of digital facsimiles of Dutch auction catalogues.

My transcription of the data from these catalogues resulted in a database of 96,798 listed books. This database records the author, title, book format and bibliographic information, if given. Prices are also transcribed when preserved in the auction catalogue. I have provided classifications for the books, indicating whether a book is on theology, history, grammar, philosophy or some other topic. The database also records when notes are made about books. For example, the catalogue for André Rivet's library makes note of when one of his books includes manuscript notes, and these are recorded in the transcription database. The information was transcribed into Microsoft Access, so that the data could be sorted and analysed by multiple criteria.

For the remaining 180 or so surviving catalogues, I have analyzed the total number of books listed in each catalogue, the sizes of books (folio, quarto, octavo and duodecimo and smaller) and the languages of books listed in each catalogue.[35] In addition to this survey of the auction catalogues, I have also made substantial use of evidence relating to the ministers' lives and careers: books, letters, synodal acts and archival sources. These sources provide vital evidence of how ministers acquired their books and how they used them.

The available sources on Dutch religious life during the seventeenth century are abundant. In addition to surviving printed works and modern editions of synodal acts, many provincial and city archives have conglomerated materials from churches in their region. While this makes a lot of diverse material available with greater convenience, there are few collections of ministers' papers. The letters and memoirs a minister wrote contain much of the information needed to understand how they acquired books. A major exception to this is the preservation of André Rivet's correspondence at the University of Leiden. Approximately 3,000 letters to and from him survive, and several hundred have been edited and published in modern editions. Rivet's letters to and from the French advisor of the Parliament of Paris Claude Sarrau were edited and published from 1978 to 1982.[36] The correspondence Rivet exchanged with Claudius Salmasius between 1632 and 1648 was published in 1987.[37] Rivet's writings combined with his auction catalogue offer an abundant and heretofore neglected source of material on building a library in the seventeenth-century Dutch Republic: how a Reformed theologian and minister interacted with the

---

35   This analysis is provided in the appendix to this volume.

36   Hans Bots and Pierre Leroy (eds.), *Correspondence Intégrale, d'André Rivet et de Claude Sarrau* (3 vols., Amsterdam: APA – Holland University Press, 1978–1982).

37   Hans Bots and Pierre Leroy (eds.), *Claude Saumaise & André Rivet, Correspondance échangée entre 1632 et 1648* (Amsterdam: APA – Holland University Press, 1987).

printed book. He regularly discussed acquiring, sending and reading books. The auction catalogue offers the most comprehensive evidence for the books he owned, and his correspondence and publications detail much of the process by which he built his library. This project will, therefore, turn to Rivet and his library more often than most other ministers.[38]

Rivet was an influential professor of theology and tutor to William II, so he is not typical of every Dutch minister. He owned a library of nearly 5,000 books. Few others had the opportunity to amass such a collection of texts. Nevertheless, analysis of surviving ministerial catalogues makes clear that Rivet is not wholly different from his ministerial colleagues. The difference between the collection owned by Rivet and those owned by less influential and less wealthy colleagues is a difference in degree, not kind. Rivet simply owned more books. His motivation to acquire books and the means by which he acquired them were largely the same as other ministers. Books were a standard feature in the lives of ministers, and the ideal minister acquired a well-stocked library. Ministers, Rivet included, valued print in their endeavour to care for their flocks as preachers and counsellors.

1 The Rise of the Book Auction Catalogue in the Netherlands

By the time that Demetrius' collection was sold in 1628, the auction of private book collections with a pre-distributed catalogue was an established part of the Dutch book trade. The first known auction of a private library with an accompanying catalogue took place in 1599 in Leiden. At least seventy-eight book collections sold at auction by the end of 1628. Printed book auction catalogues emerged as an efficient method of advertising the sale of a book collection. In 1596 Louis (II) Elzevier, whose father was the famous Leiden publisher and university beadle, was given the rights to auction books in the Great Hall of the Binnenhof in The Hague, the centre of Dutch politics and law. Such a location was ideal for book auctions because it was a hub for news, information and books. The booksellers' guild had little authority over the sales that took place in the Binnenhof. Servants of the state, administrators and jurists formed a large proportion of the book buying community at the time, creating a sufficient market at the centre of the new Republic.[39]

---

38   Forrest C. Strickland, 'Building a library in early modern Europe: André Rivet and his Books', in Graeme Kemp, et. al. (eds.), *Book Trade Catalogues in Early Modern Europe* (Leiden: Brill, 2021), pp. 161–192.

39   Bert van Selm, 'The introduction of the printed book auction catalogue: Previous history, conditions and consequences of an innovation in the book trade of the Dutch Republic around 1600', *Quaerendo*, 15 (1985), pp. 34–35.

Two years later, in 1598, Philips van Marnix, Lord of Sint Aldegonde died, leaving a substantial collection of at least 2,000 books behind. Leonard Casembroot, the executor of the estate, approached Elzevier with the idea of selling the remaining library in two parts. The jurisprudential works would be auctioned in The Hague; and the works of theology, history, and philology in the university town of Leiden. For the sale in Leiden, an auction catalogue was drawn up to advertise the sale. The auction of his books on jurisprudence in The Hague apparently did not warrant a catalogue. Marnix was one of the heroes of the Revolt, and the sale of his collection was a popular event that established a new cultural custom.[40]

Advertising the sale of private book collections with auction catalogues was a Dutch innovation, but neither the auction nor the book catalogue were novel in 1599 when the practice began. It was the peculiar genius of the Dutch to capitalize on pre-existing inventions and traditions and repurpose them for more productive ends. The auction of goods after a person's death, an 'inventory sale', was a recognized feature of the medieval and early-modern world. The goods of Elizabeth de Valois, Queen of Spain, were sold from 1569 to 1575. In 1602, Madrid saw the auction of some of the material possessions owned by Phillip II, who had died in 1598.[41] In the fifteenth and sixteenth centuries in the Low Countries, the auction of a person's estate including their books was common, especially in Leiden and The Hague.[42]

Book auctions had taken place in antiquity, and they had been taking place in the Low Countries as early as the fifteenth and sixteenth centuries.[43] Catalogues for book collections, also, were common in the early-modern world. At first, they were merely inventories of the books in a library. The catalogue for a personal collection was usually drawn up by the owner themselves or their heirs. Some institutions drew up detailed lists of their book collections. Monasteries occasionally composed a list of the books they owned.[44] The library of the University of Leiden was catalogued in 1595 as a guide to the titles in the collection.[45]

---

40   Van Selm, 'The introduction of the printed book auction catalogue', pp. 35–38.

41   Hobson, 'A Sale by Candle in 1608', p. 232.

42   Van Selm, *Een menighte treffelijcke Boecken*, pp. 13–20.

43   S. K. Padover, 'Muslim Libraries', in James Westfall Thompson (ed.), *The Medieval Library* (New York: Hafner, 1957), pp. 361–362; E. J. Worman, 'Two book-lists from the Cambridge Genizah Fragments', *Jewish Quarterly Review*, 20 (1908), p. 454; Hobson, 'A Sale by Candle in 1608', p. 232; Bert van Selm, *Een menighte treffelijcke Boeken*, pp. 11–13.

44   Archer Taylor, *Book Catalogues: Their Varieties and Uses*, p. 2. For examples of these catalogues, see idem., *Problems in German Literary History of the Fifteenth and Sixteenth Centuries* (New York: Modern Language Association of America, 1939), pp. 155–159.

45   E. Hulshoff Pol, 'The Library', in Th. H. Lunsingh Scheurleer and G. H. M. Posthumus Meyjes (eds.), *Leiden University in the Seventeenth Century: An Exchange of Learning* (Leiden: Universitaire Pers Leiden/Brill, 1975), pp. 394–459.

Within about fifty years of the invention of print around 1450, a new purpose was devised for these catalogues: they could be used to help sell books. The first stock catalogue was composed by the Venetian printer Aldus Manutius in 1498 to advertise his editions of Classical works in small formats. Two other catalogues, in 1503 and 1513, were also printed during his lifetime. In the second half of the sixteenth century, catalogues were regularly printed to advertise the books on sale at the major international book fairs in Frankfurt and Leipzig. A regular series of catalogues survives for Frankfurt from 1564 and Leipzig from 1595. It was the Frankfurt catalogues that served as the model for the first catalogue that Elzevier published.[46]

Dutch printers were exceptional in their use of printed auction catalogues. Auctioneers in Denmark, Sweden, Germany, England, France and Spain eventually began using printed auction catalogues, but they were significantly later than the Dutch. The first auction catalogue outside of the Republic came from their neighbours to the south in Brussels in 1614. The practice became common in the Southern Netherlands in 1636. Twenty years later, in 1656, a printer from Helmstedt produced the first known auction catalogue printed in the Holy Roman Empire. Five years later, in 1661, the first Danish catalogue was printed. Sweden followed in 1664. Twelve years after the Swedes, the first auction catalogue for a sale in England was printed in 1676.

The Dutch were not only the first users of book auction catalogues: they were the most prolific producers of auction catalogues in the seventeenth century. We have 430 for the British Isles, and 200 for Denmark. French booksellers were slow to take up the emerging practice of advertising a sale with a printed catalogue. One repertoire lists only sixty sales catalogues printed between 1630 and 1700 preserved in the Bibliothèque nationale de France, to which an additional eleven have since been added.[47] In using publicly available catalogues to raise national and international interest in the sale, Dutch booksellers pioneered a new method of selling books, one that eventually became common throughout Western Europe to varying degrees, but was not matched in the seventeenth century.

---

46 A. H. Laeven, 'The Frankfurt and Leipzig Book Fairs and the History of the Dutch Book Trade in the Seventeenth and Eighteenth Centuries', in C. Berkvens-Stevelinck et al. (eds.), *Le Magasin de l'Univers: The Dutch Republic as the Centre of the European Book Trade* (Leiden: Brill. 1992), p. 188. Van Selm, 'The introduction of the printed book auction catalogue, part 1', *Quaerendo*, 15 (1985), p. 43.

47 Francois Bléchet, *Les ventes publiques de livres en France 1630–1750; répertoire des catalogues conservés à la Bibliothèque Nationale* (Oxford: The Voltaire Foundation, 1991). On French catalogues, see Helwi Blom, '"Il sest vendu depuis peu une assez bonne bibliotheque": the Republic of Letters and the sale catalogue of the library of "Mr. Briot"', in Graeme Kemp, et al. (eds.), *Book Trade Catalogues in Early Modern Europe* (Leiden: Brill, 2021), pp. 361–398.

14   CHAPTER 1

2   The Dutch Context

The Dutch Republic was a prosperous nation at a time of economic and political crisis. Born out of religious persecution in the Southern Netherlands, the
Dutch Republic would transform what was a remote outpost of Charles V's
Habsburg empire into the most economically productive area in Western
Europe. The emergence of this powerful and prosperous nation out of revolt at
the end of the sixteenth century led Sir William Temple, British ambassador to
the Dutch Republic, to pronounce his hosts in 1673 'the envy of some, the fear
of others, and the wonder of all their neighbours'.[48]

Within a generation of the Fall of Antwerp in 1585, the Dutch Republic
was an economic powerhouse. Making the most of their oldest enemy, the
sea, the United Provinces of the Dutch Republic challenged Spanish trade in
the Americas and Asia, eventually becoming the dominant sea-faring nation.
At the beginning of the seventeenth century, in 1602 and 1611 respectively,
the Dutch East India company and the Amsterdam Exchange were established. Dutch economic genius in trading was in acting as middlemen, making low-risk investment in bulk trades. Cornelis Pieterszoon Hooft, father of
P. C. Hooft, once remarked, 'Most of our power and prosperity is due to the
Imperium maris and to foreign trade'.[49]

In the seventeenth century, books too could be an advantageous financial
investment, because books, by and large, retained their value. In 1649, 1679 and
1688 three copies of John Chrysostom's eight-volume *Opera* (Eton, 1612–1613)
sold for, respectively, forty-seven gulden and ten stuivers, forty-three gulden
and ten stuivers and thirty-two gulden and ten stuivers.[50] Unlike many other
household items, books could be bought and used and eventually re-sold without losing too much value from the original purchase price. The prices of books
about which Rivet inquired in 1628, after all, had changed little when his collection sold in 1657. Therefore, a decently sized collection could be used in effect
as an inheritance plan: to pay off debts ranging from a few hundred gulden

---

48   Sir William Temple, *Observations upon the United Provinces of the Netherlands*, ed. George
      Clark (Oxford: Clarendon Press, 1972), p. 1.

49   '… onse meeste kracht en weluaert bestaet bij het Imperium maris en bij de buyten-
      landtsche commercien'. P. C. Hooft, *Memoriën en adviezen van Pieter Corneliszoon Hooft*
      (2 vols., Utrecht: Kemink, 1871–1925), I, p. 236.

50   John Chrysostom, *Opera* (Eton, 1612–1613), USTC 3005371. *AC Fredrick Spanheim* 1649
      (Leiden: Severyn Matthysz ven. Gualter de Haes, 1649), USTC 1435659; *AC Jacobus Gaillard
      1689* (Leiden: Johannes du Vivié, 1689), USTC 1847229; *AC Abraham Heidanus 1679* (Leiden:
      Felix Lopez de Haro & widow and heirs Adrianus Severinus, 1679), USTC 1846941.

to several thousand, or they could serve as general financial support for the widow and heirs. In 1633, when the exiled English theologian William Ames died in Rotterdam, he left behind his books and an impoverished family. One of the first steps to alleviate this burden was to sell his library of 570 books.[51] The same was true for the collection owned by Jacob Arminius.[52]

During the Dutch Golden Age, literacy rates in the Dutch Republic became the highest in Europe. One study estimates that literacy rates in the Netherlands doubled over the course of the seventeenth century.[53] By 1650, about seventy per cent of Amsterdam grooms could sign their names, about fifty per cent of brides could do the same.[54] In comparison with their contemporaries in England, France, and Germany at the time, the Dutch were an extraordinarily literate people. It would take centuries before literacy rates in Southern Netherlands would match the levels found in the Dutch Republic during the Golden Age. Fifty-one per cent of Belgian army recruits were illiterate in 1843, compared to twenty-six per cent in the Netherlands.[55] Joseph Scaliger remarked in 1603 that 'in the Netherlands, peasant women and men, and almost all maid servants, are able to read and write'.[56] As far back as 1567, the Italian historian Lodovico Guicciardini reported the same of inhabitants of the Dutch countryside. 'Common people typically have some knowledge of grammar, and they are all, including farmers and rural people, at least able to read and write'.[57] Guicciardini even claimed, with a certain measure of exaggeration, that many Dutch citizens could speak foreign languages, even if they had never been abroad.

Literacy in the Netherlands served at least two purposes during the Dutch Golden Age: commerce and religion. In a small, industrious nation such as the

---

51 K. L. Sprunger (ed.), *The Auction Catalogue of the Library of William Ames: A Facsimile Edition with an introduction* (Utrecht: HES Publishers, 1988), pp. 5–6.

52 C. O. Bangs (ed.), *The Auction Catalogue of the Library of J. Arminius* (Leiden: Brill/Hes & De Graaf, 1984).

53 S. Hart, 'Enige Statistische gegevens inzake analfabetisme te Amsterdam in de 17e en 18e Eeuw', *Amstelodamum* 55 (1968), pp. 3–6.

54 Frijhoff and Spies, *1650: Hard-Won Unity*, pp. 236–7.

55 Jonathan Israel, *The Dutch Republic: Its Rise, Greatness, and Fall 1477–1806* (Oxford: Clarendon Press, 1995), p. 686.

56 H. J. de Jonge, 'The Latin Testament of Joseph Scaliger, 1607', *Lias*, 2 (1975), pp. 249–258.

57 'De ghemeyne lieden hebben meestendeels wat beginsels in Grammatica: ende konnen schier al t'samen jae oock de boeren ende landtlieden ten aller nunsten lesen en schryven'. Lodovico Guicciardini, *Beschryvinghe van alle de Neder-landen; anderssins ghenoemt Neder-Duytslandt* (Amsterdam: Willem Jansz Blaeu, 1612), USTC 1031392, p. 27.

Netherlands, literacy was required for a business to thrive.[58] Citizens needed the intellectual framework to navigate a complex commercial economy built on trade and exchange. The creation of an efficient communication system based on literacy was arguably the central factor of Dutch commercial expansion.[59]

Religious practice in the Netherlands was greatly indebted to literacy as well. Roman Catholics depended on books as a means of discreetly building the faith, and towards the end of the seventeenth century, the Catholic book trade flourished in Amsterdam.[60] And yet, it still remains true that the Reformed faith was a catalyst for the growth of literacy in the Dutch Republic. Jean-François Gilmont hesitated to take up the question because it had been so regularly discussed.[61] Protestant countries had higher levels of literacy on average. But there was great variation even between Protestant countries. Calvinism in the Northern Netherlands built on pre-existent civic culture of which literacy was a part.[62] In the period of confessionalization, the late sixteenth through the seventeenth century, Calvinism and Catholicism sought to make their dividing lines clear; in Willem Frijhoff's words, 'to enhance their identity by singling out elements that made them special'.[63] In contrast to the religion of images, Calvinism 'sanctified literacy', making it 'the sacrament of the individual encounter with God'.[64] Frijhoff's argument brings clarity to why such a disparity existed between Protestant countries in literacy, but it also reaffirms the point made by Gilmont. There was an undeniable connection between literacy and the Protestant Reformation. The Reformed movement and the desire to flourish economically were motivations held simultaneously by countless men and women in the Republic. The two motivations stemmed

---

58   Margaret Spufford, 'Literacy, trade and religion in the commercial centres of Europe', in Karel Davids and Jan Lucassen (eds.) *A Miracle Mirrored: The Dutch Republic in European Perspective* (Cambridge: Cambridge University Press, 1995), pp. 229–233.

59   Clé Lesger, *Handel in Amsterdam ten tijde van de Opstand. Kooplieden. Commerciële expansie en verandering in de ruimtelijke economie van de Nederlanden ca. 1550–ca. 1630* (Hilversum: Verloren, 2001), pp. 209–249.

60   Elise Watson, 'Networks of Devotion: Book Catalogues and the Catholic Print Industry in Amsterdam, 1650–1700', in Graeme Kemp, et al. (eds.), *Book Trade Catalogues in Early Modern Europe* (Leiden: Brill, 2021), 193–211.

61   Jean-François Gilmont, 'Protestant Reformations and Reading', in Guglielmo Cavallo and Roger Chartier (eds.), *A History of Reading in the West* (Polity: Cambridge, 1999), pp. 213–237.

62   Willem Frijhoff, 'Calvinism, Literacy, and Reading Culture in the Early Modern Northern Netherlands: Towards a Reassessment', *Archive for Reformation History*, 95 (2004), pp. 252–265.

63   Ibid., p. 263.

64   Ibid., p. 258.

MINISTERS AND THEIR BOOKS IN THE 17TH-CENTURY DUTCH REPUBLIC 17

from two different goals, piety and commerce. The means of accomplishing both was education.

The historical roots of literacy in the Republic are found in the Dutch emphasis on education. There was an abundance of educational opportunities.[65] By the end of the seventeenth century, there were five universities and six illustrious schools. Illustrious schools were preparatory academies for students typically destined for a university-level education, but illustrious schools did not grant formal degrees. Latin grammar schools for children, boys and girls, grew as well and were common even in smaller towns and rural villages. In 1529 Erasmus of Rotterdam called for the education of the young in the liberal arts. He contended that intellectual growth was equal in importance to physical growth. Care for the child, he argued, should be split equally between a nurse 'to nurture him in body' and a teacher 'of good character and respectable learning to whose care you may safely entrust your son to receive the proper nourishment for his mind and to imbibe, as it were, with the milk that he suckles, the nectar of education'.[66]

Though literacy and greater economic opportunity were the immediate targets, the inculcation of civic and religious virtue were the ultimate aim of education. In the *Trap der Jeugd* (*Staircase of Youth*), the Frisian Carel de Gelliers offered some example texts that students ought to learn. These were, to take a few examples, 'on diligence', 'the fear of God', and 'the suffering of Christ'.[67] One *Matery-boek* printed in Deventer in 1700 had the students practice their writing by copying proverbs. Students would repeatedly write: 'Belongings lost, nothing lost; courage lost, much lost; honour lost, more lost; soul lost, everything lost'.[68] As the title of the book makes clear, the education of youth in

---

65   Marc Wingens, 'The Motives for creating Institutions of Higher Education in the Dutch Republic during its formative Years (1574-1648)', *Paedagogica Historica*, 34 (1998), pp. 443–456.

66   Desiderius Erasmus, 'A Declamation on the Subject of Early Liberal Education for Children', trans. Beert C. Verstraete, in J. K. Sowards (ed.), *Collected Works of Erasmus*, vol. 26 (Toronto: University of Toronto Press, 1985), p. 299. Cf. J. K. Sowards, 'Erasmus and the Education of Women', *Sixteenth Century Journal*, 13 (1982), pp. 77–89.

67   Carel de Gelliers, *Trap der Jeugd* (Franeker: Joh. Arcerius, 1661), USTC 1845973.

68   'Goet verlooren, niet verlooren / Moet verlooren, veel verlooren / Eer verlooren, meer verlooren / ziel verlooren, al verlooren'. *Matery-boexken, of Voor-schriften seer bequaem voor de jonkheyt om wel te leren lezen, schryven, en een aenporringe tot alle deugden* (Deventer: A. Kurtenius 1700), USTC 1848048. Cf. Andrew Pettegree and Arthur der Weduwen, *The Bookshop of the World: Making and Trading Books in the Dutch Golden Age* (New Haven: Yale University Press, 2019), p. 156. Here, I have replaced the early-modern '/' with a semi-colon for clarity.

18   CHAPTER 1

reading and writing was for the stimulating of all virtues. Royalty and merchant alike needed such an education.

3 Available with the Booksellers

Financial prosperity, high rates of literacy and the valuing of education all combined to create an environment in which book auctions could become commonplace. The 2,092 Dutch book auction catalogues represent the libraries of all sorts of people within the Dutch Republic. Lawyers made up a considerable portion with 241 catalogues. Doctors made up a smaller portion with 153 catalogues. There were seventy-five catalogues from city magistrates, from Breda to Enkhuizen. There are twenty-six catalogues from the libraries of justices of the peace, which sold mostly in the last fifty years of the century. Auctions of six diplomats sold in The Hague, one in Leiden. Students, statesmen, and schoolmasters all had their collections sold by auction.

There were also many catalogues that list the collections of individuals who would not be expected to acquire large libraries. Libraries of brewers sold at auction in 1659 and 1698. In 1681, the auction catalogue of a glazier named Cornelis Didersz. sold in Amsterdam. Johannes du Vivié sold the collection of an instrument-maker in Leiden in 1695. The catalogue of a musician's library sold in 1693. Regardless of their profession, if someone owned a substantial library, they were keen that it should be auctioned in one of the major centres of the book trade.

Leiden dominated the auction market with Amsterdam following at some distance (Table 1.1 and Fig. 1.3). The dominance of Leiden was the result of both geographical and cultural factors. The Dutch Republic's interconnected web of rivers and canals provided the easiest and most consistent means of inland shipping on the continent. Books could be placed on barges and transported to cities with larger demand for books. The library owned by a minister in Cuijk, made the short journey to nearby Nijmegen.[69] More often than not, though, book collections were taken to Leiden. Boasting of his home city, Pieter de la Court claimed in 1659 that Leiden resided 'in a good place in the middle of Europe on both sea and rivers'.[70]

---

69   *AC Paulus Leupenius 1678* (Nijmegen: Gulielmus Meys, 1678), USTC 1846917.
70   'goede situatie in 't midden van Europen aen Zee en Rivieren', Pieter de la Court, *Het Welvaren van Leiden. Handschift uit het jaar 1659*, ed. Felix Driessen (The Hague: Martinus Nijhoff, 1911), p. 39.

MINISTERS AND THEIR BOOKS IN THE 17TH-CENTURY DUTCH REPUBLIC 19

TABLE 1.1 Known auctions of ministerial libraries by city. These figures include those auctions whose catalogues do not survive, but whose occurrence is known through newspaper advertisements, city archives and so forth

City	Auctions	City	Auctions
Leiden	178	Alkmaar	7
Amsterdam	89	Deventer	6
Rotterdam	32	Leeuwarden	4
Haarlem	30	Den Bosch	4
Dordrecht	20	Gouda	3
Utrecht	19	Groningen	3
The Hague	15	Nijmegen	2
Middelburg	12	Breda	1
Delft	9	Franeker	1
Hoorn	7	Kampen	1
Enkhuizen	7	Vlissingen	1
		s.l.	6

Leiden was also the intellectual capital of the United Provinces. With about a hundred students matriculating every year in the seventeenth century, along with numerous professors and a dozen ministers and their assistants serving in their city, there was a broader audience interested in books than was found in most other cities. Gerson Quewellerius, a one-time student of Franciscus Junius in Leiden and minister to the Walloon congregation in Wesel, had a sizable collection of 932 books. Wesel was a strategic fortress town just over the border in the Holy Roman Empire. There would not have been a substantial enough market to justify an auction of such a large book collection. Instead, his book collection was shipped down the old Rhine to Leiden where the University population would have the pick of the Reformed minister's library.[71] Leiden was a central hub in the Dutch book trade during this time. Dutch citizens recognized this. Leiden's students drove a large part of the city's auction market, and the university had to ensure auctions were not distracting them from classes too often. The rector and senate of the university decreed in May 1636 that auctions of small collections could only take place on Wednesday and Saturday, when there were no lectures, and at designated times on other days.

---

71   Bert van Selm, 'The introduction of the printed book auction catalogue, part 2', *Quaerendo*, 15 (1985), pp. 134–135.

Larger collections had to wait until vacation.[72] In 1648, the widow of Johannes Borardus, a minister in Dordrecht, requested permission from Leiden's magistrates to hold the auction of her late husband's books, 'because such a sale deserves to be held in a place with such a famous academy, since it is in Leiden that the most lovers of rare books reside'.[73] Classes were cancelled when the library owned by André Rivet sold in 1657.

The auctions of libraries owned by Dutch ministers were not elite events. The figure would seem to indicate the opposite (Fig. 1.4). Amsterdam and Leiden were the two cities where the bulk of auctions took place (fifty-nine per cent), but Amsterdam and Leiden often served as hubs in which collections owned by ministers in other cities would be sold. Though nearly sixty per cent of all auctions of ministerial libraries took place in either Amsterdam or Leiden, ministers that served in Amsterdam and Leiden account for only twenty-three per cent of all ministers whose collections sold at auction. Leiden is advertised as the place of sale for ninety-one surviving ministerial book collection in the seventeenth century. More than half of these collections were from owners who lived in other places. Ministers in towns and villages around Leiden like Katwijk, Noordwijk, Lisse and Oegstgeest had their collections sold in Leiden, but other collections came from all over the Netherlands. In 1641, the collection owned by Franciscus Gomarus was moved from Groningen, a city with its own university, for sale in Leiden, where he had taught theology.[74] The library of Carolus Schulerus, a minister in Leur (near Nijmegen), was likely placed on a barge on either the Waal or Meuse river and dispatched to Leiden for auction in 1692.[75]

The residence of ministers whose collections sold at auction mirrors the general concentration of population in the Netherlands during the seventeenth century (Fig. 1.5). The urban centres of Holland and Zeeland and the university towns of Utrecht and Groningen account for the majority of auctions, but smaller towns and rural villages are well represented in ministerial auction catalogues. The 457 auctions of ministerial libraries represent over 180 difference municipalities. Half of the auctions took place in small towns that had fewer than five auctions through the entire seventeenth century.

It was certainly the case that auctioneers had an interest in auctioning book collections that were profitable. Books were often traded for goods and services

---

72　Molhuysen, *Bronnen*, II, pp. 303, 316.

73　Erfgoed Leiden en Omstreken, Stadsbestuur II, inv. 67, f. 26or–v. Cited in Pettegree and Der Weduwen, *The Bookshop of the World*, p. 308.

74　*AC Franciscus Gomarus 1641* (Leiden: Bonaventura and Abraham Elzevier, 1641), USTC 1122202.

75　*AC Carolus Schulerus 1692* (Leiden: Fredrick Haaring, 1692), USTC 1846203.

by those in the print industry. And yet, cash was still needed, and auctioning off books was an effective means of liquidating stock for cash.[76] In some ways, this desire does not fundamentally alter our understanding of the libraries. Printers organized the catalogue to streamline what could have been a tedious process: going through numerous pages of text to find one book. By listing the books according to size, genre and language, a buyer could more easily find books that they wanted. Peeter Verhagen, the bookseller in Dordrecht, had apologized when he did not follow this pattern. Because profit was their prime motive, printers avoided providing a catalogue for smaller collections, probably of fewer than 100 books. A library with fewer than 100 books was not worth the time needed to compose and print an auction catalogue. Some ministers owned only a few books, perhaps a Bible, Psalm book for singing and a catechism. In a sense, that was the bare minimum that a minister could own. This indicates the distinction between the average minister and the average ministerial library catalogue. Many ministers likely owned a handful of books, meanwhile the average ministerial library catalogue listed over a thousand books. The average number of books listed in a ministerial auction catalogue is certainly higher than the average number owned by a minister in the Dutch Golden Age. Nevertheless, the substantial number of surviving catalogues and their similarities point to features within ministerial culture during the Dutch Golden Age that were not reserved to a select few.

Bert van Selm noted that auction catalogues must be used critically, one reason being a book auction catalogue does not always perfectly preserve the library of the owner who is advertised on the title-page of the catalogue. One reason for this is some books were passed down to children and family members, especially smaller devotional works and school-books.[77] Larger, more expensive books tend to survive more often than smaller works, as Theo Clemens demonstrated is the case with Catholic prayer books in the Netherlands from 1680–1840.[78]

Another reason auction catalogues must be used with caution is because books were sometimes added to the auction catalogue that were not originally in the owner's collection.[79] Occasionally, printers of the catalogues inserted

---

76 José de Kruif, *Liefliebbers en gewoontelezers. Leescultuur in Den Haag in de achttiende eeuw* (Zutphen: Walberg Pers, 1999), p. 120.

77 Van Selm, *Een menighte treffelijcke Boecken*, pp. 102–110.

78 Theo Clemens, *De Godsdienstigheid in de Nederlanden in de Spiegel van de Katholieke Kerkboeken 1680–1840* (Tilburg: Tilburg University Press, 1988).

79 Bert van Selm, 'Particuliere bibliotheken en boekenbezit', in his, *Inzichten en vergezichten. Zes beschouwingen over het onderzoek naar de geschiedenis van de Nederlandse boekhandel* (Amsterdam: De Buitenkant, 1992), pp. 84–85.

their own stock under the guise of being owned by the deceased.[80] This practice was forbidden by the booksellers of Leiden in 1636, though prohibitions of this sort seldom had much impact in practice.[81] This makes it more difficult to affirm that a minister definitely owned the books sold in his name, but this should not impact significantly on our overall sense of what sort of books ministers, collectively, were more likely to own. If a printer included thirty books from his stock in the auction catalogue of one minister's library, it would not substantially effect conclusions drawn from the 311,805 books listed in the ministerial auction catalogues I have analyzed or transcribed.

As will be described in more detail later, ministers sometimes read books that were not listed in their catalogues. Auction catalogues are a snapshot of the minister's books at his death. The contents of a library evolved throughout the owner's life.[82] For that reason, additional sources like a minister's letters are helpful to complement our understanding of the auction catalogue.

On 10 October 1607, the library of Johannes Halsbergius, an Amsterdam minister, sold in Leiden, accompanied by the first ministerial catalogue in the developing series of auctions.[83] In several material respects, his catalogue was similar to those ministerial catalogues that would come after. Most auction catalogues were printed in quarto format. At least 220 catalogues out of those surviving were in quarto. Only nine were printed in octavo, and five in duodecimo. Printers would often organize both large and small catalogues in this way: first they would divide the books into genres and then organize the genre by size, occasionally separating the vernacular books from the Latin. Halsbergius' catalogue is divided into eleven sections, which are further divided by size (Fig. 1.6).

Like Halsbergius' catalogue, the auction catalogue of Wilhelm Merwy, chaplain to the Dutch ambassador to Venice, is also divided by type of book and size (Fig. 1.7). Dutch books are given their own section. Occasionally, prices from the sale are written in the margins. We know that Merwy's collection sold for

---

80   Marieke van Egeraat, 'Adding Books in your Catalogues, or an ABC on how to sell left-over stock', in Graeme Kemp, et al. (eds.), *Book Trade Catalogues in Early Modern Europe* (Leiden: Brill, 2021), pp. pp. 140–159.

81   Laura Cruz, 'The secrets of success: Microinventions and bookselling in the seventeenth-century Netherlands', *Book History*, 10 (2007), p. 16.

82   Willem Frijhoff, 'Hollandse priesters en hun boekenbezit', in Willem Heijting and Sandra van Daalen (eds.) *Hollandse priesterbibliotheken uit de tijd van de Republiek: Catalogus van bibliotheken afkomstig uit de R.K. parochies te Aarlanderveen, Assendelft, Buitenveldert, Voorburg en Zevenhoven* (Amstelveen: EON Pers, 2005), pp. 15–33.

83   AC *Johannes Halsbergius 1607* (Leiden: Louis Elzevier, 1607), USTC 1122231.

MINISTERS AND THEIR BOOKS IN THE 17TH-CENTURY DUTCH REPUBLIC   23

almost 110 gulden. These prices also help show what is less clear in Halsbergius' catalogue: auctioneers would sell several books together as one lot. For example, four volumes in the duodecimo section were sold together for 8 stuivers, almost half a gulden.

Though Merwy's collection followed the developing practice in its organization, it lacks a feature that would become common in book auction catalogues: lot numbers. Over time, printers began numbering the books in each section. Of the 261 surviving catalogues, at least 215 have lot numbers. While lot numbers were useful for delineating different titles in the catalogue, some books (often bound together) are listed under one lot. Lot numbers, therefore, are not an exact representation of the number of books someone owned. Dutch printers overwhelmingly considered lot numbers a useful addition to the catalogue. On some occasions, printers would further subdivide sections into specific subsets of books. Rather than leaving *Libri Theologici* as a broad section, a few catalogues list theological books by era and confession. The auction catalogue for the books owned by Franciscus Gomarus divides theological works into biblical materials, the church fathers, the scholastics and contemporary theology.

The market for second-hand books extended beyond the town where the sale took place, encouraged by the distribution of catalogues. The catalogues were often sent to places far removed from the owner's residence, in the hope that eager buyers would bid by post or by messenger. When the library owned by a Muiden minister and medical doctor sold in 1667, the catalogue for the collection could be found in bookshops across the Netherlands. A newspaper advertisement for the sale noted, 'The catalogue is available in Amsterdam with Elias Ratelbant, in Leiden with Salomon Wagenaer, in Utrecht with Henricus Versteegh, in Haarlem with Abraham Casteleyn, in The Hague with Lescluse and in Muiden with the municipal secretary'.[84] No copy of the catalogue has been identified. Similarly, the catalogue for the collection owned by Wilhelmus Alstorphius, a minister in Deventer, was made available to those outside Overijssel. 'The catalogue can be found in Amsterdam with Joost Pluymer, in Utrecht with Johannes Ribbius, in Haarlem with Abraham

---

84   'Waer van de Catalogus is te bekomen tot Amsterdamel, by Elias Ratelbant, tot Leyden by Salomon Wagenaer, tot Uytrecht by Henricus Versteegh, tot Haerlem by Abraham Casteleyn, in den Haegh by Lescluse, en tot Muyden by den Secretaris'. *Extraordinare Haerlemse Donderdaegse Courant. 17. 29.09.1667.* Cf., Arthur der Weduwen and Andrew Pettegree, *News, Business and Public Information. Advertisements and Announcements in Dutch and Flemish Newspapers, 1620–1675* (Leiden: Brill, 2020), p. 300.

Casteleyn, and so forth'.[85] Printers occasionally assumed newspapers readers already knew the places in which auction catalogues were found. Take the advertisement for the sale of books owned by Abdias Widmarius, a professor of theology in Groningen: 'The catalogue will soon be available in various places'.[86] One advertisement stated the catalogue for the library owned by Adolph Visscher was 'available with various booksellers'.[87]

Ministers' books did not only circulate in the Netherlands alone; readers in other countries acquired books formerly owned by Dutch ministers. The auction catalogues themselves were sent to major international print centres throughout Western Europe. Pieter Leffen advertised the sale of the library owned by André Rivet in the *Tijdinghen uyt verscheyde Quartieren* [*Tidings from Various Quarters*], a newspaper published in Amsterdam. Leffen sent the catalogue to booksellers throughout Europe, in Paris, London, Denmark, and Germany.[88] In the advertisement, he noted the collection would be easily accessible to interested parties:

> On 6 November the library of the late Andreas Rivet, consisting of many beautiful and rare books, will be auctioned in Leiden at the house of Pieter Leffen. The auction catalogue is available with the booksellers.[89]

Books sold at Dutch auctions can now be found in libraries around the world. International students contributed to the circulation of books. Often, they would buy books at auctions and send them to people in their homeland, often their sponsors. Students from Hungary were required by law to bring back as many books as possible for the benefit of the Collegium where they had

---

85   *Oprechte Haerlemse Saterdaegse Courant. 21. 26.05.1668.* Cf. Arthur der Weduwen and Andrew Pettegree, *News, Business and Public Information. Advertisements and Announcements in Dutch and Flemish Newspapers, 1620–1675* (Leiden: Brill, 2020), p. 319.

86   *Oprechte Haerlemse Dingsdaegse Courant. 40. 02.10.1668* Cf. Der Weduwen and Pettegree, *News, Business and Public Information*, p. 331.

87   'de Catalogus is te bekomen by verscheyde Boeckverkopers'. *Ordinarise Middel-weeckse Courante. 15. 08.04.1653.* Cf. Der Weduwen and Pettegree, *News, Business and Public Information*, p. 144.

88   Nobel and Van der Meij, '"De Luijden sijn daer seer begeerich na"', p. 224.

89   'Den 6. November eerstkomende, sal tot Leyden ten huyse van Pieter Leffen, Boeckverkooper inde Klockstegh, by openbare Auctie werde verkoft de naergloten Bibliotheecq van d'Heer Andreas Rivetus zal bestaende in veele schoone en rare Boecken, waer van de Catalogus by de Boeckverkoopers zijn te bekomen'. *Tijdinghen uyt verscheyde Quartieren*, no. 41, 13 October 1657, and no. 43, 27 October 1657. Cf. Arthur der Weduwen, *Dutch and Flemish Newspapers of the Seventeenth Century, 1618–1700*, vol. 1 (Leiden: Brill, 2017), p. 306.

previously studied.[90] Many books from the auction of Sibrandus Lubbertus' library were taken back to modern day Romania, where they have been rediscovered by Ferenc Postma.

When, in 1629 and 1630, the library owned by Balthazar Lydius sold in Dordrecht, those interested had the opportunity to buy a huge variety of books. He owned the largest known book collection amongst ministers in the Dutch Golden Age, 5,900 books. One book, the *Acta consili Pisani* made its way into the collection of Cesar Calendrini, an Italian refugee and minister to the Dutch congregation at Austin Friars in London. It is listed in a lot containing several of books on councils in the second of Lydius' two catalogues.[91] On the title page of the *Acta*, Lydius had inscribed his name. After Calendrini died, some of his books were acquired by Daniel Williams (1643–1716), a theologian and minister in London. This particular volume survives in the Dr. Williams Library in London.[92] It is not unlikely that other books owned by ministers in the Netherlands during this time circulated in much the same way, from collection to collection.

4   Sold at Auction

From 22 June to 13 July 1639, Gualtherus de Bruyn defended four dissertations at the University of Utrecht. His professor, Gisbertus Voetius had composed all of them. On those four Saturdays, Voetius argued, through his student, against the rise of unorthodox views of the Christian faith. Anything that detracted from the pure faith led to atheism. The ideas and beliefs a person embraced led them further down one of two paths: greater godliness or eventual disbelief. In *De Atheismo* he confronted the most famous philosopher of the day, René Descartes, whose *Discourse on Method* was published two years before in 1637, but he also targeted Roman Catholics. Descartes elevated reason above divine revelation; Roman Catholic theologians elevated tradition over biblical

---

90   Ferenc Postma, 'Op zoek naar Franeker academisch drukwerk. Impressies van een drietal studiereizen naar Roemenie (1991–1993)', *Jaarboek van het Nederlands Genootschap van Bibliofielen*, 1 (1993), pp. 27–47; idem, 'Op zoek naar Franeker academisch drukwerk. Enkele impressies van een vierde studiereis naar Roemenië (1994)', *Jaarboek van het Nederlands Genootschap van Bibliofielen*, 2 (1994), 125–147.

91   AC *Balthazar Lydius 1630* (Dordrecht: Widow of Peeter Verhagen, 1630), USTC 1021757, f. Aiii.

92   With thanks to Jane Giscombe, conservator of the Dr. Williams Library, for bringing this book to my attention.

authority. Both deified human beings, leading to practical atheism in which God has no more authority than man.[93]

The venerable professor of theology was never one to allow his students and readers to forget the controversies that plagued the Roman Catholic church at the time. In this instance he hoped the poems by the Papal Nuncio, Giovanni della Cassa would be remembered in perpetuity. The Italian poet had written thinly veiled erotic poems that were alleged to have homosexual undertones.[94] One poem in particular, *Il capitolo sopra il forno* [*The Chapter on the Oven*], caused an uproar amongst Protestant ministers in the 1550s, and provided ammunition for one of the most common polemical attacks against their Roman foes.[95] Heinrich Bullinger, the nephew and successor to the Zurich Reformer Heinrich Bullinger, 'kept [*Il capitol sopra il forno*] as a monument of the abominable impurity of a papistical Bishop', as one visitor to Bullinger's library noted in 1611.[96] Voetius, in 1639, joined the tumult. To ensure the Roman Catholic authorities could not whitewash the poems from their history, Voetius encouraged all 'lovers of truth' to

> commit books of this kind ... to the locked cases and public protection which libraries afford, so that librarians can allow the interested to see them. This should be done lest, when the libraries of private individuals are dispersed at public auction, hostile persons through their agents draw all copies into their nets at any price, and destroy them.[97]

Because of the important role of print in Dutch Golden Age society, there was an abundant supply of second-hand books. From the beginnings of the seventeenth century, this second-hand trade encouraged the development of a lively

---

93   Gisbertus Voetius, *Selectarum Disputationum Theologicarum* (5 vols; Utrecht and Amsterdam: Johannes Janssonius van Waesberge, 1648–1669), USTC 1836590, II, p. 1113.

94   Helmut Puff, *Sodomy in Reformation Germany and Switzerland 1400–1600* (Chicago: University of Chicago Press, 2003), pp. 158–163.

95   Winfried Schleiner, 'Burton's Use of praeteritio in Discussing Same-Sex Relationships', in Claude J. Summers and Ted-Larry Pebworth (eds.), *Renaissance discourses of desire* (Columbia: University of Missouri Press, 1993), p. 164.

96   Thomas Coryate, *Coryat's Crudities*, vol. 2 (reprint, 1611; London: W. Cater, 1776), p. 206. With thanks to Sarah Rindlisbacher for bringing my attention to this source.

97   'Hac occasione moneo & obtestor omnes veritatis amantes, ut & hic & alibi libris ejusmodi, quorum nonc pudet Papistas, aut quos alioquin abolitos aut expurgatos velint, publicis bibliothecarum custodiis & obseratis capsis committant, quò per bibliothecarios conspectus eorum concedi possit illis, quorum interest. Hoc ni fiat, privatorum bibliothecis auctione publica distractis, quovis pretio in nassam suam per emissarios exemplara omnia pertrahent adversarii'. Voetius, *Selectarum*, I, USTC 1012125, p. 205.

market for book auctions; and, from 1599, the appearance of the first printed book auction catalogues. Prosperity and infrastructure provided the material resources; a culture of literacy and education, grounded in the need for the absorption of the Christian faith, provided the motivation.

This project poses a series of fundamental questions about ministers and their libraries. Chapter 2 ('That All May Be Instructed') considers why ministers valued print and how they understood it as a tool for spiritual growth. Chapter 3 ('Buyers of Truth') turns to the general contours of their libraries and how they acquired and afforded books. It also compares ministerial libraries to those owned by lawyers and doctors that also sold at auction. Dutch ministerial catalogues were often divided into *libri Theologici* and *libri Miscellani*. Therefore, chapter 4 ('Guardians of the Faith') focuses on the theological books ministers owned, and chapter 5 ('Learned Servants') considers the non-theological books and how ministers used them.

Ministers were the largest profession of book buyers and collectors, and hundreds of catalogues of their libraries detail their book-buying habits. The culture of seventeenth-century Dutch ministers is captured, in part, by the auction catalogues that survive today. By using these catalogues, we can begin to trace the particular relationship these men had to the intellectual material that was in abundant circulation throughout the Dutch Golden Age. A deeper understanding of their engagement with books sheds light on the intellectual climate of an era.

The ministry was a reading profession. These religious and civil servants influenced their local communities as vocal public figures. Their task was to understand the Bible and present its meaning to those under their care, impressing upon them the demands God had for them. For this, ministers not only read books, but collected them.

CHAPTER 2

That All May Be Instructed

When Franciscus Ridderus entered the ministry in 1644, few would have expected him, the son of a middling pastor, to rise to prominence in the Dutch Reformed Church. Most ministers would spend their lives in relative obscurity, toiling away in the often thankless work of preaching and counsel. Ridderus' career began in a similarly uneventful manner. Like many other new Dutch ministers at the time, after studying theology at university he was called to a small village church. The village of Schermerhorn, where he began to exercise his charge in 1644, would be far in the distance when he finished the race set before him. In two successive leaps, Ridderus climbed to the highest echelon of the ministerial class: in 1648, he left Schermerhorn for Den Briel, at the time a growing industrial town in South Holland; after eight years he made the journey up the Maas River to Rotterdam, one of the Republic's largest cities. He became a recognized leader in the Dutch Reformed Church. One of his colleagues in Rotterdam held him up as an example of erudition.[1] Utrecht University awarded him an honorary degree in 1682.[2] Ridderus' works are listed consistently in the book inventories of Norwegian Lutheran ministers in Trondheim, Bergen, and Hedmark.[3]

During his twenty-seven years in Rotterdam, Ridderus published works comprising over 27,000 printed pages, becoming one of the most prolific and popular theologians at the time. Many of his books addressed the practical concerns of Christians at the time. On 13 August 1663, Ridderus signed the preface of his book entitled *Nuttige Tiidkorter voor reizende en andere luiden* [*Useful pastimes for travelers and other people*]. The *Useful pastimes* was one of ten new works Ridderus wrote in the 1660s. The moralizing dialogue between a statesman, a minister and a skipper would go on to be modestly popular. By 1667, the work had gone through four editions and been enlarged to include Ridderus' developing thoughts.

---

1 G. van den End, *Guiljelmus Saldenus (1627–1694): Een praktisch en irenisch theoloog uit de Nadere Reformatie* (Leiden: Groen en Zoon, 1991), p. 254.

2 Gijsbert Schaap, *Franciscus Ridderus (1620–1683): Een onderzoek naar zijn theologie, bronnen en plaats in de Nadere Reformatie* (Gouda: Vereniging voor Nederlandse Kerkgeschiedenis, 2008), p. 12.

3 Gina Dahl, *Book Collections of Clerics in Norway, 1650–1750* (Leiden: Brill, 2010), pp. 41, 71, 135, 277.

THAT ALL MAY BE INSTRUCTED

The goal of the book could not have been made clearer. After the title page, Ridderus extracted three passages from the Bible, Jeremiah 2:10–11, Ezekiel 3:6 and Matthew 11:20–24. All three were intended to draw the reader to repentance. Ridderus casts himself as a seventeenth-century Ezekiel, to whom God said, 'I do not send you to people of low speech and darkness of tongue, whose words you could not understand: would they not, if I had sent you to them, hear you'?[4] If that was not enough, these words hung over the passages: 'for those who do not bow before God's law are convinced by the Heathen'.[5] Ridderus had a particular form of sin in mind: wasting time being bored, or, which is worse, devoting one's precious time to slanderous discussions or crude jokes.

Ridderus' desire to write the book came after a conversation with a colleague on 'how usefully time could be spent on the occasions by drawing good and heavenly thoughts from all kinds of incidents and histories; which I consider of such use to myself, that for my own purpose I put together several histories and applied beneficial reflections'.[6] With dialogues on such topics as writing letters, bread, wine (and drunkards), clothing, games and students, Ridderus offered the reader plenty of intellectual fodder with which to redeem the time, forty-two topics in total.

He devoted the eighth dialogue to a friendly discussion on books. Shifting the conversation from the nature of sleeping, the statesmen showed his fellow travelers the booklet he had intended to read, and so pass the time usefully. But, he admitted, the discussion was 'so pleasant to me that I do not need to read it'.[7] After the statesmen questioned 'what is a man who has no knowledge of good books', the theologian offered his thoughts on reading and the beginning of wisdom. Learning from books was a duty of all people, especially Christians. 'An open book', the theologian declared, 'is a rite of passage for a man to be wise, and especially for a Christian, an open Bible. Because books, as well as the Bible, are of no use if not studied'.[8] Reading wholesome books opened the

---

4 'Ik zende u niet tot vele volkeren diep van sprake, en zwaar van tonge, welkers woorden gij niet kond verstaan: zouden zij niet, zoo ik u tot hen gezonden had, naugehoort hebben'? Franciscus Ridderus, *Nuttige Tiidkorter voor Reizende en andere Luiden* (Rotterdam: Joannes Naeranus, 1663), USTC 1800117.

5 'Die zig voor *Godes Wet* niet beigt, Word door *de Heiden* overtuigt'. Ibid.

6 'hoe nuttig de tijd konde werden door gebracht bij alle gelegenheid door *goede* en *Hemelsche* gedachten te trekken uit allerlei *voorvallen* en *historien*; het welke ik mij zoo te nutte maakte, dat ik voor mijn eigen gebruik veel *historien* te zamen stelde, en tot goede meditatien toe paste'. Ibid., f. *3.

7 'maar ons discours valt mij soo aangenaam, dat ik daar in niet behoeve te lesen'. Ibid., p. 66.

8 'Een open boek is een recht teiken voor een wijs Man, en bijsonderlijk voor een Christen, een open Bibel: Want de Boeken, zoo ook de Bibel, doen geen nuttigheid, indien ze niet opgeslagen worden'. Ibid., p. 76.

fount of knowledge, wisdom and godliness, giving the reader access to the archives of human intellectual endeavour throughout written history.

Ridderus followed his own advice. His collection of almost 1,700 books sold at auction a few months after his death.[9] Filled to the brim with biblical commentaries, theological treatises and devotional tracts, Ridderus read deeply from the Christian tradition to develop his intellect and deepen his understanding of the faith, and so, as he understood it, leading to greater godliness. The ancient philosophers of Greece and Rome complement the contemporary works of oratory, psalters, Bibles, and English Puritan works. If he began collecting books at the age of eighteen, Ridderus would have bought an average of about thirty-five books a year until his death in 1683. Ridderus built a library worthy of a minister in the Dutch Republic in the Golden Age.

Ridderus was not alone in seeing books as tools in cultivating the heart and protecting the pious from unorthodoxy. In 1683 in the Republic, there were four other auctions of ministerial book collections. The average size of a minister's collection sold in the 1680s was 1,708 books. In Rotterdam alone, another thirteen collections owned by minister would be sold at auction before 1701. Dutch ministers in the Golden Age understood the printed word as a powerful force for a further Reformation of the heart into conformity with Christ.

Ministers competed for hearts and minds. Books were necessary and powerful tools in the culture of persuasion. For a minister, building a library was, in a sense, like building a wall against the derision of false teachers. For Protestant ministers, Protestant books were a shield against the onslaught of their Roman Catholic opponents, and many ministers thought the Catholic church would be made irrelevant by the power of the written word. This is illustrated clearly in an anonymous engraving entitled *De Bijbel op de Weegschaal* [*The Bible on the Weighing Scale*] (Fig. 2.1). The Bible was the final authority for Protestant ministers, and works by Luther, Calvin, and other ministers aided the process only when they drove readers back to the Bible. Such was a minister's goal when writing a book. Ministers held up the Bible and celebrated all ministers who wrote to free the Bible from Church Tradition. Orthodox commentaries and treatises on the Bible were not only historical and linguistic aids to understanding an ancient text. They helped solidify the Bible's weight on the scale. For this task, a robust library would be necessary to secure the authority of the Scriptures.

The ideal minister in the Netherlands was a well-educated, godly servant, shepherding his local congregation with compelling sermons and sound counsel. At provincial and national synods, in which church officials would

---

9 *AC Franciscus Ridderus 1683* (Rotterdam: Marcus van Rossus, 1683), USTC 1847118.

assemble to make resolutions binding on the represented churches, the rigorous expectations placed on ministers were regularly discussed. Article one of the acts of the general synod of Dordrecht in 1578 states that a minister must be pure in doctrine and life, with aptitude in education, and his character must be affirmed by those inside and outside of the parish.[10] The *classis*, a body of representatives from neighbouring parishes, was responsible for admitting new ministers into church ministry in their area, based on these criteria. Candidates had to demonstrate facility with the Bible. They had to pass an in-depth examination summarizing the main points of doctrine and give a defense of them from Scripture. The *classes* hoped this rigorous process would help weed out those who had not dedicated themselves to pursuing the necessary intellectual qualifications of a minister. In Dordrecht between 1578 and 1587, the *classis* was particularly strict. Though there was a desperate need for ministers to fill empty pulpits, only twelve of the twenty-nine candidates were accepted.[11] The *classis* of Sneek, from 1583 to 1625, had a similar rate of failure, with only nine out of twenty-one prospective ministers passing.[12]

Such a lofty goal was not always attained. The uneducated but godly minister fell far below the ideal. Though *classes* often had stringent requirements for entry into the ministry, they were not perfect. The Reformed Church in the Netherlands faced a logistical problem. The population of the Dutch Republic was concentrated in a few urban centres. By 1650, forty per cent of the population resided in Holland. Across the Republic, thirty-two per cent of the population lived in towns with more than 10,000 occupants. Twenty-one per cent of the population in the Southern Netherlands, by comparison, lived in similar cities; in Italy, only fourteen per cent.[13] Nevertheless, sixty-eight per cent of the Republic's 1.5 million inhabitants lived in small towns and villages, just over a million people. Many Reformed ministers were needed to serve the needs of churches in such places.

There were not enough academically trained ministers to serve the population. Rural towns often did not have the luxury of turning down a willing

---

10   F. L. Rutgers (ed.), *Acta van de Nederlandsche synoden der zestiende eeuw* (reprint; Dordrecht: J. P. van den Tol, 1980), p. 234.

11   John Paul Elliot, 'Protestantization in the Northern Netherlands, a case study: The classis of Dordrecht, 1572–1640', (PhD Dissertation, Columbia University, 1990), p. 188.

12   Ingrid Dobbe, 'Requirements for Dutch Reformed Ministers, 1570–1620', in Theo Clemens and Wim janse (eds.), *The Pastor Bonus: Papers read at the British-Dutch Colloquium at Utrecht, 18–21 September 2002* (Leiden: Brill, 2004), p. 202.

13   Willem Frijhoff and Marieke Spies, *1650: Hard-Won Unity*, trans. Myra Heerspink Scholz (Basingstoke, United Kingdom/Assen, The Netherlands: Palgrave Macmillan/Royal Van Gorcum, 2004), p. 160.

32   CHAPTER 2

pastor, educated or not. The image of a shoe-maker turned minister was commonly used by other Reformed ministers during the seventeenth century, and not entirely without warrant.[14] A group of ministers, deacons and church members reported from Klundert in 1589 were pleased with their local minister, but had one concern. 'Some of the elders and deacons as well as a few members came together and, being asked about the doctrine and conduct of the minister, replied that they can only speak well of his doctrine, and they thank God for his gifts, yet they do wish that he sometimes studied rather better'.[15] When, in 1612, members of the *classis* of Drenthe visited a minister in Odoorn, a village near the German border, they were dismayed to find he did not own a copy of the Old and New Testament. Only slightly less dismaying was the fact his entire book collection was worth less than six gulden. He probably owned a collection of ten to fifteen books. He could take pride in the fact he owned any books: his colleague in Odoorn, Meyerus van Vries, had none.[16]

Church authorities and individual churches fought to remedy this problem. The long-term strategy included ensuring more and more students were adequately trained and dispersed throughout the country. In the absence of university education, uneducated ministers would have to depend on books for their development. In June 1574, after a visitation from the *classis*, a minister in Mijnsheerenland was found to be a particularly bad orator. The minister preached as if he was writing. Leiden University would not be founded until a year later, so sending him for formal training was not an option. To be better trained in preaching, the *classis* collected money for him to buy books. A representative from Dordrecht would check-in on him after some time, to ensure his preaching was improving.[17]

Not all rural ministers were without books, however. Seventy years after the Mijnsheerenland minister was chastised for his poor preaching, the book collection of a minister in nearby Puttershoek was placed on a barge to Leiden. The 189 books were owned by Thomas Laurentius, and sold on 1 July 1645.[18]

---

14   H. H. Kuyper, *De Opleiding tot den Dienst Godts Woord bij de Gereformeerden* (The Hague: Martinus Nijhoff, 1891), p. 267.

15   'Visitations of Reformed congregations around Dordrecht, 1589', in Alastair Duke, etc., (eds.) *Calvinism in Europe, 1540–1610: A Collection of Sources* (Manchester: Manchester University Press, 1992), p. 194.

16   G. Groenhuis, *De predikanten: De sociale positie van de gereformeerde predikanten in de Republiek der Verenigde Nederlanden voor ± 1700* (Groningen: Wolters-Noordhoff, 1977), p. 165.

17   J. Reitsma and S. D. van Veen (eds.), *Acta Der Provinciale en Particuliere Synoden, Gehouden in de Noordelijke nederlanden Gedurende de Jaren 1572–1620* (8 vols., Groningen: J. B. Wolters, 1892–1899), II, p. 147.

18   *AC Thomas Laurentius* (Leiden: Hieronymus de Vogel, 1645), USTC 1122036.

THAT ALL MAY BE INSTRUCTED   33

Rural ministers often had less immediate access to books, but that did not stop many from building sizable collections. Abraham Mellinus, a minister in Sint Anthoniepolder, less than ten kilometers east of Mijnsheerenland, owned a collection of 1,451 books. At least ten rural ministers owned collections with over a thousand books.

The ability to read offered ministers and theologians a channel by which they could argue for their cause. In the eyes of Dutch ministers, literacy was a principle tool in the development of informed pious citizens who would lead more purely Reformed lives. The spiritual, philosophical, and ethical standard bearers of the Church Fathers, the Reformers, and contemporary devotional authors were open to all who could read. Even classical authors of Greece and Rome and some medieval and Roman Catholic authors could be read for spiritual benefit. Though the source material changed with the publication of new books, the aim remained constant: spiritual and civic improvement.

1   Print and Piety

Religious life during the early-modern era was a multi-media experience, in which singing, hearing sermons, and seeing religious truths depicted as prints in books and on stage all played a part. Print, too, became a fundamental component of religious life in the Netherlands during the early-modern era. Catholic devotion in the Netherlands during the sixteenth and seventeenth century made significant use of print.[19] Prior to the Reformation, devotional Roman Catholic books were easily accessible throughout the Low Countries. The Council of Trent considered the printing press a necessary tool in the advance of Catholicism.[20] Religious authorities, Protestant and Catholic, recognized the spiritual benefit that could come from reading godly books.

Amongst Protestants, ministers themselves were crucial to the normalization of reading amongst lay church members. Without the demand from ministers, the book trade may never have exploded as it did at the beginning of the Reformation.[21] Luther himself made the argument for a literate public and minister. In his ode to the wonders of print, he even called it God's greatest

---

19   Andrew G. Johnston, 'Printing and the Reformation in the Low Countries, 1520–c. 1555', in Jean-François Gilmont (ed.), *The Reformation and the Book*, trans. Karin Maag (Aldershot: Ashgate, 1998), pp. 155–183.

20   Stijn van Rossem, *Het gevecht met de Boeken. De uitgeversstrategieën van de familie Verdussen, 1589–1889* (Antwerp: Antwerpen Universiteit Pers, 2014).

21   Andrew Pettegree, *Brand Luther* (New York: Penguin Books, 2015).

34 CHAPTER 2

gift to humans.[22] If the movement to renew the church and faith were to be realised in the lives of ordinary Christians, ministers would have to make public arguments for their cause.[23]

John Foxe (1516–1587), an early English Protestant, offered readers a brief history of the invention of the printing press. His retelling of the actual process of invention, who discovered it, when, and where, is brief and restrained. He maintained that though the human inventor may be unclear, the one who bears ultimate responsibility for offering the press to human-kind was blindingly obvious. 'Not withstanding, what man so ever was the instrument, without all doubt God himself was the ordainer and disposer thereof; no other wise than he was of the gift of tongues, and that for a singular purpose'.[24] Because the gift was so wondrous, Foxe considered the date of its invention worthy of being remembered as centuries passed. 'We find this aforesaid year of our Lord 1450', he exclaimed, 'to be famous and memorable, for the divine and miraculous inventing of printing'.[25] Foxe believed that through the printed word, the papacy would be brought down and that the Reformation of the Church into her original purity would be realized. 'Either the pope must abolish printing, or he must seek a new world to reign over: for else, as this world standeth, printing doubtless will abolish him'.[26] 'That Great Antichrist of Rome could never have been suppressed', Foxe continued, 'and, being suppressed, could not have been kept under, except this most excellent science of printing had been maintained'.[27]

From the beginning of the Reformation in the Netherlands, books played a central role in forming new Reformed believers. A minister of the Reformed congregation at Antwerp wrote to the church at Emden in 1555 concerning the books they had charged him to sell.

> Tell my beloved brother Jacob Michiels that I cannot yet send him the account for the books which he charged me to sell, but I know nevertheless that I have sold more than what he has received from me, for

---

22   Martin Luther, *Werke. Tischreden, 1531–1546* (Weimar: H. Böhlaus Nachfolger, 1912), I, p. 523 (no. 1038).

23   Andrew Pettegree, *Reformation and the Culture of Persuasion* (Cambridge: Cambridge University Press, 2005), pp. 146–155. Andrew Pettegree and Matthew Hall, 'The Reformation and the Book: A Reconsideration', *The Historical Journal*, 47, no. 4 (2004), pp. 785–808.

24   John Foxe, *The Acts and Monuments of John Foxe*, vol. 3 (London: Published by R. B. Seeley and W Burnside, 1868), p. 719.

25   Foxe, *Acts and Monuments*, p. 718.

26   Ibid., p. 720.

27   Ibid., p. 721.

THAT ALL MAY BE INSTRUCTED   35

> I still sell one or two from time to time and I have already paid out the money ... but I hope soon to settle accounts with him. I also occasionally sell one of my Lord Utenhove's Psalters and I would also certainly sell more if there were not so expensive for there are those who would sometimes take a dozen copies together if they could have them for 3 daalders in order to make some profit. Some of the brethren will only pay 2 stuivers a copy and reckon that for the number of pages they are too dear: this is the reason why they have not sold.[28]

A book gave ministers a voice beyond the walls of their local congregation. While the use of print was not unique to Protestant sympathisers, the emphasis on the laity engaging with such material was itself new. Protestant ministers in the Dutch Republic had to compete with generations of embedded Roman Catholic belief. Beginning with the ministers themselves, Protestants began using print to raise up learned preachers. The first Protestant reformers were deeply ingrained with book culture and considered books a tool for convincing ordinary people of their message. As both authors and students of book production, whose legacies are due in part to their profound insights into print, Calvin and Luther had a close understandings of the press and book culture, leading Andrew Pettegree to call them 'men of the book'.[29] Following the guiding stars of the Reformation, Protestant ministers were expected to be well read, understanding and preaching the Word. Such was the case for Luther's Germany, Calvin's Switzerland, and the Dutch Republic a century later.

In the letter to his congregation prefacing his four volume *Redelyke Godtsdienst* [*The Christian's Reasonable Service*] published first in 1700, Wilhelmus à Brakel (1635–1711) reflected on the role of printing and the Reformation. Writing books extended a minister's pastoral reach beyond Sunday sermons and formal times of teaching throughout the week. A book encapsulated and promulgated the minister's reflections and teaching. Books allow the minister to continue pastoring even after his death. 'God has wonderfully compensated for both the brevity of a minister's life as well as the limited scope of his audience', à Brakel wrote,

---

28   'The first Calvinist congregation. Antwerp and Emden, 1555', in Alastair Duke, etc., (eds.) *Calvinism in Europe*, p. 135.

29   Andrew Pettegree, 'Calvin and Luther as Men of the Book,' in Karen E. Spierling (ed.), *Calvin and the Book: The Evolution of the Printed Word in Reformed Protestantism* (Göttingen: Vandenhoeck & Ruprecht, 2015), pp. 17–32. On Calvin see Jean-François Gilmont, *John Calvin and the Printed Book*, trans. Karen Maag (Kirksville, MO: Trueman State University Press, 2005).

by having given man the wisdom to become acquainted with the art of printing. It should be noted that this began during the time when the church was about to depart from Babylon. This art was brought to perfection precisely when the Reformation dawned at the beginning of the sixteenth century. Now a single minister, even centuries after his death, is capable of preaching to an entire nation, yes, even to the entire world. With joyful readiness I seize this opportunity to preach long after my death, according to the measure of the gifts the Lord has bestowed upon me.[30]

Dutch ministers were precocious users of books. The average ministerial collection that sold at auction in the seventeenth century contained 1,141 books. With an average lifespan of about 55 years, ministers acquired about twenty books a year.[31] The number could be as high 100 books a year. This was the case for Stephen le Moyne, who acquired a collection over 5,000 books. Surviving auction catalogues of ministerial book collections portray a legion of ministers bent on building robust libraries. This was a necessary task for any minister. Their library represented the theological training, academic or informal, and pastoral reflection to which they had devoted themselves.

The power of books was not only found in owning them and using them for personal benefits: Dutch ministers were prolific authors. A preliminary investigation undertaken for the Universal Short-Title Catalogue suggests well over 10,000 theological books were printed in the Netherlands from 1650–1700. The average print runs for these books would have been over a thousand.[32] Therefore, approximately ten million theological books printed in the Netherlands were in circulation during this time. Without question, publications by ministers were some of the most ubiquitous books in the entire country. Devotional works were some of the most popular books of the time. Two catechisms were best sellers, for example: *Catechizatie over den Heidelberghschen Catechismus der gereformeerde christelicke religie* [*Catechism on the Heidelberg Catechism of the Reformed Christian Religion*] by Petrus de Witte and *Christelicke catechismus*

---

30 Wilhelmus à Brakel, *The Christian's Reasonable Service*, ed. Joel R. Beeke, trans. Bartel Elshout (4 vols., Grand Rapids: Reformation Heritage Books, 1992–1995), IV, p. cxiv.

31 This average is based on the dates provided in Fred van Lieburg, *Repertorium van Nederlandse hervormde predikanten tot 1816: Predikanten* (2 vols., Dordrecht, 1996).

32 Otto S. Lankhorst, *Reinier Leers (1654–1714), uitgever & boekverkoper te Rotterdam: een Europees "libraire" en zijn fonds* (Amsterdam/Maarssen: APA-Holland University Press, 1983), p. 44: Bert van Selm, 'Onderzoek naar volkslectuur in de vroegmoderne tijd', in his, *Inzichten en vergezichten. Zes beschouwingen over het onderzoek naar de geschiedenis van de Nederlandse boekhandel* (Amsterdam: De Buitenkant, 1992), p. 68.

der Nederlandtsche gereformeerde kercken [*Christian Catechism for the Dutch Reformed Church*] by Gellius de Bouma. From 1652–1697, De Witte's catechism went through forty-five editions and was published in eight cities by thirty-seven publishers; De Bouma's went through forty-nine editions between 1621–1687. It was published in ten cities by thirty-four different printers. Well over 100,000 copies of these two catechisms would have been in circulation.

Christ's church demanded nothing less than a ministry infused with books. Theology professors and high-ranking church leaders expected all ministers to be diligent users of books, as both readers and writers. If used correctly, books were a gift from God that elevated humanity's knowledge and reason; if used wickedly, they were a destructive force, working against the Reformed church. Confessionally-sound books were the answer. Though all people in the United Provinces, men and women, were expected to read for personal improvement, ministers had a duty to be consumers of books. With knowledge of the nuanced contours of theology and the details of the Old and New Testament, ministers entered the pulpit with a lifetime of reading behind them. From the smallest villages of the inland provinces to the urban centres of Holland, Dutch ministers purchased, read and wrote books.

Theological education initiated them into the class of well-read servants of the Church. The curriculum of Dutch universities focused heavily on reading and interacting with print. Many formal lectures were discussions or explanations of books. In informal classes, students could expect a quiz on a book.[33] But, their studies did not begin with the field of theology; it began with grammar.[34] Thorough knowledge of Latin allowed the student access to the greatest theological tomes written throughout the history of the church. The authoritative religious texts were all written in Latin. Greek and Hebrew, similarly, ensured that a student could understand the Bible in its purest form, not through the eyes of a translator. Only after these linguistic skills were mastered would a student then move on to studying the catechetical points of the Reformed church and the biblical passages on which the confession was based. Once acquainted with the official theological convictions of the Reformed Church, then they could begin studying dogmatics. When studying dogmatics,

---

33 For lectures at Harderwijk, see Christaan Sepp, *Het godgeleerd onderwijs in Nederland gedurende de 16e en 17e eeuw*, vol. 2 (Leiden: De Bruek & Smits, 1874), p. 411. For lectures at Leiden, see Willem Otterspeer, *Groepsportret met dame: Het bolwerk van de vrijheid. De Leidse Universiteit*, vol. 1 (Amsterdam: Bert Bakker, 2000), p. 233.

34 F. G. M. Broeyer, 'Theological Education at the Dutch Universities in the Seventeenth Century: Four Professors on their Ideal Curriculum', in Wim Janse and Barbara Pitkin (eds.), *The Formation of Clerical and Confessional Identities in Early Modern Europe* (Leiden: Brill, 2005), pp. 115–132.

prospective ministers learned the art of persuading listeners of the Reformed faith and defending the cause from heresies. Such effort depended on being well read on the topic at hand.[35]

Several writers devoted works to the right practice of theological study. A list of recommended books was almost always included. In *De ratione studii theologici*, Heinrich von Diest, a professor of theology at Harderwijk, offered a two-hundred page introduction in duodecimo for the prospective minister. It included a manageable number of suggested books with which to begin.[36] Not all lists of suggested books would have been so helpful as that by Von Diest. The Utrecht professor, Gisbertus Voetius offered the readers of his *Exercitia et bibliotheca studiosi theologiae*, printed by Willem Strick in 1644, a seven-hundred page tome on the proper method of theological education.[37] Burdensomely comprehensive, the *Exercitia* demonstrated Voetius' erudition more effectively than pointing students and new ministers to the books necessary for their profession. It must be said that Voetius possessed one of the largest book collections amongst his ministerial colleagues, over 5,300 books. A minister in the Netherlands was supposed to be a learned and practical expositor of the Bible. Education of ministers was founded on reading, so they could more faithfully proclaim the Bible's teaching.

2 The Difficulty of the 'Reformed' Republic

Dutch ministers, often highly educated themselves, encouraged the education of the masses. The impetus behind much of the demand for education in the Republic came from the Reformed church. Education was a means by which the Reformed church could pursue national catechesis.[38] At the start of the Dutch Revolt, Protestants were a minority within the Habsburg Countries. The Reformed, while vocal and determined, nevertheless remained a minority. A few years after the Union of Utrecht established the United Provinces of the Northern Netherlands in 1579, the provincial States chastised the Reformed preachers for their criticism of the governing authorities by reminding them

---

35   Antonius Walaeus, 'Oratio de studij theologici recta institutione', in his *Opera Omnia* (2 vols., Leiden: Adriaen Wijngaerden, 1647–1648), USTC 1515253, II, p. 304.

36   Heinrich von Diest, *De ratione studii theologici* (Harderwijk: Nicolaes van Wieringen, 1634), USTC 1510759.

37   Gisbertus Voetius, *Exercitia et bibliotheca studiosi theologiae* (Utrecht: Johannes (I) Janssonius van Waesberge, 1651), USTC 1814113.

38   Leendert F. Groenendijk, 'The Reformed Church and Education During the Golden Age of the Dutch Republic', *Dutch Review of Church History*, 85 (2005), pp. 53–70.

THAT ALL MAY BE INSTRUCTED   39

only one in ten Hollanders were under the care of the Reformed church.[39] In 1600, the French ambassador observed that most of the population remained Catholic. Just two years before the Synod of Dort, Dudley Carleton quoted the Grand Pensionary Johan van Oldenbarnevelt as saying, Catholics were 'the largest and most affluent part of society'.[40] The clear majority of those who revolted were more moderate in their beliefs but saw the Reformed as an ally against their common enemy, Philip II and his surrogates. If the ministers of the public, state-supported church wanted to accomplish its mission of unifying the infant nation around a common faith and seeing the Protestant Reformation spread through all aspects of society, then levels of education and the literacy rate would have to rise.

The family was a central means to the dissemination of the faith. Education was a means of ensuring that the faith was passed down from generation to generation. The language of Deuteronomy 6:7, 'You shall teach them diligently to your children, and shall talk of them when you sit in your house, and when you walk by the way, and when you lie down, and when you rise', echoes in the encouragement given by Rotterdam minister Wilhelmus à Brakel.[41] Parents who disregarded the education and catechizing of their children prepared them for fleeing the faith and erosion of civic life. In the preface to his widely popular catechism, Petrus de Witte (1622–1669), minister in Leiden, wrote, 'Oh times, oh morals! What do parents do but bring up their children to become the prey of all kinds of seductive spirits, such as the papists, Anabaptists, Arminians, and libertines? Yes, even to become the booty of the devil, to be the heirs of eternal damnation and the fire wood of hell'.[42] To guard their children

---

39   'Het tiende deel van de ingesetene van den Lande niet is van de Gereformeerde Religie, daerom het voor een grote weldaed Gods te rekenen is, dat de gene die verre sijn de meeste in getale, geen openbare exercitie hebben, en die minste sijn Godes woord opentlijk en sonder achterdenken horen en de religie oeffenen mogen'. Pieter Bor, *Oorsprongk, begin, en vervolgh der Nederlandsche oorlogen*, vol. 2 (Amsterdam: Widow of Johannes van Someren, Abraham Wolfgangh, Hendrick en Dirck Boom, 1680), USTC 1816052, p. 976.

40   'la plus saine et plus riche partie de la population'. Jan den Tex, *Oldenbarnevelt* (2 vols., Cambridge: Cambridge University Press, 1973), II, p. 575. Alastair Duke recounts several local studies which confirm these contemporary estimates. 'The Ambivalent Face of Calvinism in the Netherlands, 1561–1618', in his, *Reformation and Revolt in the Low Countries* (London: Hambledon, 2003), pp. 269–270.

41   W. Fieret, 'Wilhelmus à Brakel – a Biographical Sketch,' in Beeke (ed.) *The Christian's Reasonable Service*, vol. 1, p. XLV. Cf. Willem Teellinck's encouragement to families in his, *The Path of True Godliness*, trans. Annemie Godbehere, ed. Joel R. Beeke (Grand Rapids: Reformation Heritage Books, 2003), p. 75.

42   'O tijden! O zeden! Wat doen die Ouders anders, dan hare kinderen op voeden tot een proye van alle verleidende geesten, van Papisten, Wederdoopers, Arminianen, Libertijnen, ofte ooc van geslagene Wereldlingen: ja zelve tot een roof van den Duivel tot Erfgenamen

40   CHAPTER 2

against such vices, children were to be instructed. De Witte would have been especially pleased if each family in the Republic decided to use his catechism.

From the beginning of the Republic through to the end of the seventeenth century, ministers regularly made the appeal for the availability of broad education. At the first synod of the Northern Provinces in 1574, ministers held that children should receive an education.[43] Ministers in Groningen in 1595 issued a regulation that each community should have a grammar school.[44] In 1606, the *classis* of Utrecht complained that the schoolmasters of Montfort and Amerongen taught from books of all sorts.[45] The schoolmaster in Abcoude taught only from Reformed textbooks, but, as reported by the local minister, 'he resorts to the taverns rather too often and he [the minister] certainly wished that he might be admonished by apt measures'.[46] A little over a decade later at the Synod of Dort, the ministers insisted that children should have the opportunity to benefit from education.[47] In an address to parents and teachers, one minister exhorted teachers to fulfil the dual role of encouraging godliness and vocational preparation. A teacher was called to 'please and glorify God by preparing youth for a public vocation, to shape their minds toward love for and service to their Creator, to further their salvation in the hereafter, and to foster their well-being here on earth'.[48] Poor parents should go out of their way to ensure their children were educated, and parents should give their children pocket money to spend on a good book.[49] A minister in Zierikzee encouraged those with the means to provide for the education of gifted children from poor families.[50]

Even in the farthest corners of the Dutch empire, ministers strove to have children educated so that they could grow to be faithful and upright

---

      der vervloeckinge en Mut zaerden voor de Helle'? Petrus de Witte, *Catechisatie over den Heydelberghschen catechismus* (Amsterdam: Baltus de Wild, 1655), USTC 1825219, sig. **4.

43   Jan de Vries and Ad van der Woude, *The First Modern* Economy: *Success, Failure, and Perseverance of the Dutch Economy 1500–1815* (Oxford: Oxford University Press, 1997), p. 170.

44   Jaap Bottema, *Naar school in de Ommelanden. Scholen, schoolmeesters en hun onderwijs in de Groninger Ommelanden, ca. 1500–1795* (Bedum: Egbert Forsten & Profiel, 1999), p. 19.

45   'State of the churches in Utrecht, 1606', in Alastair Duke, etc., (eds.) *Calvinism in Europe*, p. 197.

46   Ibid., p. 198.

47   P. Th. F. M. Boekholt and E. P. de Booy, *Geschiedenis van de school in Nederland vanaf de middeleeuwen tot aan de huidige tijd* (Assen/Maastricht: Van Gorcum, 1987), pp. 19, 42.

48   Jacobus Koelman, *The Duties of Parents*, trans. John Vriend, ed. M. Eugene Osterhaven (Grand Rapids: Reformation Heritage Books, 2003), p. 32.

49   Ibid., pp. 49, 164.

50   Godefridus Udemans, *The Practice of Faith, Hope, and Love*, trans. Annemie Godbehere, ed. Joel R. Beeke (Grand Rapids: Reformation Heritage Books, 2012), p. 246.

THAT ALL MAY BE INSTRUCTED 41

Reformed citizens. Sending word from 'New Netherland' on 11 August 1628, Jonas Michaëlius minister of the Dutch Reformed Church on 'the Island of Manhatas [sic]' wrote to Adrian Smout, a minister and member in the *classis* of Amsterdam. Smout would have been pleased to hear that,

> we must ... place [the children] under the instruction of some experienced and godly schoolmaster, where they may be instructed not only to speak, read and write in our language, but also especially in the fundamentals of our Christian religion, and where besides they will see nothing but good examples and virtuous lives.[51]

Devotional books on the Christian exercise of the trades demonstrate ministers' expectation that the lay member of their churches could read. Godefridus Udemans, for example, wrote three works on Christian seafaring: *Geetelijck Zee-Compas* [*The Spiritual Compass*] (1636), *Coopmans Jacht* [*The Merchant's Ship*] (1637), and *'t Geetelyck roer van 't coopmans schip* [*The Spiritual Rudder of the Merchant's Ship*] (1638). In the dedication to *The Spiritual Rudder*, Udemans exhorted the directors of the East and West India Companies to make it required reading for all those under their command.[52] Willem Teellinck, Udemans' co-labourer in Zeeland, dedicated his *Ecce Homo* to the directors of the East India Company, in the hope that they would provide their crews with copies.[53] Whether the Reformation principles became integral aspects of Dutch life and godliness or not, the corresponding rise in literacy rates certainly aided their cause and gave booksellers an ever-growing market. No longer selling only to public servants, ministers, academics and regents, now a common deck hand could read one of Udemans' tracts and discuss it amongst the crew. At least, that was Udemans' desire.

Print was not the exclusive domain of those ministers within the state-sanctioned church. This facet of the print world was present throughout the many theological controversies that marked the Dutch Golden Age, including the most consequential of all: the Arminian Controversy (1608–1620). What began as an academic tussle between two opposing professors of theology,

---

51   Jonas Michaëlius, *The First Minister of the Dutch Reformed Church in the United States* (The Hague: Printed by the Brothers Giunta D'Albani, 1858), p. 18.

52   Maria A. Schenkeveld-van der Dussen, 'Cultural Participation as Stimulated by the Seventeenth-Century Reformed Church', in Ann Rigney and Douwe Fokkema (eds.), *Cultural Participation: Trends Since the Middle Ages* (Amsterdam/Philadelphia: J. Benjamins, 1993), pp. 39–49, here p. 42.

53   Willem Teellinck, *Ecce homo, ofte Ooghen-salve voor die noch sitten in blintheydt des ghemoedts* (Middelburg: Hans vander Hellen, 1622), USTC 1018260, pp. 203–204.

erupted into a controversy with effects reaching far beyond Leiden University. The dispute on the nature of divine predestination in the salvation of the Christian became a proxy war between political factions. A National Synod was called to help calm the waters. Representatives from the seven provinces, along with delegates from Reformed Churches across Europe, met in Dordrecht to settle the issue. Victory, so the combatants thought, would ensure the concord of the provinces and the safety of the Church. To secure public allegiance, ministers, theologians, politicians and playwrights took to print. For over ten years, the followers of Arminius wrote passionately and abundantly for their cause. They called for an international synod to settle the issue. When the Synod of Dort convened, however, the writing was already on the wall. Remonstrant ministers were expelled from Churches, professors were dismissed from their chairs, and the political leader of the Remonstrant cause was tried and executed.

Contra-Remonstrants hoped Dort would be the final word on the debate. The plague of Arminian teaching would be expunged from the public arena, from both church and state. Yet, Remonstrant ministers continued to write, preach and teach. Remonstrant churches were formed and expelled ministers found publishers and printers who would disseminate their 'unorthodox' work. Remonstrant ministers were some of the most prolific authors of the early modern era. They churned out thousands of books, pamphlets, and printed sermons, despite being formally dismissed from public life by the victors at Dort. For example, The Synod of Deventer in 1619 condemned a minister after he 'spread copies of the godless Remonstrant [pamphlet] *Panorama* among the common folk, to the great scandal and injury of the simple'.[54]

Print, though unsanctioned, offered Remonstrant writers the opportunity to win converts to their side. The press was required to expanding their realm of influence beyond the Remonstrant churches still gathering. Leaders of the ousted faith hoped to establish a new city in which they could meet freely and from which they could steer their underground movement. They needed a beacon of hope for those embattled souls who identified with the Remonstrant faction.

In 1622 Nicolaus Grevinchovius wrote to Lord Frederick, Hereditary Prince of Norway. Grevinchovius had spent twenty years serving in Rotterdam, until his exile to Antwerp. Before the Synod, he had been a prolific writer and polemicist for his cause, and he became a leader in the struggle. The Rotterdam

---

54   J. Reitsma and S. D. van Veen (eds.), *Acta Der Provinciale en Particuliere Synoden, Gehouden in de Noordelijke Nederlanden Gedurende de Jaren 1572–1620* (8 vols., Groningen: J. B. Wolters, 1892–1899), I, p. 272.

THAT ALL MAY BE INSTRUCTED   43

minister asked the prince if he would allow the Remonstrant brotherhood to
establish a city on the Eider river, so they could earn their living in peace. He
was insistent that the new community would not be a bother to the prince.
They simply desired quiet lives. In addition to asking for liberty of religion and
exemption from excise trade, Grevinchovius enquired if could they establish
a printing press.

> Whether they, the said Remonstrants, may be allowed ... to set up a
> Printing-press there, and to sell and disperse their books, especially out
> of the dominion of your highness; and in case in the meanwhile if they
> should procure a Press for the town, whether they may have the liberty to
> make use of other Presses, within or without your Highness's jurisdiction,
> if they see fit?[55]

Regardless of the Protestant confession to which one adhered, reading perme-
ated the godly life. In church services, literacy allowed for full participation
in the experience. Ministers would read the morning's text and congregants
would follow along in their personal Bibles. Reading focused the mind to medi-
tate on divine truths. By first engaging the mind, reading prepared the heart
to glorify God. In large communities, church members would have to wait for
their turn to come to the Lord's Table.[56] During this time they could devote
themselves to meditation on the broken body and shed blood of Christ.[57] This
was done through reading.

In the frontispiece to *Het rechte gebruyck van des Heeren H. Avontmael* [*The
Right Use of the Lord's Communion*], men and women on either side of the
image have open books in front of them (Fig. 2.2). At the centre of the table, a
large, clasped Bible reminded partakers that the sacrament was beneficial for
them because it was a visual reminder of the Gospel message. In the shadows,
two women seem to discuss the significance of their books to the meal before
them. This was more common in larger communities, where communion

---

55   Geeraert Brandt, *The History of the Reformation and other Ecclesiastical Transactions in
      and about the Low-Countries* (4 vols; London: Printed by T. Wood for John Hicks, 1719–
      1723), IV, p. 417.

56   Willem J. Op 't Hof, 'Ra, ra, wat ben ik? Een speurtocht naar de traditie, de aard, het milieu
      en het gebruik van het bekendste Nederlandse avondmaalsboekje *Het rechte gebruyck
      van des Heeren H. avondtmael*', in Jan Bos and August den Hollander (eds.), *Disgenoten:
      Short-Title Catalogue van* Het recht gebruyck van des Heeren H. Avondtmael (Amstelveen:
      EON Pers, 2007), pp. 269–271.

57   Andrew Spicer, 'The Material Culture of the Lord's Supper', in Barbara Pitkin (ed.), *Semper
      Reformanda: John Calvin, Worship, and Reformed Traditions* (Göttingen: Vandenhoeck &
      Ruprecht, 2018), pp. 103–142, here pp. 104–105.

44 CHAPTER 2

required waiting. Despite numerous reprints, the frontispiece remained largely unchanged.[58]

Alongside prayer and reading the Bible, reading of devotional books became a regular expectation for the promotion of spiritual growth. In his introductory poem, Cornelius Witsius, a minister in Enkhuizen, summarized vividly how Guiljemus Saldenus' *De wech des levens* [*The Road of Life*] should affect the reader: 'A Christian Soul that reads this book // Is moved to true humility. / It works upon the Spirit fervently // And presses tears from eyes'.[59] Saldenus himself considered books medicine for the soul and body.[60] The duties of joining with other Christians on Sunday and hearing sound preaching remained central, but reading could be done in the quiet of one's home. With books, spare minutes and hours could be used for one's eternal benefit, rather than wasted on trivial pursuits.

3 Vainglorious and Irreverent Books

The abundant celebration of books and their role in the cultivation of piety is a theme with which scholars of the book trade are accustomed. Similar to Jean-Francois Gilmont's acknowledgement that there was little need to discuss Calvinism and literacy in early-modern Europe, the same sentiment can be felt about Reformed thinking on books. And yet there is another side to ministers' thinking: while books could uplift the human spiritual condition, they could also lay low the reader and eventually bring disrepute on the faith itself.

Countless disputes and controversies brought disgrace on Reformed theologians. As 'petty sophists', they would argue to the death on minute points of theology, even with those who were soundly Reformed in conviction. Herman Witsius (1637–1708), professor of theology at Utrecht and later Leiden, reflected on the atmosphere of the theological academy. Some ministers, driven by self-importance, strove after vain glory. They did this by being needlessly divisive and resorting to personal attacks. The church was burdened by the

---

58 Wilco van den Brink, 'Slijtagesporen en spiegelbeelden: Overeenkomsten en verschillen in de titelgravures', in Jan Bos and August den Hollander (eds.), *Disgenoten: Short-Title Catalogue van* Het recht gebruyck van des Heeren H. Avondtmael (Amstelveen: EON Pers, 2007), pp. 18–26.

59 'Een Christen Ziele die dit leest, / Die werdt in waer ootmoedt bewogen. / Dit werckt met yver op den Geest, / En parst de tranen uyt de oogen'. Cornelius Witsius, 'Eer Gesangh', in Guiljemus Saldenus, *De Wech des levens* (Utrecht: Jacob van Doeyenborg, 1665), USTC 1802085, fol. A9r. Here the '/' represent the lines breaks of Witsius' poem.

60 Saldenus, *De Libri varioque eorum, usu et abusu* (Amsterdam: Henrick Boom, 1688), USTC 1821540, p. 51.

THAT ALL MAY BE INSTRUCTED 45

incessant printing of hairsplitting disputations that led only to the confusion of the people, eroding simple Reformed faith. Witsius did not advocate the end of theological debate or that each opinion was worthy of appropriation by the faithful. He implicitly addresses Cartesians and explicitly the Remonstrants and Socinians. The purpose and tone of the debate, however, ought to be to the building up of the Church and winning an opponent over to see the truth of an argument. 'Solid learning, manners conformable to Christian sanctity, a peaceable disposition, and a faithful charge of our duty without noise and confusion, will procure favour much more than inconsiderate warm zeal, and the violent efforts of a passionate mind'.[61]

How should ministers then interact with each other in print so as not to bring disrepute upon themselves and damage the Church? Witsius humbly put forward his own work as an example of how to remain faithful to one's convictions but also modest in presentation. 'It is not an incurable itch of writing, a raging thirst after vain glory, an envious disposition of mind ... nor lastly, the infamous desire to make, increase, or continue strife which have occasioned my writing at this time'.[62] Witsius presented himself before a jury of professors of theology, pastors of Reformed churches, and the faithful, and he asked them to judge whether he has followed his own exhortation.

Witsius did not long fancifully for a past day when Dutch theologians were more civil and respectful, debating ideas without employing *ad hominum* attacks. That day had never existed. Hostile debate had raged for decades before Witsius was born. At the beginning of the seventeenth century, ministers' vitriolic disputes were known even to those outside the academy. There was arguably no time of greater contention than the Remonstrant controversy, 1608–1619. Dudley Carleton, English ambassador in The Hague and astute observer of Dutch daily life, noted in apparent disbelief the way ministers published against each other. Both Remonstrants and Contra-Remonstrants did 'the worst they can do to their opposites ... they fling dirt in one another's faces, the ministers themselves (of whom most temper and moderation should be expected) publishing in print all the ill they can possibly say of the other'.[63]

The crushing flow of books described by Witsius led Petrus de Witte to ponder, 'do you not have too many books'?[64] Books could bring life to a parched soul; but with too many of them, the reader would be left trying to keep their

---

61 Herman Witsius, *The Economy of the Covenants Between God and Man* (2 vols., facsimile, London, 1822; Reformation Heritage Books: Grand Rapids, 2010), I, p. 24.

62 Ibid., pp. 17–18.

63 Quoted in Jan den Tex, *Oldenbarnevelt* (2 vols., Cambridge: Cambridge University Press, 1973), II, p. 562.

64 'Hebt ghy niet vele Boeken'. Petrus de Witte, *Catechisatie over den Heydelberghschen catechismus* (Amsterdam: Baltus de Wild, 1655), USTC 1825219, f. *3.

46   CHAPTER 2

head above water. Such a complaint was common throughout the early-modern world. In England, John Owen (1616–1683) openly bemoaned the 'needless multiplying of books (whose plenty is the general customary complaint of all men versed in them)'. What then ought authors do? 'Less writing, and more praying'.[65] The irony was not lost on Witsius, Saldenus, or Owen: they were all prolific authors. Fewer books were not required of the orthodox. Authors of blasphemous, pernicious and cryptic books were those who should write less and pray more.

Though some like Carleton and Witsius thought the behavior of ministers in print eroded the hard-won reputation of the Reformed church, all orthodox thinkers thought the damage of such pernicious books would have on the faith was far worse. When the Church's enemies knocked at her gates, her defenders would take up every weapon against them. Unorthodox books were the bane of stringently orthodox theologians. These books were one of the primary tools to erode the faith and destroy the Church, and heretical books sought to undo the tireless labour of ministers preaching and writing.

When taking up the topic of impediments to the Church's conservation and growth, Gisbertus Voetius listed a host of obstacles both inside and outside the Church: enemies outside the church included heretical schools and conventicles to exercise idolatrous religion; within the church, deeds that were either superstitious, profane, carnal, or unjust.[66] Amongst impediments from outside the Church, Voetius spent the most time on malicious books. 'Blasphemous, heretical, idolatrous and superstitious books oppose, in fact prohibit honest and good morals, there is no doubt they in fact beget the opposite'.[67] 'Idolatrous, impious, heretical and schismatic books', stand in stark contrast to books of the orthodox, those that promote faith and good morals.

Occasionally, even church members aided in the distribution and dissemination of corrosive books, and in at least one instance, they faced ecclesiastical punishment in response. In 1691 Balthazar Bekker's *De betoverde wereld* [*The World Bewitched*], enflamed the Republic, leading to his dismissal from church office. Amsterdam's magistrates continued paying Bekker's salary, but

---

65   Quoted in Crawford Gribben, *John Owen and English Puritanism: Experiences of Defeat* (Oxford: Oxford University Press, 2016), p. ix.

66   Gisbertus Voetius, *Politicae ecclesiasticae* (4 vols., Amsterdam: Johannes (I) Janssonius van Waesberge, 1663–1676), IV, USTC 1561448, p. 378.

67   'Libri blasphemi, haeretici, idololatrici, superstitiosi, honestati et bonis moribus adversantes quin prohibendi, non dubito quenquam in genere negaturum'. Voetius, *Politicae ecclesiasticae*, IV, p. 378.

THAT ALL MAY BE INSTRUCTED

they could not keep their churches from exercising discipline on a 'sieur Aubin' who dared to translate Bekker's work into French.[68]

The experience of being censored by political authorities varied greatly in the Netherlands. An author whose work was censored did not always face the punishment censorship typically implied. The system of censorship was largely unable to contain heretical and seditious books.[69] Enforcement of censorship regulations could be capricious. Sheriffs occasionally turned a blind eye in return for bribes, in many cases allowing printers of censored books to work as they pleased.

Many ministers, nevertheless, strove ardently for more rigorous enforcement of censorship. During the Golden Age, 263 titles were forbidden by the secular authorities, and many of these prohibitions were initiated by ministers of the Dutch Reformed church. With the encouragement of local Reformed ministers, the provincial states of Zeeland, Holland, Utrecht, and the States General issued a general ban against Socinianism between 1651 and 1656. After the Dutch edition of Thomas Hobbes' *Leviathan* was printed in Amsterdam, in 1667 the *classis* of Amsterdam decreed people should not read it; a 1668 synod complained about its publication; in 1670, the Deputies of the Synods of South and North Holland made a formal request for the States of Holland to ban it, the same request was made again in 1671. After seven years of requests, in 1674 the Court of Holland forbade the 'printing, distributing, or selling' of *Leviathan*.[70] In Utrecht, Gisbertus Voetius petitioned the local magistrates to ban Rene Descartes' philosophical works. The ban was issued in 1642, but much to Voetius' dismay the magistrates likewise banned him from writing against Descartes.[71] Instances where ministers asked the civil authorities to ban books are common. When confronted with the reality of unorthodoxy, ministers considered censorship as a godly means to protecting the faith, ensuring there were as few hindrances as possible to the conversion of the nation.

In Franciscus Ridderus, Gisbertus Voetius had a co-labourer against the threat of wicked books and their authors. Rotterdam was a hot-bed of Remonstrant and unorthodox activity. After the dismissal of Remonstrant professors and

---

68 Edwin Bezzina, 'The Practice of Ecclesiastical Discipline in the Huguenot Refugee Church of Amsterdam, 1650–1700', in Karen E. Spierling, Erik A. de Boer, R. Ward Holder (eds.), *Emancipating Calvin: Culture and Confessional Identity in Francophone Reformed Communities* (Leiden: Brill, 2018), p. 171.

69 Ingrid Weekhout, *Boekencensuur in de noordelijke Nederlanden: de vrijheid van drukpers in de zeventiende eeuw* (The Hague: SDU Uitgevers, 1998).

70 Noel Malcolm, 'The Printing of the "Bear": New Light on the Second Edition of Hobbe's *Leviathan*,' in his *Aspects of Hobbes* (Oxford: Oxford University Press, 20), p. 381.

71 Frijhoff and Spies, *1650: Hard-Won Unity*, p. 266.

48   CHAPTER 2

ministers beginning in 1619, many settled in Rotterdam. Simon Episcopius, Johannes Wtenbogaert and others established a Remonstrant community there. In 1635, they wrote to Hugo Grotius, seeking his advice as a banished Remonstrant intellectual.[72] In 1680, at least four Remonstrant ministers served openly in Rotterdam.[73] Ridderus devoted his life to combating such deviant belief. In 1678, the widow of Arnout Leers printed Ridderus' tract *Worstelende Kercke* [*The Wrestling Church*]. In brief, digestible portions, Ridderus listed those who had misled the Church. The product was a hundred-page reference work that keen church members and other ministers could consult. Beginning with a 'Register of false spirits and heretics, and also those in error', Ridderus offered brief summaries of where these individuals were mistaken.

After a cursory biographical introduction, Ridderus summarized Nestorius' heretical view on the nature of Christ (Fig. 2.3). 'That in Christ there are two persons, the one, the Son of God, and the other, the son of Mary, and the Son of God united with the son of man not in a unity of persons, but in indwelling grace, like God is with the faithful, yet in a beneficial way.'[74] Of contemporary examples, Ridderus summarized the views of Brownists, Socinians, Arminians, Quakers, and Independents. Ridderus also addressed those 'in error [der dwalende]'. Augustine of Hippo and Martin Luther were of this sort. Rather than denying a fundamental precept like the person of Christ, Luther's error was concerning the Lord's Supper. Though he had rejected the Mass, he remained in error by believing consubstantiation.[75] Ridderus considered the heretical beliefs (and those who were in error) dangerous enough to summarize the main errors taught throughout church history, and he would respond to many of these errors in a three-volume commentary on the Bible in which he would summarize the teaching of a heretical group on a passage, and then offer the Reformed response.[76]

For all the grandeur of ministers' celebration of the spiritual good books could do, they also considered books a potential danger. While books could help lift the believer out of spiritual adolescence into mature adulthood, if the

---

72   UB Leiden, ms. PAP 2.

73   SAR, 326 Remonstrants Gereformeerde Gemeente Rotterdam (Lijst van Predikanten).

74   'Dat in Christo zijn twee persoonen, de eene, de Zoone Godts, ende de andere, de Zoone van Maria, ende dat de Zoone Godts sigh vereenight hadde met de Zoone des menschen, niet in eenigheydt des persoons, maer (1) door inwoonende genade, gelijck Godt met de geloovige vereenight is, doch evenwel op een heerlijcker maniere'. Franciscus Ridderus, *Worstelende kercke, ofte Historische vertooninge van het bestreden geloove* (Rotterdam: Widow of Arnout Leers, 1679), USTC 1815770, p. 60.

75   Ibid., p. 84.

76   Idem, *Apollos, ofte Zedige verantwoorder voor de leere der gereformeerde kercke* (3 vols., Rotterdam: Arnout Leers, 1666–1670), USTC 1803594, 1529865, 1557930.

THAT ALL MAY BE INSTRUCTED

author was unsound in spiritual matters a book could corrupt the reader or tempt them to sin. Discussing 'the temptation toward atheism', Wilhemus à Brakel argued that though the temptation is common, it is 'especially for those who have a keen intellect'.[77] Temptation to not believe in God, he argued, can be brought about by any number of reasons: some from the hand of God as a test, others directly caused by the believer's own action. One such action that could cause this state was absorbing the thought of atheists. 'Sometimes we can come into such a condition by reading atheistic books, hearing atheistic lectures or argumentation, listening to the complaints of those who are in such a state, or by carelessly giving expression to our inner thoughts'.[78] In another place, he simply stated 'Refrain from reading books authored by atheists or those who encourage atheism'.[79] Parents had a duty of ensuring that their children did not 'read or sing lighthearted ditties, or immerse themselves in bad and shallow love stories'.[80] Books were too effective in changing the reader for parents to allow their children to read frivolously.

4   'I Must Have the New Tidings'

The possibility for print to build up or tear down the faith is especially evident in the reception of newspapers amongst ministers. The ministry was a reading profession. Books lined the shelves of newly built bookcases and were used to fulfill their calling. But ministers read beyond commentaries and treatises: they read the news. This is no surprise. Newspapers were read widely across different social spheres. Regents and rural farmers alike read the *couranten*. In disbelief, the French ambassador to the Republic, Jean Antoine de Mesmes lamented in the 1680s 'everybody reads them here'.[81] This was no exaggeration. Numerous visual depictions of ordinary life in the seventeenth-century Dutch Republic portray the reading of newspapers. Typically, one person would be reading the news while at least one other seems to listen intently.[82]

While reading the newspaper was common, giving a minister a decent enough reason to do so, the news was also intimately connected to the heart of Dutch religious life in the seventeenth century. Dutch newspapers emerged

77   À Brakel, *The Christian's Reasonable Service*, IV, p. 193.
78   Ibid., IV, p. 196.
79   Ibid., I, p. 22.
80   Koelman, *The Duties of Parents*, p. 79.
81   Cited in Michiel van Groesen, 'Reading Newspapers in the Dutch Golden Age,' *Media History*, 22 (2016), p. 342.
82   Ibid., pp. 335, 338, 339, 340.

50 CHAPTER 2

in the 1610s, as the conflict between Remonstrants and Contra-Remonstrants became a political issue.[83] As political leaders aligned themselves behind theologians, the nation's international policy was called into question as the two sides, politicians and theologians, took opposing views on what should be done in the build-up for the Thirty Years' War. Even the first newsmen participated in the international process. Both Broer Jansz and Caspar van Hilten described themselves as former news writers associated with the Prince Maurice, who aligned himself with the Calvinist ministers. To encourage war to end the suffering of Calvinists across Europe, Jansz and Van Hilton 'offered welcome publicity to the tribulations of international Calvinism and certainly played a role in the encouragement of war sentiment in the Dutch Republic'.[84] For ministers in the Republic, reading the news would offer insight into the world around them and inform them about the plight of their brethren abroad.

Throughout the seventeenth century, Dutch ministers had one eye on the news and the other on the Bible. They believed God was acting in history through nations and monarchs. The news would have provided the most up-to-date information on the working out of divine providence. The Dutch closely identified with the people of Israel. Like Israel being freed from Egypt, the Dutch were liberated from Spanish slavery and now enjoyed the fruits of the promised land.[85] But, this identification also included a negative connotation. Would the Netherlands see a fate like Israel, being brought to repentance by an invading army? Would their faithfulness be rewarded with victory over their English enemies during the Anglo-Dutch war? Answers to such questions were found in the news. Under the pseudonym Ireneus Philalethius, Ewout Teellinck described the reading of newspapers and how they were a common source of public information. In discussion it is revealed that both Timotheus and Theophilus read the newspapers regularly: Timotheus shared the copies brought by his neighbour; Theophilus read both Amsterdam papers daily. Theophilus considered the *couranten* worthy of reading because they were an effective means of learning of news of other Christians and of other countries that were bound to the Republic.[86]

---

83 Arthur der Weduwen, *Dutch and Flemish Newspapers of the Seventeenth Century, 1618–1700* (2 vols., Leiden: Brill, 2017), I, p. 18.

84 Der Weduwen, *Dutch and Flemish Newspapers of the Seventeenth Century*, p. 18.

85 T. G. Koote (ed.), *De Bijbel in huis. Bijbelse verhalen op huisraad in de zeventiende en achttiende eeuw* (Utrecht: Museum Catharijneconvent, 1991).

86 'Maer in dese gelegentheyt van tyde, daer de geheele Christen Werelt gelyck als in roere staet, ben ick begeerich om te weten watter inde gelegentheyt van Boëmen, omme-gaet, want gewisselyck, na al datmen can mercken, daer syn groote saecken onderhanden, daer aen de geheele Christenheyt in 't gemeen, ende de Staet onser Landen, oock int

THAT ALL MAY BE INSTRUCTED   51

Ewout Teellinck was not alone in finding them beneficial. Included in a Delft minister's yearly budget were 'books, paper, ink and newspapers'.[87] The regularity of ministers pouring over the tidings was captured in a satirical dialogue written by an anonymous pamphleteer from the Southern Netherlands. Mennonites, Arminians, and Gomarists (Contra-Remonstrants) were all infatuated with the papers. 'Let the people stand on hope', the Mennonite declared, 'I think I will buy the new copy of the Tidings'. 'Aye', the Remonstrant responded, 'let us now hope to hear the call of the new Tiding'. The Gomarist could wait no more, 'I must read the new tidings, or I shall not have any patience'.[88] Occasionally, collections of newspapers were listed in a minister's auction catalogue. When Johannes du Vivié auctioned Nathan Vay's book collection, the English minister in Hulst owned 'Some English Newspapers [Eenige Engelsse Couranten]'.[89]

The desire to read the news, good or bad, was interpreted through Scripture. A torrent of bad national news crashed upon Ewout Teellinck in 1625: the Spanish defeated the Dutch in Bahia, Brazil; Stadholder Maurits died on 23 April; less than two months later, Breda fell to Spinola and the Army of Flanders. To understand it, Teellinck took to the Old Testament. These calamities could be nothing less than divine punishment: 'Look for I begin to bring evil upon the city which is called by my name, and ye be utterly unpunished? Ye shall not be unpunished'.[90] Like Babylon sent to chasten Israel, Spain was now the instrument of divine punishment for the nation's sins.[91] When French

---

bysondere, ten hoochsten aengelegen is, want na dat de saken daer gaen, soo sal het met ons oock waer-schynelyck hier gaen, ende nae dat de raderen haer daer keeren, daer na sullen oock onse saken haren keer nemen, midts dat ons lot oock daer in geworpen is'. Ireneus Philalethius [= Ewout Teellinck], *Boheemsch gelvyt ofte Christelyck gespreck, over het tegenwoordich Boheemsche wesen, ende de oorloge daer ontrent ontstaen* (Amsterdam: Paulus van Ravesteyn, 1620), USTC 1029470, pp. 3–4.

87   *Bewys, dat het een predicant met zyn huysvrouw alleen niet mogelijck en is op vijfhondert guld. eerlijck te leven* (Delft: Pieter de Menagie, 1658), USTC 1839928.

88   'Mennist.: Maetien ick ben welt te breden / 'T is mijn sijn ick gaen wat mede / Siet de lieden staen op hoopen / my dunckt sy nieuwe Tydingh coopen; Arminiaen. Iae maet laet ons nu wel hoepen / hoorte de nieuwe Tydingh roepen. Gom.: De nieuwe Tydingh moet ick lesen / oft ick can niet gherust ghewesen'. *Het geusen-gheschreeuw behelsende hoe de gommaristen, mennisten ende arminianen hebben gheroepen over die groote victorie* (s.l., s.a. [1635]), USTC 1001964, p. 3.

89   *AC Nathan Vay 1693* (Leiden: Johannes du Vivie and Jordaan Luchtmans, 1693), USTC 1841496, p. 111.

90   Michiel van Groesen, *Amsterdam's Atlantic: Printing Culture and the Making of Dutch Brazil*, p. 73.

91   Benjamin Schmidt, *Innocence Abroad: The Dutch Imagination and the New World, 1570–1670* (Cambridge: Cambridge University Press, 2001), p. 72.

52   CHAPTER 2

forces marched on the Republic from the east in 1672, ministers returned to a similar refrain of retribution for a sinful nation. Jacob Sceperus drew the connection between the Chaldeans and Babylonians warring with Israel and the French invading the Republic. 'The Chaldeans and the Babylonians were used by God for the chastisement of his people. To this end, God has also raised up the French, who are a rod in the hand of God, and a staff in his hand, to bring low the proud and brittle Hollanders'.[92] Victory, too, was a sign that the hand of providence directed the affairs of nations. When the Dutch triumphed over the English in the Third Anglo-Dutch War, ministers were quick to see this as a sign of divine favor. The success of the invasion of England in 1688 was an obvious sign of divine pleasure with young William's actions.[93] The flow of news informed the daily lives of ministers, and they interpreted such events through Scripture.

Not every minister was pleased with the immense popularity of reading newspapers. In contrast to his brother Ewout's celebration of the use of newspapers, Willem Teellinck considered them a convenient way to waste time; time that could be spent doing other beneficial things. The incessant weekly printing of news had captivated Christians. 'Published and printed on a weekly basis', Teellinck declared, these papers are 'read by Christians who do not bother to turn their eyes over the Scripture even once a week'.[94] To waste one's time untangling worldly lies from worldly truths contained in the *couranten* was vain. Later in the century, a Hoorn minister would repeat Teellinck's message almost to the letter: 'Church members read the newspaper two or three times (or listen to them being read), but do not read or listen to the Word of God one single time'.[95] The newspaper, like the book, was a tool in the process of developing a virtuous and godly citizenry. They could be used to build up or tear down. The necessity of disseminating beneficial material could not have been more apparent.

---

92   'De Chaldeen en Babylonieren wierden van God gebruyckt om sijn volck te kastijden: en tot dien einde gebruckt Godt nu oock de Francoisen: sy zijn een roede van Gods toorn, en een stoeck in sijne hant, om Hollandts hoogmoet en brootdronckenheyt te straffen'. Jacobus Sceperus, *De Chaldeen en Babylonieren onder de voeten van den koninck aller koningen* (Amsterdam: Jacques Boursse, 1673), USTC 1810411, p. 32. For other examples of such responses, see David Onnekink, *Reinterpreting the Dutch Forty Years War, 1672–1713* (Palgrave Macmillan: London, 2016), pp. 48–59.

93   David Onnekink, 'The Last Wars of Religion? The Dutch and the Nine Years War,' in David Onnekink (ed.), *War and Religion after Westphalia, 1648–1713* (Ashgate: Farnham, 2009), p. 78.

94   Theophilis Philopatris (= Willem Teellinck), *Geestelijcke covranten voor dit loopende quartier-iaers, over de swarigheden die ons de voorleden somer getroffen hebben* (The Hague: Aert Meuris, 1626), USTC 1031456, sig. ***v.

95   Cited in Van Groesen, 'Reading Newspapers in the Dutch Golden Age,' p. 10.

THAT ALL MAY BE INSTRUCTED 53

5 Printers and the Dissemination of Piety

Publishing and printing were a religious exercise of one's Christian duty to spread the faith. In Amsterdam, Marten Jansz Brandt was one of the most prolific publishers for the orthodox cause. He supervised the publication of at least 350 Reformed works. Most were small, cheap devotional or polemical works by some of the most stringent theologians of his day. Jacob Trigland, the 'Bishop of Amsterdam', was a fiery preacher and polemicist. When the Remonstrant controversy erupted in the 1610s, Trigland was a provocative defender of the Contra-Remonstrant side. Brandt published most of his works. Vondel identified Brandt as Calvinism's greatest champion in the print industry.[96] His shop was located at the back of the Nieuwe Kerk, under the sign of the 'Reformed Catechism'. During his twenty years of work, Brandt never published a work that was potentially damaging or in opposition to the Reformed faith.[97]

Many of Willem Teellinck's works were published by Brandt. The minister from Zeeland had two characteristics Brandt appreciated: he was a consistently popular author, and he was thoroughly Reformed. On the back of these two traits, Brandt hoped to sell books. To capitalize on Teellinck's name recognition, the publisher in the Reformed catechism produced a list of Teellinck's works. It was the first advertising list of its kind, and it went on to become a common feature of the Dutch book trade.[98] In a commentary by the English Divine Samuel Clarke, Johannes Boekholt (1656–1693), a printer in Amsterdam, included a list of the works Teellinck published.[99]

Teellinck allowed Brandt to compose the list because it was an effective method of encouraging the reading of godly books. Brandt would push commercialism too far, though, and lose one of his most popular authors in the process. In the second edition of Teellinck's *Den Spiegel der Zedicheyt* [*The Mirror of the Soul*], Brandt inserted the author's portrait. This flamboyant appeal to celebrity was vain and contrary to the simple, unadorned devotion Teellinck propagated.[100] Teellinck turned to Brandt's competitors for the publication of

---

96 Mark Aalderink, *Voor rechtzinnigheid en vroomheid, Marten Jansz Brandt (1613–1649): 37 jaar tromgeroffel van 'Soete Marten'* (PhD Thesis: University of Amsterdam, 2001), pp. 17–18.

97 Craig E. Harline, *Pamphlets, Printing, and Political Culture in the early Dutch Republic* (Dordrecht: Martinus Nijhoff, 1987), p. 91.

98 Willem Op 't Hof, 'The oldest Dutch commercial œuvre lists in print', *Quaerendo*, 23 (1993), pp. 265–290.

99 Samuel Clark, *Annotatien over't N. Testament* (Amsterdam: Johannes Boekholt, 1692), USTC 1822720.

100 Willem Op 't Hof, 'Een portret als oorzaak van verwijdering tussen een auteur en zijn uitgever', *Documentatieblad Nadere Reformatie* 16 (1992), pp. 97–102.

54   CHAPTER 2

his future works. Authors like Teellinck expected printers to join their cause and do nothing to tarnish the reputation of the faith or the author.

Not all printers agreed. Many, it would seem, simply published and printed whatever would bring in profit. The Elzeviers of Leiden were happy to print the works of fervently Reformed ministers like André Rivet and Jacob Trigland alongside works by René Descartes. Printers had to make money, and printing books from a wide-range of theological confessions opened more possibilities for higher sales. A printer in Delft acknowledged this fact when he was charged with printing heretical books. He defended himself, saying 'I have had no other design in my printing and selling, than to conquer a stuiver or two, though I have always been careful not to offend his majesty'.[101] In 1662, a writer applied an ancient maxim to the print culture of his day: '"Men will always seek their own interests even to the disadvantage of others": No one practices this more than profit-seeking booksellers'.[102] Print was a business, and there was much money to be made in printing works of questionable orthodoxy.

Some printers became famous for propagating 'seditious' books. Joan Blaeu saw to it that the dissenting works of Remonstrants and Socinians were printed. The persistence of Remonstrants in public religious discourse infuriated many stringently orthodox ministers and theologians. Socinians, too, found a home in the Dutch Republic after their expulsion from Poland in 1635. The Blaeu press abetted their rise and influence through print. The challenge from Socinians and Remonstrants was similar: though public worship was not allowed for either group, both Remonstrants and Socinians found eager printers in urban centres of the Republic, the Blaeus being the most famous example. Though the Blaeus printed some works by anti-Socinians, like the *Opera omnia* of Leiden theologian Johannes Cocceius, the handful of Socinian works they printed would be enough to tar their reputation as printers of pernicious and heretical books.[103] It certainly did not help matters when in 1668 Joan Blaeu printed Thomas Hobbes's *Leviathan*.[104]

Blaeu earned the reputation of printer *de jure* of seditious books, and his reputation was further confirmed when he dragged his feet printing orthodox books. On 24 October 1644, Gisbertus Voetius wrote a brief letter to Joan Blaeu: Voetius was cordial, yet thoroughly frustrated. The Utrecht theologian

---

101   Harline, *Pamphlets, Printing, and Political Culture in the Early Dutch Republic*, p. 91.

102   Ibid., p. 92.

103   For Socinian works printed by the Blaeus, see Philip Knijff and Sibbe Jan Visser, *Bibliographia Sociniana: A Bibliographical Reference Tool for the Study of Dutch Socinianism and Antitrinitarianism*, ed. Piet Visser (Hilversum: Verloren; Doopsgezinde Historische Kring, Amsterdam, 2004), p. 286.

104   Herman de la Fontaine Verwey, 'Dr. Joan Blaeu and his sons', *Quaerendo* 11 (1981), p. 15.

THAT ALL MAY BE INSTRUCTED   55

acknowledged that Blaeu was the acclaimed and great printer of Amsterdam, but that status did not protect him from reproof when a titan of the theological world was ready for him to publish an important book. *Contra Sectam Muhammeticam* by Johannes Maurius languished away waiting to be printed in Blaeu's celebrated type, while Blaeu, in the meantime, worked on other projects.[105] There is no clear evidence for why Blaeu may have delayed publication. The struggle against Islam demanded this response from a Christian perspective. Voetius clearly considered himself of enough weight to speed along the book's printing. Voetius was ultimately vanquished, and he looked for a new publisher for the book, settling on Johannes van Waesberge, the Utrecht printer of many of Voetius' own works.

Through thinly veiled false imprints and antedated years of publications, the Blaeu press was a primary instrument for the dissemination of heretical works.[106] Reformed ministers throughout the Dutch Republic petitioned local authorities to forbid the Blaeus from publishing heretical material. In three letters to the Socinian Martinus Ruarus (1588–1657), Stephanus Curcellaeus related the events of January 1642.[107] After being lobbied by local ministers, the schout (sheriff) of Amsterdam raided the Blaeu shop, confiscated the full run of *De Vera Religione* by the Socinian authors Volkelius and Crellius, and punished the Blaeus: a fine of 2000 gulden and the burning of the books. The fine would never be paid, however.

Once the burgomasters were informed, the fine was waived, but it was too late for the books. They had already been burned, but even this proved to be a selling point. In the 1644 Dutch translation, the title page included a reference to the events of 1642. The title page read 'condemned by the schepens in Holland, publicly executed and burnt by fire, anno 1642, in January'.[108] Johannes Naeranus of Rotterdam would use the same marketing technique to increase the allure of Becius' *Apologia*. On 17 September 1668, in a newspaper advertisement Naeranus reminded those interested that the book had been banned in Middelburg.[109] On 22 February 1672, Joan Blaeu's shop caught fire, burning for

---

105   D. Nauta (ed.), 'Drie Brieven van Gisbertus Voetius', *Dutch Review of Church History*, 60 (1980), p. 200.

106   Herman de la Fontaine Verwey, 'Willem Jansz Blaeu, "Mercator Sapiens"', in his, *Uit de wereld van het boek*, vol. 3 (Amsterdam: Nico Israel, 1979), p. 25.

107   Stephanus Curcellaeus to Martinus Ruarus, 8 February 1642, in M. Ruarus, *Epistolarum selectarum centuria* (Amsterdam: David Crispicus, 1677), USTC 1813394, pp. 405–409, esp. 406–407. J. C. van Slee, *De geschiedenis van het Socinianisme in de Nederlanden* (Haarlem: De Erven F. Bohn, 1914), p. 206n5, pp. 255–256.

108   Quoted in Verwey, 'Dr. Joan Blaeu and his sons', p. 9.

109   S. Groenveld, 'The Mecca of Authors? Sates Assemblies and Censorship in the Seventeenth-Century Dutch Republic', in A. C. Duke and C. A. Tamse (eds.), *Too Mighty to Be Free:*

56   CHAPTER 2

almost a full twenty-four hours. Daniel Elzevier offered a conservative estimate of the cost of the damages, 60,000 to 70,000 gulden. The painter Jan van
der Heyden valued the destroyed goods at 382,000 gulden. The long-awaited
Spanish edition of Blaeu's atlas was a casualty in the blaze. But one observer
considered the fire a sign of God's retribution, 'a divine punishment for the
printing of so many "Romish" books'.[110] The onlooker's comments would have
resonated with any minister who expected printers to join the Reformed cause.
Such printing was a failure by the Blaeus to use their gifts for the original purpose for which God had given them: to spread the truths of the gospel.

One minister valued the press so much that he allegedly altered another
theologian's manuscript. The changes created an incendiary and libelous
personal exposé of an intellectual opponent, rather than the reasoned, sober
assessment and critique of a philosophical argument. Martinus Schoock was
brought before the legal authorities in Utrecht in August 1645, and this was his
claim: when he sent the manuscript of *Admiranda methodus* to Johannes van
Waesberge in Utrecht, it contained none of the politically-charged rhetoric for
which he was now being questioned.[111] Martinus claimed that none other than
the Utrecht theologian, Gisbertus Voetius had distorted the text. His debate
with Descartes was nothing less than incendiary. Voetius had radically altered
the *Admiranda methodus* to cudgel Schoock into taking his side publicly
against Descartes. As evidence in defense of the defendant, Schoock presented
letters Voetius had written to him, offering to have Waesberge print some of
the Groningen professor's writings under his editorial auspices. At first, Voetius
would not confirm whether the letters were his. After all, 'it is always possible
that lies are proclaimed in controversy, that letters are fabricated and falsified,
and that my letters are attributed many additional meanings or nonsensical
inferences'.[112] After a long and cumbersome trial, the court took the side of
Voetius, but 'also emphasized that the good name and fame of the Groningen
professor remained unaffected'.[113]

     Censorship and the Press in Britain and the Netherlands (Walburg Pers: Zutphen, 1987),
     p. 85, n. 65.

110   Verwey, 'Dr. Joan Blaeu and his sons', p. 18.

111   Erik-Jan Bos, 'Epistolarum Voetianum I', *Dutch Review of Church History* 78, no. 2 (1998),
     pp. 184–191.

112   'Possunt mendacia jactari, possunt literae fingi et subornari, possunt literis meis, si quas
     ex iis alibi venati sint, multa affingi per additiones et stolidas consequentias'. Gisbertus
     Voetius to Martin Schoock, April 1644, in Erik-Jan Bos, 'Epistolarum Voetianum II', *Dutch
     Review of Church History* 79, no. 1 (1999), p. 51.

113   Ibid., p. 48.

THAT ALL MAY BE INSTRUCTED

Despite the outcome, there was much evidence of Voetius' tampering.[114] The strongest evidence, however, came from Voetius himself. When Voetius described why he thought *Admiranda methodus* should have been published, he began with the threat Cartesianism posed to the Christian faith. One must respond to the charges of Descartes in like manner to his own, Voetius declared, 'because it concerns a Jesuit and a papist who, with his opinion on the authority of Scripture, paves the way for atheists and atheism, and puts their own weapons in their hands against religion'.[115] In rejecting the supernatural theology of the Christian tradition, Descartes was in league with the chief heretics found throughout church history. 'All theologians and philosophers have so far proven their natural theology only by means of these principles against atheists, skeptics, and epicureans. The supernatural theology against the same, and as unfolded and defended against the heretics: Manicheans, Marcionites, Pelagians, Nestorians, Arians, Socinians, Anabaptists, etc.'.[116] Voetius wrote against Descartes for 'truth and rest of the Republic and Church'.[117] With such high stakes, it would not be difficult to infer that Voetius would be willing to rewrite Schoock's judicious critique of Descartes' theology. If Descartes was going to write books that sought to erode the faith of the Church and destabilize the concord of the Republic, Voetius had the duty to use whatever means were available to counteract such consequences.

Print and controversy went hand in hand from print's beginning. In André Rivet's experience with printing in the Republic, that was certainly the case. And on at least one occasion, it concerned ministers with whom he was friendly. Utrecht's great contender for orthodoxy, Voetius, employed extensive means to ensure pure Reformed doctrine was offered to the saints throughout the Republic. Struggling for the cause of truth against heresy and error brought ceaseless dispute to Utrecht. These polemics inevitably took to print: professors and high-ranking ministers would publicly quarrel over each other's printed works, especially when fraud and anonymity were involved.

---

114 Ibid., pp. 48–50. For Schoocks' charges and corroborating evidence, see the short document he presented defending himself entitled *Corte memorien*. Ibid., pp. 68–72.

115 'Tu juste huic Jesuitarum pullo retalias, tum tanquam Jesuitae et Pontificio qui sententia sua de autoritate scripturae Atheis et Atheismo viam sternunt, eosque in religionem armant'. Bos, 'Epistolarum Voetianum 11,' p. 53.

116 'Naturalis enim hactenus ex solis illis principiis ab omnibus Theologis et philosophis demonstrate fuit contra Atheos, Scepticos, Epicureos; supernaturalis vero contra eosdem, ut et contra haereticos Manicheos, marcionitas, Pelagianos, Nestorianos, Arrianos, Socinianos, Anabaptistas etc. explicate et defense fuit'. Ibid., p. 52.

117 'Voor de waerheyt en rust van Republijcq en Kerk'. Suetonius Tranquillus [= Gisbertus Voetius], *Den overtuyghden cartesiaen, ofte Clare aenwysinge uyt de bedenckingen van Irenœvs Philalethivs* (Leiden: Cornelis Banheinning, 1656), USTC 1833733, p. 40.

In 1641, Martinus Schoock, Voetius' student, stood at the centre of one such controversy. An anonymous author composed the *Exercitatio prima de Hellenistis et lingua Hellenistica ad ... D. Heinsium et C. Salmasium.* Though the attack singled-out the linguistic work of both Claude de Saumaise (Salmasius) and Daniel Heinsius, De Saumaise considered it written by Heinsius: including himself in the title was merely cover. André Rivet knew better. Voetius considered De Saumaise blinded to the truth by his fury, and Rivet confirmed as much. Writing to Claude Sarrau, Rivet opened the lid on the anonymous publication:

> You are right to believe that Heinsius is not the author of this exercise. Nevertheless, Mr. Saumaise wishes to believe it is Heinsius, and he tells me that all the eloquence in the world will not convince him otherwise. And yet, I have told him that Martinus Schoock is the author, and Mr Voetius is its godfather and the director, which I say with certainty. But he wants to hit Heinsius no matter the cost.[118]

Schoock had indeed written the *Exercitatio*, driving a wedge between the two Leiden professors. But De Saumaise would not believe Rivet. He soon wrote a response against the author of inflammatory book. For Rivet, such deception on the part of Schoock and Voetius had gone far enough. De Saumaise's response was based on the false premise that Heinsius was the original author; the rejoinder, therefore, could not go to print. Rivet leveraged his friendship with Gisbertus and his son to stop the Elzeviers from printing. He was unsuccessful. At the auction of Rivet's collection, De Saumaise's *De Lingua Hellenistica* would sell in a lot with one other book for nearly two gulden. 'Elzevier' was listed proudly beside the title.

Ministers were deeply involved in the ordinary operations of the Dutch print industry. Three ministers were crucial to the publication of Hugo Grotius' *Ordinuum Hollandiae ac Westfrisiae pietas* in 1613. Johannes Wtenbogaert, the theological leader of the Remonstrant cause, served as Grotius' middleman with the printer, Jan Paets. Wtenbogaert updated Grotius on progress of the book through the printing process: when typesetting, proofs, and

---

118 'Vous avez raison de croire que Heinsius n'est pas autheur de cette exercitation. Monsieur de Saumaise le veut croire neantmoins, et me dit que toute l'eloquence du monde ne luy persuadera pas le contraire, quoy que je luy aie dit que Martinus Schooc en est l'autheur, et Mr Voetius le parrain et le directeur, ce que je scay certainement. Mais il veut drapper Heinsius a quelque prix que ce soit.' Rivet to Claude Sarrau, 19 November 1641, in Hans Bots and Pierre Leroy (eds.), *Correspondence Intégrale, d'André Rivet et de Claude Sarrau* (3 vols., Amsterdam: APA – Holland University Press, 1978–1982), I, p. 22.

THAT ALL MAY BE INSTRUCTED 59

the final product were complete. Grotius selected Johannes Arnoldus Corvinus, a Remonstrant minister in Leiden and son-in-law to Paets, to oversee the proofreading. For composing the French translation, Samuel Naeranus was chosen.[119] Dishonest activity by ministers marked the publication of the *Ordinuum pietas*, as it did with Schoock's *Admiranda methodus*. Festus Hommius, apparently had an unspecified friend who sneaked into Petrus Bertius' study and stole Bertius' copy. Hommius likely had an informant close to the project.[120] The firmly orthodox Hommius considered Grotius' work of sufficient danger to the true faith that he was willing to organize its theft. The Church had to be defended from such false and malicious books. Print, piety and profit were intricately linked.

Rivet worked as an intermediary for authors whose books were printed in Amsterdam and Leiden.[121] Rivet convinced a theologian in Leiden to copy edit Samuel Bochart's work on the origin of peoples, *Geographia Sacra*. Rivet had been instrumental in arranging the publishing and printing of the work and likely received a copy of it for his troubles.[122] The professor of theology was most helpful to Abraham and Bonaventura Elzevier. Beyond writing numerous prefaces for colleagues' books printed in their shop, Rivet regularly mediated between Abraham and Bonaventura Elzevier and their authors. Rivet even served as their international agent on occasion. One scholar of ancient languages needed a printer for his most auspicious project, a concordance of the Hebrew Bible. He wrote to Rivet describing how difficult the process would be given the typefaces necessary. Only six presses in all of Protestant Europe could manage the project.[123] Rivet was confident that the Elzeviers could handle the complexity, and he offered himself as an intermediary.[124]

Rivet leveraged the Elzeviers to print the collected works of a Roman Catholic theologian. Pierre Picherel had Reformed sympathies, yet Picherel remained in communion with the Roman Catholic Church. Theodore Beza esteemed him

---

119 Edwin Rabbie, introduction to *Hugo Grotius: Ordinuum Hollandiae ac Westfrisiae pietas: Critical Edition with English Translation and Commentary*, ed. Edwin Rabbie (Leiden: Brill, 1995), pp. 43–45.

120 Ibid., pp. 56–57.

121 For Rivet and Blaeu, see Rivet to Isaac Vossius, 5 August 1645, UB Amsterdam, Remonstrant Kerk Amsterdam, inv. III E8-107. On Le Maire, see Rivet to G. J. Vossius, 8 October 1644, in Paulus Colomesius (ed.), *Clarorum Virorum ad Vossium* (London: Sam Smith and Benjamin Walford, 1698), p. 267.

122 *AC André Rivet* (Leiden: Pieter Leffen, 1657), USTC 1846296, p. 89.

123 Moritz Steinschneider and David Cassel, *Judische Typographic und Judischer Buchhandel* (Jerusalem: Bamberger & Wahrmann, 1938), pp. 37–55.

124 Stephen George Burnett, 'The Christian Hebraism of Johann Buxtorf (1564–1629)' (University of Wisconsin PhD dissertation, 1990), p. 234.

60   CHAPTER 2

highly. Rivet ensured Picherel's work was edited and published for broad dissemination. In 1629, the Elzeviers printed Picherel's *Opuscula Theologica*. That the Sorbonne condemned Picherel on 1 September 1629 was certainly a selling point in the Reformed Netherlands.[125]

Etienne de Courcelles (1586–1659), a professor of theology at the Remonstrant seminary in Amsterdam from 1643, wrote to Hugo Grotius to congratulate him on the publication of his defence of the faith, the 'Proof of the True Religion': he also sent Grotius his translation of the book into French. While he welcomed Grotius' judgement for edits and correction, he was especially delighted that in French it would reach a wider audience. 'Having known that you desired to see in French the book you composed for the defence of our religion, so that it may benefit so many more people, I have undertaken its translation'.[126]

Minister and printers had a symbiotic relationship. Because they were well educated, ministers were useful to printers when books needed to be proofread or translated; because they were often prolific authors, ministers made printers substantial profits. Printers were necessary to the noble task of disseminating the light of the faith, any minister's primary goal.

6   The Book and Pen

When a minister or theologian sat down to read a text, both he and the text were changed. Franciscus Gomarus was an active reader. He expected to grow intellectually and spiritually from whatever he was reading. But the book itself was changed into something unique. With a pen in hand, he scribbled notes in the margins of his collection of dissertations. It became a reference tool with which he could better construct his own arguments. Underlining important phrases and concepts, he tucked them away to be retrieved when needed. The books stored cross-references and reflections, making his own thoughts inseparable from what was printed on the page. It was a tool for the cultivation of the reader's own thought, not merely a depository of the author's ideas.

---

125   Eugéne and Èmile Haag, *La France Protestante, ou, Vies des Protestants français*, vol. 8 (Paris: Cherbuliez, 1858), p. 231.

126   'Ayant su que vous desiris de voir en francois le livre que vous aves composo pour la defensio de nostre religion, afin qu'il profitast a tant plus de personnes, i'en ai entrepris la traduction.' Etienne de Courcelles to Hugo Grotius, 2 December 1628, UB-Leiden, Sem Rem 84.

THAT ALL MAY BE INSTRUCTED

A collection of academic dissertations that had previously been in Gomarus' library were acquired by James Ussher in 1641 and were eventually incorporated into the library of Trinity College, Dublin.[127] Gomarus' dissertations spanned the entire scope of Christian theology. Many of the topics covered would be expected: dissertations on the person and work of Christ, on church ordinances of baptism and the Lord's Supper, justification. He owned several on the nature and authority of Scripture, even his own dissertation, presided over by Franciscus Junius at Heidelberg in 1585, poetically entitled "Thesis on the Word, or the Sermon of God." Gomarus collected several theses on ministry, repentance and conversion and the authority of Church councils.

Beyond general theological topics, Gomarus' collection of disputations mirrors the fraught period Gomarus would enter when he began his academic career in Leiden. He owned one volume containing ninety-nine thesis publications, the first eighty-nine from Leiden, the last ten from German institutions.[128] Of the eighty-nine Leiden theses, there is a sequence of thirty-five presided over by Jacobus Arminius and Franciscus Gomarus in rotation (and three by Lucas Trelcatius). These years saw the beginning of the Republic's first and greatest theological debate: the Remonstrant controversy, 1604–1619. Four of the disputations given in the Holy Roman Empire were also an exercise in knowing thy enemy during the Remonstrant Controversy. Conrad Vorstius, Arminius' successor, presided over them while a member of the theological faculty at Steinfurt. Gomarus even owned a manuscript copy of Arminius' third disputation on divine predestination, given in 1604 by Wilhemus Bastingius.

In this collection of disputations, Gomarus often neatly underlined important material or made cross-references in the margins of disputations. In Samuel Gruterus' thesis on predestination, over which Gomarus presided on 31 October 1604, Gomarus underlined on fewer than ten occasions and made notes on only two sections. On Gruterus' continuation on the object of predestination, Gomarus underlined "ad suos fines" ("to their ends"). He underlined the same phrase when it was used in the next section. The phrase itself was not controversial: Peter Martyr Virmigli (1499–1562), the Italian-born Zurich Reformer, used it in his definition of providence. Thomas Aquinas, likewise, used it in his explanation of the goodness of God.

---

127   On the pamphlets in this collection, see Andrew Pettegree and Arthur der Weduwen, 'The library as a weapon of state: the pamphlet collection of Gaspar Fagel in Trinity College, Dublin', in E. Boran (ed.), *Book collecting in Ireland and Britain, 1650–1850* (Dublin: Four Courts Press, 2018), pp. 223–235.

128   Trinity College, Dublin, Shelf mark B.B.hh.19. Gomarus' disputations are included in the volumes B.B.hh.18 through B.B.hh23. With thanks to Andrew Pettegree and Arthur der Weduwen for bringing this collection of theses to my attention.

The professor was not always so reticent with his pen. In several instances, the quiet restraint of a diligent note-taker gives way to an unbridled frenzy. Occasionally Gomarus filled every available blank space with his own notes. Three theses, all of which were presided over by Gomarus, are filled with manuscript notes. They cover Christ's justification of man, man's justification before God, and the sacraments.

The theses on the sacraments are illuminating of Gomarus' method. On 11 March 1609, a local student from Leiden gave a disputation on the nature of the sacraments. Aegidius F. Laovicus presented the case that the sacrament had been corrupted, little by little, by Satan, 'the pernicious and cunning.' Despite the fact this disputation was his own personal copy, and thus the student would likely never see his notes, Gomarus nevertheless fastidiously noted corrections. The published version left much room for improvement. There were small grammatical errors to fix: misuse of parenthetical marks or forgetting to put a comma before a prepositional phrase. Not all such errors appear to be the student's fault. The disputation has thirty-one articles, each building off the previous, with the intention of making one cogent, persuasive and logically consistent argument. When numbering the articles, an error was made in the numbering of 14 through twenty. The disputation has article 14 listed correctly, but a manuscript note turned XV to XVI, 17–18 continue the trend, and 19 is doubled. Rather than the correct sequence of XIV, XV, XVI, XVII, XIIX, XIX, the manuscript notes make it XIV, XVI, XVII, XVII, XIX, XIX. Perhaps there is an omitted article 15, but there is no way to know with whom the fault lies.

Other notes were less about meticulous corrections, and more about putting his own thoughts down on paper. Gomarus wrote entire sentences, occasionally entire paragraphs in the margins of his disputations. In article XXII, the disputation connects the Passover from Exodus 12 to the Lord's Supper. Connecting the rites and signs of the Old Testament to the New, the author cited Exodus 12:21–23: '... the LORD will pass over the door and will not allow the destroyer to enter your houses to strike you.' For his own benefit, Gomarus wrote that the author should also have cited verse 27. 'You shall say, "It is the sacrifice of the LORD's Passover, for he passed over the houses of the people of Israel in Egypt, when he struck the Egyptians but spared our houses."' In a statement on the necessity of obediently participating in the sign of the covenant, the disputation cites Romans 4:11 and 1 Corinthians 11:24; Gomarus suggested also referencing Mark 11:11, where Christ directly connects believing in him and being baptized. His student based much of his case on the Church Fathers: Origen, Theodoretus, Augustine, and Tertullian. Gomarus had numerous suggestions for further research.

THAT ALL MAY BE INSTRUCTED   63

At the end of a thesis on man's justification before God, Gomarus included a table of authors and their works that could be use when studying the topic. He divides the authors into two broad categories, *Catholici* and *nostri*. *Catholici* is broken down into two more specific groups, *scholastici* (including Thomas Aquinas and Bonaventura) and other Roman Catholics like Robert Bellarmine. *Nostri* is a broad list of nine Protestant reformers. Gomarus not only lists the authors of specific confessions, whether Roman Catholic or Protestant, he also gives specific section references where a student could find their expositions on the topic at hand. Such references were the fruit of years of reading. And they display Gomarus' fluency with the relevant source material for his profession, in this case, theological books. With his manuscript notes, Gomarus displayed his erudition and studiousness. Print, in this case pamphlets specifically, were seen as a tool in the necessary process of theological investigation. By actively engaging with print in this way, Gomarus created a hybrid medium.

7   **Creatures of the Book**

Reading godly books became a regular expectation for the promotion of spiritual growth. Based upon a pre-existent culture that valued literacy for civic engagement and commerce, the Reformed faith stimulated education for citizens from every economic background and pushed for greater literacy to encourage internalization of the confession. The seventeenth century also saw the proliferation of books harmful to the faith. Though censorship was a tactic to constrain such material, more books faithful to orthodoxy was the primary response.

These publications sought to tear down heterodox arguments and encourage faithfulness. The book expanded a minister's realm of influence beyond the local church and amplified their message of personal piety and confessional zeal across the Republic and, indeed, across Europe. Ministers enthusiastically encouraged their colleagues and their flocks to read. Reading could be done in the quiet of one's home. Ministers could continue developing as preachers and counselors, and church members could pursue godliness outside of Sunday gatherings. A lit candle and a godly book would be enough to redeem the time. The minutes and hours one had to spare during the week could be used for benefit rather than wasted on trivial activities. Jean Taffin (1528–1594), court minister of William of Orange in Delft and a Walloon minister, chastised his readers for lack of concern for Bible reading and established a Reformed ideal of Bible reading:

In that time we burnt of desire to read through it completely, but now, although we are allowed to do so, and although we are stimulated by daily admonition, people even don't have good books in their houses. And in case they have, they do not read them.[129]

Ministers led by example, buying and reading hundreds and sometimes thousands of books throughout their lives. An individual minister would devote much of his life to acquiring books and reading them for personal gain. Throughout the Reformed Church in the Netherlands, church officials admonished ministers to devote themselves to the buying and reading of good books.[130] When ministers were found to have failed in this, they were admonished to mend their ways. No less than the alleged arch-atheist Rene Descartes said, 'Reading good books is like engaging in conversation with the most cultivated minds of past centuries who had composed them, or rather, taking part in a well-conducted dialogue in which such minds reveal to us only the best of their thoughts'.[131] If it had been said by almost any other thinker, every Reformed minister in the Republic would have given hearty approval.

Rigorous study was a holy calling. In Rivet's understanding intellectual and spiritual gain were divine blessings that were brought about by pursuing specific means.[132] Reading godly books was one of those means. For ministers, diligent study of books was an act of service to the Church. 'In private study, be unremitting and diligent', he wrote to a young minister.[133] Rivet believed this wholeheartedly, and over the course of his life he built a book collection comparable to the largest libraries owned by other theologians of his time. Their duty as pastors required their best, and books were a means by which their best was cultivated. They read and wrote books with the goal that all might be instructed in the faith, leading congregants to grow in their personal devotion

---

129   Quoted in, Fred van Lieburg, 'Bible Reading and Pietism in the Dutch Reformed Tradition', in M. Lamberigts and A. A. den Hollander (eds.), *Lay Bibles in Europe 1450–1800* (Leuven: Leuven University Press, 2006), p. 227.

130   *Acta Der Provinciale en Particuliere Synoden*, IIX, pp. 146, 152.

131   Rene Descartes, *A Discourse on the Method of Correctly Conducting One's Reason and Seeking Truth in the Sciences*, trans. Ian Maclean (Oxford: Oxford University Press, 2006), pp. 7–8.

132·   André Rivet, *On Faith and the Perseverance of the Saints* (disp. 31), in Henk van den Belt (ed.), *Synopsis of a Purer Theology: Latin Text and English Translation*, trans. Riemer A. Faber (2 vols., Leiden: Brill, 2014–2016), II, pp. 228–275.

133   'In privatis studiis asiduus & diligens'. Rivet to Justinus van Assche, 5 April 1620, UB Leiden, ms. BPL 245.

and ministers to become more faithful shepherds.[134] Ministers built libraries to fulfill their divine callings. Whether from their earliest days as ministry candidates or long after their formal instruction was over, they could still learn from teachers of the Church.

---

134 Wilhelmus à Brakel van der Kluyt, Preface to Wilhemus à Brakel, *Edifying Discourses Regarding the Preparation for, the Partaking of, and the Reflection upon the Sacrament of the Lord's Supper*, in James A. De Jong (ed.), *In Remembrance of Him: Profiting from the Lord's Supper*, trans. Bartel Elshout (Grand Rapids: Reformation Heritage Books, 2012), p. 87.

CHAPTER 3

Buyers of Truth

By 1628 Johannes Lydius had fallen into poverty. Lydius was a minister in Oudewater, near Utrecht, and he had committed a principle error for anyone trying to maintain and build wealth: he had married a poor English woman, with whom he had three children. Lydius found himself unable to afford one of the things he most dearly desired: books. His ministerial career began like most other ministers. He first ministered to a meagre congregation in Aarlanderveen. The congregation was nearly non-existent and rife with theological confusion. He needed advice on who could properly take the Lord's Supper: believers who renounce their works and say they believe in Christ crucified, which could include Lutheran believers, or did they have to claim the Reformed faith explicitly? 'I have quite shocked the rustics, simple souls, who can scarcely tell A from B', Lydius wrote. 'This is not surprising for they have been without a minister for a good two years and they are all devoted either to Lutheranism or to the Papists. The church consists of only six men and seven women; there are no elders and only a single deacon.'[1]

By 1628, he had been promoted to Oudewater, from which he wrote to Gerardus Vossius, a family friend and, at the time, the rector of Dordrecht's Latin school. Johannes' friendship with Vossius went back to when the two were enrolled at Leiden University. Johannes' father began to worry about his son's spiritual condition while pursuing theological studies, so he asked Vossius to check in on him. Lydius' nephew, Isaac had asked to borrow a copy of the *Martyrologium Romanum*, by Caesar Baronius. Johannes sent it to Vossius for delivery to his nephew in Dordrecht. Loathe to give it up, Johannes confessed he wished he had more money for books, including many of Vossius' that he craved.[2]

Despite his self-professed fiscal deprivation, Johannes built a respectable library of 1,747 books. Amongst those ministers whose book collections sold at auction, his was well above average size. The average ministerial collection that sold at auction contained 1,141 books. Few ministers in the Netherlands during

---

1 Johannes Lydius to Franciscus Junius, 3 May 1602, published in 'Dilemma of a Calvinist minister with a rural charge', in Alastair Duke, et al., (eds.) *Calvinism in Europe, 1540–1610: A Collection of Sources* (Manchester: Manchester University Press, 1992), p. 195.

2 Johannes Lydius to Gerardus Vossius, 12 July 1628, in Paulus Colomesius (ed.), *Virorum eruditione celeberrimorum epistolae, clarorum virorum ad Vossium* (London: Sam Smith and Benjamin Walford, 1698), p. 61.

© KONINKLIJKE BRILL NV, LEIDEN, 2023 | DOI:10.1163/9789004538191_004

BUYERS OF TRUTH

the seventeenth century owned as many books as did Johannes. In that, he could take a measure of pride. His pride in his collection, however, would not last long when he considered the collections of several of his family members. Johannes came from a family of extravagant book collectors. Two of the largest book collections owned by ministers belonged to Johannes' brother, Balthazar, and Balthazar's son, Jacob, both of which contained over five thousand books. This was all the more impressive because Jacob built his own collection rather than only inheriting his father's books, which were sold on his death. Seven of the ministers in the Lydius family had collections that sold at auction during the seventeenth century. Four of their catalogues survive.[3] Pierre Bayle noted that Johannes' distant nephew Matthaeus Lydius 'had a good library'.[4] Only in a family of ministers whose fanatical acquisition of books was well known could Johannes Lydius crave more than the 1,747 books he had.

Pursuing truth meant acquiring books. Bouritius Sibema, a minister in Haarlem and unrestrained Contra-Remonstrant, wrote against the Remonstrant errors that were debated at the Synod of Dort a decade prior to him writing his popular polemical work, *Salomons Sweerdt, scheydende de remonstrantsche vande rechtsinnighe leere* [*Solomon's Sword, separating the Remonstrants from Right Teaching*].[5] By the time Sibema's work was available with Dutch booksellers, the political controversy between followers of Jacob Arminius and their opponents had largely run its course. He addressed the theological battle that continued, taking up the five points of debate the Remonstrants put forward. He summarized their false teaching in a few paragraphs. On occasion, he allowed them a few pages. He then presented his case for the Reformed position. Sibema hoped to make clear the dividing lines between the Reformed and the Remonstrants, and to encourage those who held to the Reformed position to understand the baselessness of their opponents' beliefs on human sin, predestination, the nature of Christ's atonement, and the calling and perseverance of the saints.

---

3   Those that survive: AC *Balthazar Lydius 1629 and 1630* (Dordrecht: widow of Peeter Verhagen, 1629–1630), USTC 1021755, USTC 1021757 and USTC 1021756; AC *Johannes Lydius 1643* (Leiden: Franciscus Hackius, 1643), USTC 1122163; AC *Jacobus Lydius 1680* (Dordrecht: Herman van Wessem, 1680), USTC 1816682; AC *Martinus Lydius and Wilhelmus Vis 1679* (Enkhuizen: Meynerdt Mul, 1679), USTC 1846949. Those now lost: Martinus Lydius (d. 1657), SA Leiden 74 (GERECHTSDAGBOEK FF), f. 330v (26-4-1657); Isaac Lydius, SA Leiden 77 (GERECHTSDAGBOEK II), f. 322v (12-5-1661); Matthaeus Lydius, Oprechte Haerlemse Courant (03.06.1685); Oprechte Haerlemse Courant (05.06.1685).

4   'avoit une belle Bibliotheque'. Pierre Bayle, *Dictionaire Historique et Critique* (3 vols., Rotterdam: Reinier Leers, 1697), USTC 1831857, III, p. 338.

5   *NNBW*, X, p. 917. Bouritius Sibema, *Salomons sweert, scheydende de remonstrantsche vande rechtsinnighe leere* (Amsterdam: Marten Jansz. Brandt, 1631), USTC 1031025.

68 CHAPTER 3

Such knowledge was incalculably valuable. It was the pearl of great price. Bouritius encouraged all 'lovers of truth' to heed King Solomon's timeless advice to 'buy the truth and not sell it (Proverbs 23:23)'.[6] The Haarlem minister's encouragement was nothing new: It repeated the ideal early Protestant Reformers espoused and it encapsulated the commonly accepted practice of his day. Ministers like Lydius followed this advice, even if they had not read Sibema's tract. The acquisition of right knowledge was paramount to preserving the faith. Only by knowing Scripture and the theology of those who rightly handled Scripture could a faithful Christian discern truth from error.

The Dutch Republic was the most bookish nation in early-modern Europe.[7] More people there relied on print for information and their livelihoods than any other place in the Western world. Modest book collections of up to a few hundred books were not unheard of even amongst tradesmen. But no professional group was more invested in Dutch book culture than ministers. They invested precious resources of time and money into buying and acquiring books. How these ministers afforded and acquired these books, the general nature of their collections and how their collections compare with those owned by similarly educated book buyers are the subjects of this chapter.

1 Between Opulence and Poverty

In the Netherlands the seventeenth century began with a lack of competent ministers. Consistories longed for qualified ministers to replace those who brought disrepute to the faith. In the hopes that they would return to pastor, cities began providing scholarships to local young men who were academically gifted and spiritually inclined to the ministry. Jacob Arminius received a generous stipend from the Merchants' Guild in Amsterdam so he could pursue further theological education for three or four years. When he returned, he devoted fifteen years to pastoring in Amsterdam and had to receive permission from the city before he could move to Leiden to become a professor of theology.[8]

Well-connected theology students, many of whose fathers had been ministers in good standing for many years, often began their careers in small villages

---

6 'Koopt de Waerheydt, ende en verkooptse niet'. Sibema, *Salomons sweerdt*, f. A2.

7 Andrew Pettegree and Arthur der Weduwen, *The Bookshop of the World: Making and Trading Books in the Dutch Golden Age* (New Haven: Yale University Press, 2019).

8 Carl Bangs, *Arminius: A Study in the Dutch Reformation* (second edition; Grand Rapids: Francis Asbury Press, 1985), pp. 65, 237.

and towns, only to use them as a stepping-stone to move to coveted positions in the Republic's urban centres. Such was the case for Franciscus Ridderus and Bouritius Sibema. About one in three ministers were the sons of ministers.[9] The Lydius family epitomized the cycle of ministers having sons who, in turn, became ministers. Pierre Bayle said of them 'No one family perhaps has furnished more ministers than this'.[10] Martinus Lydius (c.1539–1601), the patriarch, became a minister in Amsterdam and later professor of theology at Franeker after resigning his post in Heidelberg in 1575 when the Reformed Elector of the Palatinate, Frederick III, was succeeded by the Lutheran Ludwig VI.[11] Martinus had two sons who became ministers, Johannes and Balthazar. At least seven of Martinus' grandsons became ministers. Most of them became ministers in either prosperous towns or urban centres.[12] Martinus was a well-educated minister who became a member of the well-trained urban elite, and his sons' ministerial careers benefited greatly from his clout within the church.

In the seventeenth century, about 5,500 ministers served Reformed congregations throughout the Netherlands.[13] The ministers of other Protestant affiliations are difficult to number, as they were unsanctioned by the authorities and ministered in unrecognised churches. Most fared far worse than those from the Lydius family. Proponents to the ministry from humbler background longed for a similar career path. They preached for years, often decades, in the hopes of receiving a promotion to an urban centre. But more often than not, they languished in the town in which they began their career. And if they did transfer to a new pulpit, it was often only once and within the same province.[14] On average a minister's pastoral career in the seventeenth century lasted twenty-three years. A typical ministerial candidate, fresh from studying theology at a Dutch university, came from a middle-class background. He was the son of a city official, schoolmaster or in some cases a merchant. The Dutch Republic during this time was divided roughly into urban centres for which

---

9   F. A. van Lieburg, *Profeten en hun vaderland: De geografische herkomst van de gereformeerde predikanten in Nederland van 1572 tot 1816* (Zoetermeer: Boekencentrum, 1996), pp. 101–103.

10   'Il n'y a peut-être point de famille qui ait fourni plus de Ministres que celle-la'. Bayle, *Dictionaire*, III, p. 334.

11   R. B. Evenhuis, *Ook dat was Amsterdam: De kerk der hervorming in de gouden eeuw* (Amsterdam: W. Ten Have, 1965), I, pp. 152–153.

12   F. A. van Lieburg (ed.), *Repertorium van Nederlandse hervormde predikanten tot 1816: Predikanten* (2 vols., Dordrecht, 1996), II, p. 156.

13   This figure is an estimation derived from Van Lieburg, *Profeten*, p. 53.

14   Peter van Rooden, 'Van geestelijke stand naar beroepsgroep: De professionalisering van de Nederlandse predikant, 1625–1874', *Tijdschrift voor sociale geschiedenis*, 17 (1991), pp. 361–93.

70   CHAPTER 3

Holland is famous, smaller towns like Medemblik, Alphen, and Den Briel, and rural villages. Village congregations were more numerous, but most ministers were born in a city or town. There, the socially mobile family had convenient access to Latin schools, and the towns often had university bursaries to fund the theological studies of aspirant ministers, who would return and pastor, like Arminius in Amsterdam. If a prospective minister came originally from a village, it was more likely than not that his father was a minister there.[15]

Ministers depended on the secular authorities for their living. City magistrates had authority over ministers' salaries and benefits, but officials needed ministers' cooperation in maintaining the internal peace of the city. When a salary was not paid, ministers knew whom to confront. In Utrecht, the authorities circulated a list of city officials and their responsibilities, including those who delivered ministers' salaries.[16] Their salaries were typically enough to raise a small family. A rural minister could expect at least 450 gulden per year.[17] A new minister coming to Nijmegen in 1618 could expect a salary of 600 gulden. Two years later they could expect 800.[18] Even the organists in Enkhuizen's Westerkerk and Zuiderkerk were paid 100 gulden and 75 gulden, respectively, in 1692.[19] Several English travellers noted the payment system to ministers in the Netherlands. They reported that in the first decades of the seventeenth century, ministers in The Hague received about 800 gulden a year. In similar urban centres, salaries rose throughout the century to between 1,500 to 2,000 gulden.[20] In the province of Overijssel, several ministers had a salary between 400 and 500 gulden. One pastor earned around 500 gulden in 1616. In 1659, another received 450.[21]

Professors of theology, who often served as ministers in addition to their academic pursuits, fared better than the typical clergyman. A professor's salary was often over 1,000 gulden a year. At Leiden, Conrad Vorstius was offered

---

15   Van Lieburg, *Profeten*, pp. 149–181.
16   *Autentique lyste van de veranderingh der regeeringh van de provincie van Utrecht* (Utrecht: s.n., 1677), USTC 1813808, pp. 3, 9.
17   G. Groenhuis, *De predikanten. De sociale positie van de gereformeerde predikanten in de Republiek der Verenigde Nederlanden voor ± 1700* (Groningen: Wolters-Noordhoff, 1977), p. 125.
18   Groenhuis, *De predikanten*, p. 144.
19   *Staat van ambten waarover jaarlijks of éénmalig recognitie moet worden betaald, 30 december 1692*. WA, Oud archief stad Enkhuizen 1353-185, inv. 0120. 1374-1.
20   C. D. van Strien, *British Travellers in Holland during the Stuart Period: Edward Browne and John Locke as Tourists in the United Provinces* (Leiden: Brill, 1993), p. 205.
21   Staten van Overijssel, Ridderschap en Steden, en de op hen volgende colleges, Inventaries van de archieven van de Staten van Overijssel, Riddershap en Steden, en van de op hen volgende colleges, HCO, Inv. nr. 4858.

BUYERS OF TRUTH 71

1,200, 200 more than Franciscus Gomarus.[22] Petrus van Mastricht received 1,000 gulden when he became professor of theology in Utrecht. The city eased the transition from Doesburg by ensuring that the costs of transporting his furniture and books would be covered.[23]

Institutions that could not offer such inducements struggled to keep professors. From its beginning in 1599, the Illustrious School at Harderwijk scrounged for funds. It narrowly avoided financial collapse several times throughout the seventeenth century. Other institutions offered more money, and the professors left as quickly as they could. Harderwijk was quick to remind their professors that they could supplement their income. A professor could expect 100 gulden per boarder. Private lessons in theology added seven gulden per student for a half-year's tuition. But this was insufficient to keep prestigious theologians at the academy. Antonius Thysius became the first professor of theology at Harderwijk in 1601. He received a paltry 550 gulden. After making a name for himself at the Synod of Dort, he received an offer from the University of Leiden, and he quickly moved on. Most professors at Leiden earned about a thousand gulden. Heinrich von Diest left Harderwijk after thirteen years for a theology post at Deventer's Illustrious School in 1639, which paid him an annual salary of 900 gulden. After teaching in Harderwijk for less than a year, one minister left for Groningen in 1644. The curators acknowledged that finances kept professors from staying. The new professor's 'sober salary' was not even paid on time. After struggling for decades, in 1648 the Illustrious school became a provincial academy and professorial salaries were raised to between 800 and 1,000 gulden.[24]

André Rivet owned one of the largest libraries among ministers in the seventeenth century, but he could afford it. When he came to Leiden as a professor of theology in 1620, his yearly salary was 1,200 gulden, plus 300 gulden for housing. He had already received between 300 and 400 gulden for moving costs.[25] In addition to his salary from the university, he earned a healthy additional income from writing. The university awarded him two hundred gulden after he published his commentary on the Psalms, and 100 gulden for a book against Grotius.[26] When Rivet divided his time between the university

---

22   Edwin Raggie, introduction to *Hugo Grotius, Ordinum Hollandiae ac Westfrisiae Pietas (1613): Critical edition with English translation and commentary* (Leiden: Brill, 1995), p. 20.

23   Adriaan C. Neele, *Petrus van Mastricht (1630–1706), Reformed Orthodoxy: Method and Piety* (Leiden: Brill, 2008), p. 49.

24   Meindert Evers, 'The Illustre School at Harderwyk', *Lias*, 12 (1985), pp. 81–113.

25   H. J. Honders, *André Rivet: Als invloedrijk gereformeerd theoloog in Holland's bloeitijd* (The Hague: Martinus Nijhoff, 1930), p. 15.

26   P. C. Molhuysen (ed.), *Bronnen tot de geschiedenis der Leidensche Universiteit* (The Hague: Martinus Nijhoff, 1913–1924), II, pp. 129, 269.

72 CHAPTER 3

of Leiden and pastoring the Walloon Church in The Hague, his salary from
the Walloon church was 600 gulden a year, with an additional 200 gulden for
rent.[27] This income, not including his university salary, was more than many
ministers made. His financial status would only improve further as he joined
the court of Frederick Henry. His salary more than doubled to 3,600 gulden
per year. He received free food and lodging, and his salary was guaranteed for
the rest of his life, even if he resigned after a few years or illness kept him from
his duties.[28] With a salary of this size, Rivet could easily care for his family and
build a library of nearly five thousand books.

Five hundred gulden was much more than what a tradesman earned in a
year. A day laborer earned about 250 gulden a year.[29] Yet, complaints that their
salaries were insufficient were common from ministers. Many ministers, often
those less educated, received a far more modest remuneration and salaries
were often paid in arrears.[30] Salaries as little as 300 gulden were not unheard of
in rural villages.[31] In Delft in 1658, the minister whose budget included 'books,
paper, ink and newspapers' argued that it was not possible to support himself
and his wife on 500 gulden a year.[32] To support his case, he published his yearly
budget. His expenses were unnecessarily high, he claimed, because a minister
was expected to entertain regularly, and it was unusual for a minister's wife to
work. By his estimation, he would need at least 547 gulden to survive; and this
was a family not burdened (or blessed) by children.

Ministers' formal salaries tell only part of the story. The Dutch Republic was
the highest taxed country in the seventeenth century, yet ministers received
several benefits that alleviated that burden. Ministers were free from excise
duties on basic foodstuffs, beer, wine, peat, and other consumables. The magistrates of Rotterdam issued an ordinance that stated 'all ministers, including
Scottish and English ministers, shall be free from excise duties'.[33] They could

---

27   A. G. Van Opstal, *André Rivet: Een invloedrijk hugenoot aan het hof van Frederick Hendrik*
      (Harderwijk: Flevo, 1937), p. 12.
28   Van Opstal, *André Rivet*, p. 19.
29   A. Th. van Deursen, *Plain Lives in a Golden Age: Popular culture, religion and society in
      seventeenth-century Holland*, trans. Maarteen Ultee (Cambridge: Cambridge University
      Press, 1991), p. 7.
30   Groenhuis, *De predikanten*, pp. 133–137. Johannes Picardt, *Den Prediger, Dat is gron-
      dige verklaringe en bewys, genomen uyt Goddelycke, kerckelycke ende prophane schriften*
      (Zwolle: Jan Gerritsz., 1650), p. 3.
31   Van Strien, *British Travellers in Holland*, p. 205.
32   *Bewys, dat het een predicant met zyn huysvrouw alleen niet mogelijck en is op vijfhondert
      guld. eerlijck te leven* (Delft: Pieter de Menagie, 1658), USTC 1839928.
33   'Insghelijcks sullen vry wesen [of excise] ... alle de predicanten, daer onder de Schotse
      ende Engnelsche predicanten mede verstaen begrepen te zijn'. *Generale ordonnantie ende
      conditien* ([Rotterdam], s.n., s.d.), likely USTC 1529670, f. A2r.

BUYERS OF TRUTH

also rely on free accommodation, provided by the city council. Beyond salary and public benefits, ministers earned additional income through numerous other means. It was common for ministers to take in boarders. A remarkable instance of this can be found in a letter from John Dury to Dorothy More on 1 August 1641. A professor of theology and minister in Utrecht, Gisbertus Voetius (1589–1676) had thirteen boarders living with him at one time. For each of the three boys More was hoping to send to Voetius, it would cost about 300 gulden a year.[34] With a house full of boarders, Voetius would have had an additional gross income of 3,900 gulden.

Ministers were educated citizens, but by and large they were moderately paid. They lived between opulence and poverty. In most cities and towns, they were some of its most educated citizens. They capitalized on this to help provide for their families. Printers and publishers needed educated correctors, and ministers had the training needed to proof read in a number of languages. Stephanus Curcellaeus (Étienne de Courcelles, 1586–1659), former Remonstrant minister in Vitry, moved to Amsterdam in 1634. Without a pulpit, he earned his living as a corrector at the Blaeu shop.[35] Many ministers wrote books to supplement their income. They dedicated their works to city and provincial officials, who often paid the author if the book bolstered their reputation. Petrus Leupenius, an Amsterdam minister, received 150 gulden from the Amsterdam burgomasters after the publication of his *De Geesel der Sonden* [*The Companion of Sin*] in 1651. Festus Hommius, professor of theology, at Leiden received 200 gulden for his *De victus ratione in morbis auctis* and another 200 for his *Specimen controversiarum Belgicarum*. Jacob Trigland received an unknown sum for his *De kracht der Godsaligheyt* [*The Power of Godliness*].[36]

Cities and states contended with one another for honour in the minds of their citizens. Ministerial salaries benefited from this competition at times, when ministers flattered the authorities, but the opposite is true as well. State control of ministerial salaries constrained ministers' ability to speak and write without threat of recourse from the authorities. When ministers and authors brought shame on political officials, authorities chastised and censored them, often forcing them to pay a fine, or banished them. After publicly rebuking

---

34   John Dury to Dorothy More, 1 August 1641. The Hartlib Papers 2/5/5A-B. https://www.hri online.ac.uk/hartlib/browse.jsp?id=2%2F5%2F5a-b Accessed 10 September 2017.

35   Kęstutis Daugirdas, 'The Biblical Hermeneutics of Socinians and Remonstrants in the Seventeenth Century' in Th. Marius van Leeuwen, et al. (eds.), *Arminius, Arminianism, and Europe: Jacob Arminius (1559/60–1609)* (Leiden: Brill, 2009), p. 108. Cf. Arnold Poelenburg, 'Oratio funebris in obitum clarissimi viri D. Stephani Curcellaei', in Etienne de Courcelles, *Opera theologica* (Amsterdam: Daniel Elzevier, 1675), USTC 1811941, ff. ***2r–***3r.

36   P. J. Verkruisse, 'Holland "gedediceerd". Boekopdrachten in Holland in de 17e eeuw', in *Kunst in opdracht in de Gouden Eeuw* (1991), pp. 225–242.

74   CHAPTER 3

Rotterdam's city magistrates in 1665, Franciscus Ridderus quickly regretted his words and went to the town hall to apologize before they decided to suspend his salary.[37] Wilhemus à Brakel in 1688 was chastised by Rotterdam's magistrates after he gave an 'offensive sermon'.[38] But officials were equally lavish in generosity when an author honoured them and their jurisdiction. In the chronicle of his hometown, the Haarlem minister Samuel Ampzing (1590–1632) reinforced Haarlemmers' identity as those who valiantly resisted the Spanish during the Dutch Revolt: unlike the opportunistic Amsterdammers who capitulated and aided the Spanish against the citizens of Haarlem. Haarlem's magistrates revelled in Ampzing's description of the town's heroism, rewarded him with 600 gulden and bought fifty copies of the book for the city. News of the magistrates' generosity reached other local ministers who preceded to bombard them with book dedications. To pacify the ministers eager for some additional income, the magistrates raised their annual salaries from five hundred to six hundred gulden: on the condition that the ministers stopped dedicating books to them.[39]

2   Dusty Attics

While neither wealthy nor impoverished, ministers had sufficient income to buy and acquire books. Books at auction sold for an average of a gulden a piece. In 1636 Wilhelm Merwy's collection of 104 books sold for about 110 gulden.[40] Guilielmus Fabius in 1677 owned 449 books, of which 441 had listed prices.[41] These 441 sold for just under 550 gulden. They built collections and they gave books as gifts. During this era, sending and receiving books from fellow ministers and theologians was commonplace. When writing letters to

---

37   J. R. Callenbach, 'Kerkelijk leven', in C. te Lintum (ed.), *Rotterdam in de loop der eeuwen*, vol. 2 (Rotterdam: W. Neuvens, 1906–1907), p. 50.

38   *Extract uit de resoluties van de Weth van 1688 over een aanstootgevende preek van ds. Wilhelmus a Brakel*, SAR, 37-04_144. Cf. *Extract uyt de notulen van de [...] Staten van Zeelant. Den 21. september 1684* (S.l., s.n., 1684), USTC 1827017; G. Groenhuis, 'Calvinism and National Consciousness: the Dutch Republic as the New Israel', in A. C. Duke and C. A. Tamse (eds.), *Britain and the Netherlands: Church and State Since the Reformation*, vol. 7 (The Hague: Martinus Nijhoff, 1981), p. 129–130; A. Th. van Deursen, 'De Dominee', in H. M. Beliën, et al. (eds.), *Gestatlen van de gouden eeuw: Een Hollands groepsportret* (Amsterdam: Bert Bakker, 1995), p. 155.

39   Raingard Esser, *The Politics of Memory: The Writing of Partition in the Seventeenth-Century Low Countries* (Leiden: Brill, 2012), p. 113, n. 26.

40   *AC Wilhelm Merwy 1636* (Delft: Jan Pietersz Waelpot, 1636), USTC 1027540.

41   *AC Guilielmus Fabius 1677* (Delft: Cornelis van Heusden, 1677), USTC 1813810.

BUYERS OF TRUTH

each other, many senders wrote 'with a book' or some version thereof below the recipient's name and place. Amongst the urban elite of ministers, sending each other books was expected. They understood themselves as men of letters and supplying friends and correspondents with stimulating books was a standard practice. André Rivet (1572–1651), then a professor of theology at Leiden, was deeply involved in the academic book circuit. Anna Maria van Schurman (1607–1678), Utrecht's promoter of the education of women, once offered her thanks to Rivet for sending her a collection of volumes:

> I received most happily, as was appropriate, the volumes with which you wished to adorn my library. The gift was indeed very pleasing to me when I turned my eyes toward the person of the giver and when I turned to the argument itself, that is to the subject matter of your triumph.[42]

On at least two occasions Franciscus Junius (1545–1602) sent copies of the books he had written or translated. To Ludovico à Sein, he intended to send two copies of his translation of the Bible.[43] He sent Henricus Corputius (1536–1601), a minister in Dordrecht, a copy of his Hebrew grammar.[44] The Leiden theologian Johannes Hoornbeeck received at least two books from the Dutch missionary to China, Justus Heurnius. 'I have in my possession', Hoornbeeck stated, 'a Chinese-Latin manuscript, a gift from Justus Heurnius, a very pious man and special friend'.[45] At a later point in the same publication, Hoornbeeck noted '[Heurnius] wrote the exhortation *De legatione evangelica ad Indox capessenda*, of which he also gave a copy to us'.[46]

Ministers sent books to members of other similarly bookish professions. The Dordrecht minister Abraham vander Corput (1599–1670) sent his regular correspondent Joachim Oudaan, a Remonstrant playwright and theologian in Rotterdam, numerous books along with his letters. Two letters have the manuscript notes 'with a book' under the recipients' information. A third letter states

---

42   Anna Maria van Schurman, *Anna Maria van Schurman: Whether a Christian Woman Should Be Educated and Other Writings From Her Intellectual Circle*, ed. and trans. Joyce L. Irwin (Chicago: University of Chicago Press, 1998), 41–42.

43   Franciscus Junius to Ludvico à Sein, 24 April 1579, in Fr. W. Cuno, *Franciscus Junius der Ältere, Professor der Theologie und Pastor. (1545–1602): Sein Leben und Wirken, seine Schriften und Briefe* (Amsterdam: Scheffer and Co., 1891), p. 301.

44   Franciscus Junius to Henric Corputio, 15 September 1580, in Ibid., p. 303.

45   Johannes Hoornbeeck, *Johannes Hoornbeeck (1617–1666), On the Conversion of Indians and Heathens: An Annotated Translation of De Conversione Indorum et Gentilium (1669)*, eds. Ineke Loots and Joke Spaans (Leiden: Brill, 2018), p. 109.

46   Ibid., p. 187.

'with two books'.[47] Authors often sent books to well-known ministers, hoping they would recommend them to others. In 1661, a young Sephardic scholar named Jacob Abendana (1630–1695) sent Johannes Cocceius (1603–1669) a copy of *Mikhlal Yophi*, a commentary on the Old Testament by Shelomo ben Melekh. Abendena hoped Cocceius would send it to Guilielmus Anslaar (1633–1694), a minister (and Cocceius' son-in-law) in Zeeland.[48]

Martinus Lydius generously gave books away. Such gifts represented the encouragement to propagate the gospel as widely as possible. He gave several books intended for comforting the sick and dying to a colleague in Harlingen. Martinus hoped the gift would encourage him to write his own book on the topic.[49] The Utrecht church council received thirty-six copies of Godefridus Udemans' *Absaloms-hayr* [Absaloms Hair] in 1643, sent by Gisbertus Voetius.[50]

André Rivet received numerous books from correspondents. Letters to and from Rivet regularly mention sending and receiving books. Sentences like this from Rivet's nephew are common: 'I am sending you a booklet that you will enjoy reading'.[51] In 1626, Marin Mersenne in Paris sent André Rivet a copy of his response to Johannes Drusius' edition of the Bible.[52] The French polymath was an intelligencer for mathematicians and philosophers throughout Europe in the seventeenth century, and he hoped that Rivet could become a possible contact in his network. He regularly sent Rivet the newest and best publications from Parisian presses.[53] A few years later, Mersenne clarified the kind of information exchange he hoped would come from his correspondence with Rivet: 'From now on, I will have a particular care to maintain our communication for books and other matters of literature, only for whatever you think will

---

47 'Met een boeck'. Abraham vander Corput to Joachim Oudaan, 13 July 1662 and 29 October 1669; 'Met twee boecken'. Corput to Oudaan, 26 March 1670, UB-Leiden PAP 2 Copernicus-Cuyckius.

48 Johannes Cocceius, *Opera ANEKDOTA* (2 vols., Amsterdam: Janssonius-Waesburge, Boom, and Goethals, 1706), I, pp. 722–723.

49 Willem Op 't Hof, *Engelse pietistiche geschrift in het Nederlands, 1598–1622* (Rotterdam: Lindenberg, 1987), p. 73.

50 Dirck van Miert, 'The "Hairy War" (1640–1650): Historicizing the Bible in the Dutch Republic on the Eve of Spinoza', *Sixteenth Century Journal*, 49 (2018), p. 423.

51 'Je vous envoie un livret que vous prendrez plaisir à lire'. J. M. de Lange to Rivet, 4 November 1625, in Jean Luc-Tulot (ed.), 'Correspondence of Jean-Maximilien de Langle (1590–1674)', p. 16. Available at http://jeanluc.tulot.pagesperso-orange.fr/Rivet-Langle.pdf. Last accessed 22 October 2019.

52 Sixtinus Amama to Rivet, June 1626, in Paul Tannery, Cornelis de Waard and Armand Beaulieu (eds.), *Correspondence du P Marin Mersenne* (Paris: Presses Universitaires de France, 1945–1988), I, p. 476. Henceforth, *CM*.

53 Justin Grosslight, 'Small Skills, Big Network: Marin Mersenne as Mathematical Intelligencer', *History of Science*, 51 (2013), pp. 337–374, esp. 340.

BUYERS OF TRUTH 77

be able to bring contentment'.[54] He and Rivet would correspond often until Mersenne's death in 1645.

Rivet, however, would not keep his copy of Mersenne's work on the Drusius Bible. There is no reference to this work in Rivet's catalogue. Only one book by Mersenne is listed in Rivet's catalogue: his commentary on Genesis (Paris, 1623).[55] What happened to the book is not in question. Rivet promptly sent it Sixtinus Amama, professor of theology at Franeker. Amama would defend Drusius, his colleague at Franeker, as he would numerous times throughout his life.[56] Amama briskly composed a response to Mersenne, printed in 1628 in Franeker and Amsterdam. Amama sent Rivet a copy of his response.[57] Unlike Mersenne's publications, Rivet's catalogue contains five of Amama's works.[58] Gerardus Vossius hoped to send Rivet the new London edition of Optatus of Milevis' work, printed in 1631.[59] In 1643, he was sent a new edition of the Greek New Testament, printed by the French Royal printer.[60]

In the realm of philosophy too, Rivet's connections with French intellectuals contributed to his books. In 1638, René Descartes was stirring the intellectual world into a frenzy. His *Discourse on Method* had just been printed in Leiden by Jean La Maire.[61] Those who acquired a copy were excited finally to have the Descartes' treatise on philosophy. As an important figure amongst the international intellectual community, Rivet was well aware of the publication of the *Discourse*.[62] Rivet's catalogue includes Descartes' most controversial work: the *Discourse* sold for six gulden.[63] When Descartes completed work on his textbook of philosophy, *Principia Philosophiae*, he sent proofs to scholars throughout Western Europe. One recipient of the philosopher's work was André Rivet. During the dog-days of summer Rivet took a few minutes to

---

54 'J' auray desormais un soin particulier dentretenir nostre communication tant pour les livres et autres choses qui concernement la litterature, que pour tout ce que vous iugerez pouvoic apporter du contentement'. *CM*, II, p. 104. Van Opstal, *André Rivet*, p. 122.

55 *AC André Rivet 1657* (Leiden: Pieter Leffen, 1657), USTC 1846296, p. 10.

56 Peter T. van Rooden, *Theology, Biblical Scholarship and Rabbinical Studies in the Seventeenth Century* (Leiden: Brill, 1989), p. 75.

57 Sixtinus Amama to Rivet, 13/23 February 1628, in *CM*, II, p. 27.

58 *AC André Rivet*, pp. 28, 43, 54.

59 G. J. Vossius to Rivet, 8 April 1632, in *Virorum eruditione celeberrimorum epistolae*, p. 198. USTC 3015206.

60 De Langle to Rivet, 4 July 1643, in 'Correspondence of Jean-Maximilien de Langle', p. 70.

61 On La Maire, see Ronald Bruegelmans, *Fac et spera: Joannes Maire, publisher, printer and bookseller in Leiden 1603–1657. A Bibliography of His Publications* (Leiden: Hes & De Graaf, 2003).

62 Grosslight, 'Small Skills, Big Network', p. 351.

63 *AC André Rivet*, p. 129.

78   CHAPTER 3

compose a thank-you note for sending him three copies. Rivet insisted that he would send the two extra copies to a couple of contemporaries once the postal route was clear.[64]

Descartes' treatises were not the only provocative works from French intellectuals to come across his desk. To keep his uncle up to date, Jean-Maximilian de Langle in Rouen would send Rivet the most recent theological books printed in France.[65] At one point De Langle sent a book so Rivet would no longer hold the Rouen booksellers in such low regard.[66] In 1633, De Langle came across *La Papesse Jeanne*, a French translation of a tract by an English theologian. De Langle would promptly send it to his uncle for his enjoyment.[67] In December 1634, De Langle sent Rivet *Defense des ministers de l'Evangile contra Cacherat*. He left the package with Johannes de Laet, the director of the West India Company, and hoped he would deliver it to Rivet.[68]

In 1668 Antonius Hulsius (1615–1685), a Walloon minister in Breda, a professor of theology at Breda's Illustrious School, and rector of the city's Latin school, became regent of the *Statencollege* at Leiden and extraordinary professor of theology. For his first publication in his new role, Hulsius decided to publish a collection of letters he exchanged with Jacob Abendana. Leiden's rector intended an evangelistic discussion, hoping to win Abendana to the Christian faith through rigorous debate of the Old Testament. With short, reserved letters, Abendana made clear his desire to change the venue from written letters to a verbal debate. Whether Abendana feared the letters being made public is not clear. What is clear, however, is that communication became enflamed when Hulsius lost his temper and wrote his longest (and last) letter in response to Abendana's alleged intractability.[69] Abendana claimed he had

---

64   'J'ai reçu les trois exemplaires qu'il vous a plu m'envoyer de vos principes de philosophie. Sitôt que la navigation sera propre, je travaillerai pour envoyer ceux que vous destinez à Jean Gillot, et vous remercie humblement de celui qu'il vous a plu me donner. J'en ai déjà lu les deux premières parties avec attention'. Rivet to Renè Descartes, 19 July 1644. ePistolarum, http://ckcc.huygens.knaw.nl/epistolarium/letter.html?id=desc004/7441b is. Last Accessed 8 September 2017.

65   J. M. de Langle to Rivet, 29 November 1633, in 'Correspondence of Jean-Maximilien de Langle', p. 26.

66   J. M. de Langle to Rivet, 27 July 1641, in 'Correspondence of Jean-Maximilien de Langle', p. 58.

67   J. M. de Langle to Rivet, 6 May 1633, in 'Correspondence of Jean-Maximilien de Langle', p. 24. AC *André Rivet*, p. 134.

68   J. M. de Langle to Rivet, 6 November 1634, in 'Correspondence of Jean-Maximilien de Langle', p. 29.

69   Peter T. van Rooden and Jan Wim Wesselius, 'Two early cases of publication by subscription in Holland and Germany: Jacob Abendana's *Mikhal Yophi* (1661) and David Cohen de Lara's *Keter Kehunna* (1668)', *Quaerendo* 16 (1986), p. 114.

BUYERS OF TRUTH

in fact responded; Hulsius denied this.[70] The correspondence was broken off, but only after Abendana had devoted much time and effort to helping Hulsius build his library of Jewish books. The Sephardic scholar acted as a book agent to the professor in search of books that aided his career in Hebrew studies.

Writing from Breda in 1659 to Abendana, Hulsius exclaimed 'my desire to see your book on *Mikhal Yophi* consumes me. If it pleases you to send a folio copy, it would satisfy me'. 'Also', Hulsius continued, 'Remember my lord R. Majemonidis' work on *Mischnajoth*, which he promised to me, if he could manage an untouched and excellent copy, if the price is tolerable'.[71] Writing a month later, Abendana admitted he had not been able to acquire the book for Hulsius, despite diligent effort. Many people desired a copy. He even asked Hulsius to compile a list of those who desire the book.[72] In March Abendana told Hulsius that he had not forgotten about *Mischnajoth*, on which Abendana had good news: he could acquire it from Hamburg for a price of six gulden, and he would send it to him after he himself had received it.[73] After complaining about how long it had been since he had originally asked Abendana about the book, Hulsius mentioned he may not need the book anymore. He was able to use an edition of the 'Talmud of Babylon' to which the commentaries of Maimonides were added. This was likely a negotiating tactic, because he still encouraged Abendana to send the book, if it was for a bearable price.[74]

---

70 Ibid., p. 115.

71 'Etiam consumuntur renes mei in sinu me out videam opus tuum desiderabile super libro Michlal jophi. Si placuerit singular ejus folia impressa ad me mittere, rem mihi gratam feceris. Etiam recordabitur Dominus meus operis R. Majemonidis super Mischnajoth, quod mihi promisit, nempe si exemplar quoddam haberi possit integrum et nitidum tolerabili pretio'. Antonius Hulsius to Jacob Abendana, 24 September 1659, in Antonius Hulsius, *Wikkuah 'ivri seu Disputatio epistolaris Hebraica inter Antonium Hulsium et Jacobu Abendanah Super loco Haggaei cap. 2. v. 9* (Leiden: Joannis Nicolai à Dorp, 1669), USTC 1806032, p. 9.

72 'Hactenus acquirere nondum potui explicationem Majemonidis super mischnajoth, quaeram tamen eam diligentissimè ut serviam domino, dixit enim mihi vir quidam se exspectare quotidiè complures libros foris ad se mittendos, qui ubi advenerint transmittam domino eorum catalogum'. Jacob Abendana to Antonius Hulsius, 24 October 1659, in Hulsius, *Disputatio epistolaris Hebraica*, p. 20.

73 'Etiam non sum oblitus quaerere librum Mischnajoth, quem à me petiisti. Quaerere eum curavi Hamburgi, ubi adepti eum sunt pretio sex imperialium. Exepecto eum indics, et postquam accepero mittam Domino'. Jacob Abendana to Antonius Hulsius, 26 March 1660, in Hulsius, *Disputatio epistolaris Hebraica*, p. 58.

74 'Quantum ad libro Mischnajoth de quo scripsi Domino anno praeterito, mihique respondit, virum quondam exspectare aliquot libros foris, cujus catalogum ad me esset missurus.Sed postmodum ejus rei non meministi amplius, egoque interea mihi comparavi Talmud Babylonicum, cui additi sunt commentarii Majemonidis ad omnes codices.Adeo ut eum jam mittere non sit necesse. Tum et nimis carum mihi est ejus pretium,

When he arrived in Leiden, André Rivet had an immediate connection with Abraham and Bonaventura Elzevier. Not only did he occasionally have books printed with them and work for them on occasion, Rivet bought books from them. Three years after arriving in Leiden, Rivet was buying books from the Elzeviers and asking them to acquire books from auctions for him.[75] Abraham Elzevier wrote to the new doctor of theology to send him an invoice for books he had purchased from them and update him on how the auction went. Rivet owed the Elzeviers just over four gulden for four books: *Epistolas doctorum eucharistia* (2 gulden 8 stuivers), *Mariale* by Bernardino de Busti (1 gulden 7 stuivers), Thomas Cranmer's *De Sacramento Corporis* (6 stuivers), and Lucius' *Synopsis Antisociniana* (8 stuivers).[76] Thirty-years later when Pieter Leffen auctioned Rivet's collection, all but the *Epistolas doctorum eucharistia* sold. The three sold for nearly the original price. *Mariale* sold in a lot with one other book for a gulden and a nine stuivers. The Reformed theologian would use this regularly in his book on the Virgin Mary.[77] Cranmer's work sold for two gulden in a lot of four books, and Lucius' *Synopsis* went with a lot of six books for just over two gulden. Apparently, Rivet had requested several other books but the reserve prices were too high.

Owning a library was a principle means of ascertaining the truth about one's theological and religious opponents. Gisbertus Voetius encouraged his students to own multiple versions of the same text because, he claimed, many had been altered after the Council of Trent.[78] He was not alone in this allegation: Voetius recommended the Oxford librarian Thomas James' *A treatise of the corruption of Scripture, councels and fathers, by the prelats, pastors, and pillars of the church of Rome, for maintenance of popery and irreligion* (London, 1612).[79] Prosper Marchand, the eighteenth-century French bibliographer, agreed with Voetius' claim, and Marchand even favorably cited Voetius' text on the benefit of collecting multiple editions.[80]

---

      scripseram autem, si tolerabili pretio haberi possit'. Antonius Hulsius to Jacob Abendana, 6 April 1660, in Hulsius, *Disputatio epistolaris Hebraica*, p. 64.

75   Abraham Elzevier to Rivet, 18 May 1623, UB Leiden, ms. BPL 293 II.

76   I have not been able to identify *Epistolas doctorum eucharistia*. Rivet's catalogue lists Cranmer's *De Sacramento Corporis* as being printed in Frankfurt in 1617. Bernardino: USTC 142820; Lucius: USTC 2068663.

77   André Rivet, *Apologia pro sanctissima virgine Maria matre Domini* (Franciscus Hackers & Hegerus: Leiden, 1639), USTC 1028683, pp. 17–27, 61, 74, 104, 161, 183 and 186.

78   Gisbertus Voetius, *Exercitia et bibliotheca studiosi theologiae* (Utrecht: Johannes à Waesberge, 1651), USTC 1814113, pp. 252–262.

79   USTC 3005038. Ibid., p. 256.

80   Prosper Marchand, *Histoire de l'origine et des premiers progress de l'imprimerie* (The Hague: widow Le Vier and Pierre Paupie, 1740), part 1, pp. 106–108.

The Utrecht theologian gave his students a few tips on how to acquire the oldest, pre-Trent editions of texts. 'But where and how, you might ask, does one come by such books ... which were censured and forbidden at a later date'? Voetius offered four points of advice. First, he admonished all who hold 'learning, religion and sincerity dear' to donate their collections to public libraries so the books could be preserved. Second, the libraries of former 'monasteries, chapters, bishops and other clergy' ought similarly to be transferred to public libraries. He then addressed those actively seeking such books. Book buyers should intentionally buy from those booksellers who had 'old books regardless of how dirty and dusty they are', and from any who traveled to Spain and Italy, where old books were more readily available. Fourth, he reminded book collectors eager to obtain the oldest and best copies not to forgo those places one would not immediately associate with books of high quality:

> These books should be purchased from chemists and from people who glue paper together to make millboard for fabric salesmen. I once saw enormous stacks of such books, purchased for these purposes, in the premises of such artisans. I also once visited a bookseller whose attic was filled to overflowing with very old editions.[81]

Such book buying was an exercise in knowing one's own tradition with the best available sources. But his encouragement to gain knowledge through books extended to other faiths as well. Voetius encouraged his students to understand Islam through similar means. The connection between the Dutch Republic and Muslim countries extended back to the Dutch Revolt. They shared a common enemy, Spain. There were talks of coordinating military strategy against

---

81 'Primum est, Ut eruditionis, religionis, candoris amantes sua exemplaria, si quae privatim possideant, aut ipsi viventes, aut post obitum per haeredes suos in publicas bibliothecas inferri, ibique custoditi current. Secundum, est ut nostra ea omnia ex bibliothecis claustrorum, capitulorum, Episcoporum, aliorumque clericorum (si quae justo titulo in ipsorum potestaten veniant) in publicas & publica autoritate ac custodia munitas bibliothecas transferant. Tertium est ut a bibliopolis, qui quoscunque antiquos & fitu ac paedore squallentes libros vendere atque emere solent, ea redimant. Imprimis hic agendum cumillis bibliopolis, qui peregrinationibus, seu excursionibus per Hispaniam, Italiam &c. institutis, omnis generis excusos & MSS. libros studiose conquirunt. Quartum est, u tea redimant à seplasiariis & iis qui ex chartis conglutinates tabulas mercatoribus panni conficiunt. Vidi aliquando istius generis artifices qui ingentes strues ejusmodi Librorum ad hoc opus suum coëmerant. Vidi tabulatum bibliopolae similibus antiquissimarum editionum libris repletum'. Voetius, Exercitia, p. 261. Translation my own. Also translated in J. van Heel, 'Gisbertus Voetius on the Necessity of Locating, Collecting and Preserving Early Printed Books', Quaerendo, 39 (2009), pp. 55–56.

82 CHAPTER 3

the Spanish, though this remained only talk.[82] To curtail Spain's influence, between 1610 and 1622 the Netherlands agreed to treaties with Morocco, the Ottomans and Algiers.[83] Few Muslims, if any, lived in the Netherlands permanently. But their presence was known throughout the country. Dignitaries from these countries would visit the Netherlands and would occasionally travel through the country. Ömer Agha, a diplomat on behalf of the admiral of the Ottoman navy, visited Leiden, Haarlem, Amsterdam and Utrecht.[84] Because they were known and the conflicting beliefs between Muslims and Reformed Christians were well understood, Voetius wanted his students to understand their faith and to be able to present the Reformed alternative. He offered his students a historical overview on the rise and development of Islam and summarized some of their basic beliefs, including 'the common faith of the Turks', which was that 'there is no god but God and Muhammed is his apostle'.[85] If students desired more information on Islam and its history, he encouraged them to turn to the sources: first, the Koran, then to other texts on the faith.[86] For this, Voetius admitted, a library would be needed:

> Thirdly, among the resources necessary for [understanding Islam] is the scientific apparatus of a well-equipped library. There are books about Islam, in the first place the Koran. But it has not yet been published entirely in Arabic in Europe. The result is that an inquisitive researcher has to resort to handwritten copies, which can be found in private libraries and in public Dutch libraries in Leiden, Amsterdam, Rotterdam, and in our Utrecht library, which has the most beautiful copy. There, the curious researcher should take refuge.[87]

---

82 A. H. de Groot, *The Ottoman Empire and the Dutch Republic: A History of the Earliest Diplomatic Relations, 1610–1630* (Leiden: Nederlands Historisch-Archaeologisch Instituut Leiden/Istanbul, 1978), p. 83.

83 Ibid., pp. 247–60.

84 Benjamin J. Kaplan, *Muslims in the Dutch Golden Age: Representations and realities of religious toleration* (Amsterdam: Amsterdam University Press, 2007), p. 17.

85 Gisbertus Voetius, 'De Muhammedismo', *Selectarum disputationum theologicarum* (5 vols., Utrecht and Amsterdam: Johannes (1) Janssonius van Waesberge, 1648–1669), USTC 1836590, II, p. 664. This dissertation is available in Dutch translation in W. J. van Asselt, *Voetius* (Kampen: De Groot Goudriaan, 2007), pp. 145–154.

86 On the Koran in the Dutch Republic, see August den Hollander, 'The Qur'an in the Low Countries Early Printed Dutch and French Translations', *Quaerendo*, 45 (2015), pp. 209–239.

87 'III. Apparatus supellectilis librariae ad hanc rem necessariae. Sunt autem libri pro parte Muhammedismi, *Primo, Alcoranus*: sed qui totus Arabicè nonum in Europa editus; ita ut ad exemplaria MSS. quę exstant in Bibliothecis privatis, & publicis Belgicis Leidensi, Amsterldamensi, Roterodamensi, nostrâ Ultrajectinâ (cujus exemplar longè

BUYERS OF TRUTH

83

3 The Home of the Muses

In the Dutch Republic, local libraries where available in medium-sized towns and urban centres. Like those Voetius mentioned in passing, universities, towns and states began acquiring books for the use of the learned amongst them. A city library was a point of civic pride in early-modern Europe. In 1604 in Rotterdam, the city's preachers secured the money for a 'public library which in due course would be a renowned library in the town'.[88] It was started often with a sizeable donation or the confiscation of books from local monasteries. Local churches housed many of them: Tiel, Amsterdam, Weesp and many other cities had libraries housed in one of their churches. As educated citizens and book collectors in their own right, ministers were crucial to the establishment of these collections. The first major purchase the city of Alkmaar made for the creation of a library in 1596 came from the auction of books owned by Jeremias Bastingius (1551–1595), a former professor of theology at Leiden. The city sent the municipal secretary to the auction, and a local minister likely accompanied him.[89]

Martinus Lydius had a formative hand in the constitution of Amsterdam's city library. The churches' ruling body in Amsterdam wanted to update the library, selling unused books and acquiring more helpful texts. On 7 May 1580, they asked Martinus and Laurens Jacobsz (the famed Bible publisher) 'to enquire of Cornelis Claesz, bookbinder, whether he is ready to part with certain books which he has purchased from the library'. The minister and the publisher were asked to be consultants and 'to see what books can be dispensed with in the library so that these might be exchanged with him'. They sold unnecessary books to Claesz and reorganized the collection for more effective use.[90] Amsterdam's city library was open 'to all enthusiasts who did not have the means to buy all sorts of books themselves'.[91] Lydius' youngest son, Balthazar, was given responsibility for the library at Dordrecht's Latin School when he became its curator a few years after becoming a minister there.[92] Johannes Becius (1558–1626),

---

elegantissimum) harum rerum curioso indagatori confugiendum sit'. Voetius, 'De Muhammedismo', p. 675.

88   Quoted in, Ad Leerintveld, 'Inleiding' in Ad Leerintveld and Jan Bedeaux (eds.), *Historische stadsbibliotheken in Nederland: Studies over openbare stadsbibliotheken in de Noordelijke Nederlanden vanaf circa 1560 tot 1800* (Zutphen: Walburg Pers, 2016), p. 11.

89   Paul Dijstelberge and Kuniko Forrer, 'De Alkmaarse Librije', in Leerintveld and Bedeaux (eds.), *Historische Stadsbibliotheken in Nederland*, p. 32.

90   Herman de la Fontaine Verwey, 'The City Library of Amsterdam in the Niewe Kerk 1578–1632', *Quaerendo*, 14 (1984), p. 168.

91   Ibid., p. 165.

92   E. O. G. Haitsma Mulier and G. A. C. van der Lem (eds.), *Repertorium van Geschiedschrijvers in Nederland 1500–1800* (The Hague: Nederlands Historisch Genootschap, 1990), p. 266.

84   CHAPTER 3

Daniel Demetrius (d. 1628) and Andreas Colvius (1594–1671), all three ministers in Dordrecht during their lives, oversaw the library.[93]

Enkhuizen's library was housed in its St Gommarus or Westerkerk. Thomas Brown, a minister there from 1650 to 1679, donated at least one book, likely a copy of Pliny's *Historia* (Geneva, 1631).[94] The library housed few vernacular works intended for a lay audience. Many more were Latin scholarly books. It is hard to imagine a Reformed miller or brewer going to the local library to read Thucydides, Franciscus Gomarus' collected works or Heinrich Bullinger's *De origine erroris*.[95] The collection seems more applicable to the work of a local schoolmaster or to supplement a minister's private collection.

As the seventeenth century progressed, regulations on who could use provincial and city libraries were gradually loosened. Many university libraries were not open to students when they were first founded. Before 1621, only professors had access to the university library of Franeker.[96] In 1621, over forty years after the university opened in 1585, it seems students were given access but only between noon and 2:00 PM on Wednesdays and Saturdays.[97] In 1627 the university sold all the quartos and smaller format so they could purchase more folios. The university assumed professors and possibly some students could access cheaper, small format books.[98] Such an assumption was not entirely without foundation. Occasionally students had book collections that were large enough to warrant a sale at auction, in the event of their untimely death. Martinus van Halewyn van der Voort, a theology student whose collection sold in 1691 in Dordrecht, owned at least seven hundred books.[99] 1,201 books formerly owned by Leiden student Christopher de Graaf sold in 1699.[100] The average student strained their budget to acquire a few small books. During

---

93   Jan Alleblas, 'Gedrukt in Dordrecht: de boekenbranche', in Willem Frijhoff, et al. (eds.), *Geschiedenis van Dordrecht van 1572 tot 1813* (Hilversum: Verloren, 1998), p. 338.

94   'Staat van Boeken die na 1600 geschonken zijn aan de bibliotheek der Hervormde gemeente, 1854' WA. Gemeentebestuur Enkhuizen. 0121. 1525. *Index Cariorum, Insignium Librorum. Tam Historicorum, Medicorum, Juridicorum, quam Theologicorum, qui servantur in Bibliotheca Enchusana* (Enkhuizen: Henricus a Straalen, 1693), USTC 1841673, WA. 0219.65c€1.

95   *Index cariorum, insignium librorum, tam historicorum, medicorum, juridicorum, quam theologicorum, qui servantur in bibliotheca Enchusana* (Enkhuizen: Henricus a Straalen, 1693), p. 13 and 18. WA. 0219.65c61.

96   Jacob van Sluis, *De academie van Vriesland. Geschiedenis van de academie en het athenaeum te Franeker, 1585–1843* (Assen: Bornmeer, 2015), pp. 111–112.

97   Ibid., p. 122.

98   Ibid., p. 112.

99   *AC Martinus van Halewyn van der Voort 1691* (Dordrecht: Dirk (I) Goris, 1691), USTC 1847281.

100   *AC Christ. de Graaf 1699* (Leiden: Jordaan Luchtmans, 1699), USTC 1833276.

BUYERS OF TRUTH

his years as a theological student at Leiden University beginning in 1595, Gerardus Vossius made do with a small library of the Church Fathers, histories of the church, and some more contemporary authors. Vossius provided succour to a poorer student in need of clothes and books.[101] From the beginning of their theological studies, books were a regular feature in a minister's life. When young theology students came to university, they were expected to acquire books necessary to their study, and over time they were allowed to use the university library.

Voetius did not overestimate his cherished local library. Founded in 1584 after the confiscation of monastic and ecclesiastical possessions, Utrecht's library began as a quasi-public institution, housed in the Janskerk. In 1602, Evert van der Poll donated his library of 800 to 1,000 books. The collection owned by the former canon of Utrecht, Huybert van Buchell, added 2,000 more volumes. By 1608, Utrecht's library contained nearly 6,000 titles. Local ministers oversaw the compilation of the first catalogue, a task in their own interest as they were some of its regular users.[102] It was transformed into a university library when Utrecht's Illustrious School was given university status in 1636. Cornelis Booth, a local alderman, oversaw the transition and instituted new library regulations. It only opened for one full day and two afternoons. Those who could use the library were further restricted to 'well-known scholars or qualified individuals'.[103] This certainly included the town's local ministers. Numerous books were donated to or bought by Booth on behalf of the library. Some of the most expensive early-modern books were made available to Utrecht's scholars: the twenty-eight volume *Tractatus tractatum, sive oceanus juris*, Plantin's eight volume *Biblia Regia*, Erasmus' *Opera* printed by Froben in Basel in, and two editions of Augustine's *Opera* (1528 and 1592).[104]

Booth solicited donations from many prosperous book owners. In October 1674, Booth wrote to Franciscus Junius II, a famous philologist and owner of a remarkable collection of books and manuscripts. Booth had heard the scholar was aging and Utrecht's librarian hoped to acquire Junius' library. Booth promised 'to discharge all obligation, so that they will be guarded and locked up as carefully as the *hero Scaliger's legacy* has been kept in the library

---

101   C. S. M. Rademaker, *Life and Work of Gerardus Joannes Vossius (1577–1649)*, trans. H. P. Doezema (Assen: Van Gorcum, 1981), p. 26.

102   *Bibliothecae Trajectinae catalogus* (Utrecht: Salomon de Roy, 1608), USTC 1019386.

103   Pettegree and Der Weduwen, *The Bookshop of the World*, p. 308.

104   *Catalogus bibliothecae Ultrajectinae* (Utrecht: Meinardus à Dreunen, 1670), USTC 1807398. On Booth and Utrecht's library see the letters to and from him that are preserved in UB Leiden BPL 246.

of Leiden' (italics original).[105] Between 1664 and 1670, the university collection totaled 6.100 titles and approximately 500 manuscripts. William Nicolson, an English traveler who visited Utrecht on 11 August 1678, reported that the University's library was far more remarkable than the town itself. In the city, 'there is little here of worth'. Nicolson managed to note a few exceptions, one of which was the university library, 'their university library which has more printed books though fewer manuscripts (a catalogue of which I transcribed) than that at Leyden'.[106]

A 2 January 1683 broadsheet issued by the magistrates of Gouda concerned the times the local library would be open and those who had access to it. The library master, the magistrates said, has the right to change when the library opens. Any who wanted access would have to deal with the master directly. Access came with a price: 2 gulden for the 'great key', 8 stuivers for the key to a bookcase.[107]

In every province and in all but the smallest towns, school-masters, ministers, and regents, learned men, had regular access to libraries stocked with standard texts useful to their professions.[108] Johannes Secundus, a poet in The Hague, regaled his local library:

> Do you still perchance seek the Aonian goddesses // at the clear waters of sacred Helicon, O ignorant crowd? // The home of the Muses is now here; here the learned Apollo, // and here the Doric Divinity have established their abodes.[109]

Local ministers had convenient access to such celebrated book collections throughout the Republic. Though most were less adorned than libraries in

---

105 Cornelius Booth to Franciscus Junius II, 20 October 1674, in Sophie van Romburgh (ed.), *"For My Worthy Friend Mr Franciscus Junius": An Edition of the Correspondence of Franciscus Junius F. F. (1591–1677)* (Leiden: Brill, 2004) pp. 1052–1055.

106 Paul G. Hoftijzer, 'A Study Tour into the Low Countries and the German States: William Nicolson's *Iter Hollandicum* and *Iter Germanicum* 1678–1679', *Lias*, 15 (1988), p. 101.

107 Koninklijke Bibliotheek, Plano's en plakkaten, Plakk F 212 (44). Last Accessed 21 October 2019. https://www.geheugenvannederland.nl/nl/geheugen/view?coll=ngvn&identifier=KONB16%3A533116694.

108 On the phrase "learned men" in the Dutch Golden Age, see Karel Davids, 'Amsterdam as a centre of learning in the Dutch golden age, c. 1580–1700', in Patrick O'Brien, et al. (eds.), *Urban Achievement in Early Modern Europe: Golden Ages in Antwerp, Amsterdam and London* (Cambridge: Cambridge University Press, 2001), p. 306.

109 Quoted in Johannes Lomeier, *A Seventeenth-Century View of European Libraries: Lomeier's De Bibliothecis, Chapter X*, ed. and trans. John Warwick Montgomery (Berkeley: University of California Press, 1962), p. 38.

BUYERS OF TRUTH 87

Utrecht or Leiden, they were indicative of the Dutch aspiration for a more learned citizenry. These learned men modeled the informed life.

4   The Legion of Books

These collections were unable to satisfy ministers' desire for knowledge. Although influential on the construction of city and provincial libraries, ministers took their admiration for books and the knowledge gained from reading them a step further. They built book collections of their own, often surpassing in size and scope their local institution. Between 1607 and 1700, at least 457 book collections formerly owned by ministers sold at auction. Of these, 261 catalogues survive. At least ten per cent of ministers in the seventeenth-century Dutch Republic had book collections that were auctioned after their death. Several of their collections were listed in an auction catalogue with the books of other owners. The book collections owned by Nicolaas Ouwens, a minister in Gorinchem and Dirck van der Meer, a solicitor of the polder board of the Rijnland, were combined in one catalogue and sold in 1693. Sixteen catalogues fall into this category. It would be impossible to discern which books listed in the catalogue were owned by whom. Not all ministers owned a collection that was worthy of its own auction catalogue. Many ministerial collections were combined with other ministers' collections (or even anonymous owners) and sold in a joint catalogue. The collections owned by Strijen minister Daniel Schoonderoort and an anonymous minister from 's Gravenmoer were sold in this way.[110] So too were the collections owned by the Walloon minister in Bergen op Zoom Jacobus de Niel and an unknown owner.[111]

By sending books to their colleagues, acquiring them through agents or frequenting the dusty attics of tradesmen and booksellers, ministers acquired books for their own mental and spiritual development. Books were a tool that helped ensure light spread in the darkness of the human soul and pushed against those who would lead faithful Christians away from the Reformed faith. Surviving auction catalogues of ministerial book collections portray a legion of ministers bent on building robust libraries.

Ministerial libraries that sold at auction in the seventeenth century were quite large. After examining 234 ministerial book auction catalogues, one can draw a host of conclusions about ministers and their books. The median number listed in the auction catalogues was 1,142 books. They ranged from the

---

110   Oprechte Haerlemse Courant (17.05.1695).
111   Oprechte Haerlemse Courant (23.10.1700).

88   CHAPTER 3

chaplain to the Dutch Ambassador in Venice Wilhelm Merwy's 104 books to
the Dordrecht Minister Balthazar Lydius' 5,890 (Table 3.1). Ministers in urban
centres like Amsterdam, Leiden, Utrecht, Groningen and Middelburg typically
owned more books than their more rural contemporaries. Urban ministers
had more convenient access to bookshops. Bernard Somer in Amsterdam or
Cornelis van der Vliet in Utrecht, for example, could walk to multiple local
bookshops. Barthold Verstegen in Drempt, near Doesburg, would have to
request books from booksellers in other places. Amongst those whose books
came to auction, rural ministers on average owned 853 books, compared to
1,521 owned by ministers in cities. The key difference is at the upper margin.
Only one rural minister in this corpus owned more than 2,000 books, whereas
thirty-seven urban ministers owned collections of over 2,000.

Guilielmus Isenhagius in Emmerich owned 154 books; in Puttershoek,
Thomas Laurentius's library contained 189. Smaller book collections were not
the exclusive domain the rural ministers, however. Urban ministers, too, occasionally owned collections of only a hundred or so. The Utrecht minister Jacob
Cleaver owned 212. Josephus van de Rosiere, a minister in Haarlem, had only
258 (Table 3.2). Urban ministers were financially better off than their rural contemporaries, but wealth was not always the limiting factor for the number of
books a minister might own.

TABLE 3.1   Ten largest ministerial collections which sold at auction in the
             seventeenth century

Owner	Issue date	Residence	Total books
Balthazar Lydius	1629	Dordrecht	5,890
Gisbertus Voetius	1677	Utrecht	5,535
Jacob Lydius	1680	Dordrecht	5,391
Stephan le Moyne	1689	Leiden	5,175
Wilhelmus Anslaar	1696	Amsterdam	4,840
André Rivet	1657	Breda	4,803
Samuel Gruterus	1700	Rotterdam	4,294
Johannes Cloppenburg	1653	Franeker	3,703
Johannes Pechlinus	1690	Leiden	3,660
Abdias Widmarius	1668	Groningen	3,645

BUYERS OF TRUTH   89

TABLE 3.2   Ten smallest ministerial collections which sold at auction in the
             seventeenth century

Owner	Issue date	Residence	Total books
Wilhelm Merwy	1636	Venice	104
Gulielmus Isenhagius	1666	Emmerich	154
Theodorus van Couwenhoven	1646	Leiden	172
Johann Courten	1646	Scheveningen	176
Thomas Laurentius	1645	Puttershoek	189
Jacob Claver	1660	Utrecht	212
Rijck Dircksz	1655	Leiden	213
Theodorus van Altena	1662	Oestgeest	257
Josephus van de Rosiere	1650	Haarlem	258
Jacob Verhage	1645	Noordwijk	269

Even the library collections of ministers who were wealthy could sometimes be
unexpectedly meagre. After getting married, Sibrandus Lubbertus (1555–1625),
a professor of theology at the University of Franeker, became related to Frisian
nobles. Joseph Scaliger commented in a letter that he wished he could live in
Lubbertus' estate in Minnertsga.[112] In 1616, Lubbertus and his wife had purchased land in Oosterbierum for 3,400 gulden. His book collection was valuable, but not as extravagant as some of his other possessions. Lubbertus'
library was appraised at 1,223 gulden and ten stuivers after his death in 1625.
His family kept some of his books and paid for the auction fees from the value
of the books sold: the auction raised 1,076 gulden and 4 stuivers in profit for
the family.[113] For someone who valued education and had considerable wealth,
one would expect Lubbertus to have owned several thousand books. That was
common for similarly wealthy theology professors. Yet the catalogue for his
collection only contained 530 books.[114] Despite his wealth, Lubbertus' collection is amongst the fifty smallest in this corpus.

---

112   Joseph Scaliger, *Epistolae omnes, quae reperiri potuerunt, nunc primum collectae ac editae*
       (Leiden: Bonaventure and Abraham Elzevier, 1627), USTC 1028641, p. 583.
113   C. van der Woude, *Sibrandus Lubbertus: Leven en werken* (Kampen: J. H. Kok, 1963),
       p. 524, n. 27.
114   *AC Sibrandus Lubbertus 1623* (Franeker: Fredrick Heyns, 1623), USTC 1122248.

90 CHAPTER 3

TABLE 3.3   The size of ministerial book collections that sold at auction by decade

Decade	Average of total books	Decade	Average of total books
1600s	896	1650s	1,867
1610s	1,243	1660s	1,212
1620s	1,641	1670s	1,181
1630s	632	1680s	1,708
1640s	1,106	1690s	1,405
1600–49	1,096	1650–1700	1,409

When the 234 catalogues are arranged by the decade in which the collection sold, it is clear that the average sizes of ministerial book collections swung dramatically throughout the seventeenth century (Table 3.3). The 1650s and 1670s had the largest collections sold at auction, with an average of 1,708 and 1,747 respectively. A noticeable distinction can be made from the first half of the century (1600–1649) to the last half (1650–1700). This is due largely to one decade: the 1630s.

The years between 1615 and 1629 saw real wages stagnate throughout the Republic.[115] But the health of the national economy was not the only factor that influenced the size of libraries. The Dutch economy began slowly contracting after 1672, yet book collections remained largely unaffected. The meagre size of collections in the 1630s can be traced to the accidents of survival and the vagaries of book auctions. Eleven catalogues of ministerial book collections in the 1630s are preserved (Table 3.4). Of those, four are from rural ministers. The urban ministers whose collections sold during the decade were far smaller than the average for the urban minister's collection during the century. One facet of booksellers' auction practice complicates this further: when a collection was especially large, the bookseller who compiled the catalogue sometimes divided the collection across several auction catalogues, selling it over a few years. Balthazar Lydius' book collection was sold in three parts: one in 1629, two in 1630. The average for the 1630s would skew higher to 1,071 books, if the second and third catalogues for his collection were allocated to the 1630s. For the purpose of this analysis, however, Lydius' collection is considered as being sold in 1629. If the bookseller had not divided his collection for a more efficient auction, the entire collection would have sold in 1629.

---

115   Jan de Vries and Ad van der Woude, *The First Modern Economy: Success, Failure, and Perseverance of the Dutch Economy, 1500–1815* (Cambridge: Cambridge University Press, 1997), p. 628.

BUYERS OF TRUTH   91

TABLE 3.4   Ministerial collections which sold in the 1630s

Owner	Year of sale	Residence	Total books
Adrianus van der Borre	1632	Leiden	660
William Ames	1634	Franeker	563
Wilhelm Merwy	1636	Venice	456
Petrus Stermont	1636	Gouda	104
Johannes Westerburg	1637	Dordrecht	1,033
Samuel Basilius	1637	Lisse	741
Johannes Nevius	1637	Venlo	741
Daniel Castellanus	1637	Den Bosch	570
Samuel Middlehoven	1637	Voorschoten	347
Johannes Bogermann	1638	Franeker	1,272
Dionysius Marsbach	1638	Odijk	471

Some wealthy ministers indulged in expensive and lavish books. Abraham Heidanus was a minister in Leiden before becoming a professor of theology there in 1648. He was a leading controversialist of his day, and a noted figure in harbouring Cartesianism at the university.[116] As befitted a man in his prestigious station, he owned a remarkable collection of books. When his 3,493 books were sold at auction in 1679, they raised over 10,000 gulden, garnering an average price of almost three gulden per book, two to three times the average of other collections. Many lots of three, four, or even five books sold for under a gulden in Heidanus' collection. The overwhelming proportion of the profits came from his collection of highly-valued folios that dwarfed the prices of books in other formats. This was a trend in book auctions in England, as well as the Netherlands.[117] Twenty per cent of Heidanus' collection was folios, 686 in total. The folios sold for 6,238 gulden; the nearly three thousand other books garnered about 3,900 gulden, paltry in comparison. A few folios were largely responsible for the large amount of money. His copy of the *Biblia Regia* (Antwerp), 7 volumes, sold for 156 gulden; the London Polyglot Bible (1657) sold for 138 gulden.[118]

---

116   Theo Verbeek, *Descartes and the Dutch: Early Reactions to Cartesian Philosophy, 1637–1650* (Carbondale: Southern Illinois University Press, 1992), pp. 70–71, 82.

117   Graeme Kemp, 'Auctioning Books in Late Seventeenth-Century London: Perceptions, Stratification, and Determinants of Price in an Emergent Market', in Graeme Kemp, et al. (eds.), *Book Trade Catalogues in Early Modern Europe* (Leiden: Brill, 2021), 118–139.

118   *AC Abraham Heidanus 1679* (Leiden: Felix Lopez de Haro & widow and heirs Adrianus Severinus, 1679), USTC 1846941, p. 3.

Heidanus' library was in no way typical of the ministerial collections sold at auction. Ministerial collections focused on utilitarian books that were economically efficient. The formats of their books indicate as much. About fifteen per cent of their collections was large folio volumes. These works tended to be works of timeless theological value: the Bible, the collected works of Church Fathers, biblical commentaries, comprehensive theological treatises, and linguistic aids. Though they made up a smaller percentage of the collection, folios were often the most valuable books. They would raise a disproportionate portion of the profits when the collection sold at auction.

In ministerial collections, folios tended to be older than books in smaller formats. Of the 92,184 items in the fifty-five auction catalogues I have transcribed, 52,273 have a listed date of publication. When publication date is listed in the lot, fifty per cent of all folios were published before 1600. For comparison, just under twenty-five per cent of all quartos and twenty-two per cent of duodecimos were pre-1600. Octavos were the closest in age to folios, with forty-six per cent being printed before 1600. Folios tended to be older and more scholarly in nature. Only five per cent of folios are in vernacular languages. Quartos and smaller tended to feature more vernacular titles than folios. Nearly a quarter of all quartos and octavos are in non-Latinate, non-scholarly languages.

The largest number of titles owned were in the more practical octavo format. Ease of reading and transportation combined with low prices made these books immensely popular. A minister's collection of octavos and duodecimos often contained the printed relics of theological controversies grounding the catalogue in a specific time and place. These works were more contemporary in nature. Psalm books, New Testaments, devotional tracts or works engaging in a current controversy were also the kinds of books a minister could read on a barge while traveling. These utilitarian formats, octavos and duodecimos, account for well over half of the titles in their collections. Octavos were just under forty per cent of the titles, with duodecimos close to the number of folios (Table 3.5).

TABLE 3.5   Formats of books in ministerial book collections

Size	Proportion
Folio	15.1%
Quartos	28.2%
Octavos	39.4%
Duodecimos	16.7%

BUYERS OF TRUTH

Scholarly books like Heidanus' expensive sets were difficult to sell. A folio work by a Church Father in its original Greek would last far beyond a minister's lifetime. There was little need to buy a second copy. The prohibitive cost and the scarcity of buyers made a significant barrier to purchasing such books. The dearth of those who could both afford expensive books and benefit from a scholarly publication was a headache for those who sought to sell them.

Folios were the heirlooms of a minister's collection. They were typically sixteenth-century standardized texts that would retain their values even after decades of use. When a printer or scholar decided to re-edit the work of a Church Father, its necessity was not always apparent to the book-buying public, including to ministers. Sir Henry Saville (1549–1622), a classics scholar and provost of Eton College, Oxford, edited an eight-volume collection of John Chrysostom's works. To help him boost sales of the Church Father's *Opera* in the Netherlands, Saville asked his son-in-law to use his contacts as English Ambassador to the Netherlands. Dudley Carleton sought the aid of his friend and correspondent, Matthew Slade.[119] Slade was an obvious choice for salesman. He was deeply loyal to Carleton, so failure was not an option; and he had wide-reaching connections to Dutch scholars, especially ministers and professors of theology, so the sale should have gone smoothly. But from the start, Slade had trouble selling the eight-volume sets. 'Concerning Chrysostom', Slade reported on 1 March 1617,

> I have written and spoken with divers, who say they are desirous to have the work but cannot resolve until they know the price, whereof if it pleases your L. to advertise mee, I will, as I am bound, and as long since I professed to do, use all diligence to gratify Sr. Henry Savill and your L.[120]

By 2 May, Slade had seen some mild success with provincial and university libraries. Utrecht's library, still a city library in 1617, did not buy it 'because it is all Greek'.[121] But Amsterdam and Leiden both bought the set for 100 gulden.[122] Franeker eventually purchased a set of the books, but their celebrated theology professor, Sibrandus Lubbertus, tried to haggle over the price, and when they

---

119 Matthew Slade to Dudley Carleton, 29 November 1616, in Willem Nijenhuis (ed.), *Matthew Slade (1569–1628): Letters to the English Ambassador* (Leiden: E. J. Brill/Leiden University Press, 1986), p. 48.

120 Slade to Carleton, 1 March 1617, in Ibid., p. 48.

121 Slade to Carleton, 3 April 1617, in Ibid., p. 50.

122 Slade to Carleton, 2 May 1617, in Ibid., p. 51.

94   CHAPTER 3

agreed to a price, they were slow in sending the money.[123] An Amsterdam minister showed interest, but not long after fell ill and was 'loath to deale til hee bee recovered'.[124] Eager to set Carleton's mind at ease concerning his father-in-law's cherished publication, Slade often updated him on the sale first before moving on to other topics. By 20 November 1617, a year after he first mentioned doing this favor for Carleton, Slade was exasperated and came to agree with Carleton, who in time recognized the meagerness of the market for such an expensive set of scholarly books. Slade repeated in approval Carleton's statement that 'they who have Greeke are moniles, and they that have mony are Greekles'.[125]

In reality, ministers who had Greek did not require Saville's edition. Many editions of Chrysostom's *Opera* had already emerged from Europe's most renowned bookshops, and several sixteenth-century editions were still used 150 years later. The joint catalogue of Johannes Kuchlinus and Egbertus Aemilius, ministers in Hazerwoude and Leiden respectively, includes Froben's 1530 edition of Chrysostom's *Opera*.[126] Gisbertus Voetius, whose collection sold in 1677 and 1679, had a set of Froben's from 1547.[127] Johannes Hoornbeeck's collection, which sold in 1667, listed an Antwerp edition of Chrysostom's works from 1547.[128]

Furthermore, they could easily buy a multi-volume set of a Church Father's works at auction for significantly less than Slade hoped to earn. Saville's edition sold at thirteen auctions of ministerial books. If a minister bought the set from Slade, he had to pay at least eighty gulden and then pay more to have them bound. If he waited and bought it at auction, he paid much less. Jacobus Gaillard's catalogue lists it at thirty-two gulden, ten stuivers; André Rivet's lists it at sixty gulden. At the turn of the seventeenth century, there was no lack of available editions of the Church Father's works with which Saville's would have to compete. Rather than a lack of money being the reason the book did not sell well at first, ministers were already well supplied at the time, and the changes in an updated edition did not usually warrant buying a second set of expensive folios.

Ministers focused their collections on books intended for an educated audience that aided their work as preachers and counsellors. Sixty-eight per cent of the books in ministerial collections were written in Latin. Dutch, French, German and other vernacular books made up twenty-eight per cent of the

---

123   Slade to Carleton, 14 July 1617, in Ibid., p. 57; Slade to Carleton, 20 October 1617, in Ibid., p. 61.

124   Slade to Carleton, 3 April 1617, in Ibid., p. 50.

125   Slade to Carleton, 20 November 1617, in Ibid., p. 64.

126   USTC 626163. *AC Kuchlinus and Aemilius 1610* (Leiden: Henrick Lodewijcxsoon van Haestens, 1510 [= 1610]), USTC 1122220.

127   USTC 679610. *AC Gisbertus Voetius 1677* (Utrecht: Willem Clerck, 1677), USTC 1813323.

128   As of yet, I have not been able to identify the USTC number for this volume. *AC Johannes Hoornbeeck 1667* (Leiden: Pieter Leffen, 1667), USTC 1846494.

BUYERS OF TRUTH

collection. Books in scholarly languages (Greek, Hebrew, Chaldaic and others) made up the rest, about four per cent. Only twelve ministers had more vernacular books than Latin. The joint catalogue for the collections formerly owned by Jan Jansz. Kaeskooper and Kornelis Kornelisz., two Mennonite ministers, contained 558 books, all of which were in the vernacular. The urban-rural divide did little to change the ratio of Latin to texts in other languages. Vernacular works comprised thirty-one per cent of rural ministers' collections, and twenty-seven per cent of the collection of minister serving urban congregations. Even in their ownership of books of Greek, Hebrew, and similar academic languages, there is little difference between the two groups: 3.06% for rural ministers, 3.927% for urban.

During their university education, ministers learned, conversed, and were examined in Latin. Lacking knowledge in Latin was considered a significant shortcoming in the sixteenth century and remained so through the Golden Age. In 1555, a minister in Antwerp admitted that he had no desire to become John à Lasco's domestic servant, rather he preferred to apprentice under the Emden Reformer. He would be useful in some ways, but he lacked Latin: 'If he wanted me to do something else, such as reading, writing and so forth, I do not know what I would make of it, since I do not have the gift of Latin'.[129] Latin remained the established language of scholarship and scholarly polemic, despite ministers not preaching in Latin (Table 3.6). Books published in Latin were intended for the educated classes and were regarded as having less sway on the broader public.

TABLE 3.6   Proportions of books by language in ministerial book collections

Latin	68.6%	(918)
Scholarly	3.9%	(52.19)
Vernacular	27.7%	(371.4)
Dutch	13.39%	(179.2)
French	7.3%	(97.7)
English	4.32%	(57.8)
German	2.17%	(29)
Italian	.48%	(6.46)
Spanish	>.076%	(>1)
Other	>.076%	(>1)

129   Gaspar vander Heyden, 'The leader of the new Reformed congregation at Antwerp seeks the advice of the church at Emden, 1555', in Alastair Duke, et al., (eds.) *Calvinism in Europe*, p. 134.

Books in Dutch were the most common amongst vernacular texts. Its average share in ministerial auction catalogues, about thirteen per cent, is nearly double that of the second most common group of vernacular books, French, with just over seven per cent. Nearly half of all vernacular works in ministerial libraries were written in Dutch. Books written in other vernacular languages, German, English, Italian, Spanish, were far less common. About twenty-nine German books were the average for a minister's book sales catalogue. The average (mean) number of English books was about fifty-eight. The disparity between the popularity of Dutch and French books and other vernacular books is made clearer when the median is used. 160 out of the 234 catalogues list ten or fewer German books. The mean (adding a set of values and dividing by the number of values) obscures how uncommon other vernacular works are in ministerial book auction catalogues. Twenty-two catalogues with ninety or more German books skew the average significantly. The median number of German books was only three. English books were concentrated in a few collections. 146 collections had ten or fewer English books. Nineteen collections with over 250 distort the mean. Jacob Koelman's catalogue lists 887 English books.[130] 1,138 were listed in Richard Maden's catalogue.[131] The median number for English books owned is two. When median is used to calculate the average number of Italian books listed, it drops from about six to one.

Ownership of Latin, scholarly, Dutch and French books were much more diverse in comparison (Table 3.6). There is a twenty-one per cent difference between the mean and the median number of Latin books, 918 and 721 respectively. Only seventeen catalogues contained ten or fewer Dutch books. The median number of Dutch books was 138. French books were less common than Dutch but were more common than all other vernacular languages by far. Eighty-four catalogues list ten or fewer French books. The median number of French books was thirty-one.

A disproportionate number of books in one of the vernacular languages often indicates specific instances in the personal history of the owner. Lutheran ministers, many of whom fled to the Netherlands, had noticeably larger numbers of German books. Born in Gautsch, Germany, Casper Pfeiffer moved to the Netherlands and became a proponent in the Lutheran Church in 1609.[132] His collection sold in 1643, and it was the first known sale of a Lutheran minister's book collection with an auction catalogue in the Netherlands. The catalogue lists 935 books, 132 of which are German.[133] Native Dutch Lutherans continued

---

130   *AC Jacobus Koelman 1695* (Utrecht: François Halma, 1695), USTC 1847446.
131   *AC Richard Maden 1680* (Rotterdam: Henricus Goddaeus, 1680), USTC 1846866.
132   *NNBW*, IX, p. 500.
133   *AC Caspar Pfeiffer 1643* (Amsterdam: Joost Broersz, 1643), USTC 1013744.

BUYERS OF TRUTH

to read German-language books, because it was the devotional language in which the most influential Lutheran theologians wrote. Of his collection of 1,609 books, Adolph Visscher (1605–1652), an Amsterdam Lutheran minister, owned 506 German books and only 262 Dutch books.[134] Walloon ministers owned a disproportionately large number of French books. Born in Montauban, Jacobus Gaillard (c.1620–1688) fled to Den Bosch in 1662, later becoming a minister and professor at the Walloon College in Leiden.[135] Twenty-seven per cent of his 2,266 books were written in French. Daniel de la Vinea (d.1628) became a minister in Dordrecht's Walloon church after being confirmed by Johannes Polyander, who had left Dordrecht to become a professor at Leiden.[136] The auction catalogue of De La Vinea's book collection lists 1,191 books, twenty-two per cent of which were French. French books made up seven per cent of the corpus.[137]

Like their Walloon counterparts, Reformed ministers who moved from Germany to the Netherlands often maintained their distinctive identity as expressed in their book collections. Martinus Lydius, whose family fled from Overijssel to Germany in 1535, owned a large book collection, and he likely brought it with him when he returned to the Netherlands. Martinus was a learned and respected theologian. Johannes Wtenbogaart, the theological leader of the Remonstrants, said he was 'a very well read man in all sorts of writers, and peaceable such that he did not heap onto church differences'.[138] No catalogue of his collection survives, but it is known that he left much of his book collection to his sons, Johannes and Balthazar. Scaliger, the famous Leiden historian and a family friend to Martinus and his sons, arranged the sons' inheritance of the father's books.[139] Many of these books may have been sixteenth-century German works. Both Johannes and Balthazar had disproportionately large numbers of German books. Nearly four per cent of Johannes'

---

134 *AC Adolph Visscher 1653* (Amsterdam: Zacharias Webber, 1653), USTC 1846273.

135 D. Nauta, et al. (eds.), *Biografisch lexicon voor de geschiedenis van het Nederlandse protestantisme* (6 vols; Kampen: J. H. Kock, 1978–2006), I, p. 80. *AC Jacobus Gaillard 1689* (Leiden: Johannes du Vivié, 1689).

136 Matthys Balen, *Beschryvinge der Stad Dordrecht* (Dordrecht: Symon Onder de Linde, 1677), USTC 1813805, pp. 193–194.

137 *AC Daniel de la Vinea 1628* (Dordrecht: Jan (II) Canin, 1628), USTC 1122270.

138 'een man seer belezen in alle soorten van schrijvers, en soo vredelievend, dat hij sich geen arbeit ontrent het slissel [sic] van kerkelijke verschillen ontsagh'. Quoted in Geeraerdt Brandt, *Historie der Reformatie, en andre Kerkelyke Geschiedenissen in en ontrent de Nederlanden* (3 vols., Amsterdam: Henrik and Dirk Boom, 1674), USTC 1561244, III, p. 8. Cf. Johannes Wtenbogaart, *Johannis Uytenbogaerts leven, kerckelijcke bedieninghe ende zedighe verantwoordingh* (s.l., s.n., 1646), USTC 1034831, p. 12.

139 D. Nauta, et al. (eds.), *Biografisch lexicon voor de geschiedenis van het Nederlandse protestantisme*, IV, p. 322.

collection was German books, compared to two per cent in the corpus as a whole. Balthazar's collection had significant number of sixteenth-century books written in German. 201 of his 5,890 books were pre-1600 German language texts. By comparison, in the transcription database only 617 out of 92,184 books are pre-1600 German language texts, under one per cent.

Italian and Spanish books were rare in ministerial collections. If a minister owned only two Italian books, it was likely *Il Pastor Fido* and Giovanni Diodati's Italian translation of the Bible. *Il Pastor Fido*, Battista Guarini's romantic tragicomedy, was condemned by Robert Bellarmine: *Il Pastor Fido* 'was responsible for the depravity of countless women, and that it had done more harm to the Catholic Church than Luther and the Protestant revolt'.[140] A Spanish Bible was usually the only Spanish book, if they owned any. Thirty-nine ministers owned more than ten Italian books, and the majority of those ministers owned collections significantly over the average of 1,141 books. Amongst the 2,764 books sold when his collection was brought to auction in 1671, Andreas Colvius owned a staggering 166 Italian books and twenty-eight Spanish books, far more than the 129 Dutch books in his collection. Colvius' personal history illuminates this anomaly.[141] Before becoming a minister in Dordrecht, Colvius served the Dutch ambassador to Venice, Johan Berck, as chaplain. His five years there were spent meeting Italian scholars, collecting books and copying manuscripts. Famously, he transcribed Galileo's *Del Flusso e riflusso del mare*.[142] Even after he returned from Venice in 1627, he continued acquiring Italian books. Writing to Cornelis Booth, Utrecht's librarian, Colvius celebrated the library Booth oversaw, 'our public library', even contributing to it. And he thanked Booth for a gift: 'Thank you for the little Italian book. Della Casa's verses are impudent and hardly poetry'.[143]

When ministers read religious works in vernacular languages, they preferred books from Protestant countries. 76.12% of the Dutch and 73.3% of German books were theological. It is helpful to compare English to Spanish/Italian

---

140   Quoted in Victoria Kahn, 'The Passions and the Interests in Early Modern Europe: The Case of Guarini's Il Pastor fido', in Gail Kern Paster, et al. (eds.), *Reading the Early Modern Passions: Essays in the Cultural History of Emotion* (Philadelphia: University of Pennsylvania Press 2004), p. 222.

141   *NNBW*, I, pp. 627–628.

142   Theo Verbeek, 'Colvius, Andreas (1594–1671)', in Lawrence Nolan (ed.), *The Cambridge Descartes Lexicon* (Cambridge University Press, 2015), pp. 135–136.

143   'Gratias habeo pro misso libello italico, quim ocyssimi reddo. Verses di casa sunt impudicissimi, et vix poetici. Italia sunt ut Apostolus Adjunxi etiam quadam qua nostrarum pro, si quid sit, vir clarissimi, in Bibliotheca mea aut publica nostra, cujus usum desiderias, Quid si hosco libros pro vostra Bibliotheca desideratis, ego eos venales existimo'. Andreas Colvius to Cornelis Booth, Pridie Kal November 1654, UB Leiden, BPL 246 (met en boek).

books. While ministers choose to read religious works in English, religious works in Spanish and Italian are only sporadically present in ministerial collections. There are 619 Spanish and Italian books in total, of these 187 are religious books, only thirty per cent. Several are Protestant translations: there are seven by John Calvin, and another by Peter Martyr. 2,016 English books are listed in this database, and 1,790 were religious works, eighty-nine per cent. Adrian Smoutius' collection is illuminating in this regard. It sold in 1646. He owned a comparable number of English (21) and Spanish (30) books. All but two of the English books were religious in nature: *A collection of all the Statutes from the Beginning of the Magna Carta unto 1572* and King James' *Instructions to his sonne Henry the Prince*. Only four of the Spanish books were religious.[144] English books will be addressed more fully in the following chapter.

5 Learned Men

How did ministerial libraries compare to their similarly educated peers? Universities in the Netherlands during the seventeenth century mostly prepared students for one of three vocations: the ministry, law or medicine. After ministers, lawyers and doctors were the next largest groups of academically trained professionals. While theology was regarded as the highest field of inquiry, law and medicine were not far behind.[145] Members of all three professions collected and used books to fulfill their duties. Book auction catalogues for personal collections overwhelmingly list the books of someone from one of those callings. 853 auctions of private book collections were formerly owned by either a minister, lawyer or doctor, nearly half of all known auctions. 217 auctions of collections owned by lawyers and jurists are known to have taken place in the seventeenth century. 135 doctors' book collections sold with an auction catalogue during the same time.

Renaissance wits often satirized lawyers as greedy and concerned only with financial gain. Despite rhetorical protestations about serving for the common good, the practice of law was seen as a self-serving endeavor. Renaissance writers praised decency and good morals in stark contrast to lawyers' usual behaviour.[146] Nevertheless, the law was the profession of choice in families

---

144   AC *Adrian Smoutius 1646* (Leiden: Severyn Matthysz, 1646), USTC 1122092.

145   Eric Jorink, *Reading the Book of Nature in the Dutch Golden Age, 1575–1715*, trans. Peter Mason (Leiden: Brill, 2010), p. 59.

146   For example, Thomas More, *Utopia*, ed. and trans. Paul Turner (Harmondsworth: Penguin, 1965), bk. II, pp. 106–107; Erasmus, *The Education of a Christian Prince*, in his *Collected*

from the rising middle classes who hoped to provide a better life for their sons. Lawyers performed necessary tasks in the Dutch Republic. They had the unenviable task of understanding a labyrinth of jurisdictional laws and statutes, with which they would have to make the case for their client. They were called upon to intervene in squabbles over land, title, and wills, often during times of deep suffering. Arnoldus Buchelius in Utrecht litigated numerous cases on rightful claims to property and political authority.[147] Lawyers made judgements on the kinds of matter which shaped everyday life.[148] This required a robust knowledge of history and legal precedent.

TABLE 3.7   Median number of books by language listed in ministerial book auction catalogues

Language	Median number
Latin	721
Dutch	138
French	31
Scholarly	29
German	3
English	2
Italian	1
Spanish	0

TABLE 3.8   Percentages of book formats in lawyers' book collections

Format	Percentage
Folio	18%
Quarto	23.11%
Octavo	37.65%
Duodecimo	15.45%

Works, trans. N. M. Cheshire and M. J Heath (Toronto: University of Toronto Press, 1986), p. 273.

147   Judith Pollmann, *Religious choice in the Dutch Republic: The reformation of Arnoldus Buchelius (1565–1641)* (Manchester: Manchester University Press, 1999), p. 114.

148   William J. Bouwsma, 'Lawyers and Early Modern Culture', in his *A Usable Past: Essays in European Cultural History* (Berkeley: University of California Press, 1990), pp. 129–156.

BUYERS OF TRUTH

Of those whose collections sold at auction, lawyers and doctors owned similarly substantial libraries. After examining forty-one of the 217 surviving lawyers' catalogues, some comparisons can be drawn to ministerial collections. The law was primarily an urban profession. Lawyers resided in centres of power, where financially lucrative cases were settled. Nevertheless, the average size of their libraries was not dramatically different from ministers, a geographically diverse population. In this set of forty-one, the average is slightly less than ministerial median average: 1,042 books. Amongst these forty-one, the size of their collections ranges from a meager 251 owned by Wilhelmus Beukens, a Groningen jurist and the 3,572 owned by The Hague's Abraham van der Meer. Their collections were more Latinate than those of ministers, seventy-three per cent for lawyers' collections, sixty-seven for ministers'. Books in scholarly languages were slightly less common: just over two per cent were books in Greek, Hebrew, Chaldaic, and similar languages. Ministers read more Dutch books, on average, than lawyers did. Lawyers read more in French than most ministers.

Many medical doctors, like their university-trained peers in the law or the church, amassed similarly substantial book collections (Tables 3.7 and 3.8). As the Republic experienced a dramatic increase in economic dynamism and prosperity in the seventeenth century, scientific and medical advances followed.[149] Medicine had been studied to various degrees for centuries. During the Dutch Revolt, William of Orange formalized the independence of Holland and Zeeland with the establishment of a university. The study of medicine at a university level, first taught in Leiden after its foundation in 1575, spread as newly founded universities and illustrious schools began competing with each other for prestige.[150] The medical and scientific advances led to a degree of religiously inspired optimism. Johannes van Horne (1621–1670), a Leiden professor of medicine, noted that 'in our century that we are now going through, and in which the knowledge of anatomy has risen as high as we know it ever to have risen ... the last seal of the book of nature may be opened'.[151]

---

149   Harold J. Cook, *Matters of Exchange: Commerce, Medicine, and Science in the Dutch Golden Age* (New Haven: Yale University Press, 2007), p. 412.

150   Dirk van Miert, *Humanism in an Age of Science: The Amsterdam Athenaeum in the Golden Age, 1632–1704*, trans. Michiel Wielema with Anthony Ossa-Richardson (Leiden: Brill, 2009) pp. 310–328.

151   'Och oft onse eeuwe, die wy nu beleeven, ende in de welcke de kennisse der Anatomie tot soo hoogen top is ghereesen, als men weet dat sy oyt gheweest is; ... het laeste Seegel van het Boeck der Natuure mochte ge-oopent worden'. Johannes van Hoorne, *Waerschouwinge, aen alle Lieff-hebbers der Anatomie* (Leiden: Daniel and Abraham van Gaasbeeck, 1660), USTC 1844690, p. 6.

Such optimism did not solve a logistical problem, however. Though Leiden began teaching medicine in 1575 at its foundation, a lack of university-trained doctors remained for the course of the century. Midwives and local surgeons who had learned from the school of experience were far more common than those who had observed anatomical lessons in a university. A division existed between the medical practitioners who had studied at Leiden, Franeker, or the Amsterdam *Athenaeum* and those who had no formal training. Like the kinds of ministers and lawyers whose collections sold at auction, doctors whose collections were large enough to warrant sale with a catalogue focused on Latinate books. Vernacular books were about as common in doctors' and lawyers' catalogues, but doctors read more Dutch language books in general. Their collections focused more on smaller formats. In that way their collections were more like those of ministers than lawyers. In the set of thirty-one doctors' catalogues I have analyzed, the average is 997 books (Tables 3.9 and 3.10).

TABLE 3.9   Average proportions of lawyers' book collections by language

Language	Percentage
Latin	77.35%
Scholarly	2.28%
Vernacular	20.38%
Dutch	9.17%
French	8.18%
Italian	1.82%
English	.557%
German	.36%
Spanish	.3%

TABLE 3.10   Average doctors' book collections by format

Format	Percentage
Folio	13.51%
Quarto	21.28%
Octavo	39.46%
Duodecimo	23.52%

BUYERS OF TRUTH

The similarities between the book collecting habits owned by these three professional groups are striking. In the formats of the books and in the proportion of Latin to other language texts, they are nearly identical. The key difference is the numbers of Italian, German, and English books. Ministers typically read far more English and German books than did their peers who were lawyers and doctors. Lawyers and doctors, similarly, owned three times as many Italian books as ministers. The reason for this is self-evident: Protestant ministers had little use for Italian vernacular works that were overwhelmingly Roman Catholic, while lawyers and doctors were deeply indebted to the work of Italians in their own fields (Tables 3.11 and 3.12).

TABLE 3.11 Average presence of languages in doctors' book auction catalogues

Language	Percentage
Latin	76.57%
Scholarly	2.47%
Vernacular	20.973%
Dutch	11.91%
French	5.72%
Italian	1.713%
English	.658%
German	.887%
Spanish	>.0845%

TABLES 3.12 AND 3.13 Average percentage formats and languages of books as listed in the auction catalogues of doctors, lawyers and ministers

	Doctors	*Lawyers*	*Ministers*
Format	Percentage	Percentage	Percentage
Folio	13.51%	18.5%	15.07%
Quarto	21.28%	23.11%	28.16%
Octavo	39.46%	37.65%	39.23%
Duodecimo	23.52%	15.45%	16.76%

104   CHAPTER 3

TABLES 3.12 AND 3.13   Average percentage formats of books (*cont.*)

| | *Doctors* | *Lawyers* | *Ministers* |
Language	Percentage	Percentage	Percentage
Latin	76.27%	77.35%	68.6%
Scholarly	2.47%	2.28%	3.9%
Vernacular	20.979%	20.38%	27.7%
Dutch	11.91%	9.17%	13.39%
French	5.72%	8.18%	7.3%
Italian	1.713%	1.82%	.48%
English	.658%	.557%	4.32%
German	.887%	.36%	2.17%
Spanish	>.0845%	.3%	>.076%
Other	>.0845%	>.075%	>.076%
Median	**997 books**	**1,042 books**	**1,142 books**

Ministers, doctors and lawyers built book collections for professional gain. The authors and titles they read varied significantly, but all three owned significant numbers of books that were necessary for their profession: for lawyers, history, classics, and jurisprudence; for doctors, medicine and science; for ministers, theology, copies of the Bible, and linguistic aids. They all read beyond their own field of expertise. Theodorus Hamel (1627–1660), a lawyer practicing in The Hague, owned a respectable collection of 421 books, over 200 of which were on jurisprudence, about thirty were theological, and the rest in miscellaneous fields.[152] The catalogue of the collection of the Leeuwarden lawyer Thomas Tiberius lists 428 theological books, 378 jurisprudential and 388 books on history and literature.[153] Petrus van Willigen, a Rotterdam doctor, owned an eclectic collection of thirty-eight theological books, sixty-nine in jurisprudence, 337 on medicine, 114 on history, and another 379 covering miscellaneous topics.[154]

Learned men, ministers, lawyers and doctors, were both intrinsically motivated and expected by society to own books. Not to own a library was

---

152   AC *Theodorus Hamel 1638* (The Hague: Abraham (1) Elzevier, 1638), USTC 1122205.
153   AC *Thomas Tiberius 1678* (Leeuwarden: Jacob Hagenaar, 1678), USTC 1846920.
154   AC *Petrus van Willigen 1650* (Rotterdam: Bastiaen Wagens, 1650), USTC 1030020.

BUYERS OF TRUTH

unbecoming of anyone who claimed intellectual legitimacy or authority. It is not impossible that some ministers, doctors and lawyers built large book collections to receive praise from their peers. Yet such a pessimistic view of book ownership cannot explain why nearly a thousand known ministers, lawyers and doctors built book collections large enough to warrant a sale at auction. All of these professions valorized the acquisition of knowledge. The exemplary practitioner of law, medicine or theology devoted themselves to sharpening their skills through reading.

6   Dwelling in Sparta

A minister's calling included a command to a life of reading. They devoted their days to studying the Bible and investigating the works of other authors. If preaching, officiating in church and pastoral counsel were their public duties, devoting hours to rigorous continued learning was part of their private calling. It was a task that required as much unbroken focus as one could muster. After becoming a professor of theology at Leiden, Franciscus Junius was able to devote himself to the scholarly life without distraction. He was grateful to the university's trustees that he could now spend his time 'dwelling in Sparta'.[155]

A well-equipped study was the closest a minister could get to the monastic singlemindedness Junius cherished. Reading books in preparation for a Sunday sermon was primarily something done in the home. Ministers owned hundreds of books, and such large book collections presented a logistical problem: where to house their libraries. The auction catalogues themselves give hints to potential solutions. Bookcases and reading stands are regularly listed for sale at the end of a minister's catalogue. Johannes Pechlinus' catalogue lists 'some bookcases, reading stands, and a study-table', as did the catalogues for the libraries owned by Johannes Cocceius, Jacob Cuilemann, Jacob Lydius (1610–1679), Franciscus Ridderus (1620–1683), Bernard Somer (1579–1632), Gerardus van der Port (d. 1691) and many others.[156] Marcus van Peenen (1642–1696), a Leiden minister, had 2,441 books listed in his catalogue. 'Six book-cases, two reading stands, and various land-maps' are listed at the end.[157]

---

155   Franciscus Junius, *De theologia vera: ortu, natura, formis, partibus, et modo* (Leiden: Plantin Raphelengius, 1594), USTC 423372, p. 6.

156   AC *Johannes Pechlinus 1690* (Leiden: Pieter vander Aa, 1690), USTC 1823437.

157   AC *Marcus van Peenen 1696* (Leiden: Johannes du Vivié and Jordaan Luchtmans, 1696), USTC 1830515.

106   CHAPTER 3

Visual portrayals of ministers provide further evidence of how they managed this predicament of hundreds or thousands of books with limited space (Figs. 3.1–3.5). Etchings and prints show the minister sitting at his reading desk, open books strewn around him. Often the Bible sits on a reading stand. Their book collections remind the viewer that the minister is a scholar. It is likely for the scholarly community that such etchings were intended. They convey a message to the viewer: that the minister before them is learned and godly. Often, they are not a snapshot of the minister in his actual study. Rather, they are a compilation of the minister's portrait super-imposed over stock features, in some cases, after the minister died.[158] Those stock features, open books, bookcases, and other scholarly accoutrements, encapsulate what was in common use for the kinds of men whose portraits were taken. Pens, paper, desks, bookcases and books were the tools of the ministerial trade. Most of the depictions include a curtain, likely to protect the books from sun damage and dust. Books are shelved indiscriminately. Folio volumes are in the same case as duodecimos. Many volumes have metal clasps.

Ministers owned book collections that were useful to them. Though some bought highly regarded books of significant value, most quietly built libraries that furnished their needs as ministers of the word of God. As preachers and counsellors, they had to understand Scripture and theology to an academic level, so they had to read Latin and scholarly languages. But they also had to translate that robust theological conversation into something their congregations understood, so they could not cast aside vernacular language texts. Surviving catalogues list nearly 320,000 books collected by a group that epitomized the Dutch bourgeois society. From collections of a hundred books to libraries reaching nearly six thousand, ministers collectively amassed a legion of books.

Books had two principle uses for a minister: piety and polemic. In the quest to understand truth, books were the most efficient tool for building one's argument and deconstructing that of an opponent. Reasons to own a personal library in the seventeenth century were numerous. Prestige, entertainment, academic notoriety, intellectual curiosity, professional necessity, all were common justifications for collecting books. For ministers, such explanations only scratch the surface. Ministers were economically advantaged in comparison with many other Netherlanders, and many of these church servants acquired books to signal their intelligence and the prominent position they occupied in the community. But the relentless pursuit of truth compelled them to build

---

158   For example, Marijke Tolsma, 'Facing Arminius: Jacob Arminius in Portrait', in Th. Marius van Leeuwen, et al. (eds.), *Arminius, Arminianism, and Europe*, pp. 203–237.

libraries. The Lydius family and Johannes specifically encapsulate the spirit with which ministers throughout the Republic desired books. The pursuit of truth was constant. Editions of the works of the Church Fathers were revised. New translations of the Bible were regularly printed. Theological controversies came and went. Through it all, the need for books remained; and ministers, 'lovers of truth' turned to them instinctively.

CHAPTER 4

Guardians of the Faith

After serving in Amsterdam for fifteen years, Jacob Arminius was recommended for a chair in theology in Leiden, a decision that would nearly rend the apart Republic in two fifteen years later. Even the mere suggestion of him filling the post roused opposition. One of his colleagues in Amsterdam claimed he had been too friendly to Roman Catholics.[1] Others considered his teaching on predestination reprehensible and corrosive to pure religion. Franciscus Gomarus, Arminius' future colleague and most capable opponent, expressed his misgivings at the prospect of Arminius filling the faculty position that once belonged to Franciscus Junius. In Gomarus' estimation, Junius was the stalwart champion of the Reformed cause during the Dutch Revolt. Although after a two-day conference on Arminius' orthodoxy, Gomarus would initially grudgingly accept that Arminius' formulation of predestination was acceptable, Gomarus became one of the new professor's fiercest opponents. Arminius had changed how he articulated his understanding of the doctrine, and Gomarus later concluded that Arminius' belief that God chose those who would be saved based on his foreknowledge of them coming to faith in him, or, as it was later called, conditional election, was outside the Reformed church's confessional bounds.[2]

Gomarus, inveterate theologian that he was, saw the consequences of Arminius' error behind every corner. The new professor of theology had so corrupted the minds of proponents to the ministry that even booksellers in Leiden began selling contentious and perverse books. While Franciscus Junius was alive, Gomarus claimed, 'writings of the most excellent and most well-versed ministers of our churches were sought-after and sold in large numbers'. After Arminius began sowing the seeds of heterodoxy, 'the controversial and papist books of Thomas Aquinas, Suarez, Bellarminus and such vacuous polemicists were most in demand and used'.[3]

---

1   Carl Bangs, *Arminius: A Study in the Dutch Reformation* (Nashville: Abingdon Press, 1971), p. 236.
2   Richard A. Muller, 'Arminius and the Reformed Tradition', *Westminster Theological Journal*, 9 (2008), pp. 19–48.
3   'Jae dat meer is, de registers van de boeckvercoopers opgheslagen, sullen met hare meesters bewijsen, daer de schrijften van de treffelickste ende schriftmatichste leeraers onser kercken, te vooren ghesocht ende vercocht wierden, met menichte: dat daerentegen na de veranderinghe, in stede van die, de twistighe ende Papistische boecken van Thomas Aquinas,

---

© KONINKLIJKE BRILL NV, LEIDEN, 2023 | DOI:10.1163/9789004538191_005

GUARDIANS OF THE FAITH 109

Gomarus was not alone in his accusation. A student at Leiden from 1608 to 1609 and later minister in Deventer, Caspar Sibelius made a similar allegation. He claimed that in his private theological class with Arminius,

> We were utterly drawn away from reading the works and treatises of Calvin, Beza, Zanchius, Martyr, Ursinus, Piscator, Perkins, and other learned and valuable theologians of the church of Christ; we were commanded to examine only Holy Scripture, but equally so, the writings of Socinus, Acontiùs, Castellio, Thomas Aquinas, Molina, Suarez and other enemies of grace were commended to us.[4]

Sibelius further claimed that even auctions and booksellers were corrupted by Arminius.[5] Such allegations are straightforward. They expanded the logic of 'you shall know a tree by its fruit', to you shall know the truthfulness of someone's teaching by the books most in demand by their students. Unfortunately for Gomarus and Sibelius, the facts do not support this theory.

Even before Arminius' arrival in 1603, the kinds of books Gomarus maligned as controversial, vacuous and papist were widely available in Leiden. Petrus Bertius, the Regent of Leiden University's theological college (*Statencollege*) from 1606–1615, reminded Gomarus that 'all these books were already in use before Arminius's arrival, and concerning Thomas and Bellarminus: the late Junius himself recommended them to young students'.[6] Several private

---

Suarez, Bellarminus, ende diergelijcke onnutte questie-schrijvers, meest sijn opgesocht ende gebruyckt'. Franciscus Gomarus, *Bedencken over de lyck-orate van meester P. Bertius*, in his *Waerschouwinghe, over de vermaninghe aen R. Donteclock*. (Leiden: Jan Jansz. Orlers, 1609), USTC 1028772, p. 48.

4 'Nam in isto Collegio a lectione Operum et Tractuum Calvini, Bezae, Zanchii, Martyris, Ursini, Piscatoris, Perkinsi, aliorumque doctissimorum, et optime de Ecclesia Christi meritorum Theologorum abstrahebamur, solam scripturam sacram inspicere jubebamur; sed juxta, Socini, Acontii, Castellionis, Thomae Aquinatis, Molinae, Suarezii, aliorumque Gratiae hostium scripta summe nobis commendabantur'. Caspar Sibelius, *Historica narratio Caspari Sibelii de curriculo totius vitae et peregrinationis suae*, in H. W. Tijdeman, 'Caspar Sibelius: In Leven Predikant te Deventer, volgens zijne onuitgegeven levens beschriving', *Godgeleerde Bijdragen*, 23 (1849), p. 522.

5 'Et sane molestis illis temporibus, in publicis auctionibus et tabernis librariis, istorum Arianizantium, Samosateniozantium, et Pelagianizantium authorum scripta duplo carius veniebant quam Orthodoxorum Theologorum libri'. Ibid., p. 522.

6 'Dese alle zijn in swanghe gheweest al voor de comste van D. Arminius: ende soo veel Thomam ende Bellarminuum aengaet D. Junius zaliger heeftse self den jongen Studenten gerecommandeert'. Petrus Bertius, *Aen-spraeck, aen D. Fr. Gomarvm op zijne bedenckinghe over de lijck-oratie, ghedaen na de begraefenisse van D. Iacobvs Arminivs* (Leiden: Ian Paedts Jacobszoon, 1609), USTC 1022196, f. D3r.

110   CHAPTER 4

book collections containing Roman Catholic books sold at auction in Leiden. In 1604 at the sale of the collection owned by the university librarian, Janus Dousa, one could buy works written by Robert Bellarmine, the medieval scholastic Albertus Magnus, and a Roman Catholic Psalter.[7] Numerous works by Thomas Aquinas were available for purchase in 1607 at the sale of the library of a former professor of theology.[8] In 1606 and 1607, large stocks of books owned by Hieronymus Commelin, a deceased printer and publisher with offices in Heidelberg, Leiden and Amsterdam, sold at auction in Leiden. The catalogue for the sale lists many Roman Catholic works.[9]

It seems Arminius' teaching had not changed the book market in any meaningful way. He was, however, aware of the books with which Gomarus tarred him. His library contained many of their works.[10] But such ownership was not a subtle form of identifying with their beliefs. As Keith Stanglin and Thomas McCall write, 'To be ignorant of these writings would have been unflattering for a theologian of Arminius' calibre'.[11] For the standards ministers had to meet, the so-called Assembly at Wesel (1571) noted that reading heretical books was not cause for immediate dismissal. Churches were to inquire 'whether [a minister] has read the books of heretics more diligently than is seemly and whether he has conversed much with fanatics and men given over to their own imaginings'.[12] Ministers, professors of theology, and learned readers throughout Europe read books by those with whom they disagreed on profound levels. Arminius owned several books by Roman Catholics, but Gomarus did as well,

---

7   AC *Janus Dousa 1604* (Leiden: Thomas Basson, 1604), USTC 1122042.

8   AC *Lucas Trelcatius 1607* (Leiden: Jan Maire, 1607), USTC 1025132.

9   AC *Hieronymus Commelinus 1606* (Leiden: Jan Jansz. Orlers, 1606), USTC 1122014.

10 Carl O. Bangs (ed.), *The Auction Catalogue of the Library Catalogue of Jacob Arminius* (Leiden: Brill/HES & De Graaf, 1985). It is also available online at Book Sales Catalogues Online: https://primarysources.brillonline.com/browse/book-sales-catalogues-online /catalogvs-librorvm-collected-by-a-leiden-professor-of-theology-printed-date-16100519 -leiden-thomas-basson-1610;bscobsco1757?search=arminius&searchStart=1&search Total=2&search-go=&q=arminius&sort=true&fq=collection%3A%22book-sales-cata logues-online%22.

11 Keith Stanglin and Thomas McCall, *Jacob Arminius: Theologian of Grace* (Oxford: Oxford University Press, 2012), p. 43.

12 'vt certò constare possit an cuipiam haeresi addictus fuerit, an exoticis et curiosis quaestionibus speculationibuswue ptiosis plus aequo se oblectarit, an hereticorum libros studiosius quam par est legerit, hominumque fanaticorum et suis somniis indulgentium consuetudine multa vsus fuerit'. F. L. Rutgers (ed.), *Acta van de Nederlandsche Synoden der zestiende eeuw* (Utrecht: Kemink and Zoon, 1889), p. 14. Recent scholarship has made clear that the so-called Assembly at Wesel (1571) could not have taken place in 1571 or in Wesel. See, Jesse Sponholz, *The Convent of Wesel: The Event that Never was and the Invention of Tradition* (Cambridge: Cambridge University Press, 2017).

GUARDIANS OF THE FAITH

over forty in folio alone.[13] In folio, Gomarus owned twelve books by Thomas Aquinas, three by Gabriel Biel, two each by Albertus Magnus, William of Ockam and Bonaventure. He also owned Savanorola's *Opera*, the six volume *Opera* written by the Dominican friar Hugh of Saint-Cher and many others.

Arminius rejected the charge that he had ever recommended scandalous books. Writing to Ubbo Emmius, rector of the University of Groningen, Arminius denounced the teachers Gomarus mentioned, claiming 'Thomas, Scotus and the entire flock of Scholastics, however they may excel philosophically, are blinder than bats in their exegesis of the Scriptures'.[14] The besieged professor, for his part, owned numerous works by those Gomarus held up as the most excellent and well versed theologians: nearly thirty by Franciscus Junius; twenty-three by John Calvin; twenty by Beza; thirteen by Heinrich Bullinger; twelve by Jerome Zanchius; five by William Perkins; four by Peter Martyr Virmigli.

Despite having a family of nine surviving children, Jacob Arminius built a library that was larger than the typical collection which sold at auction during the seventeenth century. The pastor from Amsterdam acquired 1,770 books throughout his life. A few months after his death in 1609, his book collection was auctioned in Leiden. His family, left impoverished, sold the books.[15] Thomas Basson, a local printer, compiled the list of books and distributed the catalogue, so eager buyers could make arrangements to acquire the books they desired from the collection.

Theological books formed the bulk of ministers' book collections. On average a minister whose collection sold at auction owned 1,142 books, about 700 of which would have been the books most obviously suited for their pastoral endeavors, Bibles, theological treatises, biblical commentaries, catechisms and similar works. Ministers read broadly in theology. Their collections not only list those with whom they shared common religious convictions, but also those they repudiated as in error or even committing heresy. The Netherlands was a religiously diverse country with large pockets of Roman Catholics and Lutherans. Books from authors associated with those confessions were also widely available, either by import or printed locally in the Netherlands. A minister had to read a diverse range of theological books to understand his own faith and to shepherd his flock well. For Dutch citizens, daily life was shaped

---

13   *AC Franciscus Gomarus 1641* (Leiden: Bonaventura and Abraham Elzevier, 1641), USTC 1122202.

14   Jacob Arminius to Ubbo Emmius, 18 May 1608, Quoted in Jan Maronier, *Jacobus Arminius: een biographie (met portret en handteekening)* (Amsterdam: Y. Rogge, 1905), p. 271.

15   *The Auction Catalogue of the Library of J. Arminius.*

112 CHAPTER 4

by interactions with those with whom they disagreed, either in print or in person. Ministers sharpened their theological abilities by becoming aware of their opponents' arguments. This process, though, began not with Calvin, Aquinas, Bellarmine or Luther, but with the Bible.

1   The Academy of Academies

The seriousness of the allegation against Arminius by Gomarus and Sibelius goes deeper than at first seems. It was not only a matter of dissenting from an arbitrarily chosen group of human authors. Gomarus and Sibelius believed those profitable authors had come to the proper understanding of the Bible and they most clearly presented the Bible's teaching on matters of faith and life. At the heart of their allegation was the claim that Arminius rejected the Bible. For them, as for other Protestant ministers, every theological disagreement came down to an argument about the Bible.

Bibles were often the most common books in collections owned by ministers. Of the 2,783 books Gomarus owned, 110 were versions of the Christian scriptures, either complete Bibles (Old and New Testaments together) or individual parts (a New Testament, Psalter or other book). 53 of Arminius' 1,770 books were Bibles. If a Protestant minister owned one book, it had to be the Bible. The Bible was at the centre of the Protestant and Reformed traditions. Their claim that the Bible was the ultimate authority of matters of faith and practice united a disparate religious movement.[16]

Protestant ministers venerated Scripture and encouraged those in their congregation to read it. Jeremie du Pours, a minister of the Walloon church in Middelburg, composed a lengthy volume on the Psalms, entitled *La divine melodie, du sainct psalmiste ou La divinité du livre des pseaumes* [*The Divine Melody of the Holy Psalmist, or the Divinity of the Book of Psalms*]. It ran to over 800 pages. In the introductory preface written to the members of his church, his 'brothers and sisters', he called his congregation to remain faithful to the purity that first marked the Reformed Walloons.[17] He recounted the trials and travails their forefathers had suffered at the hands of the Spanish at the start of the Reformation. In addition to the synods that consecrated their confession of faith, Du Pours mentioned the books, and especially the Bibles, that

---

16   Alec Ryrie, *Protestants: The Faith that Made the Modern World* (New York: Viking, 2017).

17   Jeremie du Pours, *La divine melodie, du sainct psalmiste ou La divinité du livre des pseaumes* (Middelburg: Geeraert Moulert, 1644), USTC 1024498, f. A2. Copy consulted: ZA, 1722 Waalse Gemeente te Middelburg, 1618–2009, Inv. No. 71.

GUARDIANS OF THE FAITH

had been banned by the theologians at Louvain in May 1546. He encouraged them to take up, once again, those books which had shaped their forefathers' devotion, beginning with the Bible. He concluded with a reminder to his flock: 'All lovers of God, those loved by God, the loving God, will also love this holy book for their beginning and end'.[18] Antonius Walaeus, in his oration marking his admission to the theological faculty of the University of Leiden, reminded the ministerial candidates in attendance that if all Christians are supposed to read Scripture for their edification, how much more should ministers.[19] It is no surprise, then, that Bibles and portions of the Bible are some of the most common books in ministerial libraries.

Of the fifty-five transcribed catalogues, Bibles comprise just over two per cent of the entire corpus, 2,075 Bibles in whole or part. This nearly equals the combined total of the five most common religious authors listed in these transcribed catalogues: John Calvin (612), Theodore Beza (420), Franciscus Junius (383), Desiderius Erasmus (339) and André Rivet (324). At a bare minimum, the smallest ministerial libraries had to contain a Bible. No other single text approaches the Bible in popularity in ministerial collections. Not Augustine's *Opera*, Luther's *The Bondage of the Will*, Zachary Ursinus' *Commentary on the Heidelberg Catechism*, or even Calvin's *Institutes*: the Bible was overwhelmingly more prevalent in their collections than even these most popular theological books.

Often, some of the most expensive books in their collections were Bibles. André Rivet's three volume *Biblia Hebraea* (1618) sold for thirty-eight gulden and five stuivers.[20] Guilielmus Fabius owned a Dutch Bible that sold for forty gulden, the *Nederduytschen Bible na de Nieuwe Oversettingh* (Amsterdam, 1641).[21] Abraham Heidanus owned the London Polyglot Bible, which sold for 138 gulden, the seven volume *Biblia Regia*, which sold for 156 gulden, and the ten volume Paris edition of the *Biblia Regia*, which sold for an astounding 360 gulden.[22]

---

18   'Tout Theophile, ami de Dieu, aimé de Dieu, Dieu aimant aimera aussi ce Sainct Livre pour son entree & son issue'. Du Pours, *La divine melodie*, f. G3r. Copy consulted: ZA, 1722 Waalse Gemeente te Middelburg, 1618–2009, inv. 71.

19   Antonius Walaeus, *Oratio de studii Theologici recta institutione* (Leiden: Jacob Marcus: 1620), USTC 1015798. Cf. F. G. M. Broeyer, 'Bible for the Living Room: The Dutch Bible in the Seventeenth Century', in M. Lamberigts and A. A. den Hollander (eds.), *Lay Bibles in Europe 1450–1800* (Leuven: Leuven University Press, 2006), p. 214.

20   AC *André Rivet 1657* (Leiden: Pieter Leffen, 1657), USTC 1846296, p. 1.

21   Either USTC 1022780 or USTC 1030443. AC *Guilielmus Fabius 1677* (Delft: Cornelis van Heusden, 1677), USTC 1813810, f. A2.

22   AC *Abraham Heidanus 1679* (Leiden: Felix Lopez de Haro & widow and heirs Adrianus Severinus, 1679), USTC 1846941.

Most Bibles (forty per cent) were Latin translations. Thirty-two per cent were in the original languages or other scholarly languages like Chaldaic or Syriac. Bibles in vernacular languages made up the remaining twenty-eight per cent. These were books that did not easily lose their value. New translations were published every so often, but they rarely varied in matters of major theological importance from older editions. Often, they were characterized more by stylistic changes or updated reading notes. Bibles were passed down from father to son or sold and resold in auctions until they were used to destruction. They tended to be a bit older than most other books listed in ministerial catalogues, but only slightly. Forty-eight per cent of Bibles among this dataset were printed in the sixteenth century. For the corpus as a whole, thirty-six per cent was printed in the sixteenth century. Unlike folio volumes which had a similar timeless quality like Bibles, and therefore tended to be older, editions of the Bible were almost evenly split between sixteenth and seventeenth editions. For those lots that included the place of publication of Bibles (1,096), nearly sixty per cent came from six major print centres: Antwerp (116), Amsterdam (113), Basel (107), Leiden (102), Geneva (98) and Paris (91). Of the 204 Bibles that are listed with prices, the average price was over ten gulden. A book typically sold for anywhere between one and two gulden.

Vernacular Bibles, however, tended to be newer than their Latin and scholarly counterparts. Only two ministers, Jacob Lydius and Jacob Cuilemann, owned incunabula editions of the Delft Bible printed in 1477. The purpose of a translation indicates why older vernacular Bibles were less common. They not only had to reproduce faithfully the meaning of the original languages; they had to do so while being comprehensible to the lay readers for whom they were intended. Luther had exhorted translators of the Bible: 'we must consult the mother at home, children in the street, and the ordinary man in the marketplace, watch them mouth their words, and translate accordingly'.[23] Antonius Thysius, a professor of theology at Leiden, noted that faithful translation to the original is 'not only permitted and useful ... but also entirely necessary, so that it may be of use to all people ... so that it may be understood, read, and heard by all people and those of any kind, also lay-people'.[24] Adolph Visscher, working alongside a group of Lutheran ministers in Amsterdam, strove for this quality of readability when they adapted a Dutch Bible for the Lutheran churches

---

23   Martin Luther, *Ein Sendbrief vom Dolmetschen – An Open Letter on Translating*, trans. Howard Jones (Oxford: Taylor Institution Library, 2017), p. 17.

24   Antonius Thysius, 'Disputation 3. Concerning the Canonical and Apocryphal Books', in *Synopsis Purioris Theologiae/Synopsis of a Purer Theology: Latin Text and English Translation*, ed. Dolf te Velde, trans. Riemer A. Faber, vol. 1 (Leiden: Brill, 2014), p. 81.

GUARDIANS OF THE FAITH   115

in the Netherlands.[25] His colleagues in Amsterdam praised his work on the translation in a sermon preached at his funeral.[26] In 1606 one minister recommended translating Johan Piscator's German Bible into Dutch, because a suitable translation from the original would not be available soon.[27] As a basis for his Dutch translation of the Bible, Sixtinus Amama used Giovanni Diodati's Italian translation because the Synod of Dort had been slow to realize its stated goal of producing a new Dutch translation from the original languages.[28]

The *Statenbijbel* [States Bible], first printed in 1637 in Leiden, quickly became common in ministerial auction catalogues. It makes its first appearance in the catalogue of the library owned by Franciscus Gomarus in 1641.[29] The 1637 edition is listed eleven times. Paulus Aertsz. van Ravesteyn (1586/87–1655), the famous Bible printer, is mentioned twenty times as the printer and publisher. Even the Mennonite minister Johannes van Dijk owned a copy.[30] Usually, though, entries for the States Bible are not listed as such. They are typically listed with some variation of 'van de Nieuwe oversettinge [of the new translation]', as was the case in the catalogue of the library owned by Caspar Sibelius.[31] Catalogues on occasion went out of their way to mention when translations prior to the States Bible were for sale. In the catalogues of the books owned by Bernard Somer, Jacob Cuilemann and Guilielmus Fabius, sold in 1685, 1694 and 1677 respectively, the printers noted the Dutch Bible for sale was according to the 'oude oversetting [old translation]'.

Before the States Translation the most widely used Dutch translation was known as the Deux Aes [Two Aces] Bible. The name is drawn from a note on Nehemiah 3:5: 'The poor must bear their cross, the rich giveth nothing. Two

---

25   Adolph Visscher, 'Aen den Christelijcken Leser', in his *Biblia, Dat is, De gantsche H. Schrifture, vervattende alle de boecken des Ouden ende Nieuwen Testamenten* (Amsterdam: Rieuwert Dircksz van Baardt, [1648]), USTC 1014161, ff. *2v–r. On the so-called 'Visscher Bible', see A. A. den Hollander, 'Een bijbel voor de lutheranen in Nederland–de mythe van de vertaling van Adolf Visscher uit 1648', in Gillaerts et al. (eds.), *De Bijbel in de Lage Landen. Elf eeuwen van vertalen* (Heerenveen: Royal Jongbloed, 2015), pp. 445–450.

26   Elias Taddel, *Voor-stellinge, ende verklaringe van de woorden Daniels Cap. XII. vers 2. 3. Op de Doot ende christelijcke Begraeffenisse des eerwaerdigen, aendachtigen, wel-geleerden ende in Godt saligen Dn. M. Adolphus Visscher* (Amsterdam: Anna Serobandts and Michiel Strobach, 1653), USTC 1812102, pp. 16–17.

27   Wilhelmus Baudartius, *VVech-bereyder op de verbeteringhe van den Nederlantschen Bybel* (Arnhem: Jan Jansz., 1606), USTC 1017588.

28   Broeyer, 'Bible for the Living Room: The Dutch Bible in the Seventeenth Century', p. 210.

29   *AC Franciscus Gomarus 1641*.

30   *AC Johannes van Dijk 1685* (Amsterdam: Widow of Johannes van Someren, 1685), USTC 1847142.

31   *AC Caspar Sibelius 1658* (Deventer: Jan Colomp, 1658), USTC 1846312.

116   CHAPTER 4

aces have nothing, six fives give nothing, four threes help freely'.[32] Between 1562 and 1637, the Deux Aes Bible was published in 195 editions. About two-thirds of these were complete Bibles, the sixty-six books of the Old and New Testaments. The remaining third was New Testaments, individual books or groups of books.[33] In collections owned by ministers, the Deux Aes Bible was popular. Its popularity, however, is obscured by the fact that the Bible has a complex publication history. No one city had a monopoly on its production, and it was often published in sections. Nevertheless, one can safely say the Deux Aes Bible was one of the most common Dutch vernacular versions of the Bible within ministerial libraries, rivalled only by the States translation.

These translation efforts took place despite the fact that numerous Dutch translations were in circulation already. According to USTC data, 109 editions of the Dutch Bible, in whole or part, were printed between 1555 and 1600. The ministers owned many of these Bibles. Vernacular Bibles were less common than Latin. Latin was the dominant language of the academy and it was the language of most theological books. Ministers were sufficiently adept at Latin to permit reading of the Bible in Latin. Nevertheless, ministers preached from vernacular Bibles, and so they were needed for regular consultation. A minister would often own a vernacular copy of the Psalms. Franciscus Gomarus owned two Psalm books and a New Testament in Dutch. Such books were convenient tools in the daily life of a believer.[34] Two French psalters, a French New Testament and a Dutch Psalm book sold at the auction of Godefridus Udemans' collection.[35] Eight of these works are found in Gisbertus Voetius' collection, three of which were English translations of the Psalms.[36]

The Leiden professor André Rivet owned forty-six Bibles. Seventeen are in folio. Ten are quarto. There are two in octavo, and another seventeen in duodecimo. Latin is the most common language with nineteen. Rivet gave away two biblical texts in his last hours: one Arabic New Testament and a complete Bible.[37] There is a nearly equal number of Bibles in Greek and Hebrew, seven and six respectively. Rivet studied the Bible for personal devotion, and his six

---

32   Quoted in A. A. den Hollander and Ole Peter Grell, 'Bibles in the Dutch and Scandinavian vernaculars to c. 1750', in Euan Cameron (ed.), *The New Cambridge History of the Bible* (Cambridge: Cambridge University Press, 2016), pp. 247–248.

33   August den Hollander, 'The Edition History of the Deux Aes Bible', in August den Hollander, et al. (eds.), *Religious Minorities and Cultural Diversity in the Dutch Republic* (Leiden: Brill, 2014), pp. 41–72.

34   *AC Franciscus Gomarus 1641.*

35   *AC Godefridus Udemans 1653* (Zierikzee: Jaques Fierens, 1653), USTC 1846270.

36   *AC Gisbertus Voetius 1677* (Utrecht: Willem Clerck, 1677–79), USTC 1813323 and 1846977.

37   Marie du Moulin, *The Last Houers, of the Right Reverend Father in God Andrew Rivet*, trans. G. L. (The Hague: Samuel Brown, 1652), pp. 41–44.

GUARDIANS OF THE FAITH

French Bibles indicates this fact. Rivet ended his brief letter to the reader of the *Biblia Sacra*, an amalgamation of the Tremellius and Junius translation of Old Testament with Beza's New Testament, with a benediction for the reader: 'May God, to whom is glory and honour forever, completely satisfy the reader'.[38]

Bibles dominated the theological books ministers owned. But soon, three other important books emerged: the *Confessio belgica*, the Heidelberg Catechism and the Acts of the Synod of Dort. These confessional documents emerged after the initial waves of the Protestant Reformation when a process of clarifying beliefs and an increasing focus on training pastors began.[39] Ministers and professors of theology crafted carefully-worded statements that summarized the Bible's teaching on central points of faith: the Trinity, human nature, the Bible, Christ and redemption and the Church. Seventeenth-century Dutch ministers looked back to the confession and catechism as the pure distillation of the 'faith that was once for all delivered to the saints (Jude 3)'. Rather than creating a new authoritative tradition that added to the teachings of Scripture, these creeds and confessions were derived from Scripture and were used as guides to its teaching. By 1563 any ministry candidate who aspired to preach in Reformed churches in the Low Countries had to sign the Belgic Confession, composed in 1561 by Guy de Brès to distinguish the Reformed faith from the Mennonites.[40] In 1593, the Heidelberg Catechism and the Belgic Confession was used as a confessional guide. In June of that year, a meeting of representatives from every province gathered in Alkmaar to, among other things, chastise a Medemblik minister who was ignorant and deceptive in his teaching. He had refused to 'submit to the Dutch Confession and Catechism'.[41] Ministers who subscribed to the Belgic Confession affirmed that the Bible was without error and contained everything 'which a man ought to believe unto Salvation'.[42] No human writings were comparable to 'those divine Scriptures', because 'all men

---

38   'Id Deus in omnibus lectoribus impleat, cui honor & Gloria saecula. Amen' *Ad Lectorem*, in *Biblia Sacra sive Testamentum Vetus ab Im Tremellio et Fr Junio ex Hebraeo Latine Redditum, et Testamentum Novum á Theod. Beza a Graeco in Latinum Versum* (Amsterdam: Willem Jansz. Blaeu, 1648), USTC 1014147, f. A2v.

39   Richard A. Muller, *After Calvin: Studies in the Development of a Theological Tradition* (Oxford: Oxford University Press, 2003).

40   N. C. Kist, 'De Synoden der Nederlandsche Hervormde Kerken onder het kruis gedurende de Jaren 1563–1577', in *Nederlandsch Archief voor Kerkelijke Geschiedenis*, 20 (1849), p. 135.

41   'voorleggenweigerende die Nederlandtsche Confessie ende Catechismum te onderteickenen'. J. Reitsma and S. D. van Veen (eds.), *Acta Der Provinciale en Particuliere Synoden, Gehouden in de Noordelijke nederlanden Gedurende de Jaren 1572–1620* (8 vols., Groningen: J. B. Wolters, 1892–1899), I, p. 172.

42   'que tout ce que l'homme doit croire pour estre sauué'. Guy de Brés, *Confession de foy* (s.l., s.n., 1562), USTC 247, p. 3.

are naturally liars, and more vain than vanity itself'.[43] Theologians, councils and decrees were only authoritative insofar as they conformed to Scripture. Church confessions, therefore, were recognized as authoritative only when their teaching aligned with Scripture. When necessary, confessions were changed or clarified, as happened at the Synod of Dort.

Despite their importance to the Reformed church in the Netherlands, these confessional documents were in far fewer collections than Bibles. Despite his importance to the establishment of the Reformed Church in the Netherlands, they did, after all, use his confession as a basis for their doctrinal unity, Guy de Brès is rarely mentioned in the auction catalogue of Dutch Protestant ministers in the seventeenth century. Less than twenty copies of his confession are listed, and he is only listed as an author twelve times. The Heidelberg Catechism was slightly more common, but only slightly. It was often bound alongside other books: the Genevan Psalter edited and translated by Petrus Dathenus, for example. The typical Protestant church book included a Bible, a psalm book, a catechism, and a liturgy. If copies of a church book are listed in a minister's catalogue, the catechism would not be listed on its own. The catechism, though rarely listed on its own, is still a common presence in ministerial auction catalogues. Zacharius Ursinus, the principal author of the catechism, was one of the most popular authors listed in their auction catalogues, however: his explanation of the catechism was listed about sixty times. An additional sixty or so works on the catechism are also listed.

No theological controversy caused such catastrophic damage as the Remonstrant Controversy of 1609–1619. It led to the deposition of numerous ministers, theology faculties (such as Leiden) were purged, a civil war nearly broke out, and Grand Pensionary Johan Oldenbarnevelt was executed for, in part, his association with the ousted party. This controversy helped establish the tradition in which Dutch ministers worked. Many ministers, therefore, owned a copy of the *Acts of the Synod of Dort*. A Lutheran minister in Amsterdam even owned a copy in 1680.[44] Thirty-eight out of the forty-seven post-1619 catalogues I have transcribed owned the acts that emerged from the Synod of Dort.

The heart of theological debate during the seventeenth century was the intersection of the authority of Scripture with the confessional documents. Theologians whose works were censored by the orthodox community often sought to eschew these texts in favour of a more rigorous claim to *sola*

---

43   'aux escrits Divins ... Car tous hommes sont mēteurs, & leur sagese ne peut estre assuiettie à Dieu. Ils sont plus vains que la vaniteé mesme'. Ibid., p. 3.

44   *AC Artus Georgius Velten 1680* (Amsterdam: Widow Joannes van Someren, 1680), USTC 1816303, p. 5, lot 39.

GUARDIANS OF THE FAITH   119

scriptura. Those who were considered heterodox wielded the Protestant shibboleth against those who condemned them. In other words, those who made use of confessions and books by human authors remained ensnared in Roman Catholic trappings. A professor of theology and pastor in Steinfurt, Conrad Vorstius was appointed to succeed Jacob Arminius after the latter's untimely death in 1609. Vorstius had a reputable academic pedigree, and he had published several theological works. Immediately after his appointment opposition arose from those who had opposed Arminius for unorthodox teachings. Vorstius, they claimed, peddled anti-Trinitarian heresies.[45] Vorstius defended himself, suggesting he allowed Scripture to speak on its own terms. The framework by which his accusers understood the Christian doctrine of the Trinity was more influenced by Greek philosophers than the Apostles. He claimed to be more purely Reformed. Writing to the states of Holland, Vorstius claimed theologians like Sibrandus Lubbertus (1555–1625), Franciscus Gomarus (1563–1641) and Petrus Plancius (1551–1622) considered him heretical,

> not because I have ever rejected or cast doubt on any doctrine of the true faith expressed anywhere in the Holy Scriptures but because I examine a bit too courageously some purely human opinions that are nothing but some Scholastical teachings that in the past have been accepted under the name of Aristotelian philosophy and recently have been introduced into our religion, but nonetheless are found nowhere in God's Word, much less being taught there with clarity and perspicuity.... I have too courageously looked into the reasons by which people try to prove them, by testing them against the Holy Scriptures and true reason.[46]

Vorstius was recognized by the followers of Jacob Arminius as his successor. The appeal Vorstius made to 'testing them against the Holy Scriptures and true reason' echoed in other ostracized theological communities in the Netherlands. The Collegiants, a group who evolved from a spiritualistic group into a rationalistic religious community, claimed to have no authority but the Bible and their own individual reason or spiritual experience. In his 'twenty-one ground rules for the interpretation of Scripture', Adrian Swartepaert, a Collegiant theologian, laid out these two pillars of sola scriptura and reason, so praised by Vorstius a half century earlier. Rule one was that 'It is impossible that one and the same thing can, at the same time, both be and not be'. And later in rule 6:

---

45   C. van der Woude, *Sibrandus Lubbertus: Leven en werken, in het bijzonder naar zijn correspondentie* (Kampen: J. H. Kok, 1963), pp. 198–258.

46   Quoted in Bangs, *Arminius*, p. 480.

'That which the Scripture says of damnation and salvation ought not to be disagreed with'.[47] Joachim Oudaan, a Collegiant theologian, though a poet and playwright by profession, argued 'We have only our understanding, however great or small ...' The Mennonite minister Galenus Abrahamsz. (1622–1699), who openly associated with Collegiants, came to regret the rationalizing tendency he and other like-minded thinkers inflicted on their churches. Turning his pastoral eye to his fellow Collegiants in 1699, Abrahamsz. wrote 'These men take the Holy Scripture of the Old and New Covenant as the one rule of their belief and life, although perhaps it can be said of them that they place a little too much value on the use of human reason in the Christian religion'.[48]

Traditionally Protestant ministers and theologians rejected the supreme authority of reason: the mind had a finite ability to discern matters concerning God. Reason, therefore, could only take a person so far; though it could be used to think through issues in a clear way, it could not fully comprehend matters like the Trinity or the Incarnation. Samuel Maresius, a professor of theology at Groningen, encapsulated the Reformed response to the Collegiants and other rationalistic movements when he argued that faith informs reason, in the same way that reason shapes the senses.[49] Rather than the individualistic pursuit of biblical knowledge as informed by reason, Caspar Streso (1603–1664) suggested a more communal understanding of Scripture that, informed by those properly trained, involved far more than what Collegiants and rationalists suggested. Streso, a minister in The Hague, was confident that anyone with even mediocre understanding of the Reformed church would know the means by which the Reformed church came to a conclusion on interpreting the Bible: interpretation was a matter of 'the ecclesiastical sentence of the official ministers and other leaders of the congregation, taken from Scripture, tried, approved, and admitted by charge and order of the Christian government, and accepted not just by the high and low government, but also by all sane and regular church members'.[50]

---

47 Quoted in Andrew C. Fix, *Prophecy and Reason: The Dutch Collegiants in the Early Enlightenment* (Princeton: Princeton University Press, 1991), pp. 160–161.

48 'Die de H. Scriften des ouden en Nieuwen Verbonds, voor den eenigen regel van hun gelove en leven, houdende, eerder souden mogen bedagt worden an die sijde te veel over te slaan, datse het dictamen des menchelijken verstands'. Galenus Abrahamsz. de Haen, *Verdédiging der christenen die doopsgezinde genaamd worden* (Amsterdam: Widow of P. Arents and C. vander Sys, 1699), USTC 1836339, p. 69.

49 Samuel Maresius, *Oratio inauguralis de usu et abusu rationis in rebus theologicis & fidei* (Groningen: Hans Sas, 1648), USTC 1022694. Cf. Rienk Vermij, *The Calvinist Copernicans: the reception of the new astronomy in the Dutch Republic, 1575–1750* (Amsterdam: Koninklijke Nederlandse Akademie van Wetenschappen, 2002), p. 297.

50 'namelijck onder de Kerckelijcke decisie vande beroepene Leeraren ende dienaren des woorts, ende andere Regenten der ghemeynte, ghedaen uit de Schrifture, door last ende

GUARDIANS OF THE FAITH

Dutch Protestant ministers had to defend their theological positions with Scripture. Those whose opinions were rejected by the orthodox majority had to lean on it even more heavily to defend their beliefs. Theological debate amongst Dutch ministers started and finished with the Bible. This required robust understanding of the biblical texts, and Bibles were one of the most substantial sections of their libraries. Ministerial catalogues contain an average of thirty-five copies of the biblical text, whether whole Bibles, the Old or New Testament, the Psalter or the Gospels, or individually bound books. Bibles were easily available throughout the Netherlands. When the question of a printing a new translation of the Bible arose at the Synod of Dort, Balthazar Lydius reminded them the market was already flooded with Bibles. He claimed 60,000 Bibles were stored in print shops and warehouses throughout the Netherlands. Booksellers themselves claimed there were 80,000.[51] 'Where there were printers', A. Th. van Deursen stated, 'there too were Bibles on the press'.[52] Some listed in ministerial catalogues could be bought for less than a day's wage; others were expensive.

Classes, synods and professors valorised the Bible. Numerous synods and classes exhorted their ministers to read carefully from the Scripture both in the church service and in their private devotion.[53] Jacob Trigland, a Reformed minister and polemicist in Amsterdam, captured the Dutch Protestant ethos concerning the Bible and other sources: 'The testimony of the Holy Scriptures, the Councils, the Church Fathers, and the rightful teachers of the truth, can be confirmed by the readers themselves in that great Book, printed for all lovers of truth'.[54]

---

ordre vande Christelijcke hoog Overigheyt beproeft, geapprobeert, toegestemt ende aengenomen, niet allen by de hooge ende lage Regeeringe maer oock by alle gesonde, ende gereguleerde ledematen der ghemeynte'. [Caspar Streso], *Korte aenmerckinghen op het onbewesen bewys dat het gevoelen vander sonne stillestant ende des aertrijckx beweginghe niet strijdigh is met Godts-woort* (The Hague: Henric Hondius, 1656), USTC 1830847, p. 4.

51 Hendrik Kaajan, *De pro-acta der Dordtsche Synode in 1618* (Rotterdam: T. de Vries, 1914), pp. 80–81.

52 'Waar drukkerijen bestonden werden ook bijbels ter perse gelegd'. A. Th. van Deursen, *Bavianen en slijkgeuven. Kerk en kerkvolk ten tijden van Maurits en Oldenbarnevelt* (Franeker: Van Wijnen, 1993), p. 183.

53 Reitsma and Van Veen, *Acta*, VI, p. 344.

54 'De ghetuychenissen uyt de Heylighe Schrift: Concilien: Oudt-vaderen: ende Rechtsinnighe Leeraren achter dese Verclaringhe tot bevestinghe vande selve ghevoecht, sal de Leser vinden in dat groote Boeck, het welck voor een Lief-hebber der Waerheydt ghedruckt is'. Jacob Trigland, *Christelijcke ende nootvvendighe verclaringhe, vant ghene in seker formulier, gheintituleert Resolutie der mogende H. Staten, &c. met Godes H. woort, ende de leere der ghereformeerde kercken over een comt, of daer van verschilt* (Martin Jansz. Brandt: Amsterdam, 1616), USTC 1030656, p. 7.

122   CHAPTER 4

Protestant ministers were men of the Book. They considered Scripture as the source of their knowledge of God and his relationship to them, his creatures. Gisbertus Voetius called the Bible, 'the Book of all knowledge, the Sea of all wisdom, the Academy of the academies'.[55] Arminius himself acknowledged in true Protestant fashion, that Christians should formulate doctrine 'from the rule of Scripture, which ought to have precedence, and from the supporting guidance of the orthodox fathers'.[56] In the heated climate that so often marked the religious debates amongst ministers during this time, Scripture was the final source on which every argument had to turn. Ministers collected numerous texts and editions of the Bible so they could engage in these debates and read for their own spiritual edification.

2   The More Sound Schoolmen

By 1609, Gomarus and Arminius were locked in a theological struggle that emerged from fundamentally opposed points of view on certain biblical texts. They both worked under the assumption, and often explicitly confessed, that the Bible was the final source of their positions. But Gomarus hoped that by showing the fruit of Arminius' influence, the perversity of his belief would be clear for all to see. Those 'controversial and papist books' in such high demand by ministers in training at Leiden confirmed in Gomarus' mind what every sober observer of Arminius' theology knew: Arminius deviated from sound doctrine. The deathblow Gomarus hoped to land when he tarred and feathered Arminius with this accusation was not the most surefooted argument he made against him, to say the least. Not only were Roman Catholic books widely available in Leiden before Arminius arrived in 1603; Dutch ministers on the whole read and even openly acknowledged they benefitted from reading those 'controversial and papist books' even Aquinas, Suarez and Bellarmine.

The simple act of a minister reading medieval and Roman Catholic books gave no pause to ministers and theologians in the Dutch Golden Age. They discouraged ordinary members from reading such books, but ministers nevertheless acquired them and often cited them in their works. This was an act of retrieval. A century after the Reformation began in Wittenberg, Dutch

---

55   'Het Boeck van alle wetenschap, de Zee van alle wijsheyt, de Academie der Academien'. Gisbertus Voetius, *Sermoen van de nutticheydt der academien ende scholen* (Utrecht: Aegidius and Petrus Roman, 1636), USTC 1029443, p. 15.

56   Jacob Arminius, *The Works of Jacob Arminius*, trans. James Nichols and W. R. Bagnall (reprint, 3 vols; Grand Rapids: Baker Books, 1977), vol. 1, p. 412.

GUARDIANS OF THE FAITH

ministers still faced the question with which Roman Catholic disputants had taunted their Protestant forebears: where was your Church before Luther? Scores of Protestant ministers, including many from the Netherlands, devoted books to defending their tradition. They were convinced that the works of Christian thinkers were useful to them.

Dutch ministers self-consciously built on the tradition of the church before Luther. All branches of the Christian church claimed to be the true inheritors of the Apostolic testimony as it was preserved in the Bible, so they endeavoured to show their inheritance through the ages. The theologians who lived in times past could be used as a polemical cudgel with which seventeenth-century ministers and theologians sought to solidify their own religious convictions, all the while shaming their opponents for neglecting the true faith. Reformed versus Lutheran, Protestant versus Roman Catholic, Contra-Remonstrant versus Remonstrant: all appropriated the past in this way.

This act of retrieval was not without its difficulties. At times, seventeenth-century Dutch Protestant ministers ruthlessly attacked Roman Catholics and those from the medieval tradition. Gisbertus Voetius is only one example among many. At times, his invective against them reaches heights that are rarely matched by other Protestant theologians. Like so many of his era, he had no qualms with calling into question their political allegiance: whether or not they would follow the dictates of the Pontiff or be faithful to the Dutch Republic.[57] Nor did he shy away from decrying their religious beliefs as idolatrous and false. Such sentiments still did not preclude Protestant ministers from acquiring numerous books by medieval theologians like Thomas Aquinas or other Scholastics. In cases of conscience, Voetius considered certain Roman Catholic and medieval theologians worthy of attention. Though numerous Catholic casuists lead many to error in certain ways, Voetius wrote, 'For the rest, if these defects are understood and guarded against, we recognize that the more significant of the casuists among the papists, and the commentators on Thomas [Aquinas], are not to be despised'.[58] Despite being known as a particular scourge of Roman Catholics in his day, Voetius owned numerous books by medieval and Roman Catholic theologians: four by Aquinas, two by Bellarmine, five by Bonaventure, five by Thomas Cajetan and many others.

Voetius held up some Roman Catholic theologians as noble examples in the practice of the faith. When compiling the first volume of their father Willem's

---

57   Gisbertus Voetius, *Politicae ecclesiasticae* (4 vols., Amsterdam: Johannes (1) Janssonius van Waesberge, 1663–1676), USTC 1561164, II, p. 391.

58   John W. Beardslee III (trans.), *Reformed Dogmatics: J. Wollebius, G. Voetius, F. Turretin* (Oxford: Oxford University Press, 1965), 271.

collected works, Johannes and Theodorus Teellinck included a preface that Voetius had contributed to Willem's commentary on chapter 9 of Paul's letter to the Romans. It certainly was a reasonable choice. When the book was printed Voetius was an influential professor of theology at Utrecht and had been a key proponent of their father's Reformed ideal. Voetius, though, began his preface in an unexpected way. He grouped Teellinck with a collection of 'Practical writers' [*Practijck-scribenten*] who spanned the era from Bernard of Clairvaux to his own day.[59] For those medieval authors, Voetius acknowledged they had their faults but nevertheless were still beneficial. 'It has been seen how even under the darkness of the Papacy, there have been some practical writers (though flawed according to our judgement) of great value, like Bernard, Bonaventure, William of Paris, Harpis, Ruysbroeck, Schoonhovius, Carthusianus [Denis the Carthusian], Tauler, Thomas à Kempis, etc'.[60]

The sentiment Voetius expressed in his preface to the collected works of Teellinck echo through most of the book collections owned by other ministers at the time. In their collections medieval books tended to be more pietistic in nature. These authors were some of the few who were praised consistently by Dutch Reformed churchmen. If a Dutch minister owned two books by medieval theologians, there was a good chance they were by Bernard of Clairvaux or Thomas à Kempis. The Rotterdam minister Franciscus Ridderus encouraged Johannes Doesburg at the latter's installation as a minister with the words of Bernard of Clairvaux. Quoting Bernard of Clairvaux, he urged the new minister to flee from hypocrisy. 'The great Bernard' in Ridderus' words, 'said, "I have known a teacher who makes the poor rich, who is poor himself". Miserable state'![61] Bernard was one of the most popular medieval authors in Protestant ministerial catalogues, surpassing the readership of many professors of theology in the sixteenth and seventeenth century. His collected works were

---

59 Gisbertus Voetius, 'Praefatie van Gisbertus Voetius, anno 1631, gestelt voor het Tractaet van Mr. Willem Teellinck, over het 7 capittel tot den Romeynen', in Theodorus and Johannes Teellinck (eds.), *Het eerste stuck van de wercken van Mr. Willem Teellinck* (Utrecht: Gedruckt voor de Erfgenamen van Mr. Willem Teellinck, 1659), USTC 1840360.

60 'Men heeft gesien hoe selfs onder de duysternisse des Pausdoms soodanighe Practijcke-scribenten (al hoewel gebreckelijck onses oordeels) in weerden zijn gehouden geweest, als Bernardus, Bonaventura, Guilhelmus Parisiensis, Harpius, Ruysbroeck, Schoonhovius, Carthusianus, Taulerus, Thomas à Kempis, &c'. Ibid.

61 'De groote *Bernardus* seydt, *Ick kenne een Leeraer die Arme Rijck maeckt, en selve Arm blijft*: Ellendige state'. Franciscus Ridderus, *Voorbeeldt van een waer predikant, vertoont in een predicatie, gedaen op den 2. January 1678. uyt 1. Tim. 4 vers 12. (niemant verachte uwe jonckheydt.) op de bevestinge van D. Johannis Doesburgh, tot predikant in de bloeyende gemeynte van Rotterdam* (Rotterdam: Joannis Borstius, 1678), USTC 1814702, p. 11.

GUARDIANS OF THE FAITH

commonly listed. His *Opera* were listed in half of the catalogues transcribed in this corpus. His books are listed fifty-nine times, but most of these were his folio *Opera* in multiple editions. He is the most cited medieval theologian in Dutch Reformed writings.[62]

Godefridus Udemans invoked Bernard in defence of meditating on the Bible, not just reading it: 'These godly exercises are like the links of a chain that should not be separated, for the reading of Scripture is, as Bernard said so eloquently in *Scala Claustralium*: "Spiritual food applied to the palate of the soul; meditation chews it by its reasoning, while prayer savors it"'.[63] Like many early-modern writers, Udemans confused the work of Guigo II (d. *c*.1193), a Carthusian monk, for one written by Bernard because their method of simple, earnest devotion was so similar. Udemans accurately referenced Bernard, though, when citing the monk against predatory banking practices.[64] Udemans' catalogue lists Bernard's folio *Opera*, like so many other ministerial auction catalogues.[65]

Gisbertus Voetius wrote the foreword to a Dutch translation of Thomas à Kempis' *De imitatione Christi*.[66] He repeatedly described it as 'the golden little book'.[67] In his *Te Aesthicka sive exercitia pietatis*, a manual on Christian devotion written for academics, Voetius claimed À Kempis' *De imitatione* excelled all other Roman Catholic practical writers because of, as Willem Op 't Hof summarizes, 'its clear and simple yet penetrating style, its themes of self-denial, intimate attachment to Christ, and yearning and striving for spiritual and heavenly things; and its theme of the grace of God, excluding human virtue and merit'.[68]

This short devotional work was read throughout ministerial circles in the seventeenth century and beyond. Works by Thomas à Kempis are listed sixty times. One minister thought 'Thomas à Kempis' little book is in everyone's

---

62   Willem J. Op 't Hof, 'Willem Teellinck and Gisbertus Voetius', in Ronald K. Rittgers and Vincent Evener (eds.), *Protestants and Mysticism in Reformation Europe* (Leiden: Brill, 2019), p. 391.

63   Godefridus Udemans, *The Practice of Faith, Hope, and Love* (Grand Rapids: Reformation Heritage Books, 2012), pp. 245–246.

64   Udemans, *The Practice of Faith, Hope, and Love*, p. 441.

65   AC *Godefridus Udemans*, for. 2, lot 29.

66   On the translation of À Kempis' *De imitatione Christi*, see Max von Habsburg, 'The Devotional Life: Catholic and Protestant Translations of Thomas à Kempis', *Imitatio Christi*, *c*.1420–*c*.1620', (PhD Thesis, University of St Andrews, 2002).

67   Op 't Hof, 'Willem Teellinck and Gisbertus Voetius', p. 394.

68   Ibid., p. 394.

hands'.[69] This was no exaggeration. By 1650, over 202 editions of books by à Kempis had been printed in the Low Countries alone. An edition was likely printed in Amsterdam by Willem Jansz Blaeu under a false Cologne imprint (Fig. 4.1). Intended on deriding the Reformed, an anonymous Spinozist satirically reflected on the importance of medieval writing to Reformed pietism: a father encouraged his son to take up some devotional books, beginning with 'The works by *Taulerus, Taffin* the repentant life and *Thomas à Kempis*'.[70] The father on occasion encouraged his son to read à Kempis for three hours, the satirist claimed. This form of simple devotion appealed especially to ministers like Voetius, Teellinck and other similarly-minded pietistic theologians. But À Kempis was read well beyond these circles. The faith expressed simply without pomp, as the medieval theologian espoused, was well-received by the austere Reformed theologians.[71] À Kempis and Bernard are only surpassed by Aquinas, Cajetan and Robert Bellarmine. Bellarmine, unlike the other three, was read because he was a prolific and popular opponent of Protestant.

Protestant ministers in the Netherlands separated the simple, unadorned piety of medieval theologians like Bernard or mystics like Thomas à Kempis and Johan Tauler from the more distinctly Roman Catholic aspects of their faith. Willem Teellink understood his own conversion in the terms à Kempis used in his *Soliloquium animae*.[72] Voetius went so far as to argue that the fourth volume of *De imitatio Christi*, on the sacraments, was written by someone else. Nowhere is this separation of unadorned piety from distinctly Roman Catholic qualities clearer than in the advice of Wilhelmus à Brakel in his encouragement to the readers of his *The Christians Reasonable Service*:

> Tauler and à Kempis have little to say about the Lord Jesus as being the ransom and righteousness of sinners, about how He, by a true faith, must be used unto justification and in approaching unto God, beholding in His countenance the glory of God, and practicing true holiness as originating in Him and in union with Him. Readers must note this about both authors, keeping this in mind when they read them. They will then be able to benefit from their writings.[73]

---

69   'in alle handen is het boeksken van Thomas à Kempis'. Thadaeus de Landman, *Versameling van twintig stigtelijke en zielroerende predikatien* (The Hague: Meyndert Uytwerf, 1694), USTC 1838644, p. 141.

70   Quoted in Op 't Hof, 'Willem Teellinck and Gisbertus Voetius', p. 397.

71   Arie de Reuver, *Sweet Communion: Trajectories of Spirituality from the Middle Ages Through the Further Reformation* (Grand Rapids: Baker Academic, 2007).

72   Op 't Hof, 'Willem Teellinck and Gisbertus Voetius', p. 393.

73   Wilhelmus à Brakel, *The Christian's Reasonable Service*, ed. Joel R. Beeke, trans. Bartel Elshout (4 vol., Grand Rapids: Reformation Heritage Books, 1992–1995), II, p. 641.

GUARDIANS OF THE FAITH

TABLE 4.1   A selection of well-known Roman Catholic and medieval
authors listed in Dutch ministerial library catalogues

Author	Count
Robert Bellarmine	220
Thomas Aquinas	149
Thomas Cajetan	60
Thomas à Kempis	60
Bernard of Clairvaux	59
Peter Lombard	42
Anslem of Canterbury	21

It was common for Dutch ministers to read books by Roman Catholic and medieval theologians, though they did often encourage readers to dismiss the distinctly Roman Catholic aspects of writings by those who identified with that faith (Fig. 4.2). Beyond the pious reading Voetius and à Brakel recommended, ministers had to read Roman Catholic books because the theological debate between them continued. Protestant ministers could not ignore books by their Catholic contemporaries. Roman Catholic books were available for purchase in the Netherlands, and many Roman Catholics lived in the Netherlands despite being cast out of the public sphere.

André Rivet is a clear example of the continuing engagement with Roman Catholic theologians in which Protestant ministers had to participate. On one occasion, Jean-Maximilian de Langle told Rivet he was sending him numerous books, but he spent most of the letter dedicated to a new book by a French Huguenot. Théophile Brachet de la Milletière (1588–1665) proposed to reconcile Protestants and Catholics in France.[74] The book, *De universi orbis christiani pace et concordia* was immediately criticized by both Protestants and Catholics, and Rivet was one of its primary opponents. News of La Milletière's work reached Rivet in The Hague, and Rivet confronted the error. On 20 November 1634 (before his nephew wrote to him about it), Rivet wrote that though he had not read the book, what he had heard about it so far was enough for him to know the work was indefensible.[75] Eventually he would acquire it.[76] Even

---

74   R. J. M. van de Schoor, *The Irenical Theology of Théophile Brachet de la Milletière (1588–1664)* (Leiden: Brill, 1995), p. 33.

75   *Lettres de Messieurs Rivet, De La Milletière et du Moulin* (Sedan: Jean Jannon, 1635), USTC 6809619, p. 4.

76   AC *André Rivet*, p. 105.

128   CHAPTER 4

before reading the work, Rivet prodded La Milletière to clarify his positions. La Milletière argued that by reconciling with Roman Catholics, Calvinists like Rivet would no longer have to defend several false theological and historical claims: their belief in the spiritual presence of Christ at the Lord's Supper and the absence of any claim to the Church Fathers. La Milletière further claimed that Protestants like Rivet did not understand Roman Catholic theology. Yet Rivet was not a distant observer of Catholic thought, either. Catholic books occupied a large amount of shelf space in his collection. Rivet was proud of his knowledge and use of Catholic authors and their written works. In the titles of two of his anti-Catholic works, he stated that the opinions he summarized were taken directly from written works and one of the tracts included a list of the works consulted.[77] Rivet encouraged the reader to check his interpretation of Catholic authors against their sources.

Rivet was well aware of Roman Catholic writers. He owned several books by the founder of the Jesuits, Ignatius Loyola, and other Jesuits like Famiano Strada and Cornelius à Lapide. He owned as many books by Benedict Arias Montanus, as he did by Franciscus Gomarus, Rivet's counterpart in Groningen. His catalogue lists eight works by Thomas Aquinas, and he wrote notes in at least one of them.[78] On occasion, he even cited Roman Catholic authors favourably in his writings. Cardinal Cajetan, Rivet suggested, was the first Roman Catholic to argue that someone can legitimately interpret Scripture differently than the Church Fathers, in so far as that interpretation is derived from other passages of Scripture.[79] Rivet all but plagiarised a Jesuit professor at Alcalá when describing how biblical passages only have one meaning.[80] If Rivet had misunderstood Roman Catholic theology as La Milletière suggested, it was not because of a lack of reading.

Medieval and Roman Catholic authors were read for both piety and polemic. Some professors of theology followed the method preferred by the medieval theologians in educating students in three stages: reading, reflection and inquiry, known collectively as the scholastic method.[81] Reformed ministers

---

77   André Rivet, *The state-mysteries of the Iesuites, by way of questions and answers. Faithfully extracted out of their owne writings by themselves published* (London: George Eld, 1623), USTC 3010942; *Eschantillon des Principaux paradoxes de la Papaute, sur les poincts de la Religion controuersez en ce temps. Recueillis des propres escrits de ses plus approuuez Docteurs* (La Rochelle: Jérôme Haultin, 1603), USTC 6803696.

78   *AC André Rivet*, p. 61.

79   Rivet, *Tractatus de partum autoritate*, p. 29.

80   Anthony Ossa-Richardson, 'The Naked Truth of Scripture', in Dirk van Miert, Henk Nellen, Piet Steenbakkers, Jetze Touber (eds.), *Scriptural Authority and Biblical Criticism in the Golden Age: God's Word Questioned* (Oxford: Oxford University Press, 2017), p. 125.

81   Willem J. van Asselt, *Introduction Reformed Scholasticism*, trans. Albert Gootjes (Grand Rapids: Reformation Heritage Books, 2011), p. 59.

GUARDIANS OF THE FAITH

offered qualified approval of certain aspects of the works of a handful of medieval theologians; and on occasion, they cited some Roman Catholic thinkers positively.

Though ministers were convinced that readers would be led astray if they learned uncritically from Roman Catholic and medieval theologians, these authors occupied an important position within the book collections owned by Dutch ministers during the Golden Age. Dutch ministers read broadly within the medieval tradition. Despite rejecting many post-Tridentine dogmas, many of the most famous Roman Catholic theologians are as well represented in their collections as Protestant and Reformed theologians like Wolfgang Musculus, Johannes Piscator and Zacharius Ursinus. Over 220 copies of books by Robert Bellarmine are listed in the fifty-five transcribed catalogues. Thomas Aquinas appears 149 times in their collections. Such reading was widespread amongst those ministers whose books sold at auction. Ministers, whether Reformed, Lutheran or Mennonite, were eager to appropriate what they could from such sources.

3   Our Doctors

By the time Gomarus wrote against Arminius, there were a number of theologians whose works were recognized as necessary to the pursuit of a pure church. The second half of Gomarus' allegation against Arminius asserted the latter's deviation from the most respected Reformed theologians: books by 'the most excellent and most well-versed ministers of our churches' were in less demand under Arminius, he claimed. Here again, Gomarus' accusation has no grounding in reality. Gomarus' words echo in a letter written to Sibrandus Lubbertus, the Franeker professor. Antonius Walaeus, while a minister in Middelburg, wrote from the Synod of Dort to Lubbertus, asking the professor of theology about the twenty-second article of the Belgic Confession. Walaeus was convinced that the Remonstrants were not able to disprove Lubbertus' argument on article twenty-two of the Belgic Confession, 'On Faith in Jesus Christ'. Walaeus offered a synopsis of his theological method. First, what do the Old Testament prophets say? Second, can a theological position be shown from the New Testament apostles? Third, what does the 'Confessio Palatina-Belgica' say? He asked a fourth question for discerning the truth: 'what is the sentence of our doctors, Luther, Melanchthon, Calvin, Ursinus, Beza and others'?[82] 'Our

---

82   'Quid de eadem entiant Doctores nostril, Lutherus, Melanchthon, Calvinus, Ursinus, Beza, & alii'? Antonius Walaeus to Sibrandus Lubbertus, 6 July 1619, in Antonius Walaeus, *Opera Omnia* (2 vols., Leiden: Hackius, 1643), USTC 1512223, II, p. 420.

130   CHAPTER 4

doctors' were the authors who were the most well-read amongst ministers in the Dutch Golden Age. Arminius himself read these authors and encouraged the reading of them. Arminius deviated from the Reformed doctrine of predestination.[83] But, such differences did not prohibit reading of Calvin, Beza, Junius or any number of Reformed writers. The first auction of the book collection of a Remonstrant minister took place in 1632. In his collection were several books and commentaries by Calvin, Peter Martyr, Franciscus Junius and other Doctors of the Reformed Church.

Martin Luther was the first 'doctor' in the Protestant tradition. Luther's memory was kept long into the seventeenth century. He was still regarded as the theologian who had begun the restoration of the pure church. The Middelburg minister Abraham van de Velde (1617–1677) in his popular history *De wonderen des Alder-hoogsten* [*The Wonders of the Most High*] argued that in 1517 lightning struck an image of Christ on the lap of Mary, causing the image to fall to the ground. Thus because of Luther, Van de Velde thought, the Church would return to the pure preaching of God's word.[84] Ministers like Petrus Wittewrongel were happy to repeat Luther's encouragement to read simple parts of the Bible first.[85]

Amongst his Reformed readers, Luther was regarded as a proto-Calvinist.[86] Dutch Reformed theologians emphasized his conviction that the will of man is disastrously corrupted by sin while de-emphasizing his formulation of the Lord's Super and Sunday worship. The Reformed did not attempt to hide their interpretation of Luther and Lutheranism on this either. One minister wrote a tract in the hopes of persuading Lutherans that they should join Reformed churches because the Marburg Colloquy (1529) and the Wittenberg Concord (1536), two attempts of merging Lutheran and Reformed, had demonstrated the faiths were not incompatible.[87] Luther's scourging of Erasmus on human nature was much preferred in comparison with Luther's conviction that Christ was physically present in the bread and wine of the Lord's Supper. Heinrich

---

83   Muller, 'Arminius and the Reformed Tradition'.

84   Abraham van de Velde, *De wonderen des Alder-hooghsten* (Amsterdam: Jan Claesz. ten Hoorn, 1677), USTC 1813494, p. 262.

85   Fred van Lieburg, 'Bible Reading and Pietism in the Dutch Reformed Tradition', in M. Lamberigts and A. A. den Hollander (eds.), *Lay Bibles in Europe, 1450–1800* (Leuven: Leuven University Press/Peeters, 2006), p. 230.

86   Henk van den Belt, 'Luther in Dutch Reformed Orthodoxy: A Bag of Worms against the Lutherans', in Herman J. Selderhuis and J. Marius J. Lange van Ravenswaay (eds.), *Luther and Calvinism: Image and Reception of Martin Luther in the History and Theology of Calvinism* (Göttingen: Vandenhoek and Ruprecht, 2017), pp. 427–442.

87   Caspar Grevinchoven, *Grondelijck bericht Caspari Grevinchovii, vande dolingen der nieuwe luterschen* (Rotterdam: Felix van Sambix, 1611), USTC 1029427.

GUARDIANS OF THE FAITH   131

Alting, a professor of theology at Harderwijk, suggested Luther had presented
the true teaching of Augustine in his *De servo arbitrio*, but he rejected Luther's
formulation of the Lord's Supper.[88] 'While Reformed theology developed
the doctrine of free grace by stressing predestination and advocating a more
spiritual understanding of the *presentia realis* in the Lord's Supper', Henk van
den Belt states, 'Lutheran orthodoxy made exactly the opposite choices. The
Reformed preferred Luther in the pulpit and Melanchthon at the Table'.[89]

In theology, ministers preferred Luther over Melanchthon but that did not
translate to their book collections. Most only contain a small number of books
by the Wittenberg Reformer: either Luther's translation of the Bible, one of his
commentaries, *De servo arbitrio* or one of his catechisms. Luther's reception
was broader than one might assume from the auction catalogues of ministerial
book collections. The auction catalogues list on average four books by Luther.
Melanchthon, however, was in the top-ten most popularly listed authors in
ministerial auction catalogues.

The Netherlands was a religiously diverse country. Lutherans were a substantial proportion of the population, in both urban centres and smaller towns.
Despite being the dominant confession, Dutch ministers had to understand
their neighbours. Reformed professors, too, had to understand the work written by their Lutheran contemporaries in the Holy Roman Empire so they could
inform their students better. Dutch ministers acquired mostly sixteenth-century
editions of books by Luther. This is not surprising given the general output
of Luther editions. Before 1600, there were 7,282 editions of books by Luther
printed across Europe; between 1601 and 1650, only 455.[90] Latin was the preferred language for reading his books. Latin editions accounted for seventy-five
per cent of all books by Luther in these collections. There are only seventeen
Dutch translations of books by Luther, and seventy-one German originals.

In 1650, André Rivet received a letter from Jacob Lydius.[91] Lydius asked
Rivet the question that stretched back to Luther and Zwingli at Marburg:
what should followers of the Reformed tradition think about fellowship with
Lutheran believers? Lydius deemed reconciliation with Lutherans impossible.
The same dividing line existed in 1650 as it did for Luther and Zwingli: the
Lord's Supper. After all, Lutherans were devilishly close to Roman Catholics
on the nature of the bread and wine used in communion. Lydius was not an

---

88   Heinrich Alting, *Theologia historica, sive systematis historici loca quatuor* (Amsterdam:
      Johannes Janssonius, 1664), USTC 1801364, p. 294.
89   Van den Belt, 'Luther in Dutch Reformed Orthodoxy', p. 438.
90   USTC data last accessed 14 July 2019.
91   Jacob Lydius to Rivet, Kalendis April 1650. UB Leiden, ms. BPL 285: Bf197r.

132   CHAPTER 4

unfair critic of Lutheran sacramental theology. He quoted from Lutheran writings directly, and he suggested that an interested minister could turn to the work by Johannes Crocius.

Lydius assumed that Rivet was well aware of Lutheran books. When quoting from the Lutheran summary of the faith, Lydius gave the page number. If Rivet owned it, he could find the book on his shelf and formulate his response based on the primary source. Rivet owned numerous Lutheran works. Three works by Luther are listed: his seven volume *Opera* (Wittenberg, 1559), his postils (Nuremberg, 1545), and collection of tracts entitled *Contra Papatum Tractatus* (Strasburg, 1555). Other Lutheran theologians are similarly popular, especially late sixteenth and early seventeenth-century writers. There are over ten works by Balthazar Mentzer and four works by David Chytraeus.

Philip Melanchthon was far more popular than his mentor: thirteen works by Luther's star pupil are listed in the pages of Rivet's catalogue. His four-volume *Opera* sold for over twenty gulden.[92] Lydius' assumption that Rivet owned the *Book of Concord* was well-founded. In addition to his copy of the *Augsburg Confession*, he owned numerous commentaries and manuals on the confession.[93] One manual on the confession even included Rivet's manuscript notes, that of Johann Hulsemann's *Manuale Augustanae Confessio adversus Baltazarum Hagerum Jesuitam*.[94] Lydius certainly did not have to suggest consulting Johannes Crocius' *Commentarius de Augustanae Confessionis Societate*; Rivet owned a copy.[95] Based upon his own library, Rivet had a firm knowledge of his Lutheran contemporaries. Lydius was right to assume Rivet knew many of the printed works he referenced. Books by Lutheran theologians like Martin Luther, Philip Melanchthon and David Chytraeus were some of the most commonly read, not only amongst Lutheran ministers but the Reformed as well.

The authors whom Gomarus, Sibelius and Walaeus chose as their 'doctors' had been read widely in the sixteenth century. Reformed ministers in the Low Countries had read such works since before 1550. In 1550 a placard issued by Philip II decreed that the printing and reading of 'the books of Oecolampadius, Ulrich Zwingli, Bucer and Calvin' were forbidden.[96] All four of these were

---

92   *AC André Rivet*, p. 7.
93   *AC André Rivet*, p. 66.
94   *AC André Rivet*, p. 66.
95   *AC André Rivet*, p. 43.
96   'de boeken van Oecolampadius, Ulrich Zwingli, Bucer en Calvijn'. Quoted in H. H. Kuyper, *De opleiding tot den dienst des woords bij de gereformeerden* (The Hague: Martinus Nijhoff, 1891), p. 270.

read long into the seventeenth century. Zwingli and Oecolampadius were less common on ministerial bookshelves than Martin Bucer and Heinrich Bullinger and even less common than Calvin; nevertheless, they were all owned to some degree.

Books by the Zurich reformer Ulrich Zwingli were concentrated in larger collections, especially of those connected to the theological faculties and the urban ministerial elite. Collectors like André Rivet, Franciscus Gomarus, Johannes Cocceius and Johannes Hoornbeeck constitute the bulk of Zwingli's owners. His books are listed fifty-four times, one book per catalogue on average. Johannes Oecolampadius, the humanist scholar, assistant to Erasmus and Basel reformer, was slightly more popular with seventy works listed, most of which were his commentaries on the major and minor Prophets, the Gospel of Matthew and the Epistle to the Hebrews. Calvin's mentor and Strasburg reformer, Martin Bucer is significantly better represented in the corpus with over 150 instances.

In popularity, Zwingli is out-paced by his successor, Heinrich Bullinger. Works by both Zwingli and Bullinger were only rarely reprinted in the seventeenth century, Zwingli less than Bullinger: only two editions by Zwingli were reissued in the seventeenth century in the Dutch Republic, and seven editions by Bullinger. Franciscus Gomarus owned one volume entitled *Verscheyden Tractaten* [*Various Tracts*] (s.l., 1624), which included tracts by Zwingli, Bugenhagen, Luther and other various reformers. The Universal Short-Title Catalogue lists 448 editions by Bullinger and 264 by Zwingli. In comparison, 291 editions of books by Martin Bucer were produced, slightly more than Zwingli. But Bucer appears 156 times in ministerial auction catalogues, three times more than Zwingli's fifty-four. Bullinger is listed 292 times in ministerial catalogues, six times the number of Zwingli, despite the vast majority of his publications being available only in sixteenth-century editions. Bullinger was one of the most commonly listed authors, while Zwingli was in middle of the pack, neither common nor rare. The number of editions was not the sole factor influencing how ministers built their libraries.

John Calvin dominated the collections of ministers during this time (Table 4.2). The number of times his works are listed is outstripped only by Erasmus, whose translation of the Bible greatly increases his presence. Amongst the catalogues I have transcribed, Calvin is listed 653 times. On average he is listed ten times in each catalogue. Books by Calvin were some of the most commonly printed in the early-modern world. The USTC records 839 editions by the reformer of Geneva before 1650. In ministerial libraries, his commentaries on books of the Bible and his *Institutes* are regular features. The

Institutes alone, with ninety-nine instances, is more common than many other Reformed writers' total.

Authors cited influential contemporaries in their own defence. When one minister objected to the positions taken by another minister, a prominent professor's work could be summoned for the defence of the accused. One minister argued that the Leiden minister Jacob du Bois adhered too closely the written word of Scripture. Du Bois denied the Bible allowed room for saying the Earth rotated around the Sun. Du Bois was a Socinian in his exegesis of scripture, his opponent claimed. Du Bois defended himself by saying he took his exegesis from Festus Hommius, a professor of theology at Leiden.[97] Hommius is recorded forty-four times in this dataset. Similarly, Godefridus Udemans defended his indictment against sabbath desecration with devilish works, by using an extended quote from an earlier Leiden theologian, Lucas Trelcatius: 'We might rightfully complain as did a godly and learned man in our time ...'[98] Trelcatius and his son's works were listed about seventy times.

TABLE 4.2   The twenty most popular theological authors as listed in ministerial library catalogues. All but Augustine worked in either the sixteenth or seventeenth century. Of the early modern authors, Erasmus and Bellarmine were the only non-Protestants

Author	Count of author	Author	Count of author
John Calvin	653	William Perkins	247
Theodore Beza	420	Philip Melanchthon	228
Desiderius Erasmus	418	Martin Luther	227
Franciscus Junius	375	Augustine	226
André Rivet	326	Lambertus Danaeus	209
Johannes Cocceius	304	Hugo Grotius	201
Jerome Zanchius	288	Roberto Bellarmini	198
Conrad Vorstius	287	Wolfgang Musculus	186
William Ames	275	Zachary Ursinus	179
Heinrich Bullinger	272	Peter Martyr Vermigli	178

---

97   Jacob du Bois, *Schadelickheyt van de cartesiaensche philosophie* (Utrecht: Johannes (1) Janssonius van Waesberge, 1656), USTC 1833395, p. 10.

98   Udemans, *The Practice of Faith, Hope, and Love*, p. 298.

GUARDIANS OF THE FAITH

To shepherd Christ's flock, ministers and theologians had to stay up to date. This concern drove them to acquire new books. Ripples of controversy add shape to André Rivet's book collection. Rivet invested in the controversies occurring within his adopted nation, and amongst his mutual correspondents. But Rivet's eye remained fixed on France and the works her ministers published. Rivet loathed waiting for controversial books when time was of the essence. In addition to his concern for the havoc La Milletière would wreak on French Protestantism, Rivet was also concerned about Moïse Amyraut, professor of theology at the Academy of Saumur.[99] In 1641, Amyraut wrote to Rivet, saying he would send him send a copy of his *De Reprobatione*. But it had not arrived. 'I wait for it every hour', Rivet said, writing to Claude Sarrau.[100] Amyraut faced the charge of teaching a heterodox view of the atonement, and Rivet impatiently waited for this work to come across his desk. At Leiden, Rivet had taught one of the principal theologians now at Saumur, Paul Testard, whose work *Irenicum* is found in Rivet's catalogue with his notes.[101] During his final years, Rivet devoted himself to helping steer one of France's most celebrated academies. Rivet wrote several works to help keep Saumur on the straight and narrow. The controversy would continue after Rivet's death, but its legacy is evident even in his book collection. Moïse Amyraut was one of the most popular authors in Rivet's catalogue.

Rivet had many theological opponents: Jesuits in the Southern Netherlands, Remonstrants and Socinians in the Republic and irenical theologians in France. No other of Rivet's opponents, however, caused more ink to be spilled than Hugo Grotius. Rivet stayed abreast of the controversial Grotius through his contact in Paris, Claude Sarrau, a counsellor of the Parliaments of Rouen and Paris. Sarrau was a significant ally in Rivet's polemic against Grotius. Sarrau was a regular source of news from France and books from French presses, but he was most helpful when Rivet set his sights on the exiled Dutchman, Hugo Grotius.[102] Sarrau not only offered help on how to respond best to Grotius in the debate, he also sent Rivet the pamphlets Grotius would write in response to Rivet's numerous polemical works.[103]

---

99   On Amyraut and the Academy of Saumur, see Albert Gootjes, *Claude Pajon (1626–1685) and the Academy of Saumur* (Leiden: Brill, 2014), pp. 21–50.

100   Rivet to Claude Sarrau, 22 November 1641, in Hans Bots and Pierre Leroy (eds.), *Correspondence Intégrale, d'André Rivet et de Claude Sarrau* (3 vols., Amsterdam: APA – Holland University Press, 1978–1982), I, p. 16.

101   *AC André Rivet*, p. 53.

102   Rivet to Claude Sarrau, 19 September 1642, in *Correspondence Intégrale*, I, p. 253.

103   Henk Nellen, *Hugo Grotius: A Lifelong Struggle for Peace in Church and State, 1583–1645*, trans. J. C. Grayson (Leiden: Brill, 2017), p. 698.

136   CHAPTER 4

Rivet was the 'most productive opponent' of Grotius.[104] Grotius and Rivet sought the same end: the peace and health of the Church. But their means to that end were contradictory.[105] Rivet thought Grotius had invented a new religion separate from any known Christian group. Grotius belittled the Reformed church as nothing more than a sect, but himself did not belong to any recognized confession. Grotius' explanation of the Bible was equivalent to that offered by heretics: 'Judaico-Socinianae'.[106] Despite the vitriol with which both Grotius and Rivet attacked each other, both had read many of the other's printed works.

In 1625, within five years of joining the theological faculty at Leiden, Rivet read Grotius' *De iure belli ac pacis* and vehemently disagreed with its interpretation.[107] Grotius had denied the principle of going to war with those who persecuted Christians for their faith, and had argued against using force to secure the conversion of new believers.[108] Writing to Grotius' brother-in-law, Nicolaes van Reigersberch, Rivet knew Jesuit readers would also despise Grotius' work.[109] He read *De iure belli ac pacis* so intently that he could cite one portion from memory.[110] In his *Exercitationes CXC in Genesin*, printed in 1633, Rivet occasionally referenced Grotius' work, but often without citing his source.[111] Within ten years, Rivet would become Grotius' most ardent opponent. In 1640, three works by Grotius came off Blaeu's press in Amsterdam: *De veritate religionis christianae, De fide et operibus* and *De antichristo*.[112] Grotius could not hide his frustration that Blaeu delayed printing two of these tracts for a year.[113] But André Rivet would have been delighted if they were delayed indefinitely. Rivet wrote to his close friend Constantijn Huygens, eager for the secretary's thoughts on the new publications. Despite being busy, Huygens fired off a two-page letter offering a summary of his thoughts. Huygens was not impressed by Grotius. 'His writing is primitive and against all reason', the

---

104   H. J. M. Nellen, '"Geene vredemaeckers zijn zonder tegenspreeckers" Hugo Grotius' buitenkerkelijke positie', in *De zeventiende eeuw*, 5 (1989), p. 108.

105   Hans Bots, 'Hugo Grotius et André Rivet: Deux Lumieres Opposées, Deux Vocations Contradictoires', in Henk J. M. Nellen and Edwin Rabbie (eds.), *Hugo Grotius, Theologian: Essays in Honour of G. H. M. Posthumus Meyjes* (Leiden: Brill, 1994), pp. 145–155.

106   Rivet, *Operum Theologicorum tomus alter* (Rotterdam: Arnoud Leers, 1651), USTC 1840008, II, p. 814.

107   USTC 6026902.

108   Nellen, *Hugo Grotius*, pp. 374–375.

109   N. van Reigersberch to Hugo Grotius 8 September 1625, in P. C. Molhuysen, etc. (eds.), *Briefwisseling van Hugo Grotius* (17 vols., The Hague: Martinus Nijhoff, 2001), XVII, p. 282.

110   Nellen, *Hugo Grotius*, pp. 537–8.

111   USTC 1024329.

112   USTC 1013672. USTC 1030612. USTC 1013465.

113   Henk Nellen, 'Grotius as a Publicist in France', in Henk J. M. Nellen and Edwin Rabbie (eds.), *Hugo Grotius, Theologian: Essays in Honour of G. H. M. Posthumus Meyjes* (Leiden: Brill, 1994), p. 137n75.

GUARDIANS OF THE FAITH

Secretary snapped.[114] Rivet would certainly have agreed. By July 1642, he would write a substantive critique of Grotius' work. The Republic's greatest humanist failed the test of orthodoxy. Grotius was a danger to the health of the Church, despite Grotius' claims to the contrary.

Grotius was not only an enemy to the nation's theological health; Rivet read his political tracts and thought they could devastate the concord of the Republic. He believed Grotius' *Verantwoordingh van de wettelijcke regieringh van Holland ende West-Vrieslandt* [*Defense of the Lawful government of Holland*] delivered the final death-blow to any hope Grotius had in returning to the Republic.[115] Published in 1622, the pamphlet argued that Maurits of Nassau was an illegitimate ruler, and Grotius sought to revive Oldenbarnevelt's legacy of religious toleration. Rivet owned the Latin translation, *Apologeticus*.[116] In a letter written in 1645, Rivet remembered the work twenty years after it had been published.

Throughout the 1640s, Rivet wrote responses to Grotius' works, usually within a few months. How did Rivet acquire Grotius' books so quickly? Rivet's contact in Paris, Claude Sarrau, sent Grotius' books as soon as he could get his hands on them. In 1642, Sarrau denied the claim that he had sent Rivet proofs of Grotius' *Votum pro pace ecclesiastica*, while 'still damp from the press'.[117] Sarrau claimed Grotius had given him a presentation copy, and that it somehow made its way to Rivet in Holland. Yet despite Sarrau's protest, the accusation was accurate. On 12 September 1645, Sarrau sent Rivet a letter and swore him to secrecy. Overcoming the hurdles of embargo, Sarrau managed to send the first sheet to the eager Rivet, and the rest of the book followed two weeks later.[118] Rivet tore through the book, jotting down notes in the front.[119]

Rivet understood and read these books by Grotius in the context of published works by other authors. His library was not a collection of individual titles. Rivet used his books in conversation with one another. He reflected on how new books related to old, how arguments carried over from one book to another, often with several years between. Hugo Grotius' work *De veritate religionis christianae* could not escape comparisons with Fausto Sozzini's *De authoritate sacrae scripturae*.[120] Rivet himself made the comparison, noting

---

114 'La epist ist ecrite de vant la primitive contre touti raison'. Constantijn Huygens to Rivet, 2 June 1640, UB Leiden ms. BPL 293 II.

115 USTC 1015416. Rivet to Sarrau, 6 October 1642, in *Correspondence Intégrale*, I, p. 272.

116 USTC 6010286. *AC André Rivet*, p. 111.

117 USTC 6004921. Nellen, *Hugo Grotius*, p. 702.

118 Claude Sarrau to Rivet 12 September 1645, in *Correspondence Intégrale*, I, p. 248.

119 *AC André Rivet*, p. 117.

120 Grotius: USTC 1011736; Sozzini: USTC 2028947. This work was written by Sozzini and edited by Conrad Vorstius.

138 CHAPTER 4

in a letter where the two authors agreed.[121] He even owned Grotius' book *De Christi satisfactione*, with which Grotius sought to distance himself from Sozzini.[122] Rivet had extensive knowledge of Sozzini's works. Fourteen of his works are listed in Rivet's catalogue, with several other works by his disciples. Rivet read Sozzini's works diligently and intently. Rivet's copy of *De authoritate sacrae scripturae* contained several manuscript notes.[123]

In 1633, Rivet saw continuity in the arguments emerging from the Saumur Academy. One of its most celebrated professors simply echoed the work of his teacher. Rivet compared the thought of Paul Testard's *Eirenikon* to his teacher John Cameron. Rivet described the *Eirenikon* as 'a methodical arrangement of all those things that Cameron spoke about nature and grace scattered throughout'.[124] Rivet owned Testard's *Eirenikon* and seven of Cameron's published works. After chastising La Milletière for praising himself, Rivet remembered a book he had read thirty years before the controversy with La Milletière began.[125] La Milletière's work *La verité du sainct sacrement* reminded Rivet of *De Eucharistiae Mysterio* (Worms, 1573) by Jodocus Harchius (*c.*1500–1580).[126] Harchius, like Milletière, strove for reconciliation between Protestants and Catholics, focusing on the Lord's Supper. Rivet saw the similarities in their arguments as a clear sign that Milletière was in error. Harchius, after all, was a professing Catholic. Rivet read the book, and recalled it thirty years later, but at some point between the 1620s and 1657, it was either lost or given away. Rivet's catalogue does not record Harchius' work. But Rivet's reference does not appear to be a lapse of memory. He recalled that Harchius was a medical doctor and also recalled specific points of Harchius' argument.[127]

On 11 September 1645 word reached André Rivet that his greatest opponent, Hugo Grotius had died shortly after being shipwrecked and washing up on the shores of Rostock, in northern Germany. Grotius' final work against Rivet reached the theologian just prior to hearing of his death.[128] Though death had claimed Grotius in Rostock, his works remained influential throughout Europe. Rivet aimed his polemic not merely *ad hominum*, but sought to convince his reader that he engaged with the ideas Grotius espoused. To accomplish this,

---

121   Rivet to Claude Sarrau, 5 September 1644, in *Correspondence Intégrale*, II, p. 370.

122   AC *André Rivet*, p. 25.

123   AC *André Rivet*, p. 47.

124   USTC 6809476. Gootjes, *Claude Pajon*, p. 57.

125   Rivet to La Milletière, 29 July 1641, in Rivet, *Responses a Trois Lettres du Sieur de la Milletiere* (Quévilly: Jean Berthelin & Jacques Caïlloüé, 1642), USTC 6810069, p. 63.

126   USTC 625485.

127   For a summary of Harchius' thought, see Van de Schuur, *The Irenical Theology of Théophile Brachet de la Milletière*, pp. 181–182.

128   Rivet to Sarrau, 19 September 1645 in *Correspondence Intégrale*, III, p. 218.

GUARDIANS OF THE FAITH

he included Grotius' original work as an appendix to his own.[129] By the end of his life, Rivet had acquired twenty-four books by Grotius, from the beginning of his literary career at the turn of the seventeenth century to his last published works.

Ministers read broadly, from Luther to the contemporaries of their own day. When possible, they appropriated what they could from their 'doctors'. Johannes Wtenbogaert chastised Contra-Remonstrants by arguing that their allegiance to Calvin and Beza exceeded their commitment to Christ. Such a criticism loses its edge when we consider the book collections of a range of ministers, Lutherans, Reformed, Remonstrant and Mennonite. Arminius' followers did not spurn the reading of those authors Sibelius or Gomarus praised. Though Remonstrants rejected certain of their opponents' theological positions, Calvin and the many others who together form what we call the Reformed tradition, were well-read by Remonstrant ministers. Arminius rejected Luther's explanation that believers would in heaven comprehend how a good God could condemn innocent people.[130] Arminius owned five books by Luther. Adrianus van der Borre (1565–1630), the first Remonstrant minister whose collection sold at auction, owned more works by Franciscus Junius, twenty, than he did of Jacob Arminius and Conrad Vorstius, Arminius' influential successor.[131] The Haarlem Remonstrant minister Jacob Cuilemann (d. 1694) owned a similar number of books written by the Remonstrants Conrad Vorstius and Simon Episcopius (seventeen) as he did the Reformed Zachary Ursinus and Wolfgang Musculus (fifteen).[132]

It was reported after the Synod of Dort that John Hales, a moderate Calvinist and British delegate, 'bade John Calvin goodnight'.[133] This was hardly the case with Arminius and his followers. Despite rejecting points of Calvin's theology, the book collections of Remonstrant ministers have the indelible mark of the Genevan theologian upon them. Ministers had to be aware of the books by their many contemporaries. When one examines the dates of publications for books listed in fifty-five auction catalogues of ministerial libraries, twenty per cent of their collections were published in the twenty years before the auction catalogue was published. Influential authors, whether professors, urban ministers, or simply those whose books became popular, helped reorientate

---

129 André Rivet, *Examen animadversionum Hugonis Grotii* (Leiden: Bonaventura Elzevier, 1642), USTC 1028501.
130 Jacob Arminius, *The Works of Jacob Arminius*, II, p. 488.
131 *AC Adrianus van der Borre 1632* (Amsterdam: Broer Jansz, 1632), USTC 1021761.
132 *AC Jacob Cuilemann 1694* (Leiden: Pieter vander Aa, 1694), USTC 1847404.
133 On the legitimacy of this claim, see Anthony Milton, 'A Distorting Mirror: The Hales and Balcanquahall Letters and the Synod of Dort', Aza Goudriaan and Fred van Lieburg (eds.), *Revisiting the Synod of Dort (1618–1619)* (Leiden: Brill, 2011), p. 145.

140   CHAPTER 4

the religious landscape. They constantly referenced and responded to each other's works. The theological world was a complex system in which new books were constantly being written and old books regularly referenced. For ministers, their theological contemporaries were necessary reading. They were some of the most prolific authors at the time, so a minister had to stay abreast of this ongoing work whether they agreed with the author or not. In some cases, like Rivet and Grotius, rather than spurning the books by those with whom they disagreed, more often than not they acquired the books of their opponents as energetically as they would those of their Protestant colleagues.

4   Learning from the Britons

Theological affiliation was not typically a barrier to reading books by other theologians. Ministers recognized the need to understand their contemporaries from a variety of theological perspectives, even if that understanding was only intended to argue against them or to help others steer clear of error. Regardless of theological persuasion, ministers read broadly. There is one important exception to this broad reading: English-language books. These books were almost entirely read by a small group of ministers. This tendency goes back to events that took place between 1599 and 1606.

After touring Europe for seven years, a Dutch minister in his late-twenties resettled in his home country. Travelling with his brother, he had left a single man; now he returned with a wife and a new calling. Despite receiving his doctorate in jurisprudence from Poitiers in September 1603, Willem Teellinck returned to the windswept islands of Zeeland in 1606, boarded in his mother's house for a time and prepared to enter the ministry of the Reformed church. From 1599–1606, Teellinck visited university towns in France, England and Scotland. The final three years of his journey, 1603–1606, would be critical not only in Teellinck's own spiritual and personal growth; in fact, a powerful spiritual movement within Dutch society would trace its beginnings to those few years.

In 1603, the newly minted Doctor of Jurisprudence left Poitiers and returned to the British Isles. He settled in the town of Banbury, in Oxfordshire, and took up with the vibrant Puritan community there. In matters of Sabbath observance, the centrality of the godly family in promoting godliness of character and act, the role of the state in securing and propagating a more purely Reformed society, and many others, Teellinck left Banbury as a Dutch Puritan.[134]

---

134   Willem Op 't Hof, *Willem Teellinck (1579–1629): Leven, Geschriften en Invloed* (Kampen: De Groot Goudriaan, 2008), pp. 74–80; idem, 'The eventful sojourn of Willem Teellinck

GUARDIANS OF THE FAITH

Teellinck did not pioneer the journey from the Netherlands to Britain and back. The two nations were united in the cauldron of religious persecution and political strife. They had close economic ties, such that English merchants could be found throughout the Republic. When civil war erupted in the Habsburg Netherlands, beginning in the 1560s, thousands fled to Germany and England. These weary travellers banded together and formed substantial immigrant communities in their temporary homes. The number of Dutch refugees in London alone is staggering. In the 1560s, the Dutch stranger church tripled in size to nearly 2,000 men, women, and children.[135] At the same time, almost forty per cent of Norwich's population were Dutch refugees.[136] Less than fifty years later, tens of thousands of English and Scottish refugees would flee to the Netherlands.[137] By 1623, the English Reformed church in Amsterdam had grown to six times its size in 1607, from 68 members to 450.[138] English communities settled in Holland and Zeeland, fleeing religious persecution as their hosts had fifty years earlier.

With this cultural and religious exchange came a growing desire amongst many in the Netherlands to read the works of their contemporaries across the English Channel. Numerous works trace the development of translations from English to Dutch. Paul Hoftijzer, Willem J. op 't Hof and Cornelis W. Schoneveld demonstrate the pervasiveness of such translations.[139] The printing industries of the two nations were deeply intertwined. On 29 May 1639, William Laud, archbishop of Canterbury, heard from Jean la Maire in Leiden that the States General were willing to set out a general proclamation over all the Provinces against libelous books, and particularly those from Scotland.[140] Some Dutch ministers encouraged English ministers to write and publish for the benefit

---

(1579–1629) at Banbury in 1605', *Journal for the History of Reformed Pietism* 1 (2015), pp. 5–34.

135 Andrew Pettegree, *Foreign Protestant Communities in Sixteenth-Century London* (Oxford: Clarendon Press, 1986), p. 182.

136 Geoffrey Parker, *The Dutch Revolt* (New York: Penguin Books, 1978), p. 118.

137 Keith Sprunger, *Dutch Puritanism: A History of English and Scottish Churches of the Netherlands in the Sixteenth and Seventeenth Centuries* (Leiden: Brill, 1982), p. 5.

138 Ibid., p. 6.

139 P. G. Hoftijzer, *Engelse boekverkopers bij de Beurs: De geschiedenis van de Amsterdamse Boekhandels Bruyning en Swart, 1637–1724* (Amsterdam/Maarssen: APA-Holland Universiteits Pers, 1987); Willem Op 't Hof, *Engelse piëtistische geschriften in het Nederlands, 1598–1622* (Rotterdam: Lindenberg, 1987); Cornelis W. Schoneveld, *Intertraffic of the Mind: Studies in Seventeenth-Century Anglo-Dutch Translation with a Checklist of Books Translated from English into Dutch, 1600–1700* (Published for the Sir Thomas Browne Institute; Brill, Leiden University Press: Leiden, 1983).

140 UB Leiden PAP 2.

142   CHAPTER 4

of the Dutch Reformed. A preacher from Zoutelande in Zeeland (1626–1628) wrote from the Dutch church in London to Arthur Hildersham. Timotheus van Vleteren (d. 1641) had studied in Leiden and enjoyed the English Puritan's lectures on John 4 so much that he sent several copies to his countrymen in the Republic. The group of ministers were captivated by the book. The Dutch ministers encouraged Hildersham to print his sermons on Psalm 51 'and other lucubrations'. 'Since the Sermons already on part of the Psalme, do arise to just a full volume, be entreated to hearken to the desires of so many at home and abroad.... Do not hold back any part of their [the sermons] service to the Church, for the present time'.[141] Dutch ministers engaged in English religious life. During the Brownist controversy in the 1620s, John Forbes of Corse, an organizer of the English Synod in the United Provinces (1621–28) wrote to bring theological and organization structure to the disparate communities of exiles. His tract, *Instructiones historico-theologicae de doctrina Christiana*, was met with much approval from his Dutch counterparts. Many Dutch theologians added their endorsement, including the faculty of theology at Leiden, Gisbertus Voetius, Carolus de Maets, Johannes Hoornbeeck, Johannes Cloppenburch, Johannes Cocceius, Samuel Maresius and André Rivet.[142]

At the heart of the work to translate English to Dutch, stood Dutch Reformed ministers, who were often the translators of these works (Fig. 4.2). Willem Teellinck himself served as translator for numerous English Puritan works. Vincentius Meusevoet, minister in Schagen near Alkmaar until his death in 1624, translated forty English books into Dutch.[143] Lewis Bayly's *De practycke ofte oeffeninghe der godzaligheydt (The Practice of Piety)* went through no fewer than fifty Dutch editions from 1620–1700. By the end of the seventeenth century, 850 Puritan books were published in Dutch.[144] With average print runs of near a thousand books per edition, over 1,275,000 translated Puritan books circulated through the seventeenth-century Dutch book market.[145]

---

141   Samuel Clarke, *A Generall Martyrologie, containing a Collection of all the greatest Perse-cutions which have befallen the Church of Christ from the Creation to our present Times. Whereunto are added the lives of sundry modern Divines famous in their Generations for Learning and Piety, and most of them Great Sufferers in the Cause of Christ.* (London: Thomas Underhill and John Rothwell, 1651), p. 382.

142   James Eglinton, 'Scottish-Dutch Reformed Theological Links in the Seventeenth Century,' *Dutch Crossing: Journal of Low Countries Studies*, 37 (2013), p. 136.

143   Op 't Hof, *Engelse piëtistische geschriften in het Nederlands*, pp. 441–445.

144   Op 't Hof, 'Piety in the wake of trade: The North Sea as an intermediary of Reformed piety up to 1700', in Juliette Roding and Lex Heerma van Voss (eds.), *The North Sea and Culture (1550–1800)* (Hilversum: Verloren, 1996), p. 255.

145   Willem Op 't Hof, 'Unique Information on a Seventeenth-Century Printing House in Arnhem. The dedication by the Arnhem printer Jacob van Biesen (d. 1677) in the 1669 edition of *Fonteyne des levens* by Arthur Hildersham (1563–1632) and its implications

GUARDIANS OF THE FAITH

In the introduction to a 1685 Dutch translation of Henry Hammond's *Practikale catechismus* [*Practical Catechism*], Caspar Brandt summarized Hammond's biography because Dutch readers had little knowledge of him 'since our writer is not well known in this land, because of much ignorance of the English language and books'.[146] Though this was certainly the case amongst the general public, ministers often had some understanding of English. In the preface to his English-Dutch *Dictionary*, a retired English soldier named Henry Hexham regarded ministers as part of his target audience. He recognised 'that there are many pious theologians, students, and others, among the Dutch willing to learn our English language'.[147] Fifty years later in 1703, Jacques Bernard noted a similar phenomenon: 'there are several Churchmen who have learned enough [English] in a very short time, such that they make their profit in theology books written in English'.[148] The English Puritan theologian John Owen (1616–1683) acknowledged that the professors in Dutch academies 'have all generally learned the English tongue, to enable them for the understanding of the treatises of divinity in all kinds written therein'.[149]

Some ministers assuredly taught themselves English through the use of dictionaries, grammars, and A.B.C books. Others received some sort of formal training, either from a private tutor or through an institution of higher education. On Wednesday 18 December 1668, Joan Caegman advertised his services in the *Oprechte Haerlemse Courant*.[150] Caegman, a teacher in the French School in Hoorn, wanted it to be known he ran a well-ordered school, where reading, writing and arithmetic were taught expertly in French. Italian

---

for the history of books', *Quaerendo*, 43 (2013), pp. 214–237. On print runs in general, see Bert van Selm, 'Onderzoek naar volkslectuur in de vroegmoderne tijd', in his, *Inzichten en Vergezichten. Zes beschouwingen over het onderzoek naar de geschiedenis van de Nederlandse boekhandel* (Amsterdam: De Buitenkant, 1992), p. 68.

146 'Doch aangezien onze Schrijver hier te lande weinig bekendt is, wegens veeler onkunde van d'Engelsche taal en boecken'. Caspar Brandt, 'Voorreden aan den Christelijcken Leser', in Henrick Hammond, *Practikale catechismus, dat is Onderwijzing in de christelijke religie* (Rotterdam: Barent Bos, 1685), USTC 1825544, f. **3r.

147 "Datter vele Godtsalige *Theologanten, Studenten*, ende andere, van de Nederlanders, genegen zijn, om onse Engelsche tale te leeren." Henry Hexham, 'Voor-reden' to *A Copious English and Nederduytch* [sic] *Dictionarie* (Rotterdam: Arnoud Leers, 1648), USTC 1514701, f. *3.

148 Jacques Bernard, *Nouvelles de la République des Lettres* (Amsterdam: Henry Desbordes and Daniel Pain, January 1703), p. 50.

149 John Owen, 'The Epistolary Dedicatory', in William H. Goold (ed.), *The Works of John Owen*, vol. 12 (Edinburgh: T&T Clark, 1862), p. 7.

150 Oprechte Haerlemsche Courant *12.12.1668*. Cf. Arthur der Weduwen and Andrew Pettegree, *News, Business and Public Information. Advertisements and Announcements in Dutch and Flemish Newspapers, 1620–1675* (Leiden: Brill, 2020), p. 335. My thanks to Hanna de Lange who directed me to this advertisement.

144   CHAPTER 4

accounting, music singing and other practical tasks would be mastered by his
students. In case potential students (or their parents) were not interested in
French, he could also teach them the English language. He boasted that they
could learn it as if they were living in England.[151] During the 1610s, a band of
about one hundred English separatists bound ultimately for the New World
sojourned in Leiden. Now immortalised as the Pilgrim Fathers, these mostly
poor refugees found work in whatever ways they could. William Brewster, a
publisher of religious works and later a minister, taught English to students
at Leiden University. William Bradford, the Governor of the Plymouth Colony,
recounted that Brewster,

> Fell into a way (by reason he had the Latin tongue) to teach many stu-
> dents, who had a desire to learn the English tongue ... and by his method
> they quickly attained it with great facility; for he drew rules to learn it by,
> after the Latin manner; and many gentlemen, both Danes and Germans,
> resorted to him.[152]

Desire to read English writers in their native tongue stemmed not from a
respect to the language itself, but from the desire of Dutch ministers to return
to the sources, unsullied by the eyes of the translator. Several ministers, in fact,
despised English, but they thought it useful to know the language. A minister of
the Dutch church in Yarmouth praised some works by his adopted country men.
'I have had the opportunity of acquainting myself with English books, many have
won my highest esteem'.[153] Nevertheless when translating a work, his verdict
on the language was severe: 'The lisping English language is all languages and
almost completely botched together from all languages of Europe'.[154] Writing
during the Third Anglo-Dutch War, Franciscus Ridderus despised the English.
The Rotterdam minister and author of several historical works on various
European countries (including England) considered the English pre-eminent at
'slandering, cheating, lying, and twisting'. And the language, which was 'patched
together from various languages', was similarly reprehensible.[155]

---

151   'als zijnde natureel ervaren'. Ibid.
152   Quoted in Jeremy D. Bangs, *Strangers and Pilgrims, Travellers and Sojourners: Leiden and
      the Foundations of Plymouth Plantation* (Plymouth, MA: General Society of Mayflower
      Descendants, 2009), p. 451.
153   Charles Wolseley, *De redelykheid van 't schriftuur-geloof*, trans. Johannes Ubelman
      (Utrecht: Willem Broedelet, 1695), USTC 1833449, f. *3v.
154   Edward Stillingfleet, *Origines sacræ, heilige oorsprongkelykheden*, trans. Johannes
      Ubelman (Amsterdam: Ysabrandus Haring, 1690), USTC 1823071, f. *4v.
155   '... lasteren, liegen, verdraeyen, bedriegen, als de Engelsche Natie'. '... uyt verscheyde Talen
      is t'samen gelapt'. Franciscus Ridderus, *Historischen Engels-man, in bysondere Engelsche,*

GUARDIANS OF THE FAITH

Despite this sentiment, ministers utilized their talents in English to serve the true religion. The theological exchange that took place between the English and the Dutch was not only a matter of translating English books into Dutch. Books in the English language were extraordinarily popular within a certain segment of ministers during the Golden Age. Many owned numerous English books. The average collection in this corpus contained fifty-five English vernacular works, half the number of French books they owned and twice the number of German. But this figure is skewed wildly by a subsection of the ministers. Most catalogues of ministers' books list fewer than two English texts. A third of ministers whose collections sold at auction owned no English language books, 82 out of 234. The concentration of English books is clear when one considers the ten collections with the highest number of English books. Forty-one per cent of all English books listed in ministerial book auction catalogues are in those ten collections. Seventy-one per cent of all English-language books are listed in the twenty-five collections with the most English language books. For comparison, the twenty-five catalogues with the most Latin books only amount to thirty-two per cent of all Latin books; for the twenty-five with the most French language books, it is about forty-eight per cent.

TABLE 4.3   Collections with the most English books owned by Dutch ministers. The two
Richard Madens are two different English ministers

Owner	Residence	Total books	English
Richard Maden (1680)	Rotterdam	2,766	1,138
Jacobus Koelman (1695)	Utrecht	2,035	887
Julius Herring (1645)	Amsterdam	1,358	643
Thomas Cawton (1669)	Rotterdam	1,744	528
Johannes Thielen (1692)	Middelburg	2,512	504
Johannes Spademan (1699)	Rotterdam	955	479
Samuel Gruterus (1700)	Rotterdam	4,294	417
Petrus Gribius (1666)	Amsterdam	1,497	380
Richard Maden (1677)	Amsterdam	1,339	375
Jacob Lydius (1680)	Dordrecht	5,391	358

Schotse, en Yersche geschiedenissen, gepast op de onderdruckte staet van ons lieve vader-landt (Rotterdam: Widow of Arnout Leers, 1674), USTC 1811349, p. 20.

146   CHAPTER 4

Four of these ministers served in the English congregations in their town
(Table 4.3). One, Petrus Gribius, was the minister of the German congregation
in Amsterdam. The other five were native Dutch ministers. English language
books were highly concentrated within a few collections. Dutch, French and
German books were owned more widely. Most ministers owned one or two
English books, like they would Italian or Spanish books. Daniel Demetrius
owned three English books: The Book of Common Prayer, the Bible, and a New
Testament. Jacob Arminius owned one English book, the Bible. But some ministers owned far more. Typically ministers in larger cities owned more English
language books than their rural counterparts. Just over three per cent of the collection owned by a minister in a rural town or village were English books. This
can be compared to the eleven per cent in the collections of urban ministers.
Urban ministers had easier access to books that were less commonly available
than Dutch or Latin books. Though Henricus Berdenis in Sluis owned a large
proportion of English books, eighty-six out of 536, he was a rare exception.

Catalogues from the first three decades of the century (1600–1629) contain
less than one per cent of English books. The remaining decades saw more significant ownership of English language books, between about 2.7 per cent in
1630 and 5.9 per cent in 1680.

TABLE 4.4   Average proportion of English book by decade in Dutch
             ministerial library catalogues

Decade	Average (mean) proportion of English books
1600	0.02%
1610	0.107%
1620	0.9%
1630	2.7%
1640	4.88%
1650	2.48%
1660	4.2%
1670	3.16%
1680	6.59%
1690	5.95%

GUARDIANS OF THE FAITH

TABLE 4.5   Median proportion of English books by decade in
Dutch ministerial library catalogues

Decade	Median number of English books
1600	0%
1610	0.08%
1620	0.122%
1630	0%
1640	0.255%
1650	0.62%
1660	0.296%
1670	0.232%
1680	1.45%
1690	0.252%

Ownership of English language books was even more concentrated than these tables suggest (Table 4.4). When one controls for outliers, those figures plummet (Table 4.5). Those ministers who skewed the average of English language texts owned a large number of English Puritan books. Despite the wide availability of Dutch translations, they still acquired hundreds of English books. Theologian and minister Fredrick Spanheim owned as many books in English as he did in his native German. Of his 523 books, Petrus Leupenius (1607–1670), an Amsterdam minister in the Reformed church, owned 156 in Dutch, a high percentage but not extraordinary.[156] He also owned thirty-five English books (about six per cent of his collection), in contrast with only one books in French and six in German. A minister and author of a Dutch grammar, *Aanmerkingen op de Nederduitsche taale* [*Observations on the Dutch Language*], Leupenius may have simply been interested in linguistics.[157] Based on the authors and types of books present, however, Leupenius was interested in the intellectual material emerging from England, especially puritan works.

In Gisbertus Voetius' collection (a total of just over 5,000 works), 328 were written in English, about six per cent of his catalogue. Voetius had a reputation for his affinity with the English Divines. One student claimed, with only a little exaggeration, that Voetius' students read more English than biblical

---

156   *AC Petrus Leupenius 1670* (Amsterdam: Pieter Dircksz I Boeteman, 1670), USTC 1846619.
157   Frijhoff and Spies, *1650: Hard-Won Unity*, pp. 229–230.

148 CHAPTER 4

languages.[158] Gisbertus Voetius used English books in his pastoral endeavour to understand the Bible. While he was a minister in Heusden, at least one English translation helped in his study of the book of Job.[159] If Voetius' English language books were a stand-alone collection it would be larger than the twelve smallest surviving ministerial auction catalogues.

A minister in Arlanderveen owned enough English books to warrant special mention in the newspaper advertisement for the auction of his book collection:

> On Tuesday 9 September there will be auctioned the books of D. Johannis Naminck, former preacher at Arlanderveen, consisting of many Latin, Dutch and English books. The auction will take place at the house of Joost Pluymer in Amsterdam, where the catalogue can be found, as well as with Steven Swart in Amsterdam and with Johannes Ribbius in Utrecht.[160]

If a Dutch minister owned English-language books that were not the Book of Common Prayer or the Bible, they were almost certainly by Puritan theologians. Just under 2,000 English language books are listed in the fifty-five auction catalogues transcribed. Only 156, less than one-tenth of the total, were non-religious works: Of the theological books, almost all were written by authors with Puritan sensibilities (Table 4.6). Most of these authors advocated for a more Reformed understanding of theology and church government within the Anglican church. Ministers like Richard Sibbes, William Prynne and others are illustrative of this movement. Gisbertus Voetius recommended reading Sibbes, Bolton and others alongside Calvin's *Institutes* and other puritan-minded Dutch theologians like Godefridus Udemans and Willem Teellinck. These English authors helped provide a framework for the Reformed ideal.

---

158   Willem J. Op 't Hof, 'Geïmporteerde Vroomheid? De Zeventiende-Eeuwse Nederlandse Gereformeerde Vroomheid in Internationaal Perspectief', in Karel Davids et al. (eds.), *De Republiek Tussen Zee En Vasteland. Buitenlandse Invloeden Op Cultuur, Economie En Politiek in Nederland 1580–1800*, (Leuven: Garant, 1995), p. 88. On Voetius and his affection for English Puritans, see Helmer J. Helmers, *The Royalist Republic: Literature, Politics, and Religion in the Anglo-Dutch Public Sphere, 1639–1660* (Cambridge: Cambridge University Press, 2015), p. 67; Willem J. Op 't Hof, 'Piety in the Wake of Trade: The North Sea as an Intermediary of Reformed Piety up to 1700,' in Juliette Roding and Heerma Van Voss, *The North Sea and Culture (1550–1800): Proceedings of the International Conference Held at Leiden 21–22 April 1995* (Hilversum, Netherlands: Verloren, 1996), p. 259.

159   A. C. Duker, *Gisbertus Voetius* (4 vols., reprint; Leiden: Groen en Zoon, 1989), I, p. 374.

160   *Amsteldamsche Dingsdaegse Courant*, 35. 02.09.1670. Pettegree and Der Weduwen, *News, Business and Public Information*, p. 393.

GUARDIANS OF THE FAITH 149

TABLE 4.6 Seventeen most common authors of English language books in
Dutch ministerial library catalogues

Author	Number of instances
Richard Sibbes	30
William Prynne	24
John Downame	24
Andrew Willet	23
John Preston	22
Richard Baxter	22
Jeremiah Burroughs	21
Joseph Hall	20
Thomas Goodwin	20
John Weemse	16
Samuel Rutherford	16
John Brinsley	15
Robert Bolton, Thomas Gataker, Paul Bayne, Nicholas Byfield, William Fulke	14

Dutch ministers read the widely available Dutch translations of English
Puritan works less frequently. As listed in ministerial library catalogues, the
most popular English language author, Richard Sibbes, is far less common in
Dutch translation. Dutch translations of his works are only listed six times.
The Dutch translations of books by William Prynne are only listed three times.
Of the fifteen most common English authors, Dutch translations of their
works are listed only a third as many times as their English originals. Joseph
Hall, whose works were important to pietists on the continent, and Nicholas
Byfield were rare exceptions to this trend. The same number of Dutch trans-
lations of Hall's works were listed in ministerial auction catalogues as those
in the English original. Eleven copies of translations by Byfield are listed.
For those ministers who read books by English Puritans, the original English
was preferred.

Dutch ministers who shared the English Puritan zeal for all-encompassing
piety acknowledged this explicitly. Some Dutch theologians were charged with
pillaging sermons and books by English ministers without acknowledgment.
Bishop Thomas Sprat alleged:

150   CHAPTER 4

> Our famous Divines have been innumerable, as the Dutch Men may wit-
> ness, who, in some of their Theological Treatises, have been as Bold with
> the English Sermons, as with our Fishing; and their Robberies have been
> so manifest, that our Church ought to have Reprizals against them, as
> well as our Merchants.[161]

In the dedication to a popular Dutch translation of *Fonteyne des levens* [*The Fount of Life*] by Arthur Hildersham, the printer made special note of why he printed the book. In 1669 Jacob van Biesen described why the book was worthy of translation and publication: 'owing to their excellence and outstanding doctrines have for their merits been sent to the press and printed no fewer than three times since the year 1646 by Jacob van Biesen at Arnhem'.[162] Between 1646 and 1669, Van Biesen printed over 4,000 copies, about 1,400 copies per edition. Jacob Koelman, a minister in Sluis until he was summarily banished for causing too much trouble with the town's more moderate magistrates, owned a substantial number of English-language books. As Koelman was a translator of many Puritan books into Dutch, this is not surprising. Koelman made clear why he appreciated English Puritans as much as he did. Koelman considered them the epitome of the Reformed ideal. 'The reason why in this process I do not follow so much the Heidelberg Catechism as I do the Westminster Shorter Catechism of England, Scotland, and Ireland', Koelman wrote

> is simply that the latter is in all respects superior. Why should we not
> honestly acknowledge such an obvious truth? It would be good if the
> church of the Netherlands would be willing to learn and take over a vari-
> ety of things from the Churches of England and Scotland, things that they
> formulated in their church order and other formularies more clearly in
> accordance with God's word than our church has done.[163]

A diverse range of theological books could be found in almost any catalogue of a minister's library. But English language books were almost entirely the domain of a few. For those ministers who did acquire great numbers of books by authors like Richard Sibbes, William Perkins, Richard Baxter and John Davenant, ownership was a token of their aspiration for a particular application of the Reformed faith, one that left no aspect of life untouched. Voetius,

---

161   Quoted in Schoneveld, *Intertraffic of the Mind*, p. 123.
162   Op 't Hof, 'Unique Information on a Seventeenth-Century Printing House in Arnhem',
        p. 230.
163   Koelman, *The Duties of Parents*, p. 31.

GUARDIANS OF THE FAITH   151

Udemans, Koelman and the like considered English Puritans as the truest expression of the Christian faith, and they identified with them to such an extent that they acquired dozens and sometimes hundreds of books to signal the kinship they felt.

5   Trained in Righteousness

The theological books listed in ministerial book auction catalogues were written by a diverse range of authors. No single author and no confessional perspective had a monopoly on their collections. As good Protestants, Bibles were the most commonly listed books in their catalogues. Reading theological books, most especially the Bible, helped prepare ministers for their calling: understanding the Bible, teaching it to their flocks and encouraging them to live godly lives.

A common assumption amongst literary figures is that the library serves as the standard and defender of the owner's orthodoxy. The novelist John Updike portrayed the books of Reformed theologians contained in the library of his character Clarence Wilmont, a Presbyterian minister and former Princeton Seminary student, as a bulwark against the derision of unreformed thinkers. 'This wall of accumulated titles', Updike wrote, 'should have fortified him forever'.[164] Describing the brazen and intrepid Cousin Nancy, T. S. Eliot portrayed the books by historical figures as looking on in disdain at her smoking and modern dancing: 'Upon the glazen shelves kept watch // Matthew and Waldo, guardians of the faith, // the army of unalterable law'.[165] These descriptions ring true in certain aspects of the libraries owned by ministers in the Dutch Golden Age. Theological compatriots were certainly read to encourage and inspire the reader. Some books, especially English-language books, were owned as a reminder of the Reformed ideal to which some ministers aspired. But ministers owned many books that also directly opposed their convictions.

Dutch ministers acquired theological books with little regard for their theological orthodoxy. Even Socinian books were common in their collections. Matthew Slade entreated Dudley Carleton in January of 1618 to look after a Socinian tract that he had sent from Amsterdam. Slade claimed that finding the book required much effort and that he did not know if he could acquire another. 'The Socinian Catechism which I sent to your L[ord] I desire may

---

164   John Updike, *In the Beauty of the Lilies* (London: Penguin Books, 1996), p. 14.
165   T. S. Eliot, 'Cousin Nancy', in Christopher Ricks and Jim McCue (eds.), *The Poems of T. S. Eliot* (2 vols., Baltimore: Johns Hopkins University Press, 2015), I, p. 24.

bee safe, for I know no ready meanes to get another'.[166] A few months before in October, Slade described the book he was sending and the difficulty with which he came by it:

> The book I got from Danswijck [Danzig] with much adoe. And I have no other copy thereof. In this city [Amsterdam] there were of late certein other small works of Socinus to bee sold, but very deare. If your L[ord] desire, I will either send hereafter such others as I have, which are divers or buij for your L[ord] such as I can get.[167]

If Dutch ministers had similar issues acquiring such books, it is not obvious from their catalogues. Books by Fausto Sozzini are listed over 150 times in the fifty-five catalogues I have transcribed, an average of over three books per catalogue. The Rakow professor Johannes Crellius had at least 96 works listed in ministerial auction catalogue. Twenty-five books by Johannes Volkelius are listed.

Ministers read in the pursuit of truth. This compelled them to acquire books from a range of perspectives. Books with which a minister disagreed served not only to sharpen their own understanding of an issue, but occasionally they even profited from them. The theological process amongst Dutch ministers was one that sought to understand God and his creation. This allowed them to appropriate information from a range of sources. Human authors, even those with whom a reader often vehemently disagreed, could be helpful in striving for greater religious understanding. As Henk van den Belt states, 'The Reformed orthodox theologians rather understand theology as the pilgrim-theology of human beings that dimly but trustworthily reflects the eternal truths of God himself, the *theologia archetypa*'.[168] The first concern of a minister was to understand Scripture rightly. In order to communicate timeless truths effectively and show how they applied to their contemporaries in the pews, seventeenth-century Dutch ministers acquired hundreds and sometimes thousands of theological books.

---

166 Matthew Slade to Dudley Carleton, 17 January 1618, in Willem Nijenhuis (ed.), *Matthew Slade (1569–1628): Letters to the English Ambassador* (Leiden: E. J. Brill/Leiden University Press, 1986), p. 77.

167 Matthew Slade to Dudley Carleton, 20 October 1617, in Ibid., p. 61.

168 Van den Belt, 'Luther in Dutch Reformed Orthodoxy', pp. 438–439.

CHAPTER 5

Learned Servants

The flock of Godefridus Udemans, a pastor from Zeeland, epitomised the image of a 'Dutch seafaring people'. They built their lives on the sea and its fruits. The windswept islands bordering modern day Belgium were a central node in the web of Dutch trade. During the Dutch Golden Age, Zeeland's economic output was only outmatched by Holland. Ships from France, Portugal and the East and West Indies arrived in Zeeland, leaving salt, wine, sugar and exotic fruits for processing in one of its many factories and refineries. In the 1520s, Zeeland emerged as Europe's centre for salt-refining. By 1526, over seventy-seven salt boiling kettles operated in Zierikzee alone.[1] For the founding of the Dutch West India Company in 1621, the company's five chambers had to raise the necessary capital to get the enterprise off the ground. Zeeland contributed 1,379,775 gulden, and was only surpassed by the Amsterdam chamber, which contributed 2,846,520 gulden.[2] Men left their homes in merchant towns like Vlissingen, Middelburg and Zierikzee, to board vessels bound for new worlds. During the forty years that Udemans devoted to them from 1604 to 1649, with only brief sojourns in The Hague and Den Bosch as an interim pastor, he witnessed the birth of countless young boys, baptized them, and watched them develop into the doggedly tough men needed for a life on the open ocean, knowing that many of them would never return. A thriving hub for sea trade had its accompanying dangers and possibilities.

Zeeland was also a bastion for the Reformed faith. In the seventeenth century, the Netherlands was one of the most religiously diverse countries in Western Europe. Despite the initial spark of the Reformation sweeping through the Habsburg Lowlands in the 1520s and coming to its highest pitch in the 1560s, many did not commit to the Reformed church. Some remained loyal to Roman Catholicism; others identified with one of many Protestant churches found in the Netherlands. Most, though, attended their local Reformed church as sympathizers (*liefhebbers*), but did not place themselves under the disciplinary care of the local elders.[3] Concentrations of people with a range of expressed

---

1   Jonathan I. Israel, *Dutch Primacy in World Trade, 1585–1740* (Oxford: Clarendon Press, 1989), p. 22.

2   Ibid., p. 159.

3   Judith Pollmann, *Religious choice in the Dutch Republic: The reformation of Arnoldus Buchelius (1565–1641)* (Manchester: Manchester University Press, 1999), p. 8; Alastair Duke, 'The Ambivalent Face of Calvinism', in his *Reformation and Revolt in the Low Countries* (London:

© KONINKLIJKE BRILL NV, LEIDEN, 2023 | DOI:10.1163/9789004538191_006

religious identities could be found in cities throughout the Republic. Woerden, near Utrecht, had the highest concentration of Lutherans in the Netherlands and many Remonstrants, such that those attending the Reformed Church were in the minority.[4] Other cities and provinces were more homogenous in their religious practice, like Zeeland. Zeeland became the seedbed for a movement within the Dutch church that would join the call for a purely Reformed church and society.[5] Some of its ministers, often with the levers of political power in their hands, pushed towards the further application of Protestant doctrine into the daily lives of citizens, sailors and regents alike.

Ministers could not escape questions on the intersection of daily life and piety. How can a Christian faithfully work as a mariner? Could he pursue financial gain, and if so, how? Pastors felt a duty to take up the daily concerns of their flock and to persuade them to pursue a thoroughly Christian life. They sought to make a vast and formidable world understandable, demonstrating how Scripture applied to every area of life, from seafaring to one's hair style.[6] The Bibles was to reform every aspect of life.

During the seventeenth century, a minister and his church occupied a unique position in Dutch society. In a young, decentralized republic, the ties that bound communities together were necessary to maintain a free and peaceful society. A shared national faith helped provide stability. Church buildings themselves served a unifying purpose. The main church buildings and the city hall dwarfed all other buildings. A citizen of Leiden could not walk its streets and fail to see the Pieterskerk or Hooglandse Kerk looming over the surrounding buildings (Fig. 5.1). Dordrecht's Grote Kerk (now the Dordrecht Minster) was built on the banks of the Maas river, unavoidable by any who sailed into the town's harbour.

A local church provided social bonds and fostered communal development. More often than not, a person would not move away from the church or town in which they were born. A significant part of their life would consist of being accountable to that group, bearing the expectations and burdens

---

Hambledon and London, 2003), pp. 269–272; Herman Roodenburg, *Onder censuur: de kerkelijke tucht in de gereformeerde gemeente van Amsterdam, 1578–1700* (Hilversum: Verloren, 1990), p. 137.

4   Willem Frijhoff, *Fulfilling God's Mission: The Two Worlds of Dominie Everardus Bogardus, 1607–1647*, trans. Myra Heerspink Scholz (Leiden: Brill, 2007), p. 12.

5   Willem J. Op 't Hof, 'De Nadere Reformatie in Zeeland. Een eerste schets', in A. Wiggers, et al. (eds.), *Rond de kerk in Zeeland* (Delft: Eburon, 1991), pp. 37–82; H. Uil, 'De Nadere Reformatie en het onderwijs in Zeeland in de zeventiende eeuw', *Documentatieblad Nadere Reformatie* 25 (2001), pp. 1–18.

6   Dirk van Miert, 'The "Hairy War" (1640–50): Historicizing the Bible in the Dutch Republic on the Eve of Spinoza', *Sixteenth Century Journal*, 49 (2015), pp. 415–436.

of their community. Alexis de Tocqueville's explanation of religion's role in the American Republic certainly applies to its Dutch forebearer: 'Religion ... should therefore be considered as the first of their political institutions; for if it does not give them the taste for freedom, it singularly facilitates their use of it'.[7] Churches were the meeting houses of the Dutch Republic.

At the heart of this institution was the minister. Ministers occupied a unique position in the life and culture of a town. The congregation gathered to encourage one another in the faith, and the strongest expression of this was attentively listening to sermons. Though a church congregation in the Netherlands could range from a few souls to many hundreds, they were united under the preached word. The minister took on a civic role helping to bind the fragile communities together in shared belief and practice. He preached multiple times a week, and when possible attended to the catechising of the members, as well as comforted the sick and dying. Ministers helped shape their congregations' understanding of God, creation, and His expectations for their lives. What Harry Stout states of eighteenth-century New England ministers, equally applies to ministers in the Dutch Golden Age: they 'supplied all the key terms necessary to understand existence in this world and the next'.[8] When faithful to his charge, the minister mediated between his congregation and the occurrences that shaped their lives. From the pulpit to the deathbed, the ideal minister tirelessly encouraged and exhorted those in their flocks to pursue godliness.

Godefridus Udemans was one such minister. In 1638, he published 't geestelyck roer van 't coopmans schip [The Spiritual Rudder of the Merchant's Ship]. A moderately popular ethical handbook on the Christian method of seafaring, it would go through three editions by 1655. The Spiritual Rudder was not an abstract devotional work about loving one's neighbour, divorced from the everyday concerns of the seafarer.[9] It discussed topics of immediate relevance: there are chapters on bankruptcy, paying of servants, the dangers of brandy and tobacco, the discovery of the Americas, the duties of naval officers and much else besides. With traditional Christian proverbs and precepts, Udemans exhorted all who would pursue commercial gains to cherish virtue and a godly reputation above material prosperity. Virtue ought to reign supreme over the corrupting desire for money for its own sake.

---

7 Alexis de Tocqueville, *Democracy in America*, ed. and trans. Harvey C. Mansfield and Delba Winthrop (Chicago: University of Chicago Press, 2000), p. 280.

8 Harry S. Stout, *The New England Soul: Preaching and Religious Culture in Colonial New England* (Oxford: Oxford University Press, 1986), p. 3.

9 Maria A. Schenkeveld-van der Dussen, 'Cultural Participation as Stimulated by the Seventeenth-Century Reformed Church', in Ann Rigney and Douwe Fokkema (eds.), *Cultural Participation: Trends Since the Middle Ages* (Amsterdam/Philadelphia: J. Benjamins, 1993), pp. 39–49.

156 CHAPTER 5

Udemans' knowledge of seafaring came from two sources: conversations with local sailors and his library. The Zierikzee minister was a prolific reader on economics, politics, war and foreign lands, all topics of use to a minister hoping to care for the needs of the godly merchant or seafarer. With references ranging from the classical authors like Cicero and Plato, to the Bible and to the most popular political theorists of his day, Udemans made his case 'that *Commerce* is an *honest activity*, as long as it is pursued in justice and the fear of the Lord'.[10] Commerce, like all other aspects of life, should be governed by the application of Christian faith. Informed by his books, Godefridus Udemans took up his pen to write about a topic of public significance and sought to bring about a more Reformed society. Seeking to convince the reading public, Udemans would go on to write numerous tracts not only on theological questions, but also synthesizing other aspects of human endeavour with the Reformed faith.

Ministers devoted themselves to reading about far more than theology. While Bibles, commentaries, theological treatises and devotional works composed the bulk of their books, their collections would often include dozens, if not hundreds of books not directly intended for religious ends. Often these are listed in their catalogues as *Libri miscellani*. The average collection that sold at auction contained over 350 books in this section. Scientific and medical works, political theories, jurisprudence, handbooks on economics, military strategy and even books on agriculture: books from this broad range of topics were regularly listed in ministerial library catalogues.

During the seventeenth century, ministers were the largest group of academically trained professionals in the Dutch Republic. Ordinary citizens would have had far more personal contact with a minister than with any other similarly educated person. Unlike university trained lawyers and doctors, who were concentrated in the urban centres of Holland, ministers were dispersed around the Republic: some were part of the urban elite of Amsterdam, Leiden and Rotterdam, others working in the smallest inland villages of Overijssel or the sandy outposts of Zeeland.

Ministers played a necessary role in the structure of the nation. With the pen and pulpit, they had the means of stirring up controversy or helping to maintain concord. In 1630, one Remonstrant pamphleteer warned the magistrates of the frenzy which Orthodox ministers could spark from the pulpit: 'The magistrates would do well to be wary of those to whom they entrust the

---

10   'dat de Koopmanschap is eene eerlijcke handelinge, als die maer gedreven wordt in de gerechtigheyt, ende vreese des Heeren'. Godefridus Udemans, *'t geestelyck roer van 't coopmans schip* (Dordrecht: Françoys Boels, 1655), USTC 1820028, f. *4.

LEARNED SERVANTS

pulpit ... the listeners are stirred up as quickly as the sea by a stiff breeze'.[11] In 1650, Jacob Stermont, a minister in The Hague, wrote an invective against the regents of Amsterdam who, he alleged, were conspiring to suppress true religion, reminding them of the influence ministers exercised over the public:

> For else, seeing that their priestly garb is scorched, and true Religion undermined ... they might well awake from their sleep, and be roused to a holy zeal all over the country, so that they will publicly inform and caution the congregations against the fatal and offensive plans of many governments.... Mind, what so many hundreds of ministers as there presently are in the country could affect if they would join forces to protect their religion and the right of the Church, entrusted to them by God, and choose the righteous side of his Highness [William II].[12]

The role of a minister was not narrowly religious or theological, divorced from the ordinary cares of their congregation. Stermont, like other ministers at the time, recognized the importance he and his colleagues had for the peace and prosperity of their nation. Ministers understood themselves as public figures, with a measure of responsibility for the general welfare of their community.

1   Men of Letters

Universities equipped ministers for their roles as public figures capable of discussing issues relevant to those in the pews. They received a thorough

---

11   Johannes Wtenbogaert, *Discours op ende teghen de conscientieuse bedenckinghen, ofmen in goede conscientie trefves met Spaengien maken mach* (Haarlem: Jacob de Wit, 1630), USTC 1026450, quoted in Craig E. Harline, *Pamphlets, Printing, and Political Culture in the Early Dutch Republic* (Dordrecht: Martinus Nijhoff, 1987), p. 153.

12   '... want andersints siende dat haren Priesterlijcken mantel gesengt, ende den waren Gods-dienst onder-mijnt wert, ende datmen dan nich in openbare gal-schriften haer overhaelt, 't ist te vresen, datse uit den slaep waker gemaeckt, ende tot een Heiligen yver opgeweckt sullen werden 't gantsche Lant door, ende datese den gemeinten van de Heiloosheit en de ergerlijcke voornemens veler harer overheden openbaerlijck sullen onder-rechten ender waerschouwen ... Ick geve u te bedencken wat so veel hondert Predikanten, alsser nuin 't Landt sijn, souden konnen doen wanneer sy te samenspannende, haren Gods-dienst voorstaen, het recht der Kerke haer van Godt gegeven beschermen, ende de recht meinende zijde van sijn Hoogheyt kiesen souden willen'. C. G. [= Jacobus Stermont], *Lauweren-krans gevlochten voor syn hoocheyt, Wilhelm, de Heer de Prince van Oranjen, &c. Over sijne eeuwig roembaere handelinge, gepleegt tot ruste deser Vereenigde Lantschappen, in't Jaer 1650* (s.n., s.l. [1650]), USTC 1035032, ff. D2v–D3.

education in all theological topics, as expected: biblical studies (including Greek and Hebrew), church history and systematic theology. But their education did not prepare them solely to be a theological commentator. A typical course in theology often included studies in political theory, jurisprudence, science and medicine, ethics, economics and geography. When he completed his course of study, an aspiring minister was a man of letters.[13] Or in the words of an eighteenth-century Dutch minister, they were erudite theologians.[14]

Dutch ministers followed a long line of Christian writers who addressed every-day cares and expected other ministers to have a thorough understanding of most academic disciplines. In his dedication to *'t geestelyck roer*, Udemans favourably cited the Church Fathers Cassiodorus and John Chrysostom and the medieval scholastic Thomas Aquinas in defence of commerce.[15] The Zurich Reformer, Heinrich Bullinger (1504–1575) reminded readers of his *Ratio studiorum* that the Apostle Paul and the Church Fathers understood and made use of pagan authors.[16] Andreas Hyperius (1511–1564), professor of theology at Marburg, encouraged students to understand classical writers, mathematics, science, music, astronomy, economics, history, architecture and even agriculture.[17] John Calvin encouraged Christians to pursue their vocations with diligence and earnestness, because it was an expression of their worship of God. Calvin argued that learning from other subjects in addition to theology was not only acceptable, it was praiseworthy. 'If the Lord has willed that we be helped in physics, dialectic, mathematics and other like disciplines, by the work and ministry of the ungodly, let us use this assistance. For if we neglect God's gift freely offered in these arts, we ought to suffer just punishment for our sloth'.[18] Calvin celebrated the ability of these studies to enlighten the Christian mind.[19]

---

13   Richard Muller, 'Calling, Character, Piety, and Learning: Paradigms for Theological Education in the Era of Protestant Orthodoxy', in his *After Calvin: Studies in the Development of a Theological Tradition* (Oxford: Oxford University Press, 2003), p. 118.

14   Jona Willem te Water, *De theologo erudito* (Leiden: Sam. en Joh. Luchtmans, 1790). Cf. Joris van Eijnatten, '*Theologus Eruditus, Theologus Modestus*: The Early Modern Pastor as Communication Worker', in Theo Clemens and Wim Janse (eds.), *The Pastor Bonus: Papers read at the British-Dutch Colloquium at Utrecht, 18–21 September 2002* (Leiden: Brill, 2002), pp. 309–318.

15   Udemans, *'t geestelyck roer*, ff. *3r–*4v.

16   Muller, 'Calling, Character, and Piety', p. 107.

17   Andreas Hyperius, *De sacrae scripturae lectione ac meditatione quitidiana, omnibus omnium ordinum hominibus Christianis perquam necessaria, libri II* (Basel: Johan Oporinus, 1561), USTC 631410, pp. 45–80.

18   John Calvin, *Institutes of the Christian Religion*, ed. J. T. McNeill, trans. F. L. Battles (2 vols, Philadelphia: Westminster Press, 1960), I, p. 275 (2.2.16).

19   Ibid., p. 53 (1.5.2).

Gisbertus Voetius (1589–1676), a professor of theology at Utrecht, echoed the same message of his Reformed predecessors. He argued ministers ought to be educated in 'logic, metaphysics, politics, ethics and physics, as a minimum, plus a little knowledge of cosmography and geography'.[20] In his inaugural oration, celebrating the elevation of Utrecht's Illustrious School to a university in 1636, Voetius underscored the ways in which knowledge of a broad range of fields would be beneficial to the theologian. Theology was the highest discipline because it investigated God, but history, optics, engineering, geography and hydrography were all useful in their own ways.[21] Guijlelmus Saldenus (1627–1694), a minister in Delft and a student of Voetius, argued that portions of the Bible are difficult to understand without prior training in the 'liberal arts': grammar, rhetoric, dialectic, mathematics, music, geometry and astronomy.[22] Herman Witsius (1636–1708), a professor of theology who taught at Franeker, Utrecht and Leiden, encouraged young ministers to 'consult in no cursory manner those who are masters in the sciences of logic, grammar, and rhetoric' in his textbook on the ministry. He compared learning from the 'school of nature' to the Israelites using the craftsmanship of the Gibeonites, 'whose work was to cleave wood and draw water for use in the sanctuary'.[23]

A minister developed erudition in these diverse subjects principally through his library. Prior to seeking to persuade their congregations through preaching and the broader reading public through print, ministers first did the necessary work of thinking through issues. In his final hours, the Leiden theologian André Rivet reflected 'that I was first persuaded my selfe of the truths of the Gospel which I preached to others'.[24] Heinrich von Diest (1593–1673), a professor at Harderwijk, wrote *De ratione studii theologici necessaria instructio* to aid his students in their pursuit of building a library.[25] In his disputation exhorting ministers to educate themselves broadly, Voetius also included a list of books with which an eager trainee could begin. He included seventeen books,

---

20   'Logica, Metaphysica, Politica, Ethica, Physica ad minimū serio discenda, cū gustu aliquo doctrinae sphaericae ac geographicae ab illis ...'. Gisbertus Voetius, 'Introductio ad Philosophiam Sacram', in his *Diatribae de theologia, philologia, historia et philosophia sacra* (Utrecht: Simon de Vries, 1668), USTC 1557347, p. 130.

21   Gisbertus Voetius, *Sermoen van de nutticheydt der academien ende scholen* (Utrecht: Aegidius and Petrus Roman, 1636), USTC 1029443.

22   Guiljelmus Saldenus, *De Libri varioque eorum, usu et abusu* (Amsterdam: Henrick Boom, 1688), USTC 1821540, p. 202.

23   Herman Witsius, *On the Character of a True Theologian*, ed. J. Ligon Duncan III (Greenville, SC: Reformed Academic Press, 1994) p. 29.

24   Marie du Moulin, *The Last Houers, of the Right Reverend Father in God Andrew Rivet*, trans. G. L. (The Hague: Samuel Brown, 1652), USTC 1803725, p. 16.

25   Heinrich von Diest, *De ratione studii theologici necessari instructio* (Harderwijk: Nicolaes van Wieringen, 1634), USTC 1510759.

160   CHAPTER 5

suggesting that his students read 'Senartus, Jacob Revius, Schulerus, Du Bois, Bassendus, Stephaus Ezickus and all writings against the philosopher Rene Descartes' and six works 'concerning practical philosophy, politics, and jurisprudence'. These six were as follows: Johannes Gronovius, *De centesimos usuris* (1664); Maximilius Sandaeus, *Theologia juridica* (1629); Jacobus Gothofredus, *Tertulliani liber ad nationes, cum not.* (1625); Johan Hottinger, *Juris Hebraeorum leges 261. explicate* (1655); Gisbertus Cocquius, *Hobbes elenchomenos* (1668).[26] This brief list came from his tome, *Exercitia et bibliotheca studiosi theologiae* in which he covered nearly every topic of intellectual investigation and offered a recommended reading list.[27]

André Rivet owned well over a thousand books on topics that had little to do with Bible exposition or personal religious devotion. He was a theologian, but he was always intellectually involved in more than just theology. Twelve years after he was appointed a professor of Hebrew at Leiden University, in 1632, Rivet was chosen by Stadtholder Fredrick Henry to be the personal tutor to his son, William II.[28] While building a collection of theological books that was three or four times the size of most other ministers whose collections sold at auction, he also acquired over a thousand books on topics such as philosophy and ethics, jurisprudence, scientific exploration, and history. Such books would become the foundation of Rivet's work in the Stadtholder's court.

As tutor to William II, Rivet was responsible for helping the young prince develop into a leader on the international stage. Rivet set William on a rigorous course of education, designed to cultivate noble virtues and administrative competence.[29] The Republic needed a morally exemplary stadtholder who could efficiently lead the military. Though it was an honour, Rivet considered this a radical step down from the intellectually stimulating life of the University. 'A new occupation calls me', Rivet wrote in 1631, 'in which I must become a boy again, but in conjunction with a grand boy. If I can give him to the country and to the church as a man, I shall consider my work not badly spent'.[30] Rivet wrote

---

26   Sandaeus: USTC 2007770; Gothofredus: likely, USTC 6808927. '*Senarti, Jac. Revii, Schuleri, Du Bois, Gassendi, Stephani Ezicki*, aliorumque scripta contra Philosophemata Renati des Cartes'. 'Quae Philosophiam practica, Politicam, & jurisprudentiam attingunt'. Voetius, 'Introductio ad Philosophiam Sacram', p. 135.

27   Gisbertus Voetius, *Exercitia et bibliotheca studiosi theologiae* (Utrecht: Willem Strick, 1644), USTC 1029459.

28   Van Opstal, *André Rivet*, p. 12.

29   On William II, see Herbert H. Rowen, *The Princes of Orange: The Stadtholders in the Dutch Republic* (Cambridge: Cambridge University Press, 1988), pp. 77–94.

30   Rivet to Anna Maria van Schurman, 1 March 1632, in *Anna Maria van Schurman: Whether a Christian Woman Should Be Educated and Other Writings From Her Intellectual Circle*, ed.

LEARNED SERVANTS

to Fredrick Henry when the Prince was fifteen. The teenager's handwriting and spelling was nearly barbaric: 'his orthography is vicious and incorrect'.[31]

If not his penmanship, Rivet could help cultivate William's virtue. Reading books was the primary catalyst for turning young William into the man the Republic needed. A prince began his cultivation of martial virtue with study of the Bible.[32] In service to understanding Holy Writ, one would also read the great books of the Western tradition. On the cultivation of virtue and moderation, 'I have spoken to you beforehand about the laudable exercises of the mind in communicating with the mute doctors, by reading of good books that are worthy of you'.[33] A prince was to be well versed in the liberal arts: letters, rhetoric, history and dialectic.[34] With references to writers from antiquity, the Church Fathers, contemporary thinkers and the Bible, Rivet set out a model for the learned statesmen, leading the Republic as a virtuous administrator of the law. To fulfil his duties as the governor of William II, knowledge beyond theology was needed. Rivet was well versed in these subjects. If William had looked to his own tutor, he would have seen an example of such learning.

The intellectual curiosity with which Rivet approached his profession was not abnormal. After transcribing a total of 96,798 items in fifty-five ministerial book collections, we find that over thirty per cent of the corpus falls into these categories of non-theological books. If a minister owned a thousand books, it would not be unusual for three hundred of them to be on a diverse range of non-theological topics. About 2,000 books on political theory and government are listed in fifty-five ministerial auction catalogues, including the works of Machiavelli, Hugo Grotius and Justus Lipsius. A minister in rural Puttershoek, Thomas Laurentius owned a meagre collection of 189 books that contained fourteen books on medicine. The collection owned by Rivet included almost ninety books on political theory, twenty on astronomy and another twenty on science and mathematics.[35] Bernard Somer in Amsterdam owned a collection of books on military theory, war and fortifications, twenty-three works in

---

      and trans. Joyce L. Irwin, The Other Voice in Early Modern Europe (Chicago: University of Chicago Press, 1998) p. 40.

31   's' aheurte à l'orthographe, qui est vicieuse et incorrecte'. J. J. Poelhekke, *Frederik Hendrik: Prins van Oranje. Een biografisch drieluik* (Zutphen: De Walburg Pers, 1978), p. 148.

32   André Rivet, *Instruction du prince chrestien* (Leiden: Jan Maire, 1642), USTC 1015914, p. 59.

33   'Au reste, je vous ai parlé ci devant, des exercises louables de l'esprit, en la cómunication avec les docteurs muets, par le lecture des bons livres, dignes de vous'. Rivet, *Instruction du Prince Chrestien*, p. 454.

34   Rivet, *Instruction du Prince Chrestien*, pp. 33–53.

35   *AC André Rivet 1657* (Leiden: Pieter Leffen, 1657), USTC 1846296.

162   CHAPTER 5

total.[36] Salomon Voltelen in Waspik, a tiny community to the north of Breda, owned fifteen works on jurisprudence.[37] Udemans himself owned seven works of jurisprudence and fifteen works on medicine.[38] Informed by their libraries, ministers stepped into the public sphere to help bring about a more Christian society. They investigated the topics that most affected the lives of their congregants and they offered a synthesis of such knowledge. They endeavoured to present a cogent picture of the world to help their flocks come to terms with their earthly home, with its bewildering and formidable mysteries. The pen and the pulpit were a powerful combination for bringing about social and theological change. If used rightly, they could sooth tender consciences and fortify minds. Five genres of books, classical texts, geography, medicine, economics and astronomy and cosmography, highlight the purpose of ministers reading such a broad range of works.

2   The Philosophers

Ministers received a broad education, and they studied topics about which those in their congregation cared. The true minister was acquainted with all manner of topics, and he had considered them from his own Christian worldview. They were, in effect, Renaissance men, with competence in a wide variety of fields. Classical books like those penned by Homer, Ovid, Socrates, Plato, Aristotle and others were not common fare for farmers, brewers and weavers. But, lawyers, doctors and local administrators were educated with these works in Latin schools. Greek and Roman writers were necessary reading for any who aspired to be in a position of authority. Though a Zierikzee sailor likely cared little about Aristotle or Cicero, the elite were well acquainted with works by him and similar authors, and these urbane figures could be a significant portion of their local congregations in the major city charges. Public officials were required to be members of their local Reformed church. Like public officials, ministers were educated first in Latin schools, becoming acquainted with Greek and Roman writers.

---

36   *Catalogus variorum ac insignium librorum instructissimae bibliothecae Bernardi Someri* (Amsterdam: Henricum & Viduam Theodori Boom, 1685) Wolfenbüttel, HAB: BC Sammelband 9:20, USTC 1825590.

37   *AC Salomon Voltelen 1697* (Dordrecht: Wittegaarts, 1697), USTC 1829280.

38   *AC Godefridus Udemans 1653* (Middelburg: Jaques Fierens, 1653), USTC 1846270.

LEARNED SERVANTS 163

Greek and Roman writers were some of the most commonly read authors in the Netherlands during the Golden Age. Works by classical authors were some of the most commonly printed books in early-modern Europe. There were at least 2,338 editions printed in the Low Countries before 1650, and probably many more which cannot to identified in a surviving edition. Over 20,000 were published in Europe within the same time.[39] Schoolchildren in the Netherlands cut their intellectual teeth on classical books. They were some of the most important training tools with which students were prepared for a university education.

In 1625, the States of Holland issued a regulation to address the declining quality of their schools.[40] Under the direction of those most invested in the education of children, the senate of the University of Leiden, the rectors of the grammar schools in Holland and local ministers, the States set down the detailed curriculum through which Latin School students would have to pass. The regulation stated that Latin Schools in the Netherlands had to provide a rigorous education beginning with Latin grammar and calligraphy leading to Greek grammar and philosophy, concluding with logic and rhetoric. This curriculum took three years to complete. As ever in the Netherlands, this new school order came with a demand for books. New editions of twenty-three books by Plato, Ovid, Cicero, Aesop and other Greek or Latin authors were printed. These new editions of ancient texts were printed in small, octavo and duodecimo formats, usually with print runs of 1,000 copies.[41]

To care effectively for the needs of learned readers in their congregations, pastors in the Netherlands had to demonstrate competence in the sorts of works that indicated one's sophistication. They owned many of the works with which learned readers in the Netherlands were educated. In the fifty-five ministerial catalogues I have transcribed in full, there are 3,749 books by authors from antiquity. Most tended to be printed in the cheaper and utilitarian octavo format. Ownership of classical works in quarto is lower than the overall percentage of quartos in their libraries. This does not appear to stem from a lack of availability. According to USTC data on printing in Europe up to 1650, about thirty per cent of all classical texts were available in quarto format. Libraries

---

39   According to USTC data, last accessed 1 July 2019.

40   *School-ordre, gemaeckt ende gearresteert by de heeren Staten van Hollant ende West-Vrieslant, over de Latijnsche schoolen binnen den selve lande. Den 1. octobris sestien-hondert-vijf-en-twintig* (The Hague: widow and heirs of Hillebrant van Wouw, 1625), USTC 1012369. Ernst Jan Kuiper, *De Hollandse 'Schoolordre' van 1625* (Groningen: Wolters, 1958).

41   Andrew Pettegree and Arthur der Weduwen, *The Bookshop of the World: Making and Trading Books in the Dutch Golden Age* (New Haven: Yale University Press, 2019), pp. 164–171.

164 CHAPTER 5

owned by ministers were made up of about twenty-eight per cent quartos. There was a gradual decline of publishing the classical works in quarto beginning around 1545.

This decline does not entirely answer the question, why ministers owned a smaller proportion of classical works in quarto, because sixteenth century classical works were still widely available in quarto or other formats. Salomon Voltelen, whose collection sold in 1697, owned the Stephanus edition of Cicero's *Epistolae* (Paris, 1538).[42] Roger Blanckhart (1643–1690), a minister in Poortugaal, owned works by Virgil (1556) and Josephus (1519). The Amsterdam minister, Otto Badius (1594–1664) owned eight classical texts from Paris, all printed before 1578. It seems there was simply less need for quartos. Folios were larger and more suited to intensive study and note-taking in the study. Octavos and duodecimos could more easily be carried about on barges, to classes and so on.

The classical books ministers owned were written by a diverse range of authors (Table 5.1). No one author is as dominant as Calvin was for theological books. The most regularly listed in ministerial auction catalogues, though, is Aristotle (388BC–322BC). His works are listed 143 times. The Greek philosopher was one of the most important thinkers in post-Reformation universities. Franciscus Junius, the Leiden professor of theology, called Aristotle 'that most renowned philosopher'.[43] Reformed theologians strongly opposed the views Aristotle espoused on the eternity of creation and on God; ministers were, nevertheless, trained to think through issues using the method of analysis for which Aristotle was famous.[44] Aristotle was primarily understood through the medieval tradition, which had Christianised him. When addressing a theological topic, the medieval teacher Thomas Aquinas adapted the model of Aristotle and summarised arguments against his position, then he provided the case for his own, and finally he refuted the counter arguments.[45] Aquinas established a pattern of theological education that was adopted by ministers in the sixteenth and seventeenth centuries. Dutch ministers did not adopt the beliefs Aristotle held, but his method of working through topics. This is especially useful for providing thorough training in theological education.

---

42   AC *Solomon Voltelen 1697*. 'Epistolae & Philosophica, cum annotat Petri Victorii 2 tom I v'. USTC 147417.

43   Franciscus Junius, *A Treatise on True Theology*, trans. David C. Noe (Grand Rapids: Reformation Heritage Books, 2014), p. 146.

44   On Reformed ministers denouncing Aristotle, see Richard A. Muller, *Post-Reformation Reformed Dogmatics* (4 vols., Grand Rapids: Baker Academic, 2003), I, pp. 94, 234.

45   See, for example, Thomas Aquinas, *Summa Theologiae*, vol. 1, ed. John Gilby (London: Eyre and Spottiswoode, 1964), 1a.1.

LEARNED SERVANTS

TABLE 5.1   A selection of popular authors from antiquity
as listed in ministerial library catalogues, derived
from the author's transcription of fifty-five
ministerial library catalogues

Author	Total
Aristotle	147
Homer	89
Plato	82
Socrates	57
Juvenal	56
Josephus	41

TABLE 5.2   The five most common places of publication
for classical works listed in the auction
catalogues of libraries owned by ministers

Place of publication	Total
Paris	322
Leiden	286
Basel	277
Frankfurt	242
Antwerp	213

Because Aristotle's philosophical methodology was particularly relevant in Dutch universities, it is no surprise books by him are concentrated amongst professors of theology. Half of all the instances in which Aristotle is listed came from the collections of eleven professors of theology. For reference, the book collections owned by these eleven professors amount to thirty per cent of the entire transcribed corpus.

Ministerial libraries contained more Leiden imprints of classical texts than Basel; Leiden was second only to Paris in this respect (Table 5.1). What is striking, however, is how old the Paris and Basel imprints are. Half of all those listed with Paris as the place of publication were printed before 1600. There are only nine post-1600 Basel imprints of classical works listed. Less than a quarter of all Leiden imprints were printed before 1600. Seventeenth-century ministers did

166   CHAPTER 5

not have to request classical works from the older print centres of Basel and
Paris when they were buying new books. Leiden began producing these books
in droves. One estimate suggests over a million copies were printed by shops
in Leiden after the 1625 school order.[46] Furthermore, older sixteenth-century
copies still circulated long into the seventeenth century.

Ministers devoted time and effort to considering how best to win over others to their side. Their neighbours were overwhelmingly Christian, so the Old
and New Testaments were pertinent here. But what of those who did not recognize the authority of the Bible, those so often called pagans? Ministers considered using natural reason alone a praiseworthy method in this case. Here,
their reading of classical texts came to their aid. Franciscus Ridderus, writing
against those who denied biblical authority resorted to shaming them with
evidence from Cicero, Seneca and similar authors.[47] Johannes Hoornbeeck
encouraged his students who would encounter non-Christian beliefs in a missionary context to use natural reason, eventually leading non-Christians to
the true faith. For this, Hoornbeeck utilized classical authors. Making the case
'that God should be worshipped by human beings is agreed by all more civi-
lized people', Hoornbeeck referenced Caesar, Tacitus, Pliny, Seneca, Lactantius,
Philostraus, Aulus Gellius, Virgil and others.[48]

Johannes Hoornbeeck, like other ministers during the Dutch Golden Age,
was comfortable citing non-Christian Greek and Roman authors. References to
Aristotle, Plato, Socrates and others made up part of the theological language
of the day. But their use of these writings did not always rely on them consulting these books directly. They were happy to reference information that they
had in fact drawn from a secondary source. This is sometimes the case in their
use of classical texts. In the *Synopsis Purioris Theologiae*, a compilation of theological disputations the professors of theology at Leiden composed to demonstrate the university's return to orthodoxy in 1620, the authors cited numerous
authors from antiquity.[49] Often their references to the classical authors were
derived from other sources: lexicons of classical texts, contemporary works

---

46   Pettegree and Der Weduwen, *The Bookshop of the World*, pp. 164–171.

47   Ernestine van der Wall, 'The Religious Context of the Early Dutch Enlightenment: Moral
      Religion and Society', in Wiep van Bunge (ed.), *The Early Enlightenment in the Dutch
      Republic, 1650–1750* (Leiden: Brill, 2003), p. 45.

48   Johannes Hoornbeeck, *Johannes Hoornbeeck (1617–1666), On the Conversion of Indians and
      Heathens: An Annotated Translation of De Conversione Indorum et Gentilium (1669)*, eds.
      Ineke Loots and Joke Spaans (Leiden: Brill, 2018), pp. 260–274.

49   For a fairly detailed list, see Riemer A. Faber, 'Scholastic Continuities in the Reproduction
      of Classical Sources in the *Synopsis Purioris Theologiae*', *Church History and Religious
      Culture*, 92 (2012), pp. 562–563, nn. 3–5.

LEARNED SERVANTS

167

of biblical explanation and works by John Calvin. In disputation six, on the nature of God and his divine attributes, Antonius Thysius (1565–1640) referenced an epic poem by Publius Papinius Statius, *Thebian*. Thysius used it to demonstrate the Greek etymology for *deus*, 'God.' He quoted from *Thebian*, 'it was fear [deos] that first created the gods in this world'. Thysius rejected the idea that fear created the gods, but instead affirmed that God is to be feared. Several medieval theologians and later Greek and Roman writers took the quote and used it in their works. It is from one of those sources that Thysius likely drew his information.[50]

Though the authors of the *Synopsis Purioris Theologiae* drew on classical sources as mediated through later writings, that does not imply they were completely unacquainted with the original sources. It was unbecoming of a well-educated minister not to be familiar with Greek and Roman writings. Not only had they been educated with these texts as children, they continued acquiring their books as adults. The book catalogue for one of the authors of the *Synopsis* survives, that of André Rivet. He owned 126 classical works, including five each by Aristotle and Virgil, four by both Epictetus and Homer, and three each by Socrates, Seneca and Apollonius Rhodius. Rivet owned one of the larger book collections amongst ministers at the time, 4,803 titles. Rivet's collection of 126 classical texts is by no means small; it is just under three per cent of his entire collection. But it is proportionately much smaller than other collections. Jacob Lydius, who owned 5,391 books, owned 280 classical works. Adrianus van den Borre, a former Leiden minister and later minister in the general service of the Remonstrant church, owned 662 books, including 32 of the classics. The joint catalogue for two ministers, one the founding regent of the theological college at Leiden University, the other a Hazerswoude minister, lists 842 books. Ten per cent of their joint collection was by Thucydides, Xenophon and other classical authors.

In his *Meditations*, Marcus Aurelius denounced books as a method of self-distraction from undertaking actual responsibilities. 'Put away your books, distract yourself with them no longer.... As for your thirst for books, be done with it, so that you may not die with complaints on your lips, but with a truly cheerful mind and grateful to the gods with all your heart'.[51] The numerous Dutch ministers who carried in their pockets duodecimo editions of Marcus Aurelius'

---

50   Faber, 'Scholastic Continuities in the Reproduction of Classical Sources in the *Synopsis Purioris Theologiae*', p. 564.

51   Marcus Aurelius, *Meditations with selected correspondence*, trans. Robin Hard (Oxford: Oxford University Press, 2011), pp. 11–12.

168   CHAPTER 5

works apparently wasted their time. Yet Aurelius is listed fifteen times in
fifty-five auction catalogues of libraries owned by ministers.

In *La divine melodie, du sainct psalmiste ou La divinité du livre des pseaumes*
[*The Divine Melody of the Holy Psalmist, or the Divinity of the Book of Psalms*],
the Middelburg Walloon minister Jeremie du Pours reflected on the quality of
the poetry in which the Psalms were written. The most praised books of poetry
paled in comparison to the Psalms of David. Du Pours assumed his readers
were well acquainted with the great poets from history: Homer, Virgil and
Ovid. Nevertheless, he concluded, David surpassed even these. Du Pours took
poetic licence of his own, using a play on Homer's name and homer, a Hebrew
form of measurement. Du Pours stated, 'Homer is a great poet, but a homer of
David's poetry is far greater than Homer'.[52]

For ministers, references to Homer and similar writers were not out of place.
Homer was commonly listed in ministerial library catalogues. The authors of
the *Synopsis Purioris Theologiae* worked under the assumption that the ministers who would read their collection of disputations knew Classical authors
and their sources. Riemer A. Faber notes 'Even more unexpected, perhaps,
are the several *unattributed* [Classical] quotations in the *Synopsis*, for they
evidently assume a readership that is educated in the liberal arts and able to
identify the sources and to recall their contexts' (italics original).[53] In his *Oratio habita in Synodo Nationali Nationali Dordracena*, Simon Episcopius pleaded
the Remonstrant case for toleration. He reminded those in attendance that
the Remonstrants were united with them in the pursuit of truth. The Remonstrants only disagreed with their conclusions. He ended his appeal by saying,
'we are a friend of Plato, a friend of Socrates, a friend of the Synod, but above
all a friend of truth'.[54]

Ministers demonstrated little aversion to referencing classical texts. They
had read these works since they were children in one of many Latin schools,
and they cited their works to help understand their own faith. Lawyers, doctors
and administrators throughout the Netherlands read books by Ovid, Virgil and

---

52   'Homere est un grand Poëte, mais un homer de la poësie de David vant plus qu'Homere'.
      Jeremie du Pours, *La divine melodie, du sainct psalmiste ou La divinité du livre des pseau-
      mes* (Middelburg: Geeraert Moulert, 1644), USTC 1024498, p. 314. Copy consulted: ZA, 1722
      Waalse Gemeente te Middelburg, 1618–2009, inv. 71.

53   Faber, 'Scholastic Continuities in the Reproduction of Classical Sources in the *Synopsis
      Purioris Theologiae*', p. 563.

54   'Amicus esse debet Plato, amicus Socrates, amica Synodus, sed magis amica veritas'.
      Simon Episcopius, 'Oratio habita in Synodo Nationali Nationali Dordracena', in his *Opera
      Theologica* (Rotterdam: Arnout Leers, 1665) USTC 1802334, part 2, p. 4.

LEARNED SERVANTS

others, and those men sat in church pews and would have bought their local ministerial works in bookshops. It was an occupational necessity for the minister to demonstrate their competence with these books, and inevitably they took up a large portion of the space in their libraries and acquire dozens, and sometimes hundreds of these works.

3 Roads of the Sun

By 1669, Dutch trade reached its zenith: the seaborne empire flourished after the Treaty of Münster in 1648. On the Maas tributary, oil refineries processed whale blubber and converted it into a convenient source of fuel. Just up the Maas in Rotterdam, factories began producing processed foods from distant lands. Biscuits, spiced cakes, chocolate, mustard and exotic liqueurs made from tropical and sub-tropical fruits were ever more common. With exotic food, came news and grand tales. Travel journals from skippers and sailors offered increasingly fantastic accounts of strange people and animals, and they enraptured a reading public. They became some of the bestselling works of the Golden Age.[55] Such an expansion of knowledge led Dutch citizens to ask questions about these distant lands: how should a Reformed Dutchman understand the pagan beliefs and practices that were so luridly described in travel journals?

Many Dutch ministers attempted to answer such questions, by reflecting on how to help their congregations understand these peoples and customs from a Christian worldview. One tactic was used by Franciscus Ridderus, a minister in Rotterdam until his death in 1683. In his 1669 work, *De beschaemde christen door het geloof en leven van heydenen en andere natuerlijcke menschen* [*The Christian Shamed by the Faith and Life of Heathens and other Pagans*], he sought to exhort his Reformed readers to a life of greater piety.[56] Pagans and heathens were diligent in faith and practice of obedience to their gods, despite believing false doctrines. How much more zealous, then, ought Christians to be?[57]

Like most of his fellow citizens, Ridderus had never been to any of the lands occupied by 'pagans and heathens'. But he was deeply informed about

---

55 Pettegree and Der Weduwen, *The Bookshop of the World*, pp. 90–117.
56 Franciscus Ridderus, *De beschaemde christen door het geloof en leven van heydenen en andere natuerlijcke menschen* (Rotterdam: Johannes Borstius, 1669), USTC 1815596.
57 Bettina Noak, 'Foreign Wisdom: Ethnological Knowledge in the Work of Franciscus Ridderus', *Journal of Dutch Literature*, 3 (2012), pp. 47–64.

them. With works ranging from *Seer kort verhael van de destructie van d'Indien* [*A brief relation of the destruction of the Indians*] by Bartolomé de la Casas, the Qu'ran, to the contemporary work of the Amsterdam chorographer Olfert Dapper, Ridderus built his case for learning from so-called pagans and heathens.[58] Throughout his life, he read dozens of books on the topic. In one of his publications, he even confessed to enjoying reading of heroic voyages and travel journals. Those he did not own, a colleague in Rotterdam was prepared to lend him:

> In addition to the Journals, Voyages, Day Journeys, Land Journeys and New Descriptions that I have seen and read [from my library], my Honourable Colleague, Doctor Jacob Borstius has given me such a number, I believe more than sixty.[59]

The catalogue for the library Ridderus owned contained over 40 travel journals and histories of foreign lands. At one point, the catalogue for his book collection simply lists 'various travel narratives, journals, and descriptions of lands'.[60] Informed by his books, Ridderus took up a topic of public significance and sought to bring about a more Reformed society.

Books of this kind were widely read throughout the Dutch Republic. Jan Huygen van Linschoten (1563–1611), a Haarlem merchant and one of the first Dutchmen to travel to the East Indies, wrote three volumes based on his travels that were republished numerous times. Willem Ysbrantsz. Bontekoe was a famous author in his day, based on the virtuous stories he told from his days as a skipper with the VOC. His books were bestsellers during the seventeenth century. Bontekoe's tales were riveting and pious narratives that often encouraged the reader to maintain their trust in the benevolent provision of God for his creatures. Not only that, many were compelling stories that made for entertaining reading. Gerrit de Veer made a harrowing journey in search for the north-eastern passage. After being caught in an ice pack, the crew survived until summer eating strict rations and occasional arctic fox and polar bear. It was precisely the kind of adventure that would appeal to readers. Like many

---

58   USTC 1028137.
59   'behalven de Journalen, Voyagien, Dagreizen, Landreizen, en nieuwe Beschrijvingen, de welke ik alle die mij bekomelijk zijn geweest, heb na gezien en door lezen, gelijk daar toe mijn Eerwaardige Collega, D. Jacobus Borstius, mij heeft ter hand gesteld een getal van zoodanige, na ik meene, meer als t'zestig'. Franciscus Ridderus, *Nuttige tiidkorter voor reizende en andere luiden* (Rotterdam: Joannes Naeranus, 1663), USTC 1800117, sig. ****3r.
60   'Verscheyde reysen, journalen, land beschrijvingen'. AC *Franciscus Ridderus*, p. 14.

LEARNED SERVANTS

other residents of the Netherlands, ministers were certainly among those who read these works for pleasure. But the popularity of these works in their catalogues indicates that they also had more serious purposes.

Of the fifty-five catalogues I have transcribed, there are 1,534 books describing foreign peoples and places, about thirty per catalogue. Some ministers owned only a few of these works.[61] The Sint Anthoniepolder minister, Abraham Mellinus (d. 1622) owned thirty-five.[62] In the collection owned by Bernard Somer, there are 144 such works.[63] Within my dataset, one-third of books in this genre are only described with their title.

A handful of wealthy ministers owned the *Republics*, a series of forty volumes the Elzeviers began printing in the 1620s that quickly became collectors' items. The catalogue for the collection owned by the Amsterdam minister, Adrian Smout (d. 1646) lists twenty-four of the forty.[64] Balthazar Bekker, the controversial Amsterdam minister famous for his denunciation of those who believed in witchcraft, owned numerous books on geography and cartography, including several of the *Republics*. His catalogue includes one lot for '*Respublicae 13 vols*'.[65] Johannes Pechlinus owned the entire series.[66] The *Republics* were so commonly known amongst those who frequented book auctions that in the catalogue for the collection of Johannes Westerburg, the titles do not even include *Respublica*. The catalogue only mentions the country in consideration: *Persia, Belgica, Gallia, Dania* and so forth. *The Republics* were small books in a tiny 24mo format. When combined with a tight binding, they were difficult to read: these were volumes that were intended more as a declaration of the owners' culture, their education and societal rank. Though they were certainly helpful in some ways, other works were needed to gain thorough knowledge of the topics the *Republics* addressed. Other books on geography were as or more common than the *Republics*.

---

61   *AC Wilhelm Merwy 1636* (Delft: Jan Pietersz Waalpot, 1636), USTC 1027540; *AC Theodorus van Altena 1662* (Leiden: Petrus Hackius, 1662), USTC 1842892. Van Altena's library is listed as an appendix to a stock catalogue Hackius published.

62   *AC Abraham Mellinus 1623* (Dordrecht: Peeter Verhagen, 1623), USTC 1122090.

63   *Catalogus variorum ac insignium librorum instructissimae bibliothecae Bernardi Someri* (Amsterdam: Henricum & Viduam Theodori Boom, 1685) Wolfenbüttel, HAB: BC Sammelband 9:20, USTC 1825590.

64   *AC Adrian Smoutius 1646* (Leiden: Severyn Matthysz, 1646), USTC 1122092.

65   *AC Balthazar Bekker 1698* (Amsterdam: Daniel van den Dalen & Andries van Damme, [1698]), USTC 1847542, p. 56.

66   *AC Johannes Pechlinus 1690* (Leiden: Pieter (I) van der Aa, 1690), USTC 1823437.

172   CHAPTER 5

TABLE 5.3   A selection of popular authors of geographical works,
            as listed in fifty-five ministerial library catalogues

Author	Count
Abraham Ortelius	20
Johannes de Laet	18
Joan and Willem Jansz Blaeu	18
Olfert Dapper	17
Philip Clouwer	16
Arnoldus Montanus	13
Adam Olearius	10

Books by contemporary geographers and travellers like Philip Clouwer, Johannes de Laet, Abraham Ortelius and others were just as popular as collectors' items (Table 5.3). Duodecimo and smaller books are less frequently listed than the larger sizes. The size of the volumes indicates a utilitarian purpose: folio volumes made reading maps significantly easier than a small duodecimo. The scholarly accounts and descriptions of other places by authors like the Dutch geographer and director of the West India Company, Johannes de Laet, survive in ministerial catalogues more frequently than the popular travel narratives of the time. The languages in which ministers read them roughly follows the general trend in their collections: about sixty per cent are in Latin; the remainder are in various vernacular and academic languages. Emphasizing the scholarly nature of their geographies, several of the most reprinted authors of travel narratives are listed rarely in their collections. Despite being republished numerous times, Van Linschoten is only listed eight times in the fifty-five catalogues I have transcribed. Neither De Veer or Bontekoe is listed in any of the catalogues I have transcribed. That is not to say that ministers did not read them. These were small books, cheaply bound: perfect candidates for being used to destruction, retained by the family, given away or otherwise lost. It still is surprising that neither of these authors are listed in the nearly 100,000 items I have transcribed.

At Leiden University, two successive professors included preparation for the mission field in their teaching. Antonius Walaeus oversaw the *Seminarium Indicum* from 1622 to 1632, a preparatory school based in his home for ministers going overseas.[67] In 1669, Johannes Hoornbeeck began formally training

---

67   G. P. van Itterzon, '*Walaeus, Antonius*', in D. Nauta, et al. (eds.), *Biografisch lexicon voor de geschiedenis van het Nederlandse protestantisme* (6 vols, Kampen: J. H. Kock, 1978–2006), II, pp. 452–454.

LEARNED SERVANTS

his students to engage the peoples of the world beyond Europe, by helping them understand their language, culture and customs. Hoornbeeck encouraged his students to acquire knowledge of the language in which the 'heathen' spoke. 'People should learn languages.... In particular it is necessary to learn the more common languages, such as in East India Malay, which is in very common use, more or less like French among the Europeans: to learn this language there have now been published grammars, colloquia, dictionaries, catechisms and other similar books'.[68] On the Iroquian language spoken by the Huron in the New Netherlands, Hoornbeeck recommended *De origine gentium Americanarum* by De Laet and *Dictionnaire de la langue hurone*, by Gabriel Sagard.[69] Hoornbeeck owned many of the books he recommended: in addition to those by De Laet and Sagard, he had fifty-three other works describing foreign peoples and their customs. Samuel Gruterus, a Haarlem minister, owned a collection of 'all the books ever printed in Malay which have been printed in Holland'. His catalogue lists fifteen of them.[70] Johannes Hoornbeeck celebrated that so many places could now be reached by God-fearing Christians. He compared extending the Christian kingdom to the prophecy given for Emperor Augustus in Virgil's *Aeneid*, that it would extend beyond 'the roads of the year and of the sun'.[71]

Many ministerial catalogues end with miscellaneous items: book-cases, reading-stands and other similar objects. Often, maps and globes are listed. At the end of the catalogue for the library owned by Gerardus van der Port, '36 land maps with rods and buttons' are listed alongside 'bookcases' and 'packets'.[72] The catalogue for the collection owned by Johannes Boeken, a Rotterdam Lutheran minister, lists several items for sale that are only summarized in broad terms: '1. A Packet of School – and other Books. 2. Same. 3. A Packet of Some theological books and other tracts. 4. A Packet of life-sermons and disputations. A celestial globe by Blaeu. A great book of maps. A bookcase'.[73] These items were not the exclusive domain of the rich who aspired to demonstrate their wealth and education. Van der Port owned an average sized collection, 1,135 items. Boeken owned only 435 books. For both Van der Port and Boeken, their

---

68   Hoornbeeck, *On the Conversion of Indians and Heathens*, p. 374.

69   De Laet: USTC 1031604; Sagard: The only USTC reference to a publication by Sagard in 1632 is USTC 6021370.

70   'Alle de Maleysche Boeken die uyt in Holland gedrukt zijn'. *AC Samuel Gruterus 1700* (Leiden: Pieter (1) van der Aa, 1700), USTC 1848523, p. 1.

71   Hoornbeeck, *On the Conversion of Indians and Heathens*, p. 40. Virgil, *Aeneid* (Boston: Harvard University Press, 2015), p. 589 (6.791–800). Loeb Classical Library, DOI: 10.4159/DLCL.virgil-aeneid.1916.

72   *AC Gerardus van der Port 1691* (Amsterdam: Hendrik Boom and widow Dirk (1) Boom, 1691), USTC 1847325, p. 32.

73   *AC Johannes Boeken 1698* (Rotterdam: Barent Bos, 1698), USTC 1847535, p. 16.

174 CHAPTER 5

ownership of maps, and a globe in the case of Van der Port, stemmed from an interest in lands beyond their own. Van der Port owned several books on geography and descriptions of distant lands, including *Beschrijving van West Indien* [*Descriptions of the West Indies*] by the Spanish Chronicler Antonio de Herrera and *Compendium geographicum succincta methodo deformatus* by Abraham Göllnitz (d. 1643).

Some ministers went beyond ownership of books on geography and even beyond writing popular vernacular tracts on the subject. Arnoldus Montanus, a minister and rector of the grammar school in Schoonhoven, worked with Olfert Dapper to produce a series of descriptions of foreign lands. They were folio volumes with ornate engravings, published by Jacob van Meurs in Amsterdam and often ran to a thousand pages. If Franciscus Ridderus wrote a popular work aimed to help the ordinary Christian, Montanus and Dapper assumed their audience was the educated elite who could afford large folios. Their faith was justified: their works appear thirty times between them.

Adam Westerman (d. 1635) served four congregations in Friesland in the course of his career: Gaast (1600), Stavoren (1602), Oosterlittens (1616) and Workum (1619). All of these were port towns. In 1611, he wrote a volume entitled *Christelycke Zee-vaert* [*Christian Sea Voyage*]. This collection of twenty-six sermons was written to encourage the godly sailor through the trials that accompanied his profession.[74] In this way, Westerman was not unlike his colleagues, all of whom aspired to encourage the faith of the godly and rebuke those in sin. Westerman, a pastor of churches far removed from influential urban centres, however, was one of the best-selling authors of the century. Thirty-editions of the *Christelycke zee-vaert* were printed. The first edition that survives was printed in 1630. It was one of few books that was consistently taken on VOC ships to the East Indies.[75]

In the sweaty, humid galleys of ships bound for Malaysia, Dutch sailors could read pious devotional works written by ministers who only knew of those lands from their libraries. Some, like Justus Heurnius, a missionary to China, had served as ministers in the Republic, but most remained in their homeland. Nevertheless, people and places far removed from the United Provinces were part of everyday life. Narratives of voyages throughout the known world were one of the most popular genres of print. Matthew Slade informed Dudley Carleton in April 1618 that Amsterdam was buzzing with news about

74   J. D. Th. Wassenaar, 'Westerman, Adam', in D. Nauta, et al. (eds.), *Biografisch lexicon van de geschiedenis van het Nederlandse protestantisme*, VI, pp. 341–342.

75   Pettegree and Der Weduwen, *The Bookshop of the World*, pp. 121–122.

LEARNED SERVANTS

Sir Walter Raleigh discovering gold on his second journey to Guyana. 'Here [in Amsterdam] hath been much talk of Sir Walter Rawleighe's success in Guyana'.[76] Because information like this was part of everyday life, due in part to the great popularity of books and journals, ministers acquired books on the topic. They focused on scholarly works of geography, and they sought to help their congregants make sense of distant lands, customs and peoples.

4   Amateur Physicians

A Dutch citizen could be forgiven for having not read the latest best-selling travel journal. But all Dutch citizens were regularly plagued with concerns for the physical well-being of themselves and their loved ones. Illness and disease were a constant concern. This concern required pastoral care. Godefridus Udemans was one minister amongst many who devoted time and energy to the physical well-being of his congregation. In his explanation of the seventh commandment, 'You shall not commit adultery' (Exodus 20:14), Udemans denounced dancing as 'the bellows of indecency and instruments of frivolity'. In addition to his concern for the spiritual well-being of his reader, he added that dancing also had ill effects on the body: 'Medical doctors show us that the violent shaking of the body is dangerous, particularly after a meal. Many dancers come down with pleurisy, blood diseases, or other illnesses because of exhaustion that results from dancing'.[77] Udemans did not speak from a position of an uninformed, narrow-minded minister. Cornelis Bontekoe was one physician who discouraged dancing for similar reasons to those mentioned by Udemans.[78] Furthermore, the catalogue for the library that Udemans owned lists a section of *libri medici*, ten books in total, including the *Schat der gesontheyt* [*Treasure of Health*] by the famous Dordrecht physician Johan van Beverwijck and two works by the physician to the French court, Jean François Fernel.

---

76   Matthew Slade to Dudley Carleton, 16 April 1618, in Willem Nijenhuis (ed.), *Matthew Slade (1569–1628): Letters to the English Ambassador* (Leiden: E. J. Brill/Leiden University Press, 1986), pp. 79–80.

77   Godefridus Udemans, *The Practice of Faith, Hope, and Love*, trans. Annemie Godbehere, ed. Joel R. Beeke (Grand Rapids: Reformation Heritage Books, 2012), p. 365.

78   Anette Henriette Munt, 'The Impact of Dutch Cartesian Medical Reformers in Early Enlightenment German Culture (1680–1720)' (PhD Thesis, University of London, 2004), p. 176.

176   CHAPTER 5

The fifty-five auction catalogues I have transcribed list 1,515 medical books. Medical books are one of the more common classes of non-theological books present in libraries owned by ministers, though they were less common than travel narratives and geographies. Quality medical care was hard to find, especially for those lower down the social scale. Despite having a population of 40,000, only nine physicians worked in Haarlem in 1628.[79] Municipal governments would often pay a physician a stipend to offer basic services to the poor. Local medical practitioners, though, were often untrained surgeons or midwives who depended on medical books like the *Secreet-boek* by Carolus Battus, first printed in Dordrecht in 1600. It was written in Dutch and marketed to the kinds of readers who only bought a few books.[80] The prescriptions Battus recommended often seemed more akin to magical *hocum* than serious medical work. One such prescription encouraged anyone with inflamed ears to use the vapour from sweet milk. Another encouraged rubbing with parsley to ease swelling. As A. Th. van Deursen noted, 'It is quite possible that people found these remedies useful. But their choice and operation rested entirely on faith'.[81] Nevertheless, Dutch surgeons, midwives and even ministers drew upon the information that was widely available to them at the time. Works by Battus were listed in six ministerial catalogues.

Of course in some insistences, ministers owned only one or two medical books. Of the 343 books a minister in Cuijk owned, only one medical work is listed: *De medicina*, by the Roman teacher Serenus Sammonicus.[82] Johannes Boeken, a Lutheran minister in Rotterdam whose collection sold in 1698, owned only Thomas Bartholinus' *Anatomia* (The Hague, 1655).[83] One catalogue includes a nondescript lot including 'Various disputations on theology, law, medicine and other topics'.[84] Daniel Demetrius (d. 1628) owned two medical books; three were sold from the collection of Jan Barentsz. (*c*.1556–1609), a minister in Delft. For these ministers, a few books would have served the

---

79   Samuel Ampzing, *Beschyvinge ende lof der stad Haerlem in Holland* (Haarlem: Adriaen (1) Roman, 1628), USTC 1026151, p. 147.

80   Carolus Battus, *Secreet-boeck waer in vele diversche secreten, ende heerlicke consten in veelderleye verscheyden materien uit Latijnsche, Francoysche, Hoochduytsche, ende Nederlantsche authoren, te samen ende by een ghebracht zijn* (Dordrecht: Abraham Canin, 1600), USTC 425118.

81   A. Th. Van Deursen, *Plain Lives in a Golden Age: Popular Culture, Religion and Society in seventeenth-century Holland*, trans. Maarten Ultee (Cambridge: Cambridge University Press, 1991), p. 238.

82   *AC Paulus Leupenius 1678* (Nijmegen: Gulielmus Meys, 1678), USTC 1846917.

83   *AC Johannes Boeken 1698.*

84   *AC Otto Zaunslifer 1675* (Groningen: Rembertus Huysman, 1675), USTC 1846823, sig. B2v, lot 128.

necessary purpose of providing home remedies without the need for calling a doctor.

Forty-nine out of the fifty-five ministerial collections transcribed contain at least one medical book. Of these forty-nine, thirty-seven owned more than five medical books. The size of these collections ranged from Thomas Laurentius' 189 books, which included fourteen medical books, to collections of over 5,000 books. Of the ministers in this corpus, many owned well beyond what would have been superficially useful. Johannes Pechlinus (d. 1690), a Lutheran minister in Leiden, owned forty-five medical books. His collection totalled 3,709 books.[85] Balthazar Lydius (1576–1629) owned 282.[86] Jacobus Halsbergius (c.1560–1607) owned 120.[87] The desire to own great numbers of medical books indicates, in part, a curiosity about the medical world. Medical books were far more popular in their collections than scientific works on mathematics, physics, or similar topics.

André Rivet wrote to a young theologian named Justinus van Assche, from Zeeland, to encourage him to be diligent in private study.[88] The minister and (later in life) medical doctor, who joined the Remonstrant faction, pursued knowledge assiduously for both of his careers.[89] When he died, Van Assche's book collection amounted to 1,712 works. Theological books were only thirty-five per cent of the catalogue, 631 items. His medical books, 247 in total, rival the size of some ministers' entire collections.

Sickness, disease and the death of a mother or child (or both) during birth were ever present realities. People seldom lived beyond sixty years old, especially in the lower social orders. Franciscus Ridderus devoted an entire volume to synthesising the best medical books of the day and encouraging Christians to die well. The dialogue between a minister, a sick man, a doctor and later a widow was entitled *Historisch sterf-huys, ofte 't Samenspraeck uyt heylige, kerckelijcke en weereltsche historien over allerley voorval ontrent siecke en stervende* [*Historical Dying House, or a Dialogue from Holy, Ecclesiastical and Secular Histories concerning death and dying*].[90] In it he cited numerous

---

85   *AC Johannes Pechlinus 1690* (Leiden: Pieter van der Aa, 1690), USTC 1823437.

86   *AC Balthazar Lydius 1629–30* (Dordrecht: widow of Peeter Verhagen, 1629–1630), USTC 1021755, 1021757, 1021756.

87   *AC Johannes Halsbergius 1607* (Leiden: Thomas Basson, 1607), USTC 1122231.

88   André Rivet to Justinus van Assche, 5 April 1620, UB Leiden PAP 15.

89   *NNBW*, I, pp. 187–188. Fokko Jan Dijksterhuis, 'Labour on lenses: Isaac Beeckman's notes on lens making', in Albert van Helden, et al., (eds.), *The Origins of the telescope* (Amsterdam: Koninklijke Nederlandse Akademie van Wetenschappen, 2010), pp. 264–265.

90   Franciscus Ridderus, *Historisch sterf-huys, ofte 't Samenspraeck uyt heylige, kerckelijcke en weereltsche historien over allerley voorval ontrent siecke en stervende* (Rotterdam: Johannes Borstius, 1668), USTC 1802396.

178 CHAPTER 5

medical authorities, many of whose works were included in the fifteen medical books he owned.[91] Ridderus' *Historical Dying House* presents an image of a minister who comforts the sick with Scripture and encouraging spiritual quotations from theologians like John Chrysostom, Martin Luther and John Calvin. He understood the advice and treatments given by the doctor and reiterated their advice. He referenced influential medical doctors of the day, like the Dordrecht physician Johan van Beverwijk. In the title page to the book, three adults and two children gather around a woman on her deathbed. One person, perhaps a minister, appears to offer encouraging words to the dying woman (Fig. 5.2).

If the collections owned by other ministers are indicative of the places of publication in the collection Ridderus owned, most of the medical books Ridderus owned would have been printed in the Netherlands and the Holy Roman Empire. Unfortunately, the catalogue for his collection does not list places of publication. When other catalogues are examined for the places of publication of medical texts, the imprints most frequently listed are from locations in the Holy Roman Empire and the Netherlands. France is a distant third. Frankfurt (128) imprints account for more than all Swiss imprints combined, and nearly as many as those from France (Table 5.4).

TABLE 5.4   Medical books in ministerial auction catalogues and their countries of publication as derived from the entries for which an imprint is known or inferred

Country of imprint	Number of books
Holy Roman Empire	280
The Netherlands	251
France	156
Switzerland	103
Italian City States	53
Southern Netherlands	37
British Isles	14
Scandinavia	1

---

91   *AC Franciscus Ridderus 1683* (Rotterdam: Marcus van Rossum, 1683) USTC 1847118.

LEARNED SERVANTS

179

TABLE 5.5   A selection of the well-known medical authors as listed
in ministerial book auction catalogues

Author	Number of books
Galenus	40
Johannes Heurnius	31
Daniel Senertius	27
Hippocrates	25
Jean François Fernel	24
Celsus	19
Johan van Beverwijk	17

The medical books that ministers owned tended to be utilitarian in nature. Unlike their books on geography, which were printed in larger formats, medical texts followed the general pattern of their collection as a whole. They were slightly older than the rest of the collection, with just under sixty per cent being printed during the seventeenth century. The pre-1600 printed books in their libraries made up just over forty per cent of their titles. This is roughly the same for their collections as a whole. The enduring presence of sixteenth-century medical texts is not surprising, as two of the more popular medical authors died before or around 1600: Jean François Fernel died in 1558; Johannes Heurnius died in 1601 (Table 5.5). Furthermore, ministers' collections almost exclusively list sixteenth-century editions of Galenus, Hippocrates and Celsus.

Knowing that everyone in his flock would one day face death, a minister sought to understand the human body in its intricacies and wonders, so they could shepherd their flocks through the trials of sickness and dying. One newspaper advertised a book on death and dying, claiming that comforters of the sick, ministers, and others would benefit from reading it. 'Schat-Boeck der Onderwijsingen voor Kranck-Besoeckers, en der Vertroostingen voor Krancken [Treasure book of education for Visitors of the Sick and Consolations for the Sick], not only useful for those who care for the sick, but also for ministers, theologians, heads of households or all those who sail at sea, or cannot serve formally in church'. The title of the book also mentions another group of target buyers: 'students in holy theology'.[92] Complemented with works of spiritual

---

92   'Schat-Boeck der Onderwijsingen voor Kranck-Besoeckers, en Vertroostingen voor Krancken, niet alleen dienstigh voor Siecke-Troosters, maer oock voor Predicanten,

180   CHAPTER 5

counselling, medical books like these provided the necessary background to help the sick come to terms with their condition.

5   They That Bear Silver

If sickness, dying and medicine were at the forefront of a congregant's mind, money was a likely a close second. Everyone fell ill, and everyone needed money. In 1642, the magistrates of Utrecht asked the theological faculty for advice on the establishment of a lending bank. Citing scripture, civil law and examples from history, the theologians argued vehemently against the practice of loaning money at exorbitant rates. Usury, the theologians stated, 'drank the blood of the poor down to the very marrow'.[93] Such lenders were a cancer and plague, leading to the ruin of the poor. Publishing numerous tracts in Dutch, Gisbertus Voetius and several colleagues wrote to free the 'poor masses'.[94] He also composed several academic disputations on the evils of usury in the course of training new generations of ministers. But by taking the debate out of the academy and addressing the people and the government directly through vernacular writing, Voetius sought to build a society that had no place for this heinous economic practice.

Thirty out of the fifty-five catalogues I have transcribed contained books whose titles explicitly address matters of finance, economic supply and demand, money, banking or other such concerns. Just over 100 of these books are listed in my transcribed corpus. They are overwhelmingly written in Latin, eighty-seven in total. With five books each, French and English are the most common vernacular languages present. The relative lack of economic books compared to medical books should not be surprising. Economic principles, unlike many other topics, can be understood by everyday observation.[95]

Proponenten, Huysvaders, en die geene, die ter Zee varen, of onder 't kruys van aenspraeck niet konnen gedient werden'. *Oprechte Haerlemse Saterdaegse Courant*, 49. 06.12.1670. Cf. Arthur der Weduwen and Andrew Pettegree, *News, Business and Public Information. Advertisements and Announcements in Dutch and Flemish Newspapers, 1620–1675* (Leiden: Brill, 2020), pp. 401–402. Jacobus Sceperus, *Schat-boeck der onderwijsingen voor kranck-besoeckers* (Amsterdam: Johannes Janssonius van Waesberge, 1670), USTC 1807322.

93   Quoted in, Willem J. van Asselt, "'A Grievous Sin:' Gisbertus Voetius (1589–1676) and his anti-Lombard Polemic', in Jordan J. Ballor, et al., (eds.), *Church and School in Early Modern Protestantism: Studies in Honor of Richard A. Muller on the Maturation of a Theological Tradition* (Leiden: Brill, 2013), p. 510.

94   Doede Nauta, *Samuel Maresius* (Amsterdam: H. J. Paris, 1935), p. 297.

95   Joseph A. Schumpeter, *History of Economic Analysis* (Oxford: Oxford University Press, 1954), p. 9.

LEARNED SERVANTS   181

Furthermore, when a minister considered economics, he was concerned first with the proper order of society. Lionel Robbins, a twentieth-century British economist, offered what has become a popular definition of modern economics. 'Economics is the science which studies human behaviour as a relationship between ends and scarce means which have alternative uses'.[96] Ministers, in contrast, thought economics was a holistic endeavour, of which wealth was a part. Less concern was given to the internal machinations of Amsterdam's Exchange Bank than to the role of virtue in economic dealings. It was the study of order and justice, beginning with the husband and wife and extending out to the rest of society. Of those books on order, none are more popular than Bartholomäus Keckermann's volume on politics and economics. Keckermann (*c.*1572–1608) began his treatise on order with the home.[97] The peace and concord of the society, upon which civilization depended, began with a virtuous husband and a wife who showed honour to her husband. This familial structure was, they thought, founded by God, and it established the foundation upon which a just economic system was built.

There are two main groups of economic books listed in ministers' auction catalogues: introductory texts and books born out of controversy. Summative books on economics were largely dominated by Aristotle and discussions of his thought. Aristotle's *Politica & Oeconomica* is listed five times; there are four books commenting on Aristotle's economics, including two copies of John Case's *In oeconomica Aristotelis*.[98]

The most popular economic books mark out a public debate within the Dutch Reformed Church that, like so many other debates, spilled into a frenzied controversy. Books on usury, the practice of lending money for profit to the detriment of the recipient of the loan, dominate the genre. A third of the economic titles listed in their library catalogues mention usury in the title. Claudius Salmasius, a professor at Leiden, was the most popular author mentioned in this category. His *De modo usuris* is listed fourteen times. One of his successors who also wrote on usury, Johannes Friedrich Gronovius, was less popular, but still represented in the corpus. His *De centesimus usuris* is listed five times.

Invectives against allegedly greedy, money-grabbing bankers were not only levelled by the orthodox watchdog Gisbertus Voetius and his colleagues in

---

96 Lionel Robbins, *An Essay on the Nature and Significance of Economic Science* (London: Macmillan, 1949), p. 16.

97 Barthalomaeus Keckermann, *Synopsis disciplinae oeconomicae* (Hanau: Wilhelm Antonius, 1610). This treatise is appended to his work on politics, *Systema disciplinae politicae* (Hanau: Wilhelm Antonius, 1608 [= 1610]) USTC 2130297.

98 *AC Balthazar Lydius*; *AC Martin Ubbenius 1661* (Leiden: Pieter Leffen, 1661), USTC 1846366.

Utrecht. Voetius simply restated what the *Synopsis Purioris Theologiae* had concluded in 1620. 'The lending to the poor for financial gain that is practiced in the form of a pledge, and that is permitted by the magistrates in Christendom to a certain degree because of something good, is clearly cruel and harsh', wrote Antonius Thysius. '[A] well-established nation ought to have no place for anyone to practice this'.[99] Jacob Lydius (1610–1679), a minister in Dordrecht, reviled 'money hounds [*gelt honden*]' and all who practiced 'the acts of cunning, dodges, deceits and devilry'. Lydius considered this a failure of virtue; it was a 'sin against the old name of honour'.[100]

When Voetius and his colleagues denounced abusive banking practices, they did not do so out of ignorance. Voetius himself had investigated the subject thoroughly. In addition to those instances when usury was discussed in shorter treatments by theologians throughout the Christian tradition, Voetius had investigated both sides of the issue: of the fifteen or so books he owned, several made the case for usury, including Samuel Maresius' *Conderationes erotematicae circa foenus trapeziticum* [*Considerations of questions concerning the Loan Banker*], which argued that those who practiced usury should not be disciplined by the church, a position anathema to Voetius.[101]

At home and in business, the ideal Christian man was a godly servant, pursuing the good of those around him and ensuring the faith was not hampered by his actions. Failure to meet such a standard, however, could earn a rebuke from pulpits throughout the Netherlands. In 1655 in Rotterdam, Simon Simonides (1629–1675) denounced the businessmen in his congregation who did not apply faith to their daily lives. Despite having the pretence of godliness, their true selves were put on full display when they turned to their financial dealings. 'When he goes home from Church, does he take God's Holy Book with him to ponder the sermon'? Simonides asked. 'No. Instead he picks up the day's

---

99   Antonius Thysius, 'On Almsgiving and Fasting (disp. 37)', in Henk van den Belt (ed.) *Synopsis Purioris Theologiae/Synopsis of a Purer Theology*, trans. Riemer A. Faber (2. vols, Leiden: Brill, 2013–2016), II, p. 463.

100 'Hier leyt een gierigh mensch, een Gelt-hont in verholen, De doot, gelijck een dief, heeft hem van hier gestolen, en dit gebeurde juyst op d'onbequaemste tijt, soo dat men merken kost 't geschiede maer uyt spijt. Want op de selfde tijt wanneerse hem quam quellen, soo was hy gansch beslet met al syn gelt te tellen, en siet den snooden dief, en fellen moordenaer stal slechts alleen den man, en liet de schatten daer'. Jacobus Lydius, 'Van eenen gelt-hont', in his *Vrolycke uren, ofte Der wysen vermaeck* (Dordrecht: Hendrick van Esch, 1640), USTC 1028119, p. 100.

101 *Erotematicae* is a technical theological term, typically used in disputations to connote a logical premise in the form of a question. On it, see 'erotema' in Richard A. Muller, *Dictionary of Latin and Greek Theological Terms: Drawn Principally from Scholastic Theology* (Grand Rapids: Baker Academic, 2017).

LEARNED SERVANTS

debt book and busies himself with calculations of interest and the liquidations of debts. It would be better that on the Lord's Day he gave some accounting of himself and instead of reckoning his money reckoned up his sins'.[102]

In the 1650s, while most other countries were economically wearied by the Thirty Years War, the Dutch Republic was experiencing sustained economic growth. It was the wealthiest country in the world. After pursuing policies that established state sponsored monopoly and predatory capitalism, enshrining the nation as Europe's commodity broker, vast amounts of wealth poured into the Republic. Alongside a glut of capital came the usual trappings of wealth amongst an affluent population. Colourful, flamboyant and extravagant clothing became the norm in Amsterdam's Hof van Holland, the High Court of the Provinces of Holland and West Friesland.[103] Jacob Trigland (1583–1654), Amsterdam's most vocal minister, denounced those in his congregation who displayed wantonly their new-found wealth with gold and silver, especially those who wore such things to Sunday service. Rather than the sober wardrobes that marked the Reformed ideal, satin, brocade and damasks clothed the Amsterdammers in his care. 'How can it be that God's people could be so ornamented with silver and gold'? This criticism might also apply to the New Testaments and prayer books, decorated with silver clasps, that they carried with them to the service.[104] The Lord's judgment would surely fall on all those who indulged in with gaudy demonstrations of their wealth. Amsterdam, now exalted, should learn from the example of Antwerp, which had been brought low. The prophet Zephaniah's warning found favour with Trigland: 'Wail, O inhabitants of the Mortar! For all the traders are no more; all who weigh out silver are cut off (Zephaniah 1:11)'. For Trigland, wealth was not inherently sinful; the unchristian accumulation and presentation of wealth, however, would be punished by God.

Not all ministers were wholly in step with Trigland, Simonides and Voetius. Johannes Cloppenburg (1592–1652), a professor of theology at Harderwijk and

---

102 'Besiet eens met my, wat de Koopman verricht, als hy t' huys komt neemt hy Gods boeck, om de predicatie te her-knauwen? Neen. Hy doet het Schuldt-boeck voor den dagh halen, en is besigh met liquideren en rekenen. Och 't was beter, dat hy wat meer bekommert was, om in die grooten dagh des Heeren reeckenschap van sijn Rentmeesterschap te geven: hy is besigh om sijn geldt te tellen'. Simon Simonides, *Vrienden-raedt, gegeven aen de besochte gemeynte van de Ryp, by een merckelijck oordeel Gods over haer gegaen* (Rotterdam: Adries van Hoogen-huyse, 1655), USTC 1815758, pp. 348–349.

103 Benjamin B. Roberts and Leendert F. Groenendijk, 'Moral Panic and Holland's Libertine Youth of the 1650s and the 1660s', in *Journal of Family History* 30, no. 4 (2005), pp. 327–346.

104 'Hoe zijn sij met gouwt ende zilver behangen, hoe zijn sij verciert, soude dat Gots volk zijn'? Quoted in, R. B. Evenhuis, *Ook dat was Amsterdam* (5 vols., Amsterdam: W. Ten Have, 1966–1978), II, p. 37.

later Franeker, was one of the most able opponents of Voetius. He considered usury acceptable within certain parameters.[105] This debate was not a matter of who was more genuinely Reformed. Cloppenburg's orthodoxy in theological matters was undeniable; and Hugo Grotius (1583–1645), who was reviled by Gisbertus Voetius, made similar arguments to the Reformed Voetius.[106] The *classis* of Leiden argued that the Utrecht theologians introduced teachings on usury that were denied by Scripture, the catechism, synodal resolutions and the practice of Reformed churches. They claimed such concerns were not within the purview of the church. Political authorities had the responsibility to establish what was and was not lawful.[107] Such positions, nevertheless, were public arguments for the most faithful application of the Bible's teaching. Though the Utrecht theologians and the Leiden *classis* differed on the policy outcome, both sought the same end: they called for a more Christian society. On 30 March 1658, the States of Gelderland and Holland settled the dispute. They concluded with Cloppenburg and the Leiden *classis* that the church had no authority on these matters. If a banker followed the law, they should not be banned from the Lord's Supper.[108] Samuel Maresius (1599–1673), a professor of theology at Groningen who defended the practice alongside Cloppenburg and the Leiden *classis*, revelled in the fact that his position had won the day in both the ecclesiastical and political fields.[109]

Through everyday observation, knowledge of the Bible and the occasional reading of books on economics, ministers in the Republic exhorted congregants and those in secular authority to pursue a Christian agenda in economic matters. Ministers encouraged virtue above wealth, honour rather than glory, and humility and circumspection in place of earthly status. Armed with the knowledge of their opponents' best arguments for and against usury, ministers constructed their responses. They employed the pen to persuade readers,

---

105 Johannes Cloppenburg, *De foenore et usuris, brevis institutio, cum ejusdem epistola asd Cl. Salmasium* (Leiden: Elzevier, 1640), USTC 1028069. Cf. Neil de Marchi and Paul Harrison, 'Trading "in the Wind" and with Guile: The Troublesome Matter of the Short Selling of Shares in Seventeenth-Century Holland,' in Neil de Marchi and Mary S. Morgan (eds.), *Higgling: Transactors and their Markets in the History of Economics* (Durham: Duke University Press, 1994), p. 56.

106 Henk Nellen, *Hugo Grotius: A Lifelong Struggle for Peace in Church and State, 1583–1645*, trans. J. C. Grayson (Leiden: Brill, 2014), pp. 514–517.

107 'Aensprack tot den Christelijcken Leser', *Res judicanda, Saecke die noch state te oordeelen, van de bancken van leeninghe, by de magistrate opgerecht* (Leiden: Hendrick Verbiest, 1658), USTC 1839430, pp. 8–9.

108 Van Asselt, '"A Grievous Sin:" Gisbertus Voetius (1589–1676) and his anti-Lombard Polemic', p. 519.

109 Nauta, *Samuel Maresius*, p. 297.

LEARNED SERVANTS   185

whether ordinary citizens, local magistrates, other ministers and provincial or
national authorities.

6   Reading the Stars

Questions of sickness, death and obtaining one's daily bread were unavoidable. Every person would have been acutely aware of their frailty; and many,
the need to earn more money. These were daily, even hourly concerns. Some
events, though, captured national attention in sudden unexpected moments.
When a comet soared through the sky on a winter's night in 1664, men, women
and children stood in awe. It was one of many observed in the seventeenth
century. Astronomical events like comets, and other exceptional events like
beached whales and other natural phenomena, became shared cultural experiences that led to broad social discussion. A surge of pamphlets sought to cut
through the hubbub and explain what such heavenly spectacles meant: how
and why the comet emerged.

    Ministers jumped into the fray. Many Dutch pastors thought the comet was
a sign from God, warning the wayward nation to turn from sin and godless-
ness and return to faithful Reformed belief and action. Gisbertus Voetius suggested as much. He argued that a comet was an ominous sign, sent by God,
that ought to stir up reverence towards Him.[110] Specifically what the comet
may signify is not expressly clear, Voetius thought, but 'from the experience
of all times and the verdict of all men, they do announce drastic changes'.[111]
Similar sentiments were expressed after a gunpowder explosion levelled a portion of Delft in 1654. In the wake of these kinds of events, ministers implored
the States of Holland to impose stricter morals legislation on dancing, prosti-
tution, swearing and Sabbath observance.[112] In his *Delfschen donder-slagh ofte
Korte aensprake aen de bedroefde gemeente van Delf* [*Delft Thunderclap, or a
short address to the mourning congregation in Delft*], the Delft minister Petrus
de Witte, argued that the explosion was a providential sign against further
degeneration into immorality. Delft had already experienced a fire in 1536, and
now the fierce hand of a righteous God had chastised them again. 'Our sins, our
sins have directed the sparks and matchsticks to the powder.... The sins light

---

110   Gisbertus Voetius, *Selectarum disputationum theologicarum* (5 vols., Utrecht: Joannis à
      Wansberge 1649–1669), USTC 1836590, II, p. 912.
111   'Universali experientiâ & hominum consensus praejudicatum est, eos magnas mutations
      portendere'. Ibid., II, p. 929.
112   Jonathan Israel, *The Dutch Republic: Its Rise, Greatness, and Fall, 1477–1806* (Oxford:
      Clarendon Press, 1995), p. 662.

186 CHAPTER 5

God's wrath, here and in the hereafter, in the infernal fire. O gruesome sins'![113] His book was quickly reproduced by four other printers beyond Delft, two in Utrecht, one in Rotterdam and another in Amsterdam. Explanations that God demonstrated his displeasure for the sinfulness of human beings were common amongst observers before and after Voetius and De Witte. Yet Voetius was not wholly ignorant of the scientific advances taking place around him. When his book collection was sold in 1677 and 1679, forty-eight books on astronomy were included in the catalogue. Throughout his life, Voetius read books seeking to explain the created realm, and in concert with Scripture, he came to a reasoned conclusion.

Including cosmographical books (of which there are almost sixty), 693 books describing the Earth and the stars are listed in my database of ministerial catalogues. The catalogues I have transcribed list an average of just over ten works on the topic. This figure is skewed, because a few collections contained a far larger number. Jacob Arminius owned sixteen, including two copies of *De Sphaera Mundi* by the medieval monk and astronomer Johannes de Sacrobosco.[114] Johannes Pechlinus, a Lutheran minister in Leiden, owned thirty-nine.[115] Abraham Heidanus, a minister and later professor at Leiden, owned fifty-one, including Galileo's *Systema Mundi*.[116] Justinus van Assche owned over seventy.[117]

For some, pursuing knowledge of the heavens became an obsession. Jacob du Bois, a minister in Leiden, sought astronomical information beyond books. He wanted to become acquainted with the scientific practice himself. Du Bois had Samuel Karl Kechel tutor him in the field.[118] Kechel was the curator for astronomical instruments at Leiden University.

Astronomical and cosmographical books largely fell into three categories: classical/medieval, modern and polemical. As a group, classical and medieval

---

113 'Onse sonden, onse sonden, hebben de voncken ende zwavel-stocken aen het bus-poeder gheleydt.... De sonden ontsteken Godts torn hier, ende hier namaels in 't Helsche vuyr. O grouwelijcke sonden'! Petrus de Witte, *Delfschen donder-slagh ofte Korte aensprake aen de bedroefde gemeente van Delf* (Amsterdam: Gerrit Willemsz. Doornick, 1655), pp. 30–31. Cf. Marijke Meijer Drees '"Providential Discourse" Reconsidered: The Case of the Delft Thunderclap (1654)', *Dutch Crossings*, 40 (2016), pp. 108–121.

114 *AC Jacob Arminius* (Leiden: Thomas Basson, 1610), USTC 1506632.

115 *AC Johannes Pechlinus* (Leiden: Pieter van der Aa, 1690), USTC 1823437.

116 *AC Abraham Heidanus* (Leiden: Felix Lopez de Haro & widow and heirs Adrianus Severinus, 1679), USTC 1846941.

117 *AC Justinus van Assche* (Rotterdam: Simon Simonsz Visser, 1650), USTC 1121734.

118 Preface to Jacob du Bois, *Oude-tyds tyd-thresoor ende kerkelikke historie* (Leiden: Cornelis Banheining, 1650), USTC 1023031.

authors are the most popular in the genre. Ten copies of works by Marcus Manilius, a Roman author, were listed; Ptolemy and Proclus, seven. Gaius Julius Solinus, a third century Latin grammarian and mapmaker, was similarly popular, with ten books on the description of the world. Amongst the sixteenth- and seventeenth-century authors, none were as popular as Philip Lansbergius, Johannes Kepler and Sebastian Münster. Münster's popularity can be traced, in part, to the utility of his work. The *Cosmographia* served as an indispensable encyclopaedia that sought to describe the history and topography of the world. In a single folio volume, it 'created a universal geography, and joined to it a history which brought all the empires of man into a meaningful progression'.[119] A conspicuous absence from the most popular authors is Tycho Brahe, the famous Danish astronomer. His works are listed five times.

The most popular author present in the corpus indicates the purpose of astronomical studies for many of these ministers: Philip Lansbergius (in its non-Latinized form, Philips Lansbergen), whose various works were listed twenty times (Table 5.6). Knowledge of non-theological fields varied greatly amongst ministers. Some were content with the knowledge gleaned from experience and those Christian theologians who addressed such topics in their writings; others, however, pursued knowledge beyond religious studies with as much drive and determination as they exhibited for their pastoral care. Few did this more so than Philips Lansbergen.

TABLE 5.6   The six most popular authors of astronomical
and cosmographical works listed in ministerial
auction catalogues

Author	Number of books
Philip Lansbergius	20
Johannes Kepler	18
Sebastian Münster	17
Dionysius Alexandrinus	16
Paulus Merula	12
Johannes de Sacrobosco	12

119   Matthew McLean, *The* Cosmographia *of Sebastian Münster: Describing the world in the Reformation* (Aldershot, UK: Ashgate, 2007), p. 341.

188 CHAPTER 5

Born in Ghent in 1561, Lansbergen and his family were part of the exodus of Reformed believers to the Northern Netherlands after the fall of Antwerp in 1585. Lansbergen's interest in astronomy was likely kindled while he was a young man in the Southern Low Countries. His first publication on the topic came in 1588, only two years after he departed Leiden to become a minister in Goes. Lansbergen was a fierce proponent of Reformed theology, and he gave no quarter to those who harboured Roman Catholic sensibilities. After almost twenty years in Goes, he was relieved of his pulpit after he chastised the magistrates for their alleged forbearance towards suspected Roman Catholics. In 1613, he moved to Middelburg and dedicated the rest of his life to propagating a Copernican view of the universe that simultaneously affirmed the authority of the Bible. It was a distinctly 'Christian cosmology'.[120] In 1629, he defended the orthodoxy of his position, stating that his *Bedenckingen, op den dagelijckschen, ende iaerlijckschen loop van den aerdt-kloot,* [*Considerations on the Daily and the Yearly Course of the Terrestrial Globe*] was 'built not only upon the foundations of geometry, but also upon the testimonies of the Word of God. Both of which are so infallible, that one cannot doubt its certainty and truth'.[121] For Lansbergen and many other ministers, understanding the physical world was an exercise in piety. They sought to comprehend how God established creation, including the rotation of the stars (Table 5.7).

TABLE 5.7   A selection of well-known and celebrated astronomical authors in fifty-five Dutch ministerial catalogues

Author	Number of books
George Purbachius	10
Galileo Galilei	9
Christopher Clavius	8
Nicolaus Copernicus	8
Ptolemy	7

---

120   Rienk Vermij, *The Calvinist Copernicans: The reception of the new astronomy in the Dutch Republic, 1575–1750* (Amsterdam: Koninklijke Nederlandse Akademie van Wetenschappen, 2002), p. 88.

121   'Want gelijck de gronden vande Meet-const, geheel vast ende seker zijn, alsoo zijn oock de getuygenissen van Gods woort, 't eenemael waerachtich, jae de waerheyt selve'. Philips Lansbergen, *Bedenckingen, op den dagelijckschen, ende iaerlijckschen loop van den aerdt-kloot* (Middelburg: Zacharias Roman, 1629), USTC 1026730, f. *3r.

In 1665, Franciscus Ridderus published a tract entitled *Reys-discours op het verschijnen van de comeet-sterre, die voor d'eerstemael gesien is den 15 december des jaers 1664* [*A travel dialogue on the appearance of the Comet, which was first seen on 15 December in the year 1664*].[122] In this discourse between a student, a citizen and a traveller, the student summarized the new science which claimed the comet was a natural phenomenon with no spiritual meaning. The traveller rebukes him and offers the definitive explanation on the meaning of the comet's appearance. He argues three points: a scientific explanation is inadequate for comprehensive understanding of the comet's full meaning, predictive astrology is to be condemned, and (like Voetius argued) it is a sign of Divine hostility. Ridderus grounds the traveller's expertise not only in Scripture, but in his own proficiency gained through investigating books. He attempts to overwhelm any dissenting view with philosophical, historical, theological and scientific references. He cites works by classical authors such as Seneca and Aristotle, but also contemporary scientific theorists like Bartholomäus Keckermann and even 'the learned Star Gazer' Tycho Brahe.[123] The traveller's position is confirmed by a combination of Biblical proof and scientific observation. Ridderus, who cast himself as this learned traveller, explained his process of information gathering. 'I desired to investigate some authors and, then to summarize their conclusions'.[124] Ridderus underwent the difficult process of collecting sources, internalizing and understanding them, and presenting a biblically informed view of a topic that would have gripped his congregants' attention.

Ministers often differed on the importance of astronomy to the Christian faith. In 1608 Sibrandus Lubbertus, a professor of theology at Franeker who was happy to combat those teachings he found heretical, suggested Copernicanism was merely an astronomical hypothesis. It was simply a scientific theory that had little or no bearing on theological matters.[125] The auction catalogue composed to advertise the sale of his library does not list any works by the famed Danish astronomer.

Nevertheless, even some ministers who were less dogmatic acquired books on the topic. André Rivet was one such minister. Rivet was more ambivalent

---

122 Franciscus Ridderus, *Reys-discours op het verschijnen van de comeet-sterre, die voor d'eerstemael gesien is den 15 december des jaers 1664* (Rotterdam: Henricus Goddaeus, 1665), USTC 1802715.

123 'De gheleerde Sterre-kijcker Tycho Brahe'. Ridderus, *Reys-Discours op het verschijnen van de Comeet-sterre*, p. 15.

124 'Soo dreef mij de lust om eenighe *Autheuren* naer te sien, en dese *Regeltjes* uyt haer soo kortelijck bij een te stellen'. Ridderus, *Reys-Discours op het verschijnen van de Comeet-sterre*, f. A2v.

125 Vermij, *The Calvinist Copernicans*, p. 247.

190   CHAPTER 5

about scientific knowledge. He argued that to worship God rightly one did not need thorough knowledge of creation.[126] This ambivalence, however, did not detract from him acquiring books about the natural world. He invested time and energy in understanding the natural world and philosophy. He regularly discussed the scientific discoveries of the seventeenth century with his correspondents, and received numerous scientific books through them. In working for Leiden's printers in 1628, André Rivet oversaw the copy-editing of a book on optics by the Dutch Astronomer Willebrord Snellius.[127] Rivet acquired a copy of *Eratosthenes Batavus*, an investigation into the circumference of the Earth by Snellius (Leiden, 1617).[128] He also received numerous works of science from academics and intellectuals in France. On 4 November 1647, Marin Mersenne sent Rivet a copy of Blaise Pascal's newest work, *Expériences nouvelles touchant le vide*.[129]

Marin Mersenne often wrote to André Rivet about the scientific discoveries that were taking place throughout Europe. In 1638, Mersenne pushed his correspondent to divulge his thoughts on Nicolaus Copernicus' theory that the Earth orbited the Sun. Sensitive to what lay behind Mersenne' thinly veiled question, Rivet answered that he thought there should be little controversy over Galileo's recent defence of Copernicus. After all, theology claimed to ask and answer different questions than mathematics or philosophy.[130] If Mersenne assumed that Rivet owned a copy of any of the works by Copernicus or Galileo, however, he would have been mistaken. Rivet owned more works on astrology than he did on astronomy. One of his astrological texts, *Marmora Arundeliana* by John Selden, was a gift from Johann Gronovius while visiting Oxford.[131] His few

---

126   For Rivet on pursing knowledge of science, see his letter to Anna Maria van Schurmann, 18 March 1638, in Anna Maria van Schurman, *Verhandeling over de aanleg van vrouwen voor wetenschap*, trans. Renée ter Haar (Groningen: Xeno, 1996), p. 94. Cf. Desmond Clarke (ed.), *The Equality of the Sexes: Three Feminist Texts of the Seventeenth Century* (Oxford: Oxford University Press, 2013), p. 25.

127   C. de Pater, 'Experimental Physics', in Th. H. Lunsingh Scheurleer and G. H. M. Posthumus Meyjes (eds.), *Leiden University in the Seventeenth Century: An Exchange of Learning* (Leiden: Universitaire Pers Leiden/Brill, 1975), p. 309.

128   *AC André Rivet*, p. 98.

129   Marin Mersenne to Rivet, 4 November 1647, in Tannery, De Waard and Beaulieu (eds.), *Correspondence du P Marin Mersenne*, XC, p. 518.

130   Marin Mersenne to Rivet, 20 November 1638, in Paul Tannery, Cornelis de Waard and Armand Beaulieu (eds.), *Correspondence du P Marin Mersenne* (17 vols., Paris: Presses Universitaires de France, 1945–1988), VIII, p. 222; Marin Mersenne to Rivet, 20 December 1638, Ibid., VIII, p. 239.

131   Johann Gronovius to G. J. Vossius, 14 August 1638, in Paulus Colomesius (ed.), *Virorum Eruditione Celeberrimorum Epistolae, Clarorum Virorum ad Vossium* (London: Sam Smith and Benjamin Walford, 1698), p. 187. *AC André Rivet*, p. 91.

LEARNED SERVANTS

books on astronomy were outdated by the time Mersenne asked him about Copernicus: Bartholomäus Keckermann's *Systema geometriae, opticae, astronomiae, geographiae* and Petrus Pitatus' *Opuscula astronomica* (Basel, 1568).[132]

Understanding creation was an opportunity for controversy. Astronomical events stoked the flames of a heated debate in the academy and church. Lansbergen's reference to both geometry and the Bible hints at the debate that would erupt not long after his death. Was the sun or the Earth the centre of the universe? Du Bois' preoccupation with learning first-hand how astronomy is practiced only makes sense if much more was at stake than a scientific theory about whether the Sun or the Earth was the centre of the universe. The question was a proxy war for a debate about the authority of the Bible. Ministers and professors were some of the most vocal contributors to the debate.

Debates in obscure corners of the theological world could reach the political and cultural centres, if pursued with enough vitriol. Up and coming ministers tried to advance their position in the Dutch Reformed church during such occasions. At only twenty-five years old, Petrus van Mastricht (1630–1706), a minister in Xanten (a village near Duisburg) wrote *Vindiciae veritatis et autoritatis sacrae scripturae* against the published dissertations of the newly hired professor of theology at Duisburg, Christophor Wittich (1625–1687). Wittich argued that Cartesianism and its heliocentric view of the world were in full accord with the Bible's teaching.[133] In 1652, two professors at Duisburg University, in the Duchy of Cleves, became embroiled in a controversy about Cartesianism with Cyriacus Lenz. Wittich, the professor of theology at Duisburg, gave two disputations defending the new philosophy. The second supported Descartes' theory on the motion of the Earth, in opposition to the standard Reformed view that the Earth stood still. The brouhaha that erupted after the disputation was so intense that it was republished in 1655, in Amsterdam.[134]

Any naturalistic explanation of the rotation of the stars or phenomena like the 1664 comet failed to capture the wonder of God's operation in the world. Ministers claimed the Bible taught that such events were supernatural. Godefridus Udemans was convinced Christians should examine the heavens and marvel at their Creator, and not at the heavens themselves.

---

132   *AC André Rivet*, pp. 105, 99. Pitatus' *Opuscula Astronomica* (Basel, 1568) is likely, *Verae solaris atque lunaris anni quantitatis aliarumque rerum ad calendarii Romani emendationem pertinentium* (Basel: Peter Perna, 1568), USTC 700562.

133   Petrus van Mastricht, *Vindiciæ veritatis et authoritatis Sacræ Scripturæ in rebus philosophicis* (Utrecht: Johannes à Waesburge, 1655), USTC 1557165.

134   Theo Verbeek, *Descartes and the Dutch: Early Reactions to Cartesian Philosophy, 1637–1650* (Carbondale, Ill.: Southern Illinois University Press, 1992), p. 74.

Scripture clearly warns us against astrology, which is predicting one's fortune or misfortune from the stars ... We do not ban astronomy and the study of the course of the heavens, as long as man stays within the confines of nature and Scripture, and does not bind God's wisdom and power to it, but instead is moved to praise God the way the holy patriarchs and prophets did.[135]

When critics within the Reformed Church like Wittich began siding with René Descartes on philosophical and scientific matters, ministers like Van Mastricht and Du Bois considered it as an attack against Scripture. To bolster the faith of those Christians who might be carried along by the eloquence of such teaching, they took to print. When ordinary church members gazed into the awesome expanse above them, ministers wanted to be sure the sight encouraged their faith, as that was the purpose of the heavens in the first place. 'The heavens declare the glory of God; the skies above, his handiwork (Psalm 19:1)'.

7 Learned Servants

In the early-modern Netherlands, print had the pervasive ability to set the world ablaze with public discussion. Ministers were in the business of persuasion, and print was one of the most useful tools in their endeavour to persuade. With their book collections, ministers studied matters of public importance and offered their perspective from the pulpit and through print. Ministers attempted to bolster their congregants' knowledge of the faith and its implications for daily life, by devoting themselves to a lifetime of reading. Having learned, they then preached and wrote to bring about a more Christian society. A professor of theology at Utrecht stated, 'For it is when he goes forth from the sacred mount of contemplation, his soul manifestly replenished and radiant with the purest light, that he is best fitted to communicate that light of reflection to others'.[136]

The ministry was a reading profession, but not all ministers read diverse works merely out of the desire to glorify God in all aspects of their intellectual lives; or even to help those in their flocks pursue every aspect of life in faithfulness to Him. Some ministers had to read broadly because they were forced

---

135 Godefridus Udemans, *The Practice of Faith, Hope, and Love*, trans. Annemie Godbehere, ed. Joel R. Beeke (Grand Rapids: Reformation Heritage Books, 2012), p. 212.

136 Witsius, *On the Character of a True Theologian*, p. 38.

LEARNED SERVANTS 193

to by circumstances beyond their control. When the Synod of Dort ended in 1619, the victorious party forcibly removed the followers of Arminius from their pulpits. After the death of Prince Maurits in 1625, some banished ministers returned to the Netherlands and took up posts at newly formed Remonstrant churches, often located in Holland's urban centres. Left with few options, some Remonstrant ministers pursued other vocations instead.

Johannes Arnoldus Corvinus was one such minister. After his pastorate was taken from him in Leiden, Corvinus wandered throughout Europe for over ten years.[137] Following a controversy with his Remonstrant brethren, Corvinus made his way to Orléans to take his doctoral degree in law. In the Spring of 1634, Corvinus moved to Amsterdam and began practicing law, while offering private tuition. As a minister, Corvinus had been a man of books, and to excel in his new career, he needed more books on law. On 10 July 1634, he wrote to Petrus Cunaeus, a professor of jurisprudence at Leiden. Corvinus wanted the professor's opinion on Aegidius Hortensius' commentary on Justinian's *Institutes*.[138] If Cunaeus approved, Corvinus hoped Cunaeus would buy him a copy. 'If you are willing and able', Corvinus wrote, 'I may prefer one to be bought from either the Elzeviers or the Maires for myself, and that it may bound before my wife comes to Leiden'.[139] A week later, Corvinus thanked Cunaeus for buying it for him and he requested Vigetius' *Dialectica Juris* as well.

Ministers in the Netherlands argued that their faith presented a framework for understanding every aspect of creation, and their theological writings and libraries reflect this belief. The divide between theology and natural sciences was largely unknown in the seventeenth century. Science and economics were not completely distinct from theology and morality. Gualtherus de Bruyn, a doctoral candidate at Utrecht, gave three disputations to complete his studies. They covered the nature of evil, free will and the motion of the stars.[140]

Ministers understood themselves not only as ambassadors for a set of religious convictions, but as public intellectuals charged with helping their flocks understand every aspect of their daily lives from a biblically informed point

---

137 Johannes Arnoldus Corvinus to Petrus Cunaeus, 10 July 1634, in Wilhelmina G. Kamerbeek, 'Some Letters by Johannes Arnoldi Corvinus', *Lias*, 9 (1982), pp. 87–88.

138 Likely, Aegidius Hortensius, *Commentarii Ad IV. Institutionum Divi Iustiniani Imperatoris Libros* (Giesen: Philipp Franke, 1614), USTC 2042610.

139 'Memini me apud virum doctissimum aliquando Hortensij commentarium vidisse & ex parte legisse cum voluptate. Eum si habes et probas, velim per affinium unum mihi apud Elzevirium, vel Mairium eum emi, & interim dum uxor mea Leydam venit compingi'. Johannes Arnoldus Corvinus to Petrus Cunaeus, 10 July 1634, UB Leiden CUN 2. Cf. Kamerbeek, 'Some Letters by Johannes Arnoldi Corvinus', p. 95.

140 Vermij, *The Calvinist Copernicans*, p. 250.

of view. After years of dedicated study, acquiring hundreds and often thousands of books, the ideal minister presented an informed case to live piously as a banker, merchant, sailor, weaver, mother or father. Even when petitioning the States failed to bring about stricter Sabbath observation, virtuous lending practices, or to eradicate certain pernicious ideas from the public square, ministers attempted to persuade members of their congregations individually, to make life-changing alterations to their behaviour. Their libraries of relevant texts provided the ammunition necessary to address these demanding tasks.

Conclusion: The Ideal Ministerial Library

A few years after Johannes Lomeier became a minister in a rural village near his hometown of Zutphen, he decided to write a book on libraries: *De bibliothecis liber singularis*. Lomeier had studied at Zutphen's Latin school and Deventer's *Athenaeum*, a school that prepared young students for a university education but did not grant for formal degrees. He attended classes at the University of Utrecht before becoming a student in theology at Groningen. Lomeier was a well-connected young man who leveraged friendships, contacts and family members to help himself join the ranks of the highly-educated elite who wielded civic authority. His father was a local minister in Zutphen; his uncle was a local publisher and bookseller. Lomeier became the principal of the grammar school in Zutphen.[1] His scholarly ambition drove him to want more intellectual engagement than his rural pastorate supplied.

De bibliothecis liber singularis first appeared in 1669 (Fig. 6.1). It addressed the history of the book, the way ancient and medieval cultures preserved collective memories and he offered guides to constructing a library. He included sections on the best way for a library to be designed, facing east so books can be read in the morning.[2] The job of the library's 'prefect' was to curate a library that is useful. He reminded his readers that life is brief, so book collections should be organized in such a way that time is not needlessly wasted hunting for elusive books.[3]

In his tenth chapter the scholar set before himself the unenviable task of describing the notable libraries of the early-modern era. Many of the libraries which are famous to book historians are depicted: the Ambrosian library, the Mazarine, and others. Smaller regional and city libraries, though perhaps less renowned today, received no less attention. He began with Italy, as it was the fount of humane letters from which so many great thinkers had emerged in ancient and medieval times. His descriptions of the contents of the libraries varied drastically from one to the next. Occasionally, Lomeier noted the novel items contained in a library. On the Ambrosian library founded by Cardinal Borromeo, Lomeier noted that it contained 'the works of Virgil in folio with

---

1 Willem Frijhoff, 'Johannes Lomejer (1636–1699): From a Historian of Books to a Cultural Historian', *Quaerendo*, 42 (2012), pp. 84–113.

2 Johannes Lomeier, *De bibliothecis liber singularis* (Zutphen: Henric Berren, 1669), USTC 1806598, p. 329.

3 Ibid., p. 301.

196 CONCLUSION: THE IDEAL MINISTERIAL LIBRARY

notes by Francesco Petrarch'.[4] The city library at Dokkum, in Friesland, had the honour of housing 'a manuscript codex of the Gospels which was used by Boniface ... who preached the Christian faith in these regions, and suffered martyrdom'.[5] Despite being a book describing libraries, Lomeier rarely mentioned the specific contents of the library, beyond the novel and intriguing. Lomeier noted on several occasions that a city merely has a library: in his description of Sicilian libraries, one finds 'There is a library located in the archimandrite's palace at Messina'; or on libraries in the Low Countries 'there are libraries at Franeker, Groendael, and Groningen'.[6] Some of the libraries mentioned only in passing were no small, mediocre institutions: by the end of the seventeenth century, the university library in Franeker contained 1,087 folios and hundreds of books in other formats. Nevertheless, Lomeier rarely gave detailed descriptions of the libraries he deemed worthy of consideration in his volume.

To Lomeier's readers, this lack of detailed description was not a fault. Educated readers like Lomeier held a mutual understanding concerning the kinds of books that belonged to a library in early-modern Europe. His summaries indicate this consensus view. The library housed at the monastery of Gembloux in the Southern Netherlands consisted 'especially of works which deal with theology, and which provide Latin interpretations of Holy Scripture. Works of the poets and orators are also present, and so is anything that is a contribution to Latin literature'.[7]

The ambiguity laden in the phrase 'a contribution to Latin literature' frustrates readers interested in the specific contents of the library. Such a broad category evades easy description. Remembering Lomeier's personal and professional background may help readers come to terms with his intended meaning. He was an educated minister in the Reformed church, and he remained so despite leaving the rural pastorate for more stimulating fields. When the grammar school where Lomeier served as principal was closed during the French invasion of 1672, he returned to his first calling, the pastorate. Ministers also played important roles in getting his *De bibliothecis* to print. Wilhelm Wilhelmus wrote an introductory epistle for the first edition. Wilhelmus became the subregent of Leiden's theological college.[8] Lomeier dedicated the

---

4   Johannes Lomeier, *A Seventeenth-Century View of European Libraries: Lomeier's De bibliothecis, Chapter X*, trans. John Warwick Montgomery (Berkeley: University of California Press, 1962), p. 20.

5   Lomeier, *A Seventeenth-Century View of European Libraries*, p. 36.

6   Ibid., pp. 26, 37.

7   Lomeier, *A Seventeenth-Century View of European Libraries*, p. 37.

8   P. C. Molhuysen (ed.), *Bronnen tot de Geschiedenis der Leidensche Universiteit* (7 vols., The Hague: Martinus Nijhoff, 1913–1924), III, p. 304.

CONCLUSION: THE IDEAL MINISTERIAL LIBRARY

second edition to Johannes Rauwers (1637–1692), his brother-in-law and a minister in Harmelen near Utrecht. Rauwers had encouraged him to undertake the project, for which Lomeier expressed his thanks.[9]

Ministers were not only fundamental to the publication of *De bibliothecis*; ministers like Lomeier were some of the most prominent book collectors in the Dutch Republic. From 1607, when the first minister's collection was auctioned and advertised with a pre-distributed catalogue, to 1700, over 457 auctions of ministerial book collections took place. Nearly all of these were advertised in advance with a catalogue of the books for sale. There were about 5,500 ministers serving Reformed churches in the Netherlands during the seventeenth century. Hundreds of ministers served Protestant, but not Reformed churches. As seventy per cent of all surviving catalogues are known from only one copy, it would not be unlikely that more than one in ten Dutch ministers owned book collections that were large enough to be auctioned with an accompanying catalogue.

Book auctions were standard fare in Lomeier's time: Between 1636, the year of Lomeier's birth, and 1669, when *De bibliothecis* was published, 1,062 book auctions took place. Seventy-one auctions took place in the year he published *De bibliothecis*. In nearby Deventer, five book auctions took place between 1655 and 1669, two of which were of ministerial collections. Auctions and auction catalogues were a ubiquitous cultural phenomenon amongst people like Lomeier; that is, the educated, urbane and bookish sort.

Auction catalogues typically had a print run of five to six hundred copies.[10] 261 catalogues of ministerial books survive. Therefore, just based on surviving catalogues, at least 130,500 to 156,600 copies of ministerial book auction catalogues circulated during the seventeenth century. If one includes inferred catalogues, that figure would jump to well over 220,000. These surviving catalogues offer the clearest explanation of Lomeier's ambiguous phrase 'a contribution to Latin literature'.

To Lomeier, what was the ideal ministerial library in the Dutch Golden Age? To answer this, one must consider the role of a minister during this time. Ministers were tasked with presenting timeless biblical truths in ways that were relevant to their context, location, time and so on. They had to promulgate a faith that claimed to have authority over all people throughout history, but their own day presented unique challenges that required them to apply that knowledge in different ways than their forefathers in the faith. They had

---

9 Lomeier, *De bibliothecis liber singularis*, f. *3.
10 Arjan Nobel and Otto van der Meij, '"De Luijden sijn daer seer begeerich na": De veiling van de bibliotheek van André Rivet in 1657', in Maurits Ebben and Pieter Wagenaar (eds.), *De cirkel doorbroken* (Leiden: Instituut voor Geschiedenis, 2006), pp. 215–238.

198   CONCLUSION: THE IDEAL MINISTERIAL LIBRARY

to address new controversies and events when they arose and help their flock understand them in light of Scripture. For this twofold task of building on the tradition that came before and engaging in contemporary debate, books were essential.

1   **Timeless and Timely Libraries**

Regardless of the size of their libraries, ministerial book collections varied little in the quality or genre of books present in their libraries. All that changed was the quantity of books. Ministers who owned a smaller collection of a hundred books or so were not exempt from the task all ministers had. Rather than owning a library consisting of polemical books whose value was tied only to the controversy for which they were first written, these smaller collections had books that informed those polemical works: the Bible, the Church Fathers, the biblical commentaries of the first Protestant Reformers, classical works by Roman and Greek writers and lexicons and grammatical aids.

Books with enduring intellectual value were in constant demand. To be worthy of being auctioned, ministers had to own books that were desired by other buyers. Many of these buyers were typically ministers themselves. Books with the highest value were those that cut across confessional and geographical lines. The works of one of the Church Fathers in a Latin folio commanded a higher price partly because more ministers wanted it than they did an obscure vernacular work in a less well-known language. The size of the book certainly influenced the cost to a large extent, but some of the increase in price is also related to demand. When the prices of folios are analysed from fifty-five ministerial library catalogues, the average price of folios in ministerial libraries was ten gulden. Many folios sold for far less than this average: 122 folios sold for less than one gulden, about the same price as a moderately priced devotional book in far smaller formats.

The books that had some of the widest readership amongst ministers were Latin folio volumes. Amongst these, the first signs of an ideal ministerial library begin to emerge. Comparing the Latin folios listed in their catalogues gives a sense of the similarity between ministerial collections. With few exceptions, ministerial auction catalogues begin with these books. Booksellers used auction catalogues to sell books, and the first books they listed were most often theological folios. Nearly all ministers desired these kinds of books for their library. With rare exception, ministers throughout the seventeenth century acquired these books because they offered more enduring value than a book or pamphlet on a particular controversy. Even the smallest ministerial

CONCLUSION: THE IDEAL MINISTERIAL LIBRARY   199

collections that sold at auction contained them. Theodorus van Couwenhoven owned 173 books, a meagre collection compared to the average of 1,142 books, but Van Couwenhoven owned thirty-three folio volumes, including Johann Scapula's *Lexicon*, several *Operae* by Classical authors, eight commentaries by Cornelis à Lapide and similar books.[11] Of the 103 books owned by Wilhelm Merwy, chaplain to the Dutch ambassador to Venice, there were nine folio works, all of the same kind as the folios owned by Van Couwenhoven.[12] The Haarlem minister Samuel Gruterus owned 4,284 books (forty times the size of Merwy's collection and nearly twenty-five times Van Couwenhoven's). Of his books, 1,099 were folio works, and most of those listed were nearly identical in genre to the smaller collections owned by Merwy and Van Couwenhoven.[13] Gruterus simply owned more of them. When one considers the categories of folios Gruterus, Van Couwenhoven and Merwy owned, rather than the total number, little distinguishes the three collections.

The theological world of the early-modern Netherlands was turbulent and constantly changing, with scores of new books being written and published by ministers and professors. This terrain offered much gain for those hoping to read pious books, but also countless opportunities for authors to stir up controversy (or, in many cases, for authors to be dragged into controversy). Theological storms emerged regularly. This required books that specifically addressed the issues at hand, and a minister's auction catalogue often leaves insight into the controversies of the owner's day. These catalogues remind modern readers of the most controversial figures of the sixteenth and seventeenth centuries. One of the most controversial authors of the era is also one of the most popular: Conrad Vorstius. Far more so than his predecessor at Leiden Jacob Arminius, Vorstius is one of the most listed authors amongst auction catalogues of ministerial libraries. This popularity is due to the frenzy his works caused amongst his Reformed readers in the Netherlands. After he was nominated for a position on the University of Leiden's theology faculty in 1610, many ministers denounced the decision, claiming he dabbled in heresy. The uproar, with its mass of publications, set the terms of theological debate for over a decade. Given the fallout from Vorstius' nomination to the most prestigious theological faculty in the Dutch Republic, a minister at any time in the century could not go without knowing about Vorstius, his life and works. His popularity in auction catalogues has little to do with his importance as a theologian of enduring value, but as a flashpoint in the theological world.

---

11   *AC Theodorus van Couwenhoven 1646* (Leiden: Philippe de Croy, 1646), USTC 1121798.
12   *AC Wilhelm Merwy 1636* (Delft: Jan Pietersz Waalpot, 1636), USTC 1027540, ff. A2, A3.
13   *AC Samuel Gruterus 1700* (Leiden: Pieter van der Aa, 1700), USTC 1848523.

Hugo Grotius, the statesmen, scholar and theologian, was popular for similar reasons to Vorstius. Rather than being remembered for his constructive writings intended for a broad audience, in ministers' collections he is a polemicist who is remembered because of his arguments placing the authority of the church under that of the magistrates, his moderate theological positions and his friendliness towards Roman Catholics. Some ministers undoubtedly drew enduring theological value from books by Vorstius and Grotius, but that does not fully explain their popularity in this dataset. Their works caused controversies that reoriented the Dutch religious landscape for generations. To understand their own time and minister to their flock, a minister had to read books by those who had shaped the religious landscape in their time. Authors like Grotius and Vorstius, therefore, had to be read in similar numbers to other authors from whom the Reformed more immediately benefited: Franciscus Junius, André Rivet and Jerome Zanchius.

2 Ministerial Libraries in a Golden Age

Libraries were an unavoidable part of life for any who aspired to civil and religious authority during the Dutch Golden Age. Scholars of all sorts, including Lomeier, knew the kinds of books they could expect to find in libraries throughout Europe or in the homes of fellow scholars. Ministers were a substantial part of the book buying market: on the evidence of auction catalogues, libraries owned by ministers were the most common category of personal libraries in the Netherlands. The history of libraries and print are inextricably linked with ministers. In any estimation of the book world, these religious servants must play a substantial role.

No scholar would deny the important role Christian devotion played in the print world. Devotional books and theological texts written by ministers were the wheels upon which the entire print industry turned; they were 'pillars of the trade'.[14] The same could be said for ministerial libraries in early modern Europe. While the Mazarine, Ambrosian, Bodleian and other similar libraries are celebrated for their grandeur and sophistication, they were extravagant exceptions to the usual practice of building a library in the seventeenth century: it was ministers who built and used the most libraries. Their libraries represent the heart of library building during this time. If a citizen of the

---

14   Andrew Pettegree and Arthur der Weduwen, *Bookshop of the World: Making and Trading Books in the Dutch Golden Age* (New Haven: Yale University Press, 2019), p. 119.

CONCLUSION: THE IDEAL MINISTERIAL LIBRARY

Netherlands wanted to explore a library during the seventeenth century, their best opportunity to do so was to turn to their local minister.

Book collecting was not only a practice of elite scholars and wealthy patrons of the arts. Ministers were generally from middling backgrounds, yet they were educated to the highest possible level at the time, and they often built collections that confirm that level of education. Ministerial libraries with hundreds of books were not anomalies. Such ownership indicates that ownership of a book collection was no longer an extravagance to be enjoyed by only a few buyers.

As important ministerial book collections are to the history of libraries in early modern Europe, so too are they fundamental to our understanding of religious life during the time. Print was a fundamental component of religious life in the Netherlands, as it was too in other countries during the early modern era. Before the Reformation took root in the Netherlands in 1520, Catholic devotional works were easily available. Both Catholics and Protestants considered print necessary in the struggle for confessional dominance. Emphasis on the printing press was a central policy outcome of the Council of Trent.[15] Protestant works between 1520 and 1540 were printed in almost the same numbers as Roman Catholic books, despite harsh censure from the Habsburg Regime.[16] For the fulfilment of their pastoral duties, ministers turned to print, and over time they built impressive libraries. Ownership of a well-stocked library was a defining feature of the ministerial career. Ministers considered their libraries to be central to their work. They turned to them for personal devotion, intellectual formation and professional development. Ministers did read and own some books purely for their entertainment, but by and large their libraries served as tools. Ministers were held up as examples of pious learning in their communities and this required them to build a library. This degree of seriousness often meant some ministers possessed libraries that were much larger than was actually needed. That collection signalled to their flock the seriousness with which they took their pastoral calling.

As has been shown throughout this work, the information they drew from books in their libraries often made their way into their public work, preaching, counsel and writing. Systematic knowledge of the books owned and read by ministers sheds light on the history of church in the Netherlands, because

---

15   Stijn van Rossem, *Het gevecht met de Boeken. De uitgeversstrategieën van de familie Verdussen, 1589–1889* (Antwerp: Antwerpen Universiteit Pers, 2014).

16   Andrew G. Johnston, 'Printing and the Reformation in the Low Countries, 1520–c. 1555', in Jean-François Gilmont (ed.), *The Reformation and the Book*, trans. Karin Maag (Aldershot: Ashgate, 1998), pp. 155–183.

their libraries reflect both the expectations that were placed upon them by other ministers and by their congregations and the sources they turned to for their vital work.

We cannot understand the religious culture of the Dutch Golden Age until we come to terms with the way ministers used print. Print was vital to the survival of the Reformation in the Netherlands, and it remained a substantial factor in the process of bringing about a more Reformed Netherlands after other Protestant groups were officially banned from public meeting. Ministers of churches outside the Reformed confession and Roman Catholic priests similarly turned to print for the very same purpose. Censorship could be capricious and arbitrary in the Netherlands, but they nevertheless used print in the same ways as their Reformed counterparts. They too built similarly impressive libraries. Ministers considered print to be a vital tool in the pursuit of a more Christian society. Ministers read and acquired books with the ultimate goal of becoming better ministers, growing in godliness so they could better model the Christian life to their flock.

Libraries were possessions of central importance to the ministers who owned them. Knowing the kinds of books with which ministers interacted adds vital information into the daily life of a minister. One cannot tell the story of the history of Christianity in Netherlands without considering ministers' understanding of print, how these ministers used print to encourage godliness and the nature of their book collections.

3   The Ideal Ministerial Library

Between 1607 and 1700, over 315,000 books from ministerial collections were sold at auction in the Dutch Republic. That figure is derived from their 234 surviving auction catalogues. If the 200 or so inferred catalogues are included in this, and if they contained about the same as was average in surviving catalogues, the number of books sold from ministerial collections soars to around 450,000. From the Generality Lands on the southern border to Groningen in the north, Dutch ministers acquired libraries. Some were small and unadorned, others were comprehensive and unwieldy, with thousands of books lining their shelves; if indeed, they could find space to shelve them: some used the vestry of their churches for storing their books. Auction catalogues detail the collections of an extensive range of ministers: from towering theological professors who trained the next generation of ministers like Gisbertus Voetius with his 5,535 books to rural parish preachers with barely a hundred. Each catalogue is a monument to a minister's interaction with the printed word.

CONCLUSION: THE IDEAL MINISTERIAL LIBRARY

Despite such diversity, these catalogues nevertheless shared a certain resemblance with each other, as if an archetypal theological collection existed. The ideal library, according to Lomeier and as evidenced by the auction catalogues of ministerial book collections during the seventeenth century, was one that served the user according to their professional need. Lomeier acknowledged that even the ideal size of a collection depended on the owners' ability to acquire books, 'larger or smaller according to one's situation'.[17] The bare minimum that was needed to perform their pastoral duties would have included a Bible, a psalm book, a catechism, and perhaps a few devotional works and commentaries. The ideal, however, was much more robust, encompassing all genres of books.

The similarities in ministerial book collections can be traced to the culture and context in which Dutch ministers served. For ministers, the book collection that served their station in life was one that both helped them understand the faith as it had been received through the centuries and kept them informed about their own time. The necessary core was much smaller than they actually possessed, but the ministerial profession, by and large, worked under the assumption that reading was necessary to the minister's calling, and they often built substantial libraries because of that assumption. Their personal libraries indicate this conviction. In a constant process of theological conversation, they responded to each other's works and sought to build on the legacy that came before them. They built book collections to understand better the long tradition of biblical interpretation and theological systemization to which they claimed lineage. With books, they sought to understand the physical world around them so they could guide their flocks through the daily trials and tribulations that accompanied life in the seventeenth-century Dutch Republic. The ideal library for a minister was one with a core of certain types of books upon which all ministers had to build and the printed relics of controversies grounding the library in a specific time and place. Their collections were timeless and timely, for the development of their congregations and the further implementation of Christian convictions in the Dutch Republic.

---

17   Lomeier, *A Seventeenth-Century View of European Libraries*, p. 12.

Appendix: Analysed Ministerial Library Catalogues

Owner	Year	Residence		Location of Auction	Total	20	40	80	120	Latin	Vernac.	Dutch	Germ.	Fren.	Ital.	Span.	English
Johannes Halsbergius	1607	Amsterdam		Leiden	1426	334	299	724	69	1178	205	82	6	106	4	7	0
Lucas Trelcatius	1607	Leiden		Leiden	620	156	104	306	42	531	63	13	0	50	0	0	0
Gerson Quewellerius	1608	Wesel		Leiden	932	110	144	588	90	596	322	35	71	199	17	0	0
Johannes Barentsz	1609	Delft		Leiden	767	157	115	392	84	424	305	157	58	89	0	0	1
Joannes Bernardus	1609	Delft		Delft	736	157	117	384	78	442	260	147	59	54	0	0	0
Egbertus Aemelius/Jacobus Kuchlinus	1610	Leiden/ Hazerswoude		Leiden	842	163	193	404	82	643	214	73	0	81	0	0	2
Jacob Arminius	1610	Leiden	Rem.	Leiden	1634	238	219	706	101	1308	156	67	23	96	23	4	1
Dominicus Baudius/Andre Harckoni	1614	Leiden/ Groning		Leiden	1253	362	281	509	101	935	245	46	2	135	61	0	1
Abraham Mellinus	1623	Sint Anthoniepolder		Dordrecht	1451	346	301	728	42	1146	270	75	7	136	1	0	16
Isaac Hagius	1625	Delft		Leiden	879	106	184	433	156	566	260	207	1	35	1	0	16
Sibrandus Lubbertus	1625	Franeker		Franeker	530	164	99	256	11	475	4	0	3	1	0	0	0
Richard Niraeus/Daniel Quesnoy	1628			Leiden	2577	468	547	1198	364	1686	719	51	18	512	102	0	36
Johannes Wirink	1628	Leiden		Leiden	1361	191	243	580	182	994	324	167	6	148	2	1	0

206 APPENDIX: ANALYSED MINISTERIAL LIBRARY CATALOGUES

(cont.)

Owner	Year	Residence	Location of Auction	Total	20	40	80	120	Latin	Vernac.	Dutch	Germ.	Fren.	Ital.	Span.	English
Johannes Becius	1628	Zierikzee	Zierikzee	1269	142	309	692	126	896	313	281	12	17	2	1	0
Daniel Demetrius	1628	Dordrecht	Dordrecht	898	197	162	361	178	726	406	95	1	19	10	1	3
Daniel da la Vinea	1628	Dordrecht	Dordrecht (Wall.)	1191	154	260	652	125	765	129	138	1	267	0	0	0
Balthazar Lydius	1629	Dordrecht	Dordrecht	5890	877	1521	3076	416	4862	701	245	328	46	1	3	78
Petrus Pullaeus	1629	Amsterdam	Amsterdam	361	85	74	159	43	286	34	32	0	1	1	0	0
Adrianus van der Borre	1632	Leiden	Amsterdam (Rem.)	660	66	146	364	84	499	132	23	0	97	2	1	9
William Ames	1634	Franeker	Amsterdam	563	115	159	235	54	446	100	0	0	14	0	0	86
Petrus Stermont	1636	Gouda	Leiden	456	65	94	222	58	341	102	74	18	5	5	0	0
Wilhelm Merwy	1636	Venice	Delft	104	9	22	51	22	81	18	18	0	0	0	0	0
Johannes Westerburg	1637	Dordrecht	Dordrecht	1033	239	183	436	144	965	7	0	0	6	1	0	0
Samuel Basilius	1637	Lisse	Leiden	741	137	151	318	135	557	152	65	20	42	15	3	7
Johannes Nevius	1637	Venlo	Leiden	741	139	146	321	135	566	149	71	23	35	14	2	4
Daniel Castellani	1637	Den Bosch	Amsterdam	570	58	112	195	205	284	287	43	3	159	0	0	82
Samuel Middlehoven	1637	Voorschoten	Leiden	347	32	66	171	78	271	62	46	1	15	0	0	0
Johannes Bogermann	1638	Franeker	Leiden	1272	220	281	648	123	1073	128	73	35	17	2	1	0
Dionysius Marsbach	1638	Odijk	Leiden	471	65	94	226	86	373	72	39	5	25	3	0	0
Franciscus Gomarus	1641	Groningen	Leiden	2783	518	826	1151	281	2088	374	181	44	95	7	4	41
Caspar Pfeiffer	1643	Amsterdam	Amsterdam (Luth.)	935	119	262	479	75	662	73	111	132	2	0	1	0
Johannes Lydius	1643			1747	399	408	840	100	1571	246	4	63	6	0	0	0
Ludovic de Dieu	1643	Leiden	Leiden	784	176	344	194	70	603	140	58	2	69	0	0	11
Davidis Louwiick	1644	Barendrecht	Leiden	1144	96	313	540	195	644	483	326	1	26	0	1	129
Eido Campegius	1645	Pietersbierum	Franeker	3268	233	465	1644	376	2748	375	214	138	13	7	1	2

APPENDIX: ANALYSED MINISTERIAL LIBRARY CATALOGUES

(*cont.*)

Owner	Year	Residence		Location of Auction	Total	20	40	80	120	Latin	Vernac.	Dutch	Germ.	Fren.	Ital.	Span.	English
Daniel a Gys	1645	Leiden		Leiden	1387	258	333	564	189	902	448	92	3	205	3	0	145
Julius Herring	1645	Amsterdam		Leiden	1358	166	442	589	161	670	664	0	2	13	3	0	643
Marcus Boerhave	1645	Medemblik		Leiden	454	78	92	212	72	410	25	2	0	10	0	0	13
Jacob Verhage	1645	Noordwijk		Leiden	269	40	46	99	84	206	60	57	3	0	0	0	0
Thomas Laurentius	1645	Puttershoek		Leiden	189	91	33	65	0	161	27	10	5	2	1	1	8
Adrian Smoutis	1646	Amsterdam		Leiden	2709	443	648	1200	339	2259	246	11	61	94	29	30	21
Johannes a Campius	1646	Haarlem		Leiden	677	93	147	337	100	587	65	43	16	5	1	0	0
Petrus Busquerius	1646	Haarlem		Leiden	513	70	112	213	118	452	45	17	7	17	4	0	0
Johann Courten	1646	Scheveningen		Leiden	176	27	56	64	29	119	52	51	0	1	0	0	0
Theodorus van Couwenhoven	1646	Leiden		Leiden	172	34	15	67	47	159	7	6	0	1	1	0	0
Johannes Conringh	1647	Utrecht	Luth.	Utrecht	478	67	145	242	24	332	132	4	127	1	0	0	0
Jeremias Bastinck	1648	Strijen		Leiden	521	66	49	181	225	459	56	6	0	10	0	0	40
Petrus Facius	1648	Zandvort		Utrecht	351	59	71	146	57	221	118	69	6	43	0	0	0
Hieronymus Hirnius	1649	Rotterdam	Luth.	Rotterdam	1507	290	360	758	99	1229	495	129	53	6	2	0	0
Fredrick Spanheim	1649	Leiden		Leiden	1819	293	484	450	592	1284	190	51	83	276	3	0	82
Jesaias du Pre	1650	Leiden		Leiden	1206	342	207	536	121	758	455	52	4	350	0	0	1
Josephus van de Rosiere	1650	Haarlem		Haarlem	258	40	64	139	15	185	407	61	0	1	0	0	0
Justinus van Assche	1650	Rotterdam	Rem.	Rotterdam	1711	196	444	883	188	1150	62	183	91	84	58	6	33
Carolus de Maets	1651	Utrecht		Utrecht	1450	386	440	624	0	1223	227	60	0	139	0	0	28
Petrus Corderius	1652	Leiden		Leiden	771	133	190	263	185	585	152	16	31	2	34	0	69
Adolph Visscher	1653	Amsterdam	Luth.	Amsterdam	1609	191	530	528	360	823	276	262	506	0	0	0	0

(cont.)

Owner	Year	Residence	Location of Auction	Total	20	40	80	120	Latin	Vernac.	Dutch	Germ.	Fren.	Ital.	Span.	English
Johannes Cloppenburg	1653	Franeker	Leiden	3660	355	1012	1906	387	3255	895	63	73	12	10	7	111
Gualtherus de Bruyn	1653	Utrecht	Utrecht	1836	241	772	607	189	1239	560	188	0	39	2	0	331
Godefridus Udemans	1653	Zierikzee	Zierikzee	1449	180	329	653	247	825	768	410	5	99	0	0	67
Adam Rotarius	1653	Colijnsplaat and Kats	Middelburg	900	115	204	406	175	517	581	177	67	63	0	0	70
Carolus Niellius	1653	Amsterdam Rem.	Amsterdam	3014	281	724	1591	418	2094	377	378	91	425	1	0	0
Johan Jacob du Bois	1654	Utrecht	Utrecht	1714	369	421	924	0	1268	446	46	31	294	0	0	75
Rijck Dircksz	1655	Leiden	Leiden	213	21	52	93	47	5	207	207	0	0	0	0	0
Conrad Vietor	1657	Leiden Luth.	Leiden	2410	189	701	1020	500	877	900	833	673	0	0	0	0
Andre Rivet	1657	Breda	Leiden	4803	743	1274	2191	595	3661	294	3	0	868	25	4	0
Guilielmus Apollonius	1657	Middelburg	Middelburg	2900	544	692	1043	308	2560	306	104	1	162	17	10	0
Antonius Thysius	1657	Leiden	Leiden	2897	482	826	1457	132	2399	1506	104	74	100	15	3	10
Johannes Derramout* Much of the catalogue is missing. End of LT8, beginning of LT12, end of LM12	1658	Leiden	Leiden	2635	497	830	1244	64	1840	741	308	43	257	51	2	80
Caspar Sibelius	1658	Deventer	Deventer	1247	268	347	417	215	1032	153	102	42	5	2	1	1
Jacob van Ewyck	1658	Leiden	Leiden	658	77	119	285	166	491	140	136	3	0	0	0	1
Arnoldus van Elten	1660	Woudrichem	Leiden	1146	156	299	374	317	756	356	192	0	48	0	0	116
Jacob Claver	1660	Utrecht	Utrecht	212	13	54	82	59	193	19	19	0	0	0	0	0
Martin Ubbenius	1661	Leiden	Leiden	2268	351	600	1058	259	1860	182	122	27	13	3	0	22

APPENDIX: ANALYSED MINISTERIAL LIBRARY CATALOGUES

(cont.)

Owner	Year	Residence		Location of Auction	Total	20	40	80	120	Latin	Vernac.	Dutch	Germ.	Fren.	Ital.	Span.	English
Arnold uyt de Niepoort	1662	Schoonhoven		Schoonhoven	811	59	218	275	238	648	163	93	10	31	0	0	29
Theodorus van Altena	1662	Oestgeest		Leiden	257	19	62	143	33	210	46	34	0	8	0	0	4
Abraham Rambour/ Jacob Bizou	1663	Sedan/Utrecht		Leiden	1434	281	343	810	0	963	421	46	3	372	0	0	0
Abraham Thielenius	1663	Nijmegen		Nijmegen	843	174	201	377	91	588	255	92	119	41	0	0	3
Caspar te Haar	1663	Leimuiden		Amsterdam	681	49	110	310	212	448	214	105	5	96	8	0	0
Albertus Huttenus	1664	Nijmegen		Nijmegen	2912	383	685	1384	460	2244	554	110	28	246	7	0	163
Rudolphus Heggerus	1665	Leiden	Luth.	Leiden	921	119	278	436	88	560	416	67	289	0	0	0	0
Wessel Praetorius	1665	Emmerich		Leiden	1604	155	364	804	281	1157	185	302	97	12	0	1	4
Jacob Trigland	1665	Amsterdam		Amsterdam	1141	272	310	407	152	880	356	171	4	0	0	0	0
Petrus Gribius	1666	Amsterdam	(Ger)	Amsterdam	1497	186	486	556	269	782	664	213	51	20	0	0	380
Elias Taddel II	1666	Amsterdam	Luth.	Amsterdam	1341	208	418	612	103	1208	117	25	92	0	0	0	0
Johannes le Long	1666	Middelburg		Middelburg	820	138	179	375	128	478	317	23	0	291	2	0	1
Gulielmus Isenhagius	1666	Emmerich		Utrecht	154	41	49	64	0	134	20	3	1	0	0	0	16
Johannes Hoornbeeck	1667	Leiden		Leiden	3108	474	981	1214	439	2357	620	163	69	140	11	4	232
Hermanus Langelius	1667	Amsterdam		Amsterdam	1366	186	397	539	244	945	397	332	1	16	0	0	48
Andreas Lansman	1667	Amsterdam		Amsterdam	1016	261	295	313	147	694	217	190	1	5	1	0	79
Timotheus Rolandus	1667	Helvoirt		Leiden	722	143	157	258	164	508	276	54	13	44	1	1	0
Vincentius Snellius	1667	Piershil		Leiden	654	33	150	268	203	434	113	183	1	7	0	0	1

210   APPENDIX: ANALYSED MINISTERIAL LIBRARY CATALOGUES

(cont.)

Owner	Year	Residence	Location of Auction	Total	20	40	80	120	Latin	Vernac.	Dutch	Germ.	Fren.	Ital.	Span.	English
Aegeius Kellenaar	1667	Koudekerk aan den Rijn	Leiden	402	53	113	104	132	287	192	99	1	0	0	0	0
Arnold Poelenburg	1667	Amsterdam	Amsterdam, Rem.	1333	250	435	491	157	1030	158	183	6	7	2	2	17
Johannis Monachius	1667	Utrecht	Utrecht, Rem.	594	61	135	240	158	419	100	151	0	6	0	0	1
Rochus Arenz Immerzeel	1668	Enkhuizen	Enkhuizen, Luth.	676	65	226	242	143	490	485	83	90	1	0	0	0
Abdias Widmarius	1668	Groningen	Groningen	3645	442	986	1691	526	3036	221	268	96	118	1	0	1
Petrus Cabeljau	1668	Leiden	Leiden	1736	446	533	569	188	1458	559	182	16	4	2	0	17
Johannis ab Otten	1668	Beets	Leiden	1459	188	379	546	346	874	174	184	2	345	12	0	16
Levinus Becius	1668	Nieuw-Vossemeer	Zierikzee	484	103	134	140	107	333	142	107	0	34	1	0	0
Fridericus Swetgius	1669	Utrecht	Utrecht, Luth.	1911	133	418	913	447	1419	460	167	280	10	0	0	3
Thomas Cawton	1669	Rotterdam	Rotterdam	1744	223	544	601	283	967	690	128	5	20	5	4	528
Cornelius Lemannus	1669	Den Bosch	Den Bosch	1008	279	255	327	147	733	261	199	2	4	0	0	56
Wilhelmus Isenhagius	1669	Bunschoten	Utrecht	550	15	110	270	155	308	56	237	0	1	0	0	0
Petrus Taurinus	1669	Utrecht	Utrecht, Rem.	755	89	188	222	205	681	238	50	0	2	6	0	0
Petrus de Witte	1670	Leiden	Leiden	3062	607	1006	1010	439	2127	852	526	3	200	0	0	123
Jacob Rennet	1670	Leiden	Leiden	1547	121	419	674	333	1213	315	131	78	75	30	0	1
Gibbo Theodorus van Eerst	1670	Oudewater	Leiden	1241	179	332	515	215	892	331	309	19	1	0	0	2
Bartholomaeus Donius	1670	Rotterdam	Rotterdam	1058	98	298	323	254	398	651	404	0	20	7	0	220

APPENDIX: ANALYSED MINISTERIAL LIBRARY CATALOGUES

(cont.)

Owner	Year	Residence		Location of Auction	Total	20	40	80	120	Latin	Vernac.	Dutch	Germ.	Fren.	Ital.	Span.	English
Johann Heidan	1670	Amsterdam		Amsterdam	751	143	362	0	235	587	163	147	1	15	0	0	0
Petrus Leupenius	1670	Amsterdam		Amsterdam	523	109	124	114	60	320	196	156	4	1	0	0	35
Cornelius de Leeuw	1670	Doorn		Utrecht	303	26	59	132	86	238	172	51	0	0	0	0	0
Bartholomaeus Prevostius	1670	Amsterdam	Rem.	Amsterdam	510	45	110	246	109	335	51	78	92	0	0	0	2
Conrad Hoppe	1671	Amsterdam	Luth.	Amsterdam	325	92	82	85	66	279	746	22	10	0	0	0	0
Andreas Colvius	1671	Dordrecht		Dordrecht	2764	315	802	1177	457	1984	207	129	0	411	166	28	12
Johannes Coccejus	1671	Leiden		Leiden	2082	399	663	667	353	1547	344	50	61	76	7	2	5
Otto Badius	1671	Amsterdam		Amsterdam	1792	315	459	802	215	1431	349	153	103	82	3	0	2
Nicolaar Overeem	1671	Steenwijk		Amsterdam	1365	174	407	465	319	980	350	253	28	66	0	0	2
Jean Leger	1671	Leiden		Leiden	879	145	273	304	157	510	316	25	0	307	17	0	1
Johannes Crucius	1671	Haarlem		Haarlem	661	115	201	243	102	341	92	189	9	15	0	0	103
Johannes Paschasius	1671	Ankevee		Utrecht	461	83	122	168	88	355	32	44	0	0	0	0	48
Johan Adam Hunerfanger	1672	Utrecht	Luth.	Utrecht	828	82	291	272	183	416	557	82	306	13	1	1	1
Lodewijk Gerard van Renesse	1672	Breda		Leiden	2185	384	610	829	362	1574	153	432	17	63	0	1	14
Daniel Ouzel	1672	Voorschoten		Leiden	889	207	241	260	181	705	403	144	0	1	0	0	8
Samuel Maresius	1673	Groningen		Den Haag	2587	449	715	972	451	1879	673	127	1	531	9	5	0
Matthias Liesselius	1673	Hoorn		Hoorn	845	75	187	396	187	617	394	198	4	15	1	0	0
Johannes Korbag	1673	Amsterdam		Amsterdam	685	171	216	172	126	527	218	126	1	5	1	1	0
Michael Spranger	1673	Gameran		Amsterdam	566	79	147	206	134	230	133	326	1	1	0	0	3
Gedeon Curcellaeus	1673	Den Haag	Rem.	Rotterdam	1457	140	364	609	309	963	331	78	1	303	11	1	0

212   APPENDIX: ANALYSED MINISTERIAL LIBRARY CATALOGUES

(cont.)

Owner	Year	Residence		Location of Auction	Total	20	40	80	120	Latin	Vernac.	Dutch	Germ.	Fren.	Ital.	Span.	English
Fredericus 'tatinghoff	1674	Amsterdam	Luth.	Amsterdam	1264	119	381	567	197	1124	108	68	33	7	0	0	0
Vincent Meyer	1674	Haarlem	Luth.	Haarlem	583	52	162	223	146	437	270	84	50	0	0	0	0
Jacob Artopaeus	1674	Haarlem	Luth.	Haarlem	417	34	125	155	103	301	495	90	6	0	0	0	6
John Plooy	1674	Weesp	Luth.	Amsterdam	297	27	82	151	37	251	278	40	6	0	0	0	0
Johannes Teekmann	1674	Rotterdam		Rotterdam	1235	141	309	509	276	927	259	205	2	30	15	1	17
Johannes Kickius	1674	Loenen aan de Vect		Amsterdam	1118	99	256	521	242	794	88	183	1	71	1	0	22
Johannes à Beusecom	1674	Gouda		Leiden	934	67	227	309	331	656	134	252	1	6	0	0	0
Guilelmus Faber	1674	Delft		Delft	440	55	126	192	67	316	107	104	0	3	0	0	0
Andre Walschaart	1674	Amsterdam	Rem.	Amsterdam	1226	132	366	591	137	722	102	418	0	77	0	0	0
Theodorus Franconius	1674	Moordrecht	Rem.	Rotterdam	715	55	145	300	215	595	46	65	0	23	0	0	0
Otto Zaunsilfer	1675	Groningen		Groningen	590	112	204	204	70	490	92	34	45	13	0	0	0
Salomon Echtenius	1676	Haarlem		Haarlem	1184	149	312	545	178	788	322	163	0	62	0	0	97
Samuel van Horne	1676	Schiedam		Haarlem	781	130	237	223	191	570	189	189	0	0	0	0	0
Gisbertus Voetius	1677	Utrecht		Utrecht	5535	525	1677	2503	830	3956	1356	696	55	266	25	2	312
Johannes Rulaeus	1677	Haarlem		Haarlem	1800	219	450	704	382	1135	625	393	0	210	22	0	0
Richard Maden	1677	Amsterdam		Amsterdam	1339	382	599	305	53	935	383	4	0	0	3	1	375
Johannes Kalff	1677	Goes		Haarlem	805	81	206	274	244	487	300	294	0	1	0	0	5
Guilielmius Fabius	1677	Delft		Delft	444	54	130	191	69	315	110	108	0	2	0	0	0
Vochard Visscher	1678	Amsterdam	Luth.	Amsterdam	524	128	180	141	75	364	267	84	0	0	0	0	40
Johannes van den Bosch	1678	Woerden		Leiden	654	63	183	258	150	367	124	250	3	4	4	0	5

APPENDIX: ANALYSED MINISTERIAL LIBRARY CATALOGUES

(cont.)

Owner	Year	Residence		Location of Auction	Total	20	40	80	120	Latin	Vernac.	Dutch	Germ.	Fren.	Ital.	Span.	English
Jacobus Sceperus	1678	Gouda		Leiden	357	111	69	133	44	334	11	11	0	0	0	0	0
Paulus Leupenius	1678	Cuijk		Nijmegen	343	48	98	120	77	284	42	42	0	0	0	0	0
Abraham Heidanus	1679	Leiden		Leiden	3493	686	1188	1225	394	2619	615	180	64	330	3	1	36
Martinus Lydius/ Wilhelmus Vis	1679	Grootebroek/ Spanbroek en Opmeer		Enkhuizen	1251	180	337	433	301	634	607	238	24	42	7	3	293
Artus Georgus Veltus	1680	Amsterdam	Luth.	Amsterdam	588	145	184	159	100	549	1378	25	1	0	0	0	0
Jacob Lydius	1680	Dordrecht		Dordrecht	5391	607	1500	2362	921	3674	1149	495	211	246	66	2	358
Richard Maden	1680	Rotterdam		Rotterdam	2766	434	1192	1029	111	1485	224	4	1	5	0	1	1138
Jacobus Alting	1680	Groningen		Groningen	1649	199	481	747	198	1388	290	86	109	26	1	1	1
Franciscus Burman	1680	Utrecht		Leiden	1575	184	562	515	314	1189	116	172	4	105	0	0	9
Wilhemus Momma	1680	Middelburg		Amsterdam	628	134	194	219	81	462	26	22	7	86	0	0	1
Nicolaas Laurentius	1681	Middelburg	Luth.	Amsterdam	1414	203	331	547	333	958	426	176	241	7	2	0	0
Johannes Calander	1681	Kalslagen		Leiden	1285	102	440	461	282	951	323	295	22	5	0	0	1
Sebastiaan Crusius	1681	Zutphen		Deventer	1133	127	290	443	273	806	218	105	7	55	2	0	48
Johannes Van Niewenhuisen	1681	Amsterdam		Amsterdam	743	115	233	261	134	522	218	146	12	40	0	0	20
Barthold Verstegen	1681	Drempt/Oldenkeppel		Deventer	714	88	188	274	165	556	134	115	3	16	0	0	0
Adrianus Moll	1682	Nootdorp		Leiden	1399	249	414	474	262	1118	193	131	3	50	4	0	5
Cornelis vander Vliet	1683	Utrecht		Utrecht	2255	329	727	744	455	1229	930	356	1	242	3	0	328
Franciscus Ridderus	1683	Rotterdam		Rotterdam	1696	167	463	568	498	946	704	568	0	19	1	1	115
Johannes van Dijk	1685	Amsterdam	Menn.	Amsterdam	1480	320	409	428	323	692	814	516	14	186	10	4	2
Bernard Somer	1685	Amsterdam		Amsterdam	3459	699	1018	1107	635	2236	732	333	2	229	13	1	236

(cont.)

Owner	Year	Residence		Location of Auction	Total	20	40	80	120	Latin	Vernac.	Dutch	Germ.	Fren.	Ital.	Span.	English
Pierre de la Fontaine	1685	Gouda		Leiden	1474	301	509	405	259	881	454	74	9	332	34	4	1
Petrus Hollebeek	1685	Leiden		Leiden	990	174	291	328	197	641	321	312	2	6	1	0	0
Petrus Boreel	1686			Leiden	1333	265	353	413	302	773	765	29	7	464	6	2	22
Cornelius Lycochoton	1686	Amsterdam		Amsterdam	1274	138	377	523	236	716	530	178	0	21	0	0	338
Otto Belkampius	1686	Amsterdam		Amsterdam	765	184	220	251	110	481	537	167	0	3	0	0	93
Geeraert Brandt	1686	Amsterdam	Rem.	Amsterdam	1526	206	359	591	370	754	263	435	0	327	0	0	3
Jacob Klerk	1688	Hilversum		Amsterdam	1095	163	277	386	269	701	331	272	1	23	0	0	35
Henricus Bysterius	1688	Rotterdam	Rem.	Amsterdam	611	78	147	206	180	307	252	154	0	90	5	1	2
Stephan le Moyne	1689	Leiden		Leiden	5175	747	1915	1853	660	3932	1243	22	0	1003	29	5	184
Petrus Coolsonius/ Henricus Le Beuf	1689	Poortvliet		Leiden	2489	286	696	779	719	1441	1012	405	5	400	52	1	148
Rogerius Blanckhart	1689	Poortugaal		Rotterdam	1604	124	520	526	434	719	754	721	2	55	4	1	62
Henricus Ryndyk	1689	Amsterdam		Amsterdam	756	199	174	241	142	429	845	234	1	78	0	0	1
Jacobus Gaillard	1689	Leiden	Wall.	Leiden	2266	646	636	825	159	1381	314	55	1	600	11	0	87
Johannes Pechlinus	1690	Leiden	Luth.	Leiden	3703	512	1293	1239	659	2608	901	420	300	150	20	1	10
Quirinus Bosch	1690	Warmond		Leiden	2254	189	647	783	635	1579	626	457	1	140	6	0	22
Theodorus Wincklemans	1690	Oosterhout		Leiden	1581	289	425	557	310	896	592	414	12	77	16	5	68
Stoepe	1690	Den Haag		Den Haag	1088	138	342	391	217	196	878	261	1	267	24	2	323
Johannes Ronaldus	1690	Enkhuizen		Enkhuizen	981	149	270	273	289	441	533	246	0	0	0	0	280
Alexander Hodge	1690	Amsterdam		Amsterdam	732	142	198	215	177	323	401	54	0	2	0	0	345
Petrus Plancius	1691	Harderwijk		Leiden	1593	178	450	631	334	1229	1098	234	2	81	0	0	2

(cont.)

Owner	Year	Residence		Location of Auction	Total	20	40	80	120	Latin	Vernac.	Dutch	Germ.	Fren.	Ital.	Span.	English
Ludovici Wolzogen	1691	Amsterdam		Amsterdam	1167	189	320	321	337	789	319	73	0	247	0	0	2
Gerardus Van Der Port	1691	Amsterdam		Amsterdam	1135	214	324	332	265	721	322	257	0	122	0	0	0
Johannes Vlack	1691	Zutphen		Amsterdam	1097	119	294	414	270	874	379	173	7	16	2	1	1
Theophilus Copius	1691	Rijnsburg		Leiden	1085	125	341	326	293	782	200	145	22	100	1	0	0
Gosenius van Nyendael	1691	Den Hague	Rem.	Den Hague	2445	297	617	825	706	1307	268	571	26	442	3	0	56
Regner Verwey	1692	Alkmaar	Luth.	Rotterdam	2930	257	785	1233	655	1701	1226	882	0	160	2	0	182
Johannes Thielen	1692	Middelburg		Middelburg	2512	447	783	851	431	1306	1087	531	1	45	5	1	504
Rumoldus Rombouts	1692	Leiden		Leiden	1659	204	522	592	341	931	696	458	1	217	2	0	14
Carolus Schulerus	1692	Leur		Leiden	1388	103	469	497	319	786	566	417	0	142	1	0	6
Theodorus Colvinus	1692	Dordrecht		Leiden	1171	134	427	430	180	496	654	412	5	125	2	0	110
Willem de Valois	1692	Den Bommel		Leiden	455	51	113	183	108	300	139	131	0	6	0	0	2
Abraham Beller	1693	Amsterdam		Amsterdam	781	116	212	250	203	461	289	249	0	40	0	0	0
Henric Ramhorst	1693	Lutjebroek		Enkhuizen	731	63	220	253	195	443	274	270	2	2	0	0	0
Petrus Couwenburg	1694	Leiden		Leiden	1875	396	739	457	283	1124	662	595	4	53	4	0	6
Cornelius Danckerts	1694	Amsterdam		Amsterdam	1265	227	401	287	150	733	237	501	1	0	0	0	1
Andreas/Nicolaes Winckel	1694	Naarden		Amsterdam	806	121	251	280	154	596	503	184	0	15	0	0	0
Wijnandus van Doesburg	1694	Rotterdam		Rotterdam	605	96	219	240	50	368	199	222	0	1	0	0	0
Andreas Wenning	1694	Benthuizen		Leiden	507	181	113	102	111	332	223	155	0	9	0	0	0
Jacobus de Baudoes	1694	Noorden		Leiden	473	37	174	170	92	266	164	171	0	16	1	0	1

(cont.)

Owner	Year	Residence		Location of Auction	Total	20	40	80	120	Latin	Vernac.	Dutch	Germ.	Fren.	Ital.	Span.	English
Johannes Cuilemann	1694	Leiden	Rem.	Leiden	1412	250	461	477	224	1102	189	223	2	11	0	0	1
Mainhard Hoppe	1695	Rotterdam	Luth.	Rotterdam	335	60	110	94	71	199	1211	101	2	0	0	0	13
Jacobus Koelman	1695	Utrecht		Utrecht	2035	165	624	732	514	802	477	224	1	99	0	0	887
Godofredus à Kempen	1695	Leiden		Leiden	1483	365	504	363	251	937	512	145	0	280	9	0	42
Johannes Visscer	1695	Amsterdam		Amsterdam	1409	228	425	756	0	897	291	257	0	0	0	0	255
Henricus Berdenis	1695	Sluis		Rotterdam	536	84	146	167	113	222	116	131	3	67	4	0	86
Johannes Wilkens	1696	Haarlem	Luth.	Haarlem	816	76	306	284	150	491	888	283	17	0	0	0	1
Wilhelmus Anslaar	1696	Amsterdam		Amsterdam	4840	782	1895	1406	757	3165	834	465	15	347	3	0	58
Marcus van Peenen	1696	Leiden		Leiden	2441	266	747	891	537	1517	523	357	2	440	32	0	3
Conradus Ruysch	1696	Katwijck aan Zee		Leiden	1454	177	478	447	352	839	597	380	11	196	7	0	3
Caspar Brandt	1696	Amsterdam	Rem.	Amsterdam	1499	209	348	621	321	906	301	370	1	122	1	0	29
Henricus Francken	1696	Voorburg		Amsterdam	456	129	147	94	86	305	105	35	0	47	22	1	0
Salomon Voltelen	1697	Waspik		Dordrecht	1434	195	607	387	245	852	535	314	5	150	58	1	7
Johannis Boeken	1698	Rotterdam	Luth.	Rotterdam	487	58	200	111	118	327	645	112	48	0	0	0	0
Johannes Varnier	1698	Groningen		Groningen	1477	114	309	696	358	780	602	0	1	614	26	2	0
Balthasar Bekker	1698	Amsterdam		Amsterdam	1439	266	492	441	240	783	507	375	42	169	7	2	7
Jacobus Matthieu	1698	Montfoort		Utrecht	1118	81	199	437	401	582	144	3	0	388	0	1	115
Laurentius van den Veen	1698	Vught		Den Bosch	881	91	212	316	262	679	160	106	3	34	0	0	1
Johannes Muntendam	1698	Rotterdam		Rotterdam	364	57	131	97	79	221	135	133	0	2	0	0	0

(cont.)

Owner	Year	Residence	Location of Auction	Total	20	40	80	120	Latin	Vernac.	Dutch	Germ.	Fren.	Ital.	Span.	English
Jan Jansz/Kornelis Kornelisz	1699	Alkmaar	Menn. Alkmaar	558	62	224	152	120	0	475	558	0	0	0	0	0
Jacobus van Brakel	1699	Leiden	Rem. Leiden	1176	111	292	453	320	859	317	256	0	61	0	0	0
Christopher De Graaf	1699	Leiden	Leiden	1201	169	314	507	211	667	483	247	3	220	3	0	2
Johannes Spademan	1699	Rotterdam	Rotterdam	955	141	484	238	92	447	558	1	0	2	0	1	479
Samuel Gruterus	1700	Rotterdam	Leiden	4294	1099	1479	1125	591	2638	1487	453	18	541	57	1	417
Danielis vander Burgh	1700	Rotterdam	Leiden	1574	183	373	605	413	934	589	344	10	227	7	0	1
Cornelis van Suren	1700		Leiden	1422	103	392	531	396	967	414	345	1	65	2	0	1
Johannes Asseliers	1700	Hoorn	Leiden	1368	169	353	524	322	750	595	347	8	127	1	0	112

Bibliography

Primary Source

AC *Abraham Heidanus 1679* (Leiden: Felix Lopez de Haro & widow and heirs of Adrianus Severinus, 1679), USTC 1846941.

AC *Abraham Mellinus 1623* (Dordrecht: Peeter Verhagen, 1623), USTC 1122090.

AC *Adolf Visscher 1653* (Amsterdam: Zacharias Webber, 1653), USTC 1846273.

AC *Adrian Smoutius 1646* (Leiden: Severyn Matthysz, 1646), USTC 1122092.

AC *Adrianus van der Borre 1632* (Amsterdam: Broer Jansz, 1632), USTC 1021761.

AC *André Rivet 1657* (Leiden: Pieter Leffen, 1657), USTC 1846296.

AC *Artus Georgius Velten 1680* (Amsterdam: Widow Joannes van Someren, 1680), USTC 1816303.

AC *Balthazar Bekker 1698* (Amsterdam: Daniel van den Dalen & Andries van Damme, [1698]), USTC 1847542.

AC *Balthazar Lydius 1629 and 1630* (Dordrecht: widow of Peeter Verhagen, 1629–1630), USTC 1021755, 1021757, 1021756.

AC *Carolus Schulerus 1692* (Leiden: Fredrick Haaring, 1692), USTC 1846203.

AC *Caspar Pfeiffer 1643* (Amsterdam: Joost Broersz, 1643), USTC 1013744.

AC *Caspar Sibelius 1658* (Deventer: Jan Colomp, 1658), USTC 1846312.

AC *Christ. de Graaf 1699* (Leiden: Jordaan Luchtmans, 1699), USTC 1833276.

AC *Daniel Demetrius 1628* (Dordrecht: Peeter Verhagen, 1628), USTC 1122269.

AC *Daniel de la Vinea 1628* (Dordrecht: Jan (II) Canin, 1628), USTC 1122270.

AC *Franciscus Gomarus 1641* (Leiden: Bonaventura and Abraham Elzevier, 1641), USTC 1122202.

AC *Franciscus Ridderus 1683* (Rotterdam: Marcus van Rossus, 1683), USTC 1847118.

AC *Fredrick Spanheim 1649* (Leiden: Severyn Matthysz ven. Gualter de Haes, 1649), USTC 1435659.

AC *Gerardus van der Port 1691* (Amsterdam: Hendrik Boom and widow Dirk (I) Boom, 1691), USTC 1847325.

AC *Gisbertus Voetius 1677* (Utrecht: Willem Clerck, 1677–79), USTC 1813323 and 1846977.

AC *Godefridus Udemans 1653* (Middelburg: Jaques Fierens, 1653), USTC 1846270.

AC *Guilielmus Fabius 1677* (Delft: Cornelis van Heusden, 1677), USTC 1813810.

AC *Hieronymus Commelinus 1606* (Leiden: Jan Jansz. Orlers, 1606), USTC 1122014.

AC *Jacob Arminius* (Leiden: Thomas Basson, 1610), USTC 1506632.

AC *Jacob Cuilemann 1694* (Leiden: Pieter vander Aa, 1694), USTC 1847404.

AC *Jacobus Gaillard 1689* (Leiden: Johannes du Vivié, 1689), USTC 1847404.

AC *Jacobus Koelman 1695* (Utrecht: François Halma, 1695), USTC 1847446.

AC *Jacobus Lydius 1680* (Dordrecht: Herman van Wessem, 1680), USTC 1816682.

BIBLIOGRAPHY 219

AC Janus Dousa 1604 (Leiden: Thomas Basson, 1604), USTC 1122042.

AC Johannes Boeken 1698 (Rotterdam: Barent Bos, 1698), USTC 1847535.

AC Johannes de Planque 1698 (Leiden: Boudewijn (1) van der Aa, 1698).

AC Johannes Halsbergius 1607 (Leiden: Louis Elzevier, 1607), USTC 1122231.

AC Johannes Hoornbeeck 1667 (Leiden: Pieter Leffen, 1667), USTC 1846494.

AC Johannes Lydius 1643 (Leiden: Franciscus Hackius, 1643), USTC 1122163.

AC Johannes Pechlinus 1690 (Leiden: Pieter vander Aa, 1690), USTC 1823437.

AC Johannes van Dijk 1685 (Amsterdam: Widow of Johannes van Someren, 1685), USTC 1847142.

AC Justinus van Assche (Rotterdam: Simon Simonsz Visser, 1650), USTC 1121734.

AC Kuchlinus and Aemilius 1610 (Leiden: Henrick Lodewijcxsoon van Haestens, 1510 [= 1610]), USTC 1122220.

AC Lucas Trelcatius 1607 (Leiden: Jan Maire, 1607), USTC 1025132.

AC Marcus van Peenen 1696 (Leiden: Johannes du Vivié and Jordaan Luchtmans, 1696), USTC 1830515.

AC Martinus Lydius and Wilhelmus Vis 1679 (Enkhuizen: Meynerdt Mul, 1679), USTC 1846949.

AC Martin Ubbenius 1661 (Leiden: Pieter Leffen, 1661), USTC 1846366.

AC Martinus van Halewyn van der Voort 1691 (Dordrecht: Dirk (1) Goris, 1691), USTC 1847281.

AC Nathan Vay 1693 (Leiden: Johannes du Vivie and Jordaan Luchtmans, 1693), USTC 1841496.

AC Paulus Leupenius 1678 (Nijmegen: Gulielmus Meys, 1678), USTC 1846917.

AC Petrus Leupenius 1670 (Amsterdam: Pieter Dircksz I Boeteman, 1670), USTC 1846619.

AC Petrus van Willigen 1650 (Rotterdam: Bastiaen Wagens, 1650), USTC 1030020.

AC Otto Zaunslifer 1675 (Groningen: Rembertus Huysman, 1675), USTC 1846823.

AC Richard Maden 1680 (Rotterdam: Henricus Goddaeus, 1680), USTC 1846866.

AC Salomon Voltelen 1697 (Dordrecht: Wittegaarts, 1697), USTC 1829280.

AC Samuel Gruterus 1700 (Leiden: Pieter (1) van der Aa, 1700), USTC 1848523.

AC Sibrandus Lubbertus 1625 (Franeker: Fredrick Heyns, 1625), USTC 1122248.

AC Theodorus Hamel 1638 (The Hague: Abraham (1) Elzevier, 1638), USTC 1122205.

AC Theodorus van Altena 1662 (Leiden: Petrus Hackius, 1662), USTC 1842892.

AC Theodorus van Couwenhoven 1646 (Leiden: Philippe de Croy, 1646), USTC 1121798.

AC Thomas Laurentius 1645 (Leiden: Hieronymus de Vogel, 1645), USTC 1122036.

AC Thomas Tiberius 1678 (Leeuwarden: Jacob Hagenaar, 1678), USTC 1846920.

AC Wilhelm Merwy 1636 (Delft: Jan Pietersz Waelpot, 1636), USTC 1027540.

Alting, Heinrich, *Theologia historica, sive systematis historici loca quatuor* (Amsterdam: Johannes Janssonius, 1664), USTC 1801364.

Ampzing, Samuel *Beschyvinge ende lof der stad Haerlem in Holland* (Haarlem: Adriaen (1) Roman, 1628), USTC 1026151.

'Aensprack tot den Christelijcken Leser', *Res judicanda, saecke die noch staet te oordeelen, van de bancken van leeninghe* (Leiden: Hendrick Verbiest, 1658), USTC 1839430.

Aquinas, Thomas, *Summa Theologiae*, vol. 1, ed. John Gilby (London: Eyre and Spottiswoode, 1964).

Arminius, Jacob, *The Works of Jacob Arminius*, trans. James Nichols and W. R. Bagnall (reprint, 3 vols., Grand Rapids: Baker Books, 1977).

Aurelius, Marcus, *Meditations with selected correspondence*, trans. Robin Hard (Oxford: Oxford University Press, 2011).

Autentique lyste van de veranderingh der regeeringh van de provincie van Utrecht (Utrecht: s.n., 1677), USTC 1813808.

Balen, Matthys, *Beschryvinge der stad Dordrecht* (Dordrecht: Symon Onder de Linde, 1677) USTC 1813805.

Bangs, C. O. (ed.), *The Auction Catalogue of the Library of J. Arminius* (Leiden: Brill/ Hes & De Graaf, 1984).

Bangs, J. D. (ed.), *The Auction Catalogue of the Library of Hugh Goodyear, English Reformed Minister at Leiden* (Leiden: Brill/Hes & De Graaf, 1984).

Battus, Carolus *Secreet-boeck waer in vele diversche secreten, ende heerlicke consten in veelderleye verscheyden materien uit Latijnsche, Francoysche, Hoochduytsche, ende Nederlantsche authoren, te samen ende by een ghebracht zijn* (Dordrecht: Abraham Canin, 1600), USTC 425118.

Bayle, Pierre, *Dictionaire Historique et Critique* (2 vols., Rotterdam: Reinier Leers, 1697), USTC 1831857.

Baudartius, Wilhelmus, *VVech-bereyder op de verbeteringhe van den Nederlantschen Bybel* (Arnhem: Jan Jansz., 1606), USTC 1017588.

Beardslee III, John W. (trans.), *Reformed Dogmatics: J. Wollebius, G. Voetius, F. Turretin* (Oxford: Oxford University Press, 1965).

Bernard, Jacques, *Nouvelles de la République des Lettres* (Amsterdam: Henry Desbordes and Daniel Pain, January 1703).

Bertius, Petrus, *Aen-spraeck, aen D. Fr. Gomarvm op zijne bedenckinghe over de lijck-oratie, ghedaen na de begraefenisse van D. Iacobvs Arminivs* (Leiden: Ian Paedts Jacobszoon, 1609), USTC 1022196.

Bewys, dat het een predicant met zyn huysvrouw alleen niet mogelijck en is op vijfhondert guld. eerlijck te leven (Delft: Pieter de Menagie, 1658), USTC 1839928.

Bibliothecae Trajectinae catalogus (Utrecht: Salomon de Roy, 1608), USTC 1019386.

Bois, Jacob du, *Schadelickheyt van de cartesiaensche philosophie* (Utrecht: Johannes (1) Janssonius van Waesberge, 1656), USTC 1833395.

Bois, Jacob du, *Oude-tyds tyd-thresoor ende kerkelikke historie* (Leiden: Cornelis Banheining, 1650), USTC 1023031.

BIBLIOGRAPHY

Bor, Pieter, *Oorsprongk, begin, en vervolgh der Nederlandsche oorlogen*, vol. 2 (Amsterdam: Widow of Johannes van Someren, Abraham Wolfgangh, Hendrick en Dirck, 1680), USTC 1816052.

Bos, Erik-Jan (ed.), 'Epistolarium Voetianum II', *Dutch Review of Church History*, 79 (1999), pp. 39–73.

Bos, Erik-Jan, and F. G. M. Broeyer (eds.), 'Epistolarium Voetianum I', *Dutch Review of Church History*, 78 (1998), pp. 184–215.

Bots, Hans, and Pierre Leroy (eds.), *Claude Saumaise & André Rivet, Correspondance échangée entre 1632 et 1648* (Amsterdam: APA – Holland University Press, 1987).

Bots, Hans, *Correspondence Intégrale, d'André Rivet et de Claude Sarrau* (3 vols., Amsterdam: APA – Holland University Press, 1978–1982).

Brakel, Wilhelmus à, *Logikê latreia, dat is Redelyke godtsdienst* (3 vols., Rotterdam: Hendrik van den Aak, 1713–1714).

Brakel, Wilhelmus à, *The Christian's Reasonable Service*, ed. Joel R. Beeke, trans. Bartel Elshout (4 vols., Grand Rapids: Reformation Heritage Books, 1992–1995).

Brandt, Caspar, 'Voorreden aan den Christelijcken Leser', in Henrick Hammond, *Practikale catechismus, dat is Onderwijzing in de christelijke religie* (Rotterdam: Barent Bos, 1685), USTC 1825544.

Brandt, Geeraerdt, *Historie der Reformatie, en andre kerkelyke geschiedenissen in en ontrent de Nederlanden* (3 vols., Amsterdam: Henrik and Dirk Boom, 1674), USTC 1561244.

Brés, Guy, *Confession de foy* (s.l., s.n., 1562), USTC 247.

Calvin, John, *Institutes of the Christian Religion*, ed. J. T. McNeill, trans. F. L. Battles (2 vols., Philadelphia: Westminster Press, 1960).

'The Canons of Dort (1618–1619)', in James T. Dennison, Jr. (ed.), *Reformed Confessions of the 16th and 17th Centuries in English Translation: Volume 4, 1600–1693* (Grand Rapids: Reformation Heritage Books, 2014), pp. 120–153.

Catalogus bibliothecae Ultrajectinae (Utrecht: Meinardus à Dreunen, 1670), USTC 1807398.

Catalogus variorum ac insignium librorum instructissimae bibliothecae Bernardi Someri (Amsterdam: Henricum & Viduam Theodori Boom, 1685) Wolfenbüttel, HAB: BC Sammelband 9:20, USTC 1825590.

Clark, Samuel, *Annotatien over't N. Testament* (Amsterdam: Johannes Boekholt, 1692), USTC 1822720.

Clarke, Samuel, *A Generall Martyrologie, containing a Collection of all the greatest Persecutions which have befallen the Church of Christ from the Creation to our present Times. Whereunto are added the lives of sundry modern Divines famous in their Generations for Learning and Piety, and most of them Great Sufferers in the Cause of Christ.* (London: Thomas Underhill and John Rothwell, 1651).

Clarke, Desmond (ed.), *The Equality of the Sexes: Three Feminist Texts of the Seventeenth Century* (Oxford: Oxford University Press, 2013).

Cloppenburg, Johannes, *De foenore et usuris, brevis institutio, cum ejusdem epistola ad Cl. Salmasium* (Leiden: Elzevier, 1640), USTC 1028069.

Colomesius, Paulus (ed.), *Virorum eruditione celeberrimorum epistolae, clarorum virorum ad Vossium* (London: Sam Smith and Benjamin Walford, 1698).

Cocceius, Johannes, *The Doctrine of the Covenant and Testament of God*, trans. Casey Carmichael (Grand Rapids: Reformation Heritage Books, 2016).

Cocceius, Johannes, *Opera ANEKDOTA* (2 vols., Amsterdam: Janssonius-Waesburge, Boom, and Goethals, 1706).

Coryate, Thomas, *Coryat's Crudities*, vol. 2 (1611; reprint, London: W. Cater, 1776).

'The Counter Remonstrance', in James T. Dennison, Jr. (ed.), *Reformed Confessions of the 16th and 17th Centuries in English Translation: Volume 4, 1600–1693* (Grand Rapids: Reformation Heritage Books, 2014), pp. 45–48.

Court, Pieter de la, *Het Welvaren van Leiden. Handschift uit het jaar 1659*, ed. Felix Driessen (The Hague: Martinus Nijhoff, 1911).

Dekker, E., J. Knoop and C. M. L. Verdegaal (eds.), *The Auction Catalogue of the Library of F. Gomarus (Leiden, 1641)* (Leiden: Brill/Hes & De Graaf, 1996).

Descartes, Rene, *A Discourse on the Method of Correctly Conducting One's Reason and Seeking Truth in the Sciences*, trans. Ian Maclean (Oxford: Oxford University Press, 2006).

Diest, Heinrich von, *De ratione studii theologici* (Harderwijk: Nicolaes van Wieringen, 1634), USTC 1510759.

Donteclock, Reynier, *Proeve des Gouschen catechismi* (Delft: Jan Andriesz., 1608), USTC 1028772.

Duke, Alastair, Gillian Lewis and Andrew Pettegree (eds.), *Calvinism in Europe, 1540–1610: A Collection of Sources* (Manchester: Manchester University Press, 1992).

Episcopius, Simon, 'Oratio habita in Synodo Nationali Nationali Dordracena', in his Opera Theologica (Rotterdam: Arnout Leers, 1665), USTC 1802334, part 2, pp. 1–4.

Erasmus, Desiderius, *The Education of a Christian Prince*, in his *Collected Works*, trans. N. M. Cheshire and M. J. Heath (Toronto: University of Toronto Press, 1986).

Erasmus, Desiderius, 'A Declamation on the Subject of Early Liberal Education for Children', trans. Beert C. Verstraete, in J. K. Sowards (ed.), *Collected Works of Erasmus*, vol. 26 (Toronto: University of Toronto Press, 1985), pp. 291–346.

Extract uit de resoluties van de Weth van 1688 over een aanstootgevende preek van ds. Wilhelmus a Brakel, SA Rotterdam, 37-04_144.

Extract uyt de notulen van de [...] Staten van Zeelant. Den 21. september 1684 (S.l., s.n., 1684), USTC 1827017.

Foxe, John, *The Acts and Monuments of John Foxe*, vol. 3 (London: Published by R. B. Seeley and W Burnside, 1868).

BIBLIOGRAPHY

Gelliers, Carel de, *Trap der Jeugd* (Franeker: Joh. Arcerius, 1661), USTC 1845973.

Generale ordonnantie ende conditien (Rotterdam, s.n., s.d.), USTC 1529670.

C. G. [=Jacobus Stermont], *Lauweren-krans gevlochten voor syn hoocheyt, Wilhelm, de Heer de Prince van Oranjen, &c. Over sijne eeuwig roembaere handelinge, gepleegt tot ruste deser Vereenigde Lantschappen, in't Jaer 1650* (s.n., s.l. [1650]), USTC 1035032.

Grevinchoven, Caspar, *Grondelijck bericht Caspari Grevinchovii, vande dolingen der nieuwe luterschen* (Rotterdam: Felix van Sambix, 1611), USTC 1029427.

Gomarus, Franciscus, *Bedenckingen, op den dagelijckschen, ende iaerlijckschen loop van den aerdt-kloot* (Middelburg: Zacharias Roman, 1629), USTC 1026730.

Gomarus, Franciscus, *Bedencken over de lijck-oratie van meester P. Bertius*, in his *Waerschouwinghe, over de Vermaninghe aen R. Donteclock.* (Leiden: Jan Jansz. Orlers, 1609), USTC 1028772.

Gomarus, Franciscus, 'Undisputed Freedom: A Disputation of Franciscus Gomarus (1563–1641)', in Willem J. van Asselt, et al. (eds.), *Reformed Thought on Freedom: The Concept of Free Choice in Early Modern Reformed Theology* (Grand Rapids: Baker Books, 2010), pp. 127–144.

Guicciardini, Lodovico, *Beschryvinghe der Nederlanden* (Amsterdam: Willem Jansz Blaeu, 1612), USTC 1031392.

Gunter, W. Stephen (ed.), *Arminius and His Declaration of Sentiments: An Annotated Translation with Introduction and Theological Commentary* (Waco: Baylor University Press, 2012).

Haen, Galenus Abrahamsz. de, *Verdédiging der christenen die doopsgezinde genaamd worden* (Amsterdam: Widow of P. Arents and C. vander Sys, 1699), USTC 1836339.

Het Geusen-gheschreeuw: Behelsende hoe de Gommaristen, Mennisten ende Arminianen hebben gheroepen over die groote Victorie (s.l., s.n. [1635]), USTC 1001964.

Hexham, Henry, 'Voor-reden' to *A Copious English and Nederduytch* [sic] *Dictionarie* (Rotterdam: Arnout Leers, 1648), USTC 1514701.

Hooft, P. C., *Memorieën en adviezen van Pieter Corneliszoon Hooft* (2 vols., Utrecht: Kemink, 1871–1925).

Hoornbeeck, Johannes, *Johannes Hoornbeeck (1617–1666), On the Conversion of Indians and Heathens: An Annotated Translation of De Conversione Indorum et Gentilium (1669)*, eds. Ineke Loots and Joke Spaans (Leiden: Brill, 2018).

Hoorne, Johannes van, *Waerschouwinge, aen alle lieff-hebbers der anatomie* (Leiden: Daniel and Abraham van Gaasbeeck, 1660), USTC 1844690.

Hortensius, Aegidius *Commentarii Ad IV. Institutionum Divi Iustiniani Imperatoris Libros* (Giesen: Philipp Franke, 1614), USTC 2042610.

Hulsius, Antonius, *Wikkuah 'ivri seu Disputatio epistolaris Hebraica inter Antonium Hulsium et Jacobu Abendanah Super loco Haggaei cap. 2. v. 9* (Leiden: Joannis Nicolai à Dorp, 1669), USTC 1806032.

Hyperius, Andreas, *De sacrae scripturae lectione ac meditatione quotidiana, omnibus omnium ordinum hominibus Christianis perquam necessaria, libri II* (Basel: Johan Oporinus, 1561), USTC 631410.

Index cariorum, insignium librorum, tam historicorum, medicorum, juridicorum, quam theologicorum, qui servantur in bibliotheca Enchusana (Enkhuizen: Henricus a Straalen, 1693), USTC 1841673. Westfries Archief. 0219.65c61.

Junius, Franciscus, *A Treatise on True Theology*, trans. David C. Noe (Grand Rapids: Reformation Heritage Books, 2014).

Junius, Franciscus, 'An Image of Its Maker: Theses on Freedom in Franciscus Junius (1545–1602)', in Willem J. van Asselt, et al. (eds.), *Reformed Thought on Freedom: The Concept of Free Choice in Early Modern Reformed Theology* (Grand Rapids: Baker Books, 2010), pp. 95–126.

Junius, Franciscus, *De theologia vera: ortu, natura, formis, partibus, et modo* (Leiden: Plantin Raphelengius, 1594), USTC 423372.

Kamerbeek, Wilhelmina G. (ed.), 'Some Letters by Johannes Arnoldi Corvinus', *Lias*, 9 (1982), 85–109.

Keckermann, Bartholomäus, *Synopsis disciplinae oeconomicae* (Hanau: Wilhelm Antonius, 1610), USTC 2130298.

Keckermann, Bartholomäus, *Systema Disciplinae Politicae* (Hanau: Wilhelm Antonius, 1608 [=1610]), USTC 2130297.

Kernkamp, G. W., *Acta et Decreta Senatus* (3 vols., Utrecht: Broekhoff; Kemink en Zoon, 1936–1940).

Kluyt, Wilhelmus à Brakel van der, Preface to Wilhemus à Brakel, *Edifying Discourses Regarding the Preparation for, the Partaking of, and the Reflection upon the Sacrament of the Lord's Supper*, in James A. De Jong (ed.), *In Remembrance of Him: Profiting from the Lord's Supper*, trans. Bartel Elshout (Grand Rapids: Reformation Heritage Books, 2012).

Koelman, Jacobus, *The Duties of Parents*, trans. John Vriend, ed. M. Eugene Osterhaven (Grand Rapids: Reformation Heritage Books, 2003).

Lansbergen, Philips, *Bedenckingen, op den dagelijckschen, ende iaerlijckschen loop van den aerdt-kloot* (Middelburg: Zacharias Roman, 1629), USTC 1026730.

Landman, Thadaeus de, *Versameling van twintig stigtelijke en zielroerende predikatien* (The Hague: Meyndert Uytwerf, 1694), USTC 1838644.

Lomeier, Johannes, *A Seventeenth-Century View of European Libraries: Lomeier's De bibliothecis, Chapter X*, trans. John Warwick Montgomery (Berkeley: University of California Press, 1962).

Lomeier, Johannes, *De bibliothecis liber singularis* (Zutphen: Henric Berren, 1669), USTC 1806598.

Luc-Tulot, Jean (ed.), 'Correspondence of Jean-Maximilien de Langle (1590–1674)', available at http://jeanluc.tulot.pagesperso-orange.fr/Rivet-Langle.pdf.

BIBLIOGRAPHY

Luther, Martin, *Werke. Tischreden, 1531–1546*, vol. 1 (Weimar: H. Böhlaus Nachfolger, 1912).

Luther, Martin, *Ein Sendbrief vom Dolmetschen – An Open Letter on Translating*, trans. Howard Jones (Oxford: Taylor Institution Library, 2017).

Lydius, Jacobus, 'Van eenen gelt-hont', in his *Vrolycke uren, ofte Der wysen vermaeck* (Dordrecht: Hendrick van Esch, 1640), USTC 1028119.

Marchand, Prosper, *Histoire de l'origine et des premiers progres de l'imprimerie* (The Hague: widow Le Vier and Pierre Paupie, 1740).

Maresius, Samuel, *Oratio inauguralis de usu et abusu rationis in rebus theologicis & fidei* (Groningen: Hans Sas, 1648), USTC 1022694.

Mastricht, Petrus van, *Vindiciæ veritatis et authoritatis Sacræ Scripturæ in rebus philosophicis* (Utrecht: Johannes à Waesburge, 1655), USTC 1557165.

Matery-boexken, of Voor-schriften seer bequaem voor de jonkheyt om wel te leren lezen, schryven, en een aenporringe tot alle deugden (Deventer: A. Kurtenius 1700).

Molhuysen, P. C. (ed.), *Bronnen tot de geschiedenis der Leidensche Universiteit* (7 vols., The Hague: Martinus Nijhoff, 1913–1924).

More, Thomas, *Utopia*, ed. and trans. Paul Turner (Harmondsworth: Penguin, 1965).

Moulin, Marie du, *The Last Houers, of the Right Reverend Father in God Andrew Rivet*, trans. G. L. (The Hague: Samuel Brown, 1652), USTC 1803725.

Naudé, Gabriel, *Advice on Establishing a Library* (Berkeley: University of California Press, 1950).

Nauta, D. (ed.), 'Drie Brieven van Gisbertus Voetius', *Dutch Review of Church History*, 60 (1980), pp. 193–202.

Nijenhuis, Willem (ed.), *Matthew Slade (1569–1628): Letters to the English Ambassador* (Leiden: E. J. Brill/Leiden University Press, 1986).

Owen, John 'The Epistolary Dedicatory', in William H. Goold (ed.), *The Works of John Owen*, vol. 12 (Edinburgh: T&T Clark, 1862).

Philalethius, Ireneus, [=Ewout Teellinck], *Boheemsch gelvyt ofte Christelyck gespreck, over het tegenwoordich Boheemsche wesen, ende de oorloge daer ontrent ontstaen* (Amsterdam: Paulus van Ravesteyn, 1620), USTC 1029470.

Philopatris, Theophilis, [=Willem Teellinck], *Geestelijcke covranten voor dit loopende quartier-iaers, over de swarigheden die ons de voorleden somer getroffen hebben* (The Hague: Aert Meuris, 1626), USTC 1031456.

Picardt, Johannes, *Den Prediger, Dat is grondige verklaringe en bewys, genomen uyt Goddelycke, kerckelycke ende prophane schriften* (Zwolle: Jan Gerritsz., 1650).

Pitatus, Petrus, *Verae solaris atque lunaris anni quantitatis aliarumque rerum ad calendarii Romani emendationem pertinentium* (Basel: Peter Perna, 1568), USTC 700562.

Poelenburg, Arnold, 'Oratio funebris in obitum clarissimi viri D. Stephani Curcellaei,' in Etienne de Courcelles, *Opera theologica* (Amsterdam: Daniel Elzevier, 1675), USTC 1811941.

226   BIBLIOGRAPHY

Pours, Jeremie du, *La divine melodie, du sainct psalmiste ou La divinité du livre des pseaumes* (Middelburg: Geeraert Moulert, 1644), USTC 1024498.

Reitsma, J., and S. D. van Veen (eds.), *Acta Der Provinciale en Particuliere Synoden, Gehouden in de Noordelijke Nederlanden Gedurende de Jaren 1572–1620* (8 vols., Groningen: J. B. Wolters, 1892–1899).

'The Remonstrance (1610)', trans. James T. Dennison, Jr., in idem (ed.), *Reformed Confessions of the 16th and 17th Centuries in English Translation: Volume 4, 1600–1693* (Grand Rapids: Reformation Heritage Books, 2014), pp. 40–44.

Revius, Jacobus, *Jacobus Revius: A Theological Examination of Cartesian Philosophy, Early Criticisms (1647)*, ed. Aza Goudriaan (Leiden: Brill, 2002).

Ridderus, Franciscus, *Apollos, ofte Zedige verantwoorder voor de leere der gereformeerde kercke* (3 vols., Rotterdam: Arnout Leers, 1666–1670), USTC 1803594, 1529865, 1557930.

Ridderus, Franciscus, *De beschaemde christen door het geloof en leven van heydenen en andere natuerlijcke menschen* (Rotterdam: Johannes Borstius, 1669), USTC 1815596.

Ridderus, Franciscus, *Historisch sterf-huys, ofte 't Samenspraeck uyt heylige, kerckelijcke en weereltsche historien over allerley voorval ontrent siecke en stervende* (Rotterdam: Johannes Borstius, 1668), USTC 1802396.

Ridderus, Franciscus, *Historischen Engels-man, in bysondere Engelsche, Schotse, en Yersche geschiedenissen, gepast op de onderdruckte staet van ons lieve vaderlandt* (Rotterdam: Widow of Arnout Leers, 1674), USTC 1811349.

Ridderus, Franciscus, *Nuttige tiidkorter voor reizende en andere luiden* (Rotterdam: Joannes Naeranus, 1663), USTC 1800117.

Ridderus, Franciscus, *Reys-discours op het verschijnen van de comeet-sterre, die voor d'eerstemael gesien is den 15 december des jaers 1664* (Rotterdam: Henricus Goddaeus, 1665), USTC 1802715.

Ridderus, Franciscus, *Voorbeeldt van een waer predikant, vertoont in een predicatie, gedaen op den 2. January 1678. uyt 1. Tim. 4 vers 12. (niemant verachte uwe jonckheydt.) op de bevestinge van D. Johannis Doesburgh, tot predikant in de bloeyende gemeynte van Rotterdam* (Rotterdam: Joannis Borstius, 1678), USTC 1814702.

Ridderus, Franciscus, *Worstelende kercke, ofte Historische vertooninge van het bestreden geloove.* (Rotterdam: Widow of Arnout Leers, 1679), USTC 1815770.

Rivet, André, *Ad Lectorem, in Biblia Sacra sive Testamentum Vetus ab Im Tremellio et Fr Junio ex Hebraeo Latine Redditum, et Testamentum Novum á Theod. Beza a Graeco in Latinum Versum* (Amsterdam: Blaeu, 1648), USTC 1014147.

Rivet, André, *Apologia pro sanctissima virgine Maria matre Domini* (Leiden: Franciscus Hegerus, 1639), USTC 1028683.

Rivet, André, *Eschantillon des Principaux paradoxes de la Papaute, sur les poincts de la Religion controuersez en ce temps. Recueillis des propres escrits de ses plus approuuez Docteurs* (La Rochelle: Havltin, 1603), USTC 6806864.

BIBLIOGRAPHY 227

Rivet, André, *Examen animadversionum Hugonis Grotii* (Leiden: Bonaventura Elzevier, 1642), USTC 1028501.

Rivet, André, *Instruction Chretienne pour les Enfans & Autres, qui se preparent à la participation de la Sainte Cene* (The Hague: Abraham Troyel, 1692), UB Leiden: BIBWAL L416, USTC 1822829.

Rivet, André, *Instruction du prince chrestien* (Leiden: Jan Maire, 1642), USTC 1015914.

Rivet, André, *Isagoge, seu Introductio generalis ad Scripturam Sacram Veteris & Novi Testamenti* (Amsterdam: Isaac Commelin, 1627), USTC 1016298.

Rivet, André, *Lettres de Messieurs Rivet, De La Milletière et du Moulin* (Sedan: Jean Jannon, 1635), USTC 6809619.

Rivet, André, 'On Faith and the Perseverance of the Saints (disp. 31)', in Henk van den Belt (ed.), *Synopsis of a Purer Theology: Latin Text and English Translation*, vol. 2, trans. Riemer A. Faber (2 vols., Leiden: Brill, 2014–2016), pp. 228–275.

Rivet, André, *Operum Theologicorum tomus alter* (Rotterdam: Arnoud Leers, 1651), USTC 1840008.

Rivet, André, *Responses a Trois Lettres du Sieur de la Milletiere* (Quévilly: Jean Berthelin & Jacques Cailloüé, 1642), USTC 6810069.

Rivet, André, *The state-mysteries of the Iesuites, by way of questions and answers. Faithfully extracted out of their owne writings by themselves published* (London: George Eld, 1623), USTC 3010942.

Rivet, André, *Tractatus de partum autoritate*, in his *Critici Sacri libr IV* (Geneva: Jacob Chouët, 1652).

Ruarus, Martinus, *Epistolarum selectarum centuria* (Amsterdam: Davidus Crispicus, 1677), STCN 127304797.

Rutgers, F. L. (ed.), *Acta van de Nederlandsche synoden der zestiende eeuw* (reprint; Dordrecht: J. P. van den Tol, 1980).

Saldenus, Guiljemus, *De Libri varioque eorum, usu et abusu* (Amsterdam: Henrick Boom, 1688), USTC 1821540.

Scaliger, Joseph, *Epistolae omnes, quae reperiri potuerunt, nunc primum collectae ac editae* (Leiden: Bonaventure and Abraham Elzevier, 1627), USTC 1028641.

Sceperus, Jacobus, *De Chaldeen en Babylonieren onder de voeten van den koninck aller koningen* (Amsterdam: Jacques Boursse, 1673), USTC 1810411.

Sceperus, Jacobus, *Schat-boeck der onderwijsingen voor kranck-besoeckers* (Amsterdam: Johannes Janssonius van Waesberge, 1670), USTC 1807322.

School-ordre, gemaeckt ende gearresteert by de heeren Staten van Hollant ende West-Vrieslant, over de Latijnsche schoolen binnen den selve lande. Den 1. octobris sestien-hondert-vijf-en-twintig (The Hague: widow and heirs of Hillebrant van Wouw, 1625), USTC 1012369.

Schurman, Anna Maria van, *Verhandeling over de aanleg van vrouwen voor wetenschap*, trans. Renée ter Haar (Groningen: Xeno, 1996).

Schurman, Anna Maria van, *Anna Maria van Schurman: Whether a Christian Woman Should Be Educated and Other Writings From Her Intellectual Circle*, ed. and trans. Joyce L. Irwin, (Chicago: University of Chicago Press, 1998).

Sibelius, Caspar, *Historica narratio Caspari Sibelii de curriculo totius vitae et peregrinationis suae*, in H. W. Tijdeman, 'Caspar Sibelius: In Leven Predikant te Deventer, volgens zijne onuitgegeven levens beschriving', *Godgeleerde Bijdragen* 23 (1849), pp. 481–533.

Sibema, Bouritius, *Salomons sweert, scheydende de remonstrantsche vande rechtsinnighe leere* (Amsterdam: Marten Jansz. Brandt, 1631), USTC 1031025.

Simonides, Simon, *Vrienden-raedt, gegeven aen de besochte gemeynte van de Ryp, by een merckelijck oordeel Gods over haer gegaen* (Rotterdam: Adries van Hoogen-huyse, 1655), USTC 1815758.

Sprunger, K. (ed.), *The Auction Catalogue of William Ames* (Leiden: Brill/Hes & De Graaf, 1987).

Staat van ambten waarover jaarlijks of éénmalig recognitie moet worden betaald, 30 december 1692. Westfries Archief, Oud archief stad Enkhuizen 1353-185, inv. 0120. 1374-1.

'Staat van Boeken die na 1600 geschonken zijn aan de bibliotheek der Hervormde gemeente, 1854' WA. Gemeentebestuur Enkhuizen. 0121. 1525.

Stillingfleet, Edward, *Origines sacræ, heilige oorsprongkelykheden*, trans. Johannes Ubelman (Amsterdam: Ysabrandus Haring, 1690), USTC 1823071.

[Streso, Caspar], *Korte aenmerckinghen op het onbewesen bewys dat het gevoelen vander sonne stillestant ende des aertrijckx beweginghe niet strijdigh is met Godts-woort* (The Hague: Henric Hondius, 1656), USTC 1830847.

Taddel, Elias, *Voor-stellinge, ende verklaringe van de woorden Daniels Cap. XII. vers 2. 3. Op de Doot ende christelijcke Begraeffenisse des eerwaerdigen, aendachtigen, wel-geleerden ende in Godt saligen Dn. M. Adolphus Visscher* (Amsterdam: Anna Serobandts and Michiel Strobach, 1653), USTC 1812102.

Tannery, Paul, Cornelis de Waard and Armand Beaulieu (eds.), *Correspondence du P Marin Mersenne* (17 vols., Paris: Presses Universitaires de France, 1945–1988).

Teellinck, Willem, *The Path of True Godliness*, trans. Annemie Godbehere, ed. Joel R. Beeke (Grand Rapids: Reformation Heritage Books, 2003).

Teellinck, Willem, *Ecce Homo, ofte ooghen-salve voor die noch sitten in blintheydt des ghemoedts* (Middelburg: Hans vander Hellen, 1622), USTC 1018260.

Temple, Sir William, *Observations Upon the United Provinces of the Netherlands*, ed. Sir George Clark (Oxford: Clarendon Press, 1972).

Thysius, Antonius, 'Concerning the Canonical and Apocryphal Books (disp. 3)', in Dolf te Velde (ed.), *Synopsis Purioris Theologiae/Synopsis of a Purer Theology: Latin Text and English Translation*, vol. 1, trans. Riemer A. Faber (2 vols., Leiden: Brill, 2014–2016).

BIBLIOGRAPHY 229

Thysius, Antonius, 'On Almsgiving and Fasting (disp. 37)', in Henk van den Belt (ed.) *Synopsis Purioris Theologiae/Synopsis of a Purer Theology*, vol. 2, trans. Riemer A. Faber (2 vols., Leiden: Brill, 2014–2016).

Tijdinghen uyt verscheyde Quartieren, no. 41, 13 October 1657, and no. 43, 27 October 1657.

Tranquillus, Suetonius [=Gisbertus Voetius], *Den overtuyghden cartesiaen, ofte Clare aenwysinge uyt de bedenckingen van Irenævs Philalethivs* (Leiden: Cornelis Banheinning, 1656), USTC 1833733.

Trigland, Jacob, *Christelijcke ende nootvvendighe verclaringhe, vant ghene in seker formulier, gheintituleert Resolutie der mogende H. Staten, &c. met Godes H. woort, ende de leere der ghereformeerde kercken over een comt, of daer van verschilt* (Martin Jansz. Brandt: Amsterdam, 1616), USTC 1030656.

Udemans, Godefridus, *'t geestelyck roer van 't coopmans schip* (Dordrecht: Françoys Boels, 1655), USTC 1820028.

Udemans, Godefridus, *The Practice of Faith, Hope, and Love*, trans. Annemie Godbehere, ed. Joel R. Beeke (Grand Rapids: Reformation Heritage Books, 2012).

Velde, Abraham van de, *De wonderen des Alder-hooghsten* (Amsterdam: Jan Claesz. ten Hoorn, 1677), USTC 1813494.

Virgil, *Aeneid* (Boston: Harvard University Press, 2015), Loeb Classical Library, DOI: 10.4159/DLCL.virgil-aeneid.1916.

Visscher, Adolf, 'Aen den Christelijcken Leser', in his *Biblia, Dat is, De gantsche H. Schrifture, vervattende alle de boecken des Ouden ende Nieuwen Testamenten* (Amsterdam: Rieuwert Dircksz van Baardt, [1648]), USTC 1014161.

Voetius, Gisbertus, *Drie tracten Gisberti Voetii* (Amsterdam: Jan Pietersz Kuypen, 1656), USTC 1828807.

Voetius, Gisbertus, *Eerste predicatie in de Dom-Kerke tot Utrecht te negen uren den 16. Novembris 1673* (Utrecht: Willem Clerck, 1674), USTC 1811366.

Voetius, Gisbertus, *Exercitia et bibliotheca studiosi theologiae* (Utrecht: Johannes (I) Janssonius van Waesberge, 1651), USTC 1814113.

Voetius, Gisbertus, 'Introductio ad Philosophiam Sacram', in his *Diatribae de theologia, philologia, historia et philosophia sacra* (Utrecht: Simon de Vries, 1668), USTC 1557347.

Voetius, Gisbertus, *Politicae ecclesiasticae* (4 vols., Amsterdam: Johannes (I) Janssonius van Waesberge, 1663–1676), USTC 1561164.

Voetius, Gisbertus, 'Praefatie van Gisbertus Voetius, anno 1631, gestelt voor het Tractaet van Mr. Willem Teellinck, over het 7 Capittel tot den Romeynen', in Theodorus and Johannes Teellinck (eds.), *Het eerste stuck van de wercken van Mr. Willem Teellinck* (Utrecht: Gedruckt voor de Erfgenamen van Mr. Willem Teellinck, 1659), USTC 1840360.

Voetius, Gisbertus, *Selectarum disputationum theologicarum* (5 vols., Utrecht and Amsterdam: Johannes (I) Janssonius van Waesberge, 1648–1669), USTC 1012125, 1803813, 1565688, 1805685, 1836590.

Voetius, Gisbertus, *Sermoen van de nutticheydt der academien ende scholen* (Utrecht: Aegidius and Petrus Roman, 1636), USTC 1029443.

Voetius, Gisbertus, 'The Will as Master of Its Own Act: A Disputation Rediscovered of Gisbertus Voetius (1589–1676) on Freedom of the Will', in Willem J. van Asselt, et al. (eds.), *Reformed Thought on Freedom: The Concept of Free Choice in Early Modern Reformed Theology* (Grand Rapids: Baker Books, 2010), pp. 145–170.

Walaeus, Antonius, *Opera Omnia* (2 vols., Leiden: Adriaen Wijngaerden, 1647–1648), USTC 1515253.

Walaeus, Antonius, *Oratio de studii Theologici recta institutione* (Leiden: Jacob Marcus: 1620), USTC 1015798.

Witsius, Cornelius, 'Eer Gesangh', in Guiljelmus Saldenus, *De Wech des levens* (Utrecht: Jacob van Doeyenborg, 1665), USTC 1802085.

Witsius, Herman, *The Economy of the Covenants between God and Man* (2 vols., facsimile; Grand Rapids: Reformation Heritage Books, 2010).

Witsius, Herman, *On the Character of a True Theologian*, ed. J. Ligon Duncan, III (Greenville, S.C.: Reformed Academic Press, 1994).

Witte, Petrus de, *Catechisatie over den Heydelberghschen catechismus* (Amsterdam: Baltus de Wild, 1655), USTC 1825219.

Witte, Petrus de, *Catechizing upon the Heidelbergh Catechisme* (Amsterdam: Gillis Joosten Saeghman, 1654), 841124124.

Witte, Petrus de, *Delfschen donder-slagh ofte Korte aensprake aen de bedroefde gemeente van Delf* (Amsterdam: Gerrit Willemsz. Doornick, 1655).

Wolseley, Charles, *De redelykheid van't schriftuur-geloof*, trans. Johannes Ubelman (Utrecht: Willem Broedelet, 1695), USTC 1833449.

Worp, J. A. (ed.), *De Briefwisseling van Constantijn Huygens* (6 vols., The Hague: Martinus Nijhoff, 1911–1917).

Wtenbogaart, Johannes, *Discours op ende teghen de conscientieuse bedenckinghen, ofmen in goede conscientie trefves met Spaengien maken mach* (Haarlem: Jacob de Wit, 1630), USTC 1026450.

Wtenbogaart, Johannes, *Johannis Uytenbogaerts leven, kerckelijcke bedieninghe ende zedighe verantwoordingh* (s.l., s.n., 1646), USTC 1034831.

Literature

Aalderink, Mark, 'Voor rechtzinnigheid en vroomheid, Marten Jansz Brandt (1613–1649): 37 jaar tromgeroffel van 'Soete Marten'' (PhD Thesis, University of Amsterdam, 2001).

Alleblas, Jan, 'Gedrukt in Dordrecht: de boekenbranche', in Willem Frijhoff, Hubert Nusteling and Marijke Spies (eds.), *Geschiedenis van Dordrecht van 1572 tot 1813* (Hilversum: Verloren, 1998), pp. 326–340.

BIBLIOGRAPHY

Arnade, Peter, *Beggars, Iconoclasts, and Civic Patriots: The Political Culture of the Dutch Revolt* (Ithaca: Cornell University Press, 2008).

Arnade, Peter and Henk van Nierop, 'The Political Culture of the Dutch Revolt: Introduction', *Journal of Early Modern History*, 11 (2007), pp. 253–261.

Asselt, Willem J. van, '"A Grievous Sin:" Gisbertus Voetius (1589–1676) and his anti-Lombard Polemic', in Jordan J. Ballor, David Systema and Jason Zuidema (eds.), *Church and School in Early Modern Protestantism: Studies in Honor of Richard A. Muller on the Maturation of a Theological Tradition* (Leiden: Brill, 2013), pp. 505–520.

Asselt, Willem J. van, *Introduction to Reformed Scholasticism*, trans. Albert Gootjes (Grand Rapids: Reformation Heritage Books, 2011).

Asselt, Willem J. van. *Voetius* (Kampen: De Groot Goudriaan, 2007).

Asselt, Willem J. van, 'Cocceius Anti-Scholasticus?', in Willem J. van Asselt and Eef Dekker (eds.), *Reformation and Scholasticism: An Ecumenical Enterprise* (Grand Rapids: Baker Academic, 2001), pp. 227–252.

Asselt, Willem J. van and Paul H. A. M. Abels, 'The Seventeenth Century', in Herman J. Selderhuis (ed.), *Handbook of Dutch Church History* (Göttingen: Vandenhoeck and Ruprecht, 2015), pp. 259–360.

Bangs, Carl, *Arminius: A Study in the Dutch Reformation* (Grand Rapids: Francis Asbury Press, 1985).

Bangs, Jeremy D., *Strangers and Pilgrims, Travellers and Sojourners: Leiden and the Foundations of Plymouth Plantation* (Plymouth, M.A.: General Society of Mayflower Descendants, 2009).

Beck, Andreas J., '"Expositio Reverentialis": Gisbertus Voetius's (1589–1676) Relationship with John Calvin', *Church History and Religious Culture*, 91 (2011), pp. 121–133.

Beck, Andreas J., 'Gisbertus Voetius (1589–1676): Basic Features of His Doctrine of God', in Willem J. van Asselt and Eef Dekker (eds.), *Reformation and Scholasticism: An Ecumenical Enterprise* (Grand Rapids: Baker Academic, 2001), pp. 205–226.

Beck, Andreas J., 'Melanchthonian Thought in Gisbertus Voetius' Scholastic Doctrine of God', in Maarten Wisse, Marcel Sarot and Willemien Otten (eds.), *Scholasticism Reformed: Essays in Honour of Willem J. van Asselt* (Leiden: Brill, 2010), pp. 107–127.

Begheyn, Paul, s.J., *Jesuit Books in the Dutch Republic and its Generality Lands 1567–1773* (Leiden: Brill, 2014).

Belt, Henk van den, 'Luther in Dutch Reformed Orthodoxy: A Bag of Worms against the Lutherans', in Herman J. Selderhuis and J. Marius J. Lange van Ravenswaay (eds.), *Luther and Calvinism: Image and Reception of Martin Luther in the History and Theology of Calvinism* (Göttingen: Vandenhoek and Ruprecht, 2017), pp. 427–442.

Bezzina, Edwin, 'The Practice of Ecclesiastical Discipline in the Huguenot Refugee Church of Amsterdam, 1650–1700', in Karen E. Spierling, Erik A. de Boer and R. Ward Holder (eds.), *Emancipating Calvin: Culture and Confessional Identity in Francophone Reformed Communities* (Leiden: Brill, 2018), pp. 147–174.

Bléchet, Francois, *Les ventes publiques de livres en France 1630–1750; répertoire des catalogues conservés à la Bibliothèque Nationale* (Oxford: The Voltaire Foundation, 1991).

Blom, Helwi, "'Il sest vendu depuis peu une assez bonne bibliotheque": the Republic of Letters and the sale catalogue of the library of "Mr. Briot", in Graeme Kemp, Andrew Pettegree and Arthur der Weduwen (eds.), *Book Trade Catalogues in Early Modern Europe* (Leiden: Brill, 2021), pp. 361–398.

Boekholt, P. Th. F. M. and E. P. de Booy, *Geschiedenis van de school in Nederland vanaf de middeleeuwen tot aan de huidige tijd* (Assen/Maastricht: Van Gorcum, 1987).

Bogaard, M. Th. Uit den, *De Gereformeerden en Oranje tijdens het eerste stadhouderloze tijdperk* (Groningen: J. B. Wolters, 1954).

Bots, Hans, 'Hugo Grotius et André Rivet: Deux Lumieres Opposées, Deux Vocations Contradictoires', Henk Nellen and Edwin Rabbie (eds.), *Hugo Grotius, Theologian: Essays in Honor of G. H. M. Posthumus Meyjes* (*Leiden: Brill, 1994*), pp. 145–158.

Bottema, Jaap, *Naar school in de Ommelanden. Scholen, schoolmeesters en hun onderwijs in de Groninger Ommelanden, ca. 1500–1795* (Bedum: Egbert Forsten and Profiel, 1999).

Bouwsma, William J., 'Lawyers and Early Modern Culture', in his *A Usable Past: Essays in European Cultural History* (Berkeley: University of California Press, 1990), pp. 129–156.

Brecht, Martin and Christian Peters, *Martin Luther. Annotierungen zu den Werken des Hieronymus, Archive zur Weimarer Ausgabe der Werke Martin Luthers, Texte und Untersuchungen*, vol. 8 (Cologne: Böhlau, 2000).

Breugelmans, Ronald, *Fac et Spera: Joannes Maire, Publisher, Printer and Bookseller in Leiden, 1603–1657* (Leiden: Hes & De Graaf, 2003).

Brink, Wilco van den, 'Slijtagesporen en spiegelbeelden: Overeenkomsten en verschillen in de titelgravures', in Jan Bos and August den Hollander (eds.), *Disgenoten: Short-Title Catalogue van* Het recht gebruyck van des Heeren H. Avondtmael (Amstelveen: EON Pers, 2007), pp. 18–26.

Broeyer, F. G. M., 'Bible for the Living Room: The Dutch Bible in the Seventeenth Century', in M. Lamberigts and A. A. den Hollander (eds.), *Lay Bibles in Europe 1450–1800* (Leuven: Leuven University Press, 2006), pp. 207–221.

Broeyer, F. G. M., 'Gisbertus Voetius, God's Gardener. The Pattern of Godliness in the *Selectae Disputationes*', in Maarten Wisse, Marcel Sarot and Willemien Otten (eds.), *Scholasticism Reformed: Essays in Honour of Willem J. van Asselt* (Leiden: Brill, 2010), pp. 127–154.

Broeyer, F. G. M., 'Theological Education at the Dutch Universities in the Seventeenth Century: Four Professors on their Ideal Curriculum', in Wim Janse and Barbara Pitkin (eds.), *The Formation of Clerical and Confessional Identities in Early Modern Europe* (Leiden: Brill, 2005), pp. 115–132.

BIBLIOGRAPHY

Broeyer, F. G. M., 'William III and the Church in Utrecht after the French Occupation (1672–1673)', in J. van den Berg and P. G. Hoftijzer (eds.), *Church, Change and Revolution: Transactions of the Fourth Anglo-Dutch Church History Colloquium* (Leiden: Brill, 1991), pp. 179–191.

Callenbach, J. R., 'Kerkelijk leven', in C. te Lintum (ed.), *Rotterdam in de loop der eeuwen*, vol. 2 (4 vols., Rotterdam: W. Neuvens, 1906–1909).

Clemens, Theo, *De godsdienstigheid in de Nederlanden in de spiegel van de Katholieke kerkboeken 1680–1840* (Tilburg: Tilburg University Press, 1988).

Cook, Harold J., *Matters of Exchange: Commerce, Medicine, and Science in the Dutch Golden Age* (New Haven: Yale University Press, 2007).

Cramer, J. A. *De Theologische Faculteit te Utrecht ten tijde van Voetius* (Utrecht: Kemink en Zoon, 1932).

Crew, Phyllis Mack, *Calvinist Preaching and Iconoclasm in the Netherlands 1544–1569* (Cambridge: Cambridge University Press, 1978).

Cruz, Laura 'The Epic Story of the Little Republic That Could: The Role of Patriotic Myths in the Dutch Golden Age', in Laura Cruz and Willem Frijhoff (eds.), *Myth in History, History in Myth* (Leiden: Brill, 2009), pp. 159–174.

Cruz, Laura, 'The Secrets of Success: Microinventions and bookselling in the seventeenth-century Netherlands', *Book History*, 10 (2007), pp. 1–28.

Cruz, Laura, 'Turning Dutch: Historical Myths in Early Modern Netherlands', *Sixteenth Century Journal*, 39 (2008), pp. 3–22.

Cuno, Fr. W., *Franciscus Junius der Ältere, Professor der Theologie und Pastor. (1545–1602): Sein Leben und Wirken, seine Schriften und Briefe* (Amsterdam: Scheffer and Co., 1891).

Dahl, Gina, *Book Collections of Clerics in Norway, 1650–1750* (Leiden: Brill, 2010).

Daugirdas, Kęstutis, 'The Biblical Hermeneutics of Socinians and Remonstrants in the Seventeenth Century' in Th. Marius van Leeuwen, Keith D. Stanglin and Marijke Tolsma (eds.), *Arminius, Arminianism, and Europe: Jacob Arminius (1559/60–1609)* (Leiden: Brill, 2009), pp. 87–113.

Davids, Karel, 'Amsterdam as a centre of learning in the Dutch golden age, c. 1580–1700', in Patrick O'Brien, Derek Keene, Marjolein 't Hart and Herman van der Wee (eds.), *Urban Achievement in Early Modern Europe: Golden Ages in Antwerp, Amsterdam and London* (Cambridge: Cambridge University Press, 2001), pp. 287–326.

Deursen, A. Th. van, *Plain Lives in a Golden Age: Popular Culture, Religion, and Society in Seventeenth Century Holland*, trans. Maarten Ultee (Cambridge: Cambridge University Press, 1991).

Deursen, A. Th. van, *Bavianen en Slijkgeuzen: Kerk en kerkvolk ten tijde van Maurits en Oldenbarnevelt* (Assen: Van Gorcum, 1974).

Deursen, A. Th. van 'De Domine', in H. M. Beliën, A. Th. van Deuresen and G. J. van Setten (eds.), *Gestatlen van de gouden eeuw: Een Hollands groepsportret* (Amsterdam: Bert Bakker, 1995), pp. 131–156.

Dijksterhuis, Fokko Jan, 'Labour on Lenses: Isaac Beckman's Notes on Lens Making', in Albert van Helden, Sven Dupré, Rob van Gent, and Huib Zuidervaart (eds.), *The Origins of the Telescope* (Amsterdam: Koninklijke Nederlandse Akademie van Wetenschappen, 2010), pp. 257–270.

Dijstelberge, Paul and Kuniko Forrer, 'De Alkmaarse Librije', in Ad Leerintveld and Jan Bedaux (eds.), *Historische stadsbibliotheken in Nederland: Studies over openbare stadsbibliotheken in de Noordelijke Nederlanden vanaf circa 1560 tot 1800* (Zutphen: Walburg Pers, 2016), pp. 29–36.

Dobbe, Ingrid, 'Requirements for Dutch Reformed Ministers, 1570–1620', in Theo Clemens and Wim Janse (eds.), *The Pastor Bonus: Papers read at the British-Dutch Colloquium at Utrecht, 18–21 September 2002* (Leiden: Brill, 2004), pp. 191–203.

Duke, Alastair, *Reformation and Revolt in the Low Countries* (London: Hambledon, 2003).

Duker, Arnold Cornelius, *Gisbertus Voetius* (3 vols., Leiden: Brill, 1897–1910).

Egeraat, Marieke van, 'Adding Books in your Catalogues, or an ABC on how to sell left-over stock', in Graeme Kemp, Andrew Pettegree and Arthur der Weduwen (eds.), *Book Trade Catalogues in Early Modern Europe* (Leiden: Brill, 2021), pp. 140–159.

Eijnatten, Joris van, *Liberty and Concord in the United Provinces: Religious Toleration and the Public in the Eighteenth-Century Netherlands* (Leiden: Brill, 2003).

Eijnatten, Joris van, '*Theologus Eruditus, Theologus Modestus*: The Early Modern Pastor as Communication Worker', in Theo Clemens and Wim Janse (eds.), *The Pastor Bonus: Papers read at the British-Dutch Colloquium at Utrecht, 18–21 September 2002* (Leiden: Brill, 2002), pp. 309–318.

Eliot, T. S., 'Cousin Nancy', in Christopher Ricks and Jim McCue (eds.), *The Poems of T. S. Eliot* (2 vols., Baltimore: Johns Hopkins University Press, 2015), I, p. 24.

Elliott, John Paul. 'Protestantization in the Northern Netherlands, a Case Study: The Classis of Dordrecht (1572–1640).' (PhD Thesis, Columbia University, 1990).

End, G. van den, *Guiljelmus Saldenus (1627–1694): Een praktisch en irenisch theoloog uit de Nadere Reformatie* (Leiden: Groen en Zoon, 1991).

Esser, Raingard, *The Politics of Memory: The Writing of Partition in the Seventeenth-Century Low Countries* (Leiden: Brill, 2012).

Evenhuis, R. B., *Ook dat was Amsterdam* (3 vols., Amsterdam: W. Ten Have, 1965–1971).

Evers, Meindert, 'The Illustre School at Harderwyk', *Lias*, 12 (1985), pp. 81–113.

Faber, Riemer A., 'Scholastic Continuities in the Reproduction of Classical Sources in the *Synopsis Purioris Theologiae*', *Church History and Religious Culture*, 92 (2012), pp. 561–579.

BIBLIOGRAPHY

Fieret, W., 'Wilhelmus à Brakel – a Biographical Sketch,' in Wilhelmus à Brakel, *The Christian's Reasonable Service*, ed. Joel R. Beeke, trans. Bartel Elshout (4 vols., Grand Rapids: Reformation Heritage Books, 1992–1995), I, pp. XXXI–LXXXI.

Fix, Andrew C., *Prophecy and Reason: The Dutch Collegiants in the Early Enlightenment* (Princeton: Princeton University Press, 1991).

Fontaine Verwey, Herman de la, 'The City Library of Amsterdam in the Nieuwe Kerk 1578–1632.' *Quarendo*, 14 (1984), pp. 163–205.

Fontaine Verwey, Herman de la, 'Dr. Joan Blaeu and his sons', *Quaerendo*, 11 (1981), pp. 5–23.

Fontaine Verwey, Herman de la, 'Willem Janz Blaeu as a Publisher of Books.' *Quaraendo*, 3 (1973), pp. 141–146.

Forclaz, Bertrand, 'The Emergence of Confessional Identities: Family Relationships and Religious Coexistence in Seventeenth-Century Utrecht', in C. Scott Dixon, Dagmar Freist and Mark Greengrass (eds.), *Living with Religious Diversity in Early Modern Europe* (Farnham: Ashgate, 2009), pp. 249–279.

Frijhoff, Willem, 'Calvinism, Literacy, and Reading Culture in the Early Modern Northern Netherlands: Towards a Reassessment', *Archiv für Reformationsgeschichte*, 95 (2004), pp. 252–265.

Frijhoff, Willem, *Embodied Belief: Ten Essays on Religious Culture in Dutch History* (Hilversum: Verloren, 2002).

Frijhoff, Willem, *Fulfilling God's Mission: The Two Worlds of Dominie Everardus Bogardus, 1607–1647*, trans. Myra Heerspink Scholz (Leiden: Brill, 2007).

Frijhoff, Willem, 'Hollandse priesters en hun boekenbezit', in Willem Heijting and Sandra van Daalen (eds.) *Hollandse priesterbibliotheken uit de tijd van de Republiek: Catalogus van bibliotheken afkomstig uit de R.K. parochies te Aarlanderveen, Assendelft, Buitenveldert, Voorburg en Zevenhoven* (Amstelveen: EON Pers, 2005), pp. 15–33.

Frijhoff, Willem, 'How Plural Were the Religious Worlds in Early-Modern Europe? Critical Reflections from the Netherlandic Experience', in C. Scott Dixon, Dagmar Freist and Mark Greengrass (eds.), *Living with Religious Diversity in Early Modern Europe* (Farnham: Ashgate, 2009), pp. 21–52.

Frijhoff, Willem, 'Inspiration Instruction, Competence? Questions autour de le selection des pasteurs Réformés aux Pays-Bas, XVIE–XVIIE Siècles', *Paedagogica Historica*, 30 (1994), pp. 13–38.

Frijhoff, Willem, 'Johannes Lomejer (1636–1699): From a Historian of Books to a Cultural Historian', *Quaerendo* 42 (2012), pp. 84–113.

Frijhoff, Willem, 'Was the Dutch Republic a Calvinist Community? The State, the Confessions, and Culture in the Early Modern Netherlands', in André Holenstein, Thomas Maissen and Maarten Prak (eds.), *The Republican Alternative: The*

Netherlands and Switzerland Compared (Amsterdam: Amsterdam University Press, 2008), pp. 99–122.

Frijhoff, Willem and Marieke Spies, *1650: Hard-Won Unity*, trans. Myra Heerspink Scholz (Basingstoke, United Kingdom/Assen, The Netherlands: Palgrave Macmillan/Royal Van Gorcum, 2004).

Ganoczy, Alexandre, *La bibliothèque de l'académie de Calvin: le catalogue de 1572 es ses enseignments* (Geneva: Librarie Droz, 1969).

Gelderen, Martin van, 'Hot Protestants: Predestination, the Freedom of Will and the Making of the Modern European Mind', in Gijsbert van den Brink and Harro M. Höpfl (eds.), *Calvinism and the Making of the European Mind* (Leiden: Brill, 2014), pp. 131–154.

Gilmont, Jean-François, *John Calvin and the Printed Book*, trans. Karen Maag (Kirksville, MO: Trueman State University Press, 2005).

Gilmont, Jean-François, 'Protestant Reformations and Reading,' in Guglielmo Cavallo and Roger Chartier (eds.), *A History of Reading in the West* (Polity: Cambridge, 1999), pp. 213–237.

Gootjes, Albert, *Claude Pajon (1626–1685) and the Academy of Saumur* (Leiden: Brill, 2014).

Gootjes, Nicholaas H., *The Belgic Confession: Its History and Sources* (Grand Rapids: Baker Academic, 2007).

Gorski, Philip Stephen, 'The Disciplinary Revolution: Calvinism and State Formation in Early Modern Europe, 1550–1750.' (PhD Thesis, University of California at Berkeley, 1996).

Gorski, Philip Stephen, *The Disciplinary Revolution: Calvinism and the Rise of the State in Early Modern Europe* (Chicago: University of Chicago Press, 2003).

Goudriaan, Aza, 'Justification by Faith and the Early Arminian Controversy', in Maarten Wisse, Marcel Sarot and Willemien Otten (eds.), *Scholasticism Reformed: Essays in Honour of Willem J. van Asselt* (Leiden: Brill, 2010), pp. 155–179.

Goudriaan, Aza, *Reformed Orthodoxy and Philosophy, 1625–1750: Gisbertus Voetius, Petrus van Mastricht, and Anthonius Driessen* (Leiden: Brill, 2006).

Goudriaan, Aza and Fred van Lieburg (eds.), *Revisiting the Synod of Dort (1618–1619)* (Leiden: Brill, 2011).

Gribben, Crawford, *John Owen and English Puritanism: Experiences of Defeat* (Oxford: Oxford University Press, 2016).

Groenendijk, L. F., 'De Oorsprong van de Uitdrukking "Nadere Reformatie"', *Documentatieblad Nadere Reformatie*, 9 (1985), pp. 128–134.

Groenendijk, L. F., 'The Reformed Church and Education During the Golden Age of the Dutch Republic', *Dutch Review of Church History*, 85 (2005), pp. 53–70.

Groenhuis, G., 'Calvinism and National Consciousness: The Dutch Republic as the New Israel', in A. C. Duke and C. A. Tamse (eds.), *Britain and the Netherlands*, vol. 7 (The Hague: Martinus Nijhoff, 1981), pp. 118–133.

BIBLIOGRAPHY

Groenhuis, G., *De predikanten: De sociale positie van de gereformeerde predikanten in de Republiek der Verenigde Nederlanden voor ± 1700* (Groningen: Wolters-Noordhoff, 1977).

Groenveld, S., 'The Mecca of Authors? Sates Assemblies and Censorship in the Seventeenth-Century Dutch Republic', in A. C. Duke and C. A. Tamse (eds.), *Too Mighty to Be Free: Censorship and the Press in Britain and the Netherlands* (Zutphen: Walburg Pers, 1987), pp. 63–86.

Groesen, Michiel van, *Amsterdam's Atlantic: Print Culture and the Making of Dutch Brazil* (Philadelphia: University of Pennsylvania Press, 2017).

Groesen, Michiel van, 'Reading Newspapers in the Dutch Golden Age,' *Media History*, 22 (2016), pp. 334–352.

Groot, A. H. de, *The Ottoman Empire and the Dutch Republic: A History of the Earliest Diplomatic Relations, 1610–1630* (Leiden: Nederlands Historisch-Archaeologisch Instituut Leiden/Istanbul, 1978).

Grosslight, Justin, 'Small Skills, Big Network: Marin Mersenne as Mathematical Intelligencer', *History of Science*, 51 (2013), pp. 337–374.

Habsburg, Max von, 'The Devotional Life: Catholic and Protestant Translations of Thomas à Kempis', Imitatio Christi, C. 1420–C.1620', (PhD Thesis, University of St Andrews, 2002).

Hakkenberg, Michael Abram, 'The Predestinarian Controversy in the Netherlands, 1600–1620', (PhD Thesis, University of California at Berkeley, 1989).

Harline, Craig E., *Pamphlets, Printing, and Political Culture in the Early Dutch Republic* (Dordrecht: Martinus Nijhoff, 1987).

Hart, S., 'Enige Statistische gegevens inzake analfabetisme te Amsterdam in de 17e en 18e Eeuw,' *Amstelodamum*, 55 (1968), pp. 3–6.

Heel, Jos van, 'Gisbertus Voetius on the Necessity of Locating, Collecting and Preserving Early Printed Books', *Quaerendo*, 39 (2009), pp. 45–56.

Heijting, Willem, 'Beyond the Printed Book. The Media in Reformation Historiography', in Ulrike Hascher-Berger, August den Hollander and Wim Janse (eds.), *Between Lay Piety and Academic Theology: Studies Presented to Christopher Burger on the Occasion of his 65th Birthday* (Leiden: Brill, 2010), pp. 415–432.

Helmers, Helmer J., *The Royalist Republic: Literature, Politics, and Religion in the Anglo-Dutch Public Sphere, 1639–1660.* (Cambridge: Cambridge University Press, 2015).

Hobson, Anthony, 'A Sale by Candle in 1608', *The Library*, 26 (1971), pp. 215–233.

Hof, W. J. op 't, 'Een portret als oorzaak van verwijdering tussen een auteur en zijn uitgever', *Documentatieblad Nadere Reformatie*, 16 (1992), pp. 97–102.

Hof, W. J. op 't, *Engelse piëtistische geschriften in het Nederlands, 1598–1622* (Rotterdam: Lindenberg, 1987).

Hof, W. J. op 't, 'The eventful sojourn of Willem Teellinck (1579–1629) at Banbury in 1605', *Journal for the History of Reformed Pietism*, 1 (2015), pp. 5–34.

238 BIBLIOGRAPHY

Hof, W. J. op 't, 'Geïmporteerde Vroomheid? De Zeventiende-Eeuwse Nederlandse Gereformeerde Vroomheid in Internationaal Perspectief', in Karel Davids, M. 't Hart, H. Kleijer and J. Lucassen. (eds.), *De Republiek Tussen Zee En Vasteland. Buitenlandse Invloeden Op Cultuur, Economie En Politiek in Nederland 1580–1800*, (Leuven: Garant, 1995), pp. 83–105.

Hof, W. J. op 't. 'Het culturele gehalte van de Nadere Reformatie', *De zeventiende eeuw*, 5 (1989), pp. 129–140.

Hof, W. J. op 't. 'De Nadere Reformatie in Zeeland. Een eerste schets', in A. Wiggers, P. H. A. M. Abels, H. ten Boom, P. J. Bos and H. Uil (eds.), *Rond de kerk in Zeeland* (Delft: Eburon, 1991), pp. 37–82.

Hof, W. J. op 't. 'Piety in the Wake of Trade. The North Sea as an Intermediary of Reformed Piety up to 1700', Juliette Roding and Lex Heerma van Voss (eds.), *The North Sea and Culture (1550–1800)* (Hilversum: Verloren, 1996), pp. 248–265.

Hof, W. J. op 't. 'The Oldest Dutch Commercial Oeuvre Lists in Print.' *Quaerendo*, 23 (1993), pp. 265–290.

Hof, W. J. op 't, 'Puritan Emotions in Seventeenth-Century Dutch Piety', in Alec Ryrie and Tom Schwanda (eds.), *Puritan Emotions in the Early Modern World* (New York: Palgrave Macmillan, 2016), pp. 213–240.

Hof, W. J. op 't, 'Ra, ra, wat ben ik? Een speurtocht naar de traditie, de aard, het milieu en het gebruik van het bekendste Nederlandse avondmaalsboekje *Het rechte gebruyck van des Heeren H. avondtmael*', in Jan Bos and August den Hollander (eds.), *Disgenoten: Short-Title Catalogue van* Het recht gebruyck van des Heeren H. Avondtmael (Amstelveen: EON Pers, 2007), pp. 241–275.

Hof, W. J. op 't, 'Unique Information on a Seventeenth-Century Printing House in Arnhem. The dedication by the Arnhem printer Jacob van Biesen (d. 1677) in the 1669 edition of Fonteyne des levens by Arthur Hildersham (1563–1632) and its implications for the history of books', *Quaerendo*, 43 (2013), pp. 214–237.

Hof, W. J. op 't, *Willem Teellinck: Leven, Geschriften en Invloed* (Kampen: De Groot Goudriaan, 2008).

Hof, W. J. op 't, 'Willem Teellinck and Gisbertus Voetius', in Ronald K. Rittergers and Vincent Evener (eds.), *Protestants and Mysticism in Reformation Europe* (Leiden: Brill, 2019), pp. 389–408.

Hof, W. J. op 't, August den Hollander, F. W. Huisman. *De Praktijk der Godzaligheid: Studies over De practycke ofte oeffeninghe der godtzaligheydt (1620) van Lewis Bayly* (Amstelveen: EON Pers, 2009).

Hoftijzer, Paul G., *Engelse boekverkopers bij de Beurs: De geschiedenis van de Amsterdamse boekhandels Bruyning en Swart, 1637–1724* (Amsterdam/Maarssen: APA-Holland Universiteit Pers, 1987).

Hoftijzer, Paul G., '"A Sickle unto Thy Neighbour's Corn": Book Piracy in the Dutch Republic.' *Quarendo*, 27 (1997), 4–18.

BIBLIOGRAPHY

Hoftijzer, Paul G., 'A Study Tour into the Low Countries and the German States: William Nicolson's *Iter Hollandicum* and *Iter Germanicum* 1678–1679', *Lias*, 15 (1988), pp. 73–128.

Hoftijzer, Paul G., 'Metropolis of print: the Amsterdam book trade in the seventeenth century', in Patrick O'Brien, Derek Keene, Marjolein 't Hart and Herman van der Wee (eds.), *Urban Achievement in Early Modern Europe: Golden Ages in Antwerp, Amsterdam and London* (Cambridge: Cambridge University Press, 2001), pp. 249–263.

Hollander, August den, 'Christian Hebraism and Early Printed Dutch Bibles', in Ulrike Hascher-Berger, August den Hollander and Wim Janse (eds.), *Between Lay Piety and Academic Theology: Studies Presented to Christopher Burger on the Occasion of his 65th Birthday* (Leiden: Brill, 2010), pp. 521–532.

Hollander, August den, 'The Edition History of the Deux Aes Bible', in August den Hollander, Alex Noord, Mirjam van Veen and Anna Voolstra (eds.), *Religious Minorities and Cultural Diversity in the Dutch Republic* (Leiden: Brill, 2014), pp. 41–72.

Hollander, August den, 'Een bijbel voor de lutheranen in Nederland – de mythe van de vertaling van Adolf Visscher uit 1648', in Gillaerts et al. (eds.), *De Bijbel in de Lage Landen. Elf eeuwen van vertalen* (Heerenveen: Royal Jongbloed, 2015), pp. 445–450.

Hollander, August den, 'Illustrations in Early Printed Latin Bibles in the Low Countries (1477–1547)', in Bruce Gordon and Matthew McLean (eds.), *Shaping the Bible in the Reformation: Books Scholars and their Readers in the Sixteenth Century* (Leiden: Brill, 2012), pp. 41–61.

Hollander, August den, 'The New Testament, which … surpasses all books. Adriaen van Berghen, 1533', *Quaerendo*, 36 (2006), pp. 35–50.

Hollander, August den, 'The Qur'an in the Low Countries Early Printed Dutch and French Translations', *Quaerendo*, 45 (2015), pp. 209–239.

Hollander, August den and Ole Peter Grell, 'Bibles in the Dutch and Scandinavian vernaculars to c. 1750', in Euan Cameron (ed.), *The New Cambridge History of the Bible*, vol. 3 (Cambridge: Cambridge University Press, 2016), pp. 239–262.

Honders, H. J., *André Rivet: Als invloedrijk gereformeerd theoloog in Holland's bloeitijd* (The Hague: Martinus Nijhoff, 1930).

Hsia, R. Po-Chia and Henk van Nierop (eds.), *Calvinism and Religious Toleration in the Dutch Golden Age* (Cambridge: Cambridge University Press, 2010).

Huisman, Gerda C., 'Bibliothecae instructissimae: Geleerd boekenbezit in Groningen in de 17e en 18e eeuw', in A. H. Huussen, Jr. (ed.), *Onderwijs en onderzoek: studie en wetenschap aan de academie van Groningen in de 17e en 18e eeuw* (Hilversum: Verloren, 2003).

Israel, Jonathan I. *The Dutch Republic: Its Rise, Greatness, and Fall 1477–1806* (Oxford: Clarendon Press, 1995).

Johnston, Andrew G. 'Printing and the Reformation in the Low Countries, 1520–c. 1555', in Jean-François Gilmont (ed.), *The Reformation and the Book*, trans. Karin Maag (Aldershot: Ashgate, 1998), pp. 155–183.

Jong, O. J. de. 'Voetius en de Tolerantie', in J. van Oort, C. Graafland, A. de Groot and O. J. de Jong (eds.), *De onbekende Voetius* (Kampen: J.H. Kok, 1989), pp. 109–116.

Jonge, H. J. de, 'The Latin Testament of Joseph Scaliger, 1607', *Lias*, 2 (1975), pp. 249–258.

Jorink, Eric, *Reading the Book of Nature in the Dutch Golden Age, 1575–1715*, trans. Peter Mason (Leiden: Brill, 2010).

Kahn, Victoria, 'The Passions and the Interests in Early Modern Europe: The Case of Guarini's Il Pastor fido', in Gail Kern Paster, Katherine Rowe and Mary Floyd-Wilson (eds.), *Reading the Early Modern Passions: Essays in the Cultural History of Emotion* (Philadelphia: University of Pennsylvania Press 2004), pp. 217–239.

Kamp, J. van de., A. Goudriaan and W. van Vlastuin (eds.). *Pietas Reformata: Religieuze vernieuwing onder gereformeerden in de vroegmoderne tijd* (Zoetermeer: Boekencentrum, 2015).

Kaplan, Benjamin J., '"For They Will Turn Away Thy Sons": the Practice and Perils of Mixed Marriage in the Dutch Golden Age', in Marc R. Forster and Benjamin J. Kaplan (eds.), *Piety and Family in Early Modern Europe: Essays in Honour of Steven Ozment* (Aldershot, UK: Ashgate, 2005), pp. 115–134.

Kaplan, Benjamin J., *Muslims in the Dutch Golden Age: Representations and realities of religious toleration* (Amsterdam: Amsterdam University Press, 2007).

Kist, N. C., 'De Synoden der Nederlandsche Hervormde Kerken onder het kruis gedurende de Jaren 1563–1577', *Nederlandsch Archief voor Kerkelijke Geschiedenis*, 20 (1849), pp. 113–208.

Kivimäe, Jüri, 'Books and Preachers: The Microcosm of Reval in the Age of the Reformation', in Heinrich Assel, Johann Anselm Steiger, Axel E. Walter (eds.), *Reformatio Baltica: Kulturwirkungen der Reformation in den Metropolen des Osteeraums* (Berlin: De Gruyter, 2018), pp. 655–668.

Knijff, Philip and Sibbe Jan Visser, *Bibliographia Sociniana: A Bibliographical Reference Tool for the Study of Dutch Socinianism and Antitrinitarianism*, ed. Piet Visser (Hilversum: Verloren/Doopsgezinde Historische Kring, Amsterdam, 2004).

Kooi, Christine. *Calvinists and Catholics During Holland's Golden Age: Heretics and Idolaters* (Cambridge: Cambridge University Press, 2012).

Koote, T. G. (ed.), De Bijbel in huis. Bijbelse verhalen op huisraad in de zeventiende en achttiende eeuw (Utrecht: Museum Catharijneconvent, 1991).

Kruif, José de, *Liefliebbers en gewoontelezers. Leescultuur in Den Haag in de achttiende eeuw* (Zutphen: Walberg Pers, 1999).

Kuiper, Ernst Jan, *De Hollandse 'Schoolordre' van 1625* (Groningen: Wolters, 1958).

Kuyper, H. H., *De opleiding tot den dienst des osit bij de gereformeerden* (The Hague: Martinus Nijhoff, 1891).

Laeven, A. H., 'The Frankfurt and Leipzig Book Fairs and the History of the Dutch Book Trade in the Seventeenth and Eighteenth Centuries', in C. Berkvens-Stevelinck, H. Bots, Paul G. Hoftijzer and Otto S. Lankhorst (eds.), *Le Magasin de l'Univers: The Dutch Republic as the Centre of the European Book Trade* (Leiden: Brill. 1992), pp. 185–198.

Lankhorst, Otto S., 'Les ventes de livres en Hollande et leurs catalogues (XVIIe–XVIIIe siècles)', in Annie Charon and Élisabeth Parinet (eds.), *Les ventes de livres et leurs catalogues: XVIIe–XXe siècle. Actes des journées organisées par l'École nationale des chartes (Paris, 15 janvier 1998) et par l'ENSSIB (Villeurbanne, 22 janvier 1998)* (Paris: École nationale des chartes, 2000), pp. 11–28.

Lankhorst, Otto S., *Reinier Leers (1654–1714), uitgever & boekverkoper te Rotterdam: een Europees 'libraire' en zijn fonds* (Amsterdam/Maarssen: APA-Holland Universiteit Pers, 1983).

Lankhorst, Otto S., 'Dutch Book Auctions in the Seventeenth and Eighteenth Century', in Robin Myers, Michael Harris and Giles Mandelbrote (eds.), *Under the Hammer: book auctions since the seventeenth century* (New Castle: Oak Knoll Press, 2001), pp. 65–87.

Lee, Brian J. *Johannes Cocceius and the Exegetical Roots of Federal Theology: Reformation Developments in the Interpretation of Hebrews 7–10* (Göttingen: Vandenhoeck & Ruprecht, 2009).

Lee, Brian J. 'Johannes Cocceius as Federal Polemicist: The Usefulness of the Distinction between the Testaments', in Jordan J. Ballor, David Systema and Jason Zuidema (eds.), *Church and School in Early Modern Protestantism: Studies in Honor of Richard A. Muller on the Maturation of a Theological Tradition* (Leiden: Brill, 2013), pp. 567–582.

Leerintveld, Ad, 'Inleiding', in Ad Leerintveld and Jan Bedeaux (eds.), *Historische Stadsbibliotheken in Nederland: Studies over openbare stadsbibliotheken in de Noordelijke Nederlanden vanaf circa 1560 tot 1800* (Zutphen: Walburg Pers, 2016), pp. 6–12.

Leo, Russ, 'Geeraardt Brandt, Dutch Tolerance, and the Reformation of the Reformation', *Journal of Medieval and Early Modern Studies*, 46 (2016), pp. 485–511.

Lesger, Clé, *Handel in Amsterdam ten tijde van de Opstand. Kooplieden. Commerciële expansie en verandering in de ruimtelijke economie van de Nederlanden ca. 1550–ca. 1630* (Hilversum: Verloren, 2001).

Leu, Urs B. and Sandra Weidmann, *Heinrich Bullingers Privatbibliothek*, in *Heinrich Bullinger Werke*, Abt. 1, Bd. 3 (Zurich: Theologischer Verlag, 2004).

Leu, Urs B., *Huldrych Zwingli's Private Library* (Leiden: Brill, 2019).

Lieburg, F. A. van, 'Bible Reading and Pietism in the Dutch Reformed Tradition', in M. Lamberigts and A. A. den Hollander (eds.), *Lay Bibles in Europe 1450–1800* (Leuven: Leuven University Press, 2006), pp. 223–244.

Lieburg, F. A. van, *De Nadere Reformatie in Utrecht ten tijde van Voetius: Sporen in de gereformeerde kerkeraadsacta* (Rotterdam: Lindenberg, 1989).

Lieburg, F. A. van, 'The Dutch book trade, Christian Enlightenment and the National bibliography. The catalogues of Johannes van Abkoude (1703–60) and Reinier Arrenberg (1733–1812)', *Quaerendo*, 31 (2001), pp. 3–16.

Lieburg, F. A. van. 'Dynamics of Dutch Calvinism: Early Modern Programs for Further Reformation', in Gijsbert van den Brink and Harro M. Höpfl (eds.), *Calvinism and the Making of the European Mind* (Leiden: Brill, 2014), pp. 43–66.

Lieburg, F. A. van, 'From Pure Church to Pious Culture: The Further Reformation in the Seventeenth-Century Dutch Republic', in W. Fred Graham (ed.), *Later Calvinism: International Perspectives* (Kirksville, MO: Sixteenth Century Journal Publishers, 1992), pp. 409–429.

Lieburg, F. A. van, 'Preachers Between Inspiration and Instruction: Dutch Reformed Ministers without Academic Education (Sixteenth-Eighteenth Centuries)', *Dutch Review of Church History*, 83 (2003), pp. 166–190.

Lieburg, F. A. van, *Profeten en hun vaderland: de geografische herkomst van de gereformeerde predikanten in Nederland van 1572 tot 1816* (Zoetermeer: Boekencentrum, 1996).

Lieburg, F. A. van, *Repertorium van Nederlandse hervormde predikanten tot 1816: Predikanten* (2 vols., Dordrecht, 1996).

Lieburg, F. A. van, 'Warning against the Pietists: The World of Wilhelmus à Brakel', in Joke Spaans and Jetze Touber (eds.), *Enlightened Religion: From Confessional Churches to Polite Piety in the Dutch Republic* (Leiden: Brill, 2019), pp. 346–370.

Lim, Paul C. H., 'Not Solely *Sola Scriptura*, or, a Rejoinder to Brad S. Gregory's *The Unintended Reformation*', *Journal of Medieval and Early Modern Studies*, 46 (2016), pp. 555–582.

Linden, David van der, *Experiencing Exile: Huguenot Refugees in the Dutch Republic, 1680–1700* (Farnham: Ashgate, 2015).

Luc-Tulot, Jean (ed.), 'Les pasteurs en maris et pères, au travers des coresondances adressées à André Rivet, 1620–1650', *Bulletin de la Société de l'Histoire du Protestantisme Français*, 159 (2013), pp. 79–92.

Marchi, Neil de and Paul Harrison, 'Trading "in the Wind" and with Guile: The Troublesome Matter of the Short Selling of Shares in Seventeenth-Century Holland,' in Neil de Marchi and Mary S. Morgan (eds.), *Higgling: Transactors and their Markets in the History of Economics* (Durham: Duke University Press, 1994), pp. 47–65.

Malcom, Noel, *Aspects of Hobbes* (Oxford: Clarendon Press, 2002).

Marnef, Guido, 'The Netherlands', in Andrew Pettegree (ed.), *The Reformation World* (London: Routledge, 2000), pp. 344–364.

Maronier, Jan, *Jacobus Arminius: een biographie (met portret en handteekening)* (Amsterdam: Y. Rogge, 1905).

McLean, Matthew, *The* Cosmographia *of Sebastian Münster: Describing the world in the Reformation* (Aldershot, UK: Ashgate, 2007).

Michaëlius, Jonas, *The First Minister of the Dutch Reformed Church in the United States* (The Hague: Printed by the Brothers Giunta D'Albani, 1858).

Miert, Dirk van, *Humanism in an Age of Science: The Amsterdam Athenaeum in the Golden Age, 1632–1704*, trans. Michiel Wielema, with Anthony Ossa-Richardson (Leiden: Brill, 2009).

Miert, Dirk van, 'The "Hairy War" (1649–50): Historicizing the Bible in the Dutch Republic on the Eve of Spinoza', *Sixteenth Century Journal*, 48 (2018), pp. 415–436.

Miert, Dirk van, 'Making the States' Translation (1637): Orthodox Calvinist Biblical Criticism in the Dutch Republic', *Harvard Theological Review*, 110 (2017), pp. 440–463.

Milton, Anthony, 'A Distorting Mirror: The Hales and Balcanquahall Letters and the Synod of Dort', in Aza Goudriaan and Fred van Lieburg (eds.), *Revisiting the Synod of Dort (1618–1619)* (Leiden: Brill, 2011), pp. 135–161.

Molhuysen, P. C. and P. J. Blok (eds.), *Nieuw Nederlandsch Biografisch Woordenboek* (10 vols., Leiden: A. W. Sijthoff, 1911–1937).

Mulier, E. O. G. Haitsma and G. A. C. van der Lem (eds.), *Repertorium van geschied-schrijvers in Nederland 1500–1800* (The Hague: Nederlands Historisch Genootschap, 1990).

Muller, Richard A., *After Calvin: Studies in the Development of a Theological Tradition* (Oxford: Oxford University Press, 2003).

Muller, Richard A., 'Arminius and the Reformed Tradition', *Westminster Theological Journal*, 9 (2008), pp. 19–48.

Muller, Richard A., *Dictionary of Latin and Greek Theological Terms: Drawn Principally from Scholastic Theology* (Grand Rapids: Baker Academic, 2017).

Muller, Richard A., *God, Creation, and Providence in the Thought of Jacob Arminius: Sources and Directions of Scholastic Protestantism in the Era of Early Orthodoxy* (Grand Rapids: Baker Books, 1991).

Muller, Richard A., *Post-Reformation Reformed Dogmatics* (4 vols., Grand Rapids: Baker Academic, 2003).

Mulsow, Martin and Jan Rohls (eds.), *Socinianism and Arminianism: Antitrinitarians, Calvinists and Cultural Exchange in Seventeenth-Century Europe* (Leiden: Brill, 2005).

Munt, Anette Henriette, 'The Impact of Dutch Cartesian Medical Reformers in Early Enlightenment German Culture (1680–1720)' (PhD Thesis, University of London, 2004).

Nauta, Doede, *Samuel Maresius* (Amsterdam: H. J. Paris, 1935).

Nauta, Doede, et al. (eds.), *Biografisch lexicon voor de geschiedenis van het Nederlandse protestantisme* (6 vols., Kampen: J. H. Kock, 1978–2006).

Neele, Adriaan C. *Petrus van Mastricht (1630–1706), Reformed Orthodoxy: Method and Piety* (Leiden: Brill, 2009).

Nellen, Henk J. M., 'Disputando Inclarescet Veritas: Grotius as a Publicist in France', in Henk Nellen and Edwin Rabbie (eds.), *Hugo Grotius, Theologian: Essays in Honour of G. H. M. Posthumus Meyjes (Leiden: Brill, 1994)*, pp. 120–144.

Nellen, Henk J. M., *Hugo Grotius: A Lifelong Struggle for Peace in Church and State, 1583–1645*, trans. J. C. Grayson (Leiden: Brill, 2017).

Nellen, Henk J. M., '"Geene vredemaeckers zijn zonder tegenspreeckers" Hugo Grotius' buitenkerkelijke ositive', *De zeventiende eeuw*, 5 (1989), pp. 103–112.

Nellen, Henk J. M. and Cornelia M. Ridderikhoff (eds.), *Briefwisseling van Hugo Grotius*, vol. 17 (The Hague: Martinus Nijhoff, 2001).

Nellen, Henk J. M. and Edwin Rabbie (eds.), *Hugo Grotius, Theologian: Essays in Honour of G. H. M. Posthumus Meyjes* (Leiden: Brill, 1994).

Nierop, Henk van, *Treason in the Northern Quarter: War, Terror, and the Role of Law in the Dutch Revolt*, trans. J. C. Grayson (Princeton: Princeton University Press, 2009).

Noak, Bettina, 'Foreign Wisdom: Ethnological Knowledge in the Work of Franciscus Ridderus', *Journal of Dutch Literature*, 3 (2012), pp. 47–64.

Nobbs, Douglas, *Theocracy and Toleration: A Study of the Disputes in Dutch Calvinism From 1600 to 1650* (Cambridge: Cambridge University Press, 1938).

Nobel, Arjan and Otto van der Meij, 'De Luijden sijn daer seer begeerich na: De veiling van de bibliotheek van André Rivet in 1657', in Maurits Ebben and Pieter Wagenaar (eds.), *De cirkel doorbroken* (Leiden: Instituut voor Geschiedenis, 2006), pp. 215–238.

Oates, Rosamund, *Moderate Radical: Tobie Matthew and the English Reformation* (Oxford: Oxford University Press, 2018).

Onnekink, David, *Reinterpreting the Dutch Forty Years War, 1672–1713* (Palgrave Macmillan: London, 2016).

Onnekink, David, 'The Last Wars of Religion? The Dutch and the Nine Years War', in David Onnekink (ed.), *War and Religion after Westphalia, 1648–1713* (Ashgate: Farnham, 2009), pp. 69–88.

Oosterhout, Moniek van, 'Hugo Grotius in Praise of Jacobus Arminius: Arminian Readers of an Epicedium in the Dutch Republic and England', in Jan Bloemendal, Arjan van Dixhoorn and Elsa Strietman (eds.), *Literary Cultures and Public Opinion in the Low Countries, 1450–1650* (Leiden: Brill, 2011), pp. 151–179.

Opstal, A. G. van, *André Rivet: Een invloedrijk hugenoot aan het hof van Frederick Hendrik* (Harderwijk: Flevo, 1937).

Osborne, Troy David, 'Saints into Citizens: Mennonite Discipline, Social Control, and Religious Toleration in the Dutch Golden Age', (PhD Thesis, University of Minnesota, 2007).

Ossa-Richardson, Anthony, 'Gijsbert Voet and *Discretio Spirituum* after Descartes', in Clare Copeland and Jan Machielsen (eds.), *Angels of Light? Sanctity and the Discernment of Spirits in the Early Modern Period* (Leiden: Brill, 2013), pp. 235–254.

BIBLIOGRAPHY   245

Ossa-Richardson, Anthony, 'The Naked Truth of Scripture: André Rivet between Bellarmine and Grotius', in Dirk van Miert, Henk Nellen, Piet Steenbakkers and Jetze Touber (eds.), *Scriptural Authority and Biblical Criticism in the Golden Age: God's Word Questioned* (Oxford: Oxford University Press, 2017), pp. 109–130.

Otterspeer, Willem, *Groepsportret met dame: Het bolwerk van de vrijheid. De Leidse Universiteit*, vol. 1 (Amsterdam: Bert Bakker, 2000).

Padover, S. K., 'Muslim Libraries', in James Westfall Thompson (ed.), *The Medieval Library* (New York: Hafner, 1957), pp. 347–368.

Pater, C. de, 'Experimental Physics', in Th. H. Lunsingh Scheurleer and G. H. M. Posthumus Meyjes (eds.), *Leiden University in the Seventeenth Century: An Exchange of Learning* (Leiden: Universitaire Pers Leiden/Brill, 1975), pp. 309–329.

Parente, Jr., James A., *Religious Drama and the Humanist Tradition* (Leiden: Brill, 1987).

Parker, Geoffrey, *The Dutch Revolt* (New York: Penguin Books, 1978).

Pettegree, Andrew, *The Book in the Renaissance* (New Haven: Yale University Press, 2011).

Pettegree, Andrew, *Brand Luther* (New York: Penguin Books, 2015).

Pettegree, Andrew, 'Calvin and Luther as Men of the Book', in Karen E. Spierling (ed.), *Calvin and the Book: The Evolution of the Printed Word in Reformed Protestantism* (Göttingen: Vandenhoeck & Ruprecht, 2015), pp. 17–32.

Pettegree, Andrew, 'Centre and Periphery in the European Book World', *Transactions of the Royal Historical Society*, 18 (2008), pp. 101–128.

Pettegree, Andrew, *Reformation and the Culture of Persuasion* (Cambridge: Cambridge University Press, 2005).

Pettegree, Andrew, *Foreign Protestant Communities in Sixteenth-Century London* (Oxford: Clarendon Press, 1986).

Pettegree, Andrew, 'The Renaissance Library and the Challenge of Print', in Alice Crawford (ed.), *The Meaning of the Library: A Cultural History* (Princeton: Princeton University Press, 2015), pp. 72–90.

Pettegree, Andrew and Arthur der Weduwen, *The Bookshop of the World: Making and Trading Books in the Dutch Golden Age* (New Haven: Yale University Press, 2019).

Pettegree, Andrew and Arthur der Weduwen, 'The library as a weapon of state: the pamphlet collection of Gaspar Fagel in Trinity College, Dublin', in E. Boran (ed.), *Book collecting in Ireland and Britain, 1650–1850* (Dublin: Four Courts Press, 2018), pp. 223–235.

Pettegree, Andrew and Matthew Hall, 'The Reformation and the Book: A Reconsideration', *The Historical Journal*, 47 (2004), pp. 785–808.

Pipkin, Amanda, *Rape in the Republic, 1609–1725: Formulating Dutch Identity* (Leiden: Brill, 2013).

Platt, John, *Reformed Thought and Scholasticism: The Arguments for the Existence of God in Dutch Theology, 1575–1650* (Leiden: Brill, 1982).

Poelhekke, J. J., *Frederik Hendrik: Prins van Oranje. Een biografisch drieluik* (Zutphen: Walburg Pers, 1978).

Pol, E. Hulshoff, 'The Library', in Th. H. Lunsingh Scheurleer and G. H. M. Posthumus Meyjes (eds.), *Leiden University in the Seventeenth Century: An Exchange of Learning* (Leiden: Universitaire Pers Leiden/Brill, 1975), pp. 394–459.

Pol, Frank van der, 'Religious Diversity and Everyday Ethics in The Seventeenth-Century Dutch City Kampen', *Church History*, 71 (2002), pp. 16–62.

Pollman, Judith, 'Catholics and Community in the Revolt of the Netherlands', in C. Scott Dixon, Dagmar Freist and Mark Greengrass (eds.), *Living with Religious Diversity in Early Modern Europe* (Farnham: Ashgate, 2009), pp. 183–202.

Pollman, Judith, *Catholic Identity and the Revolt of the Netherlands* (Oxford: Oxford University Press, 2011.

Pollman, Judith, 'Countering the Reformation in France and the Netherlands: Clerical Leadership and Catholic Violence 1560–1585', *Past and Present*, 190 (2006), pp. 83–120.

Pollman, Judith, '"Each Should Tend His Own Garden": Anna Bijns and the Catholic Polemic Against the Reformation', *Church History and Religious Culture*, 87 (2007): 29–45.

Pollman, Judith, 'From Freedom of Conscience to Confessional Segregation? Religious Choice and Toleration in the Dutch Republic', in Richard Bonney and D. J. B. Trim (eds.), *Persecution and Pluralism: Calvinists and Religious Minorities in Early Modern Europe 1550–1700* (Oxford: Peter Lang, 2006), pp. 123–148.

Pollman, Judith, 'Off the Record: Problems in the Quantification of Calvinist Church Discipline', *Sixteenth Century Journal*, 33 (2002), pp. 423–438.

Pollman, Judith, *Religious Choice in the Dutch Republic: The Reformation of Arnoldus Buchelius (1565–1641)* (Manchester: Manchester University Press, 1999).

Post, R. R., *The Modern Devotion: Confrontation with Reformation and Humanism* (Leiden: Brill, 1968).

Postma, Ferenc, 'Op zoek naar Franeker academisch drukwerk. Impressies van een drietal studiereizen naar Roemenie (1991–1993)', *Jaarboek van het Nederlands Genootschap van Bibliofielen*, 1 (1993), pp. 27–47.

Postma, Ferenc, 'Op zoek naar Franeker academisch drukwerk. Enkele impressies van een vierde studiereis naar Roemenië (1994)', *Jaarboek van het Nederlands Genootschap van Bibliofielen*, 2 (1994), 125–147.

Prak, Maarten, 'The Dutch Republic as a Bourgeois Society', *Low Countries Historical Review*, 125 (2010), pp. 107–139.

Prak, Maarten, *The Dutch Republic in the Seventeenth Century*, trans. Diane Webb (Cambridge: Cambridge University Press, 2002).

Puff, Helmet, *Sodomy in Reformation Germany and Switzerland 1400–1600* (Chicago: University of Chicago Press, 2003).

BIBLIOGRAPHY

Price, J. L., *Holland and the Dutch Republic in the Seventeenth Century: The Politics of Particularism* (Oxford: Clarendon Press, 1994).

Rabbie, Edwin, introduction to *Hugo Grotius: Ordinuum Hollandiae ac Westfrisiae pietas: Critical Edition with English Translation and Commentary*, ed. Edwin Rabbie (Leiden: Brill, 1995).

Rademaker, C. S. M., *Life and Work of Gerardus Joannes Vossius (1577–1649)* (Assen, The Netherlands: Van Gorcum, 1981).

Reuver, Arie de, *Sweet Communion: Trajectories of Spirituality from the Middle Ages through the Further Reformation*, trans. James A. De Jong (Grand Rapids: Baker Academic, 2007).

Robbins, Lionel, *An Essay on the Nature and Significance of Economic Science* (London: Macmillan, 1949).

Roberts, Benjamin B. and Leendert F. Groenendijk, 'Moral Panic and Holland's Libertine Youth of the 1650s and 1660s', *Journal of Family History*, 30 (2005), pp. 327–346.

Romburgh, Sophie van, (ed.), *'For My Worthy Friend Mr Franciscus Junius': An Edition of the Correspondence of Franciscus Junius F. F. (1591–1677)* (Leiden: Brill, 2004).

Rooden, Peter van, 'Van geestelijke stand naar beroepsgroep: De professionalisering van de Nederlandse predikant, 1625–1874', *Tijdschrift voor sociale geschiedenis*, 17 (1991), pp. 361–93.

Rooden, Peter van, *Theology, Biblical Scholarship and Rabbinical Studies in the Seventeenth Century* (Leiden: Brill, 1989).

Rooden, Peter van and Jan Wim Wesselius, 'Two early cases of publication by subscription in Holland and Germany: Jacob Abendana's *Mikhal Yophi* (1661) and David Cohen de Lara's *Keter Kehunna* (1668)', *Quaerendo*, 16 (1986), pp. 110–130.

Roodenburg, Herman, *Onder censuur: de kerkelijke tucht in de gereformeerde gemeente van Amsterdam, 1578–1700* (Hilversum: Verloren, 1990).

Rossem, Stijn van, *Het gevecht met de Boeken. De uitgeversstrategieën van de familie Verdussen, 1589–1889* (Antwerp: Antwerpen Universiteit Pers, 2014).

Rowen, Herbert H. *John De Witt: Statesman of the 'True Freedom'* (Cambridge: Cambridge University Press, 1986).

Rowen, Herbert H., *The Princes of Orange: The Stadholders in the Dutch Republic* (Cambridge: Cambridge University Press, 1988).

Ryrie, Alec, *Protestants: The Faith that Made the Modern World* (New York: Viking, 2017).

Schaap, Gijsbert, *Franciscus Ridderus (1620–1683): Een onderzoek naar zijn theologie, bronnen en plaats in de Nadere Reformatie* (Gouda: Vereniging voor Nederlandse Kerkgeschiedenis, 2008).

Schenkeveld-van der Dussen, Maria A., 'Cultural Participation as Stimulated by the Seventeenth-Century Reformed Church', in Ann Rigney and Douwe Fokkema (eds.), *Cultural Participation: Trends Since the Middle Ages* (Amsterdam/Philadelphia: J. Benjamins, 1993), pp. 39–49.

Schilling, Heinz. *Civic Calvinism in Northwestern Germany and the Netherlands: Six-teenth to Nineteenth Centuries* (Kirksville, MO: Sixteenth Century Journal Publishers, 1991).

Schleiner, Winfried, 'Burton's Use of praeteritio in Discussing Same-Sex Relationships', in Claude J. Summers and Ted-Larry Pebworth (eds.), *Renaissance discourses of desire* (Columbia: University of Missouri Press, 1993), pp. 159–178.

Schmidt, Benjamin, *Innocence Abroad: The Dutch Imagination and the New World, 1570–1670* (Cambridge: Cambridge University Press, 2001).

Schoneveld, Cornelis W., *Intertraffic of the Mind: Studies in Seventeenth-Century Anglo-Dutch Translation with a Checklist of Books Translated from English in Dutch, 1600–1700* (Leiden: Brill/Universitaire Pers Leiden, 1983).

Schoor, R. J. M. van de, *The Irenical Theology of Théophile Brachet de la Milletière (1588–1664)* (Leiden: Brill, 1995).

Schumpeter, Joseph A., *History of Economic Analysis* (Oxford: Oxford University Press, 1954).

Schuringa, Gregory D., 'Embracing Leer and Leven: The Theology of Simon Oomius in the Context of Nadere Reformatie Orthodoxy', (PhD Thesis, Calvin Theological Seminary, 2003).

Schuringa, Gregory D., 'Orthodoxy and Piety in the Nadere Reformatie', *Mid-America Journal of Theology*, 20 (2009), pp. 95–103.

Schwanda, Tom, 'Soul Recreation: Spiritual Marriage and Ravishment in the Contemplative-Mystical Piety of Isaac Ambrose', (PhD Thesis, Durham University, 2009).

Sepp, Christaan, *Het godgeleerd onderwijs in Nederland gedurende de 16e en 17e eeuw*, vol. 2 (Leiden: De Bruek & Smits, 1874).

Selderhuis, Herman J. and Peter Nissen, 'The Sixteenth Century', in Herman J. Selderhuis (ed.), *Handbook of Dutch Church History* (Göttingen: Vandenhoeck and Ruprecht, 2015), pp. 157–258.

Selm, Bert van, *Een menighte treffelijcke Boeken: Nederlandse boekhandelscatalogi in het begin van de zeventiende eeuw* (Utrecht: HES, 1987).

Selm, Bert van, 'The introduction of the printed book auction catalogue: Previous history, conditions and consequences of an innovation in the book trade of the Dutch Republic around 1600 – Part 1', *Quaerendo*, 15 (1985), pp. 16–53.

Selm, Bert van, 'The introduction of the printed book auction catalogue: Previous history, conditions and consequences of an innovation in the book trade of the Dutch Republic around 1600 – Part 2', *Quaerendo*, 15 (1985), pp. 115–149.

Selm, Bert van, *Inzichten en vergezichten. Zes beschouwingen over het onderzoek naar de geschiedenis van de Nederlandse boekhandel* (Amsterdam: De Buitenkant, 1992), pp. 62–77.

Selm, Bert van, 'Schama and the Library of Gulielmus Goesius (1687)', *Quaerendo*, 18 (1988), pp. 222–224.

Sierhuis, Freya, *The Literature of the Arminian Controversy: Religion, Politics, and the Stage in the Dutch Republic* (Oxford: Oxford University Press, 2015).

Sinnema, Donald, 'The Origin of the Form of Subscription in the Dutch Reformed Tradition', *Calvin Theological Journal*, 42 (2007), pp. 256–282.

Slee, J. C. van, *De geschiedenis van het Socinianisme in de Nederlanden* (Haarlem: De Erven F. Bohn, 1914).

Sluis, Jacob van, *De academie van Vriesland. Geschiedenis van de academie en het athenaeum te Franeker, 1585–1843* (Assen: Bornmeer, 2015).

Smolenaars, Marja and Ann Veenhoff, 'Hugh Goodyear and His Books' (Phd Thesis, Leiden University, 1993).

Sowards, J. K., 'Erasmus and the Education of Women', *Sixteenth Century Journal*, 13 (1982), pp. 77–89.

Spicer, Andrew, 'The Material Culture of the Lord's Supper', in Barbara Pitkin (ed.), *Semper Reformanda: John Calvin, Worship, and Reformed Traditions* (Göttingen: Vandenhoeck & Ruprecht, 2018), pp. 103–142.

Sponholz, Jesse, *The Convent of Wesel: The Event that Never was and the Invention of Tradition* (Cambridge: Cambridge University Press, 2017).

Sprunger, Keith L., *Dutch Puritanism: A History of English and Scottish Churches of the Netherlands in the Sixteenth and Seventeenth Centuries* (Leiden: Brill, 1982).

Sprunger, Keith L., *The Learned Doctor William Ames: Dutch Backgrounds of English and American Puritanism* (Urbana: University of Illinois Press, 1972).

Sprunger, Keith L., *Trumpets from the Tower: English Puritan Printing in the Netherlands, 1600–1640* (Leiden: Brill, 1994).

Spufford, Margaret, 'Literacy, trade and religion in the commercial centres of Europe', in Karel Davids and Jan Lucassen (eds.) *A Miracle Mirrored: The Dutch Republic in European Perspective* (Cambridge: Cambridge University Press, 1995), pp. 229–233.

Stanglin, Keith D., *Arminius on the Assurance of Salvation: The Context, Roots, and Shape of the Leiden Debate, 1603–1609* (Leiden: Brill, 2007).

Stanglin, Keith D. and Thomas H. McCall, *Jacob Arminius: Theologian of Grace* (Oxford: Oxford University Press, 2012).

Steen, Jasper van der, *Memory Wars in the Low Countries, 1566–1700* (Leiden: Brill, 2015).

Steinmetz, Max, 'Thomas Müntzer und die Bücher', *Zeitschrift für Geschichtswissenschaft*, 32 (1984), 603–612.

Stout, Harry S. *The New England Soul: Preaching and Religious Culture in Colonial New England* (Oxford: Oxford University Press, 1986).

Strien, C. D. van, *British Travellers in Holland during the Stuart Period: Edward Browne and John Locke as Tourists in the United Provinces* (Leiden: Brill, 1993).

Stronks, Els, *Negotiating Differences: Word, Image and Religion in the Dutch Republic* (Leiden: Brill, 2011).

Stronks, Els, 'Working the Senses with Words: The Act of Religious Reading in the Dutch Republic', in Celeste Brusati, Karl A. E. Enenkel and Walter Melion (eds.), *The Authority of the Word: Reflecting on Image and Text in Northern Europe, 1400–1700* (Leiden: Brill, 2012), pp. 667–702.

Stupperich, Robert, 'Martin Bucers Bücherverzeichnis von 1518', *Archiv für Kulturgeschichte*, 57 (1975), pp. 162–185.

Taylor, Archer, *Book Catalogues: Their Varieties and Uses* (Chicago: The Newberry Library, 1957).

Taylor, Archer, *Problems in German Literary History of the Fifteenth and Sixteenth Centuries* (New York: Modern Language Association of America, 1939).

Thomson, Jonas Thorup, 'Gejstlig læsning i det tidligt moderne Danmark – Danske sognepræsters rolle i udbredelsen af nye tanker og strømninger 1660–1810', (PhD Thesis, Aarhus University, forthcoming).

Tolsma, Marijke, 'Facing Arminius: Jacob Arminius in Portrait', in Th. Marius van Leeuwen, Keith D. Stanglin and Marijke Tolsma (eds.), *Arminius, Arminianism, and Europe: Jacob Arminius (1559/60–1609)* (Leiden: Brill, 2009), pp. 203–237.

Tocqueville, Alexis de, *Democracy in America*, ed. and trans. Harvey C. Mansfield and Delba Winthrop (Chicago: University of Chicago Press, 2000).

Touber, Jetze, 'The Culture of Catechesis and Lay Theology: Lay Engagement with the Bible in the Dutch Reformed Church, 1640–1710', *Church History and Religious Culture*, 98 (2018), pp. 31–55.

Touber, Jetze, 'God's Word in the Dutch Republic', in William J. Bulman and Robert G. Ingram (eds.), *God in the Enlightenment* (Oxford: Oxford University Press, 2016), pp. 157–175.

Trueman, Carl R., 'Puritanism as Ecumenical Theology', *Dutch Review of Church History*, 81 (2001), pp. 326–336.

Tex, Jan den, *Oldenbarnevelt* (2 vols., Cambridge: Cambridge University Press, 1973).

Uil, H., 'De Nadere Reformatie en het onderwijs in Zeeland in de zeventiende eeuw', *Documentatieblad Nadere Reformatie*, 25 (2001), pp. 1–18.

Updike, John, *In the Beauty of the Lilies* (London: Penguin Books, 1996).

Verbeek, Theo, *Descartes and the Dutch: Early Reactions to Cartesian Philosophy, 1637–1650* (Carbondale: Southern Illinois University Press, 1992).

Verbeek, Theo, 'Colvius, Andreas (1594–1671)', in Lawrence Nolan (ed.), *The Cambridge Descartes Lexicon* (Cambridge University Press, 2015), pp. 135–136.

Verkruisse, P. J., 'Holland "gedediceerd". Boekopdrachten in Holland in de 17e eeuw', *Kunst in opdracht in de Gouden Eeuw* (1991), pp. 225–242.

Vermij, Rienk, *The Calvinist Copernicans: The Reception of the New Astronomy in the Dutch Republic, 1575–1750.* (Amsterdam: Koninklijke Nederlandse Akademie van Wetenschappen, 2002).

BIBLIOGRAPHY

Verwey, Herman de la Fontaine, 'The City Library of Amsterdam in the Nieuwe Kerk 1578–1632.' *Quarendo*, 14 (1984), pp. 163–205.

Verwey, Herman de la Fontaine, 'Dr. Joan Blaeu and his sons', *Quaerendo*, 11 (1981), pp. 5–23.

Verwey, Herman de la Fontaine, 'Willem Janz Blaeu as a Publisher of Books.' *Quaraendo*, 3 (1973), pp. 141–146.

Verwey, Herman de la Fontaine, 'Willem Jansz Blaeu, "Mercator Sapiens"', in his, *Uit de wereld van het boek*, vol. 3 (Amsterdam: Nico Israel, 1979).

Visser, Piet. '"Blasphemous and Pernicious": the Role of Printers and Booksellers in the Spread of Dissident Religious and Philosophical Ideas in the Netherlands in the Second Half of the Seventeenth Century', trans. John A. Lane, *Quaerendo*, 26 (1996), pp. 303–326.

Visser, Sibbe Jan., *Samuel Naeranus (1582–1641) en Johannes Naeranus (1608–1679): Twee Remonstrantse theologen op de bres voor godsdienstige verdraagzaamheid* (Hilversum: Verloren, 2011).

Vries, Jan de and Ad van der Woude, *The First Modern Economy: Success, Failure, and Perseverance of the Dutch Economy 1500–1815* (Oxford: Oxford University Press, 1997).

Wall, Ernestine van der, 'The Dutch Enlightenment and the Distant Calvin', in Irena Backus and Philip Benedict (eds.), *Calvin and His Influence, 1509–2009* (Oxford: Oxford University Press, 2011), pp. 202–223.

Wall, Ernestine van der, 'The Religious Context of the Early Dutch Enlightenment: Moral Religion and Society', in Wiep van Bunge (ed.), *The Early Enlightenment in the Dutch Republic, 1650–1750* (Leiden: Brill, 2003), pp. 39–60.

Water, Jona Willem te, *De theologo erudito* (Leiden: Sam. en Joh. Luchtmans, 1790).

Weduwen, Arthur der, *Dutch and Flemish Newspapers of the Seventeenth Century, 1618–1700* (2 vols., Leiden: Brill, 2017).

Weduwen, Arthur der and Andrew Pettegree, *News, Business and Public Information. Advertisements and Announcements in Dutch and Flemish Newspapers, 1620–1675* (Leiden: Brill, 2020).

Weedon, Alexis, 'The Uses of Quantification', in Simon Eliot and Jonathan Rose (eds.), *A Companion to the History of the Book* (Oxford: Blackwell, 2007), pp. 33–49.

Weekhout, Ingrid, *Boekencensuur in de noordelijke Nederlanden: de vrijheid van druk-pers in de zeventiende eeuw* (The Hague: SDU Uitgevers, 1998).

Witte, Leneth, 'The English Book in the Dutch Golden Age: Three Well-Read Men and their Libraries in the Seventeenth Century', (MA Thesis, Leiden University, 2017).

Wingens, Marc, 'The Motives for creating Institutions of Higher Education in the Dutch Republic during its formative Years (1574-1648)', *Paedagogica Historica*, 34 (1998), pp. 443–456.

Worman, E. J., 'Two book-lists from the Cambridge Genizah Fragments', *Jewish Quarterly Review*, 20 (1908), pp. 450–463.

Woude, C. van der, *Sibrandus Lubbertus: Leven en Werken, in het Bijzonder naar zijn Correspondentie* (Kampen: J. H. Kok, 1963).

Zanden, Jan Luiten van, 'The Prices of the most important consumer goods, and indices of wages and the cost of living in the western part of the Netherlands, 1450–1800', available at www.iisg.nl/hpw/brenv.php (Last Accessed 29 October 2018).

ILLUSTRATIONS

109 Nicol. Clenard. cum annot.Antefign. & Fr.Sylburg. 1590. 4.Fran.
110 Dictionarium German-latin. Tiguri, 1561. 4.
111 XII. Imperatores cum Iconib. Levin.Hulfij, Franc. 1597. 4.
112 Hadr. Iunij Batavia, Leydæ 1588. 4.
113 Dom. Baudius vant Beftant, 1616. in 4. Amfterd.
114 Hiftoria Sacra & Exot. Iac. Capelli, Sedani, 1613. 4.
115 Phil. Cluveri comment. de trib. Rhen.alveis, Leydæ 1611. 4.
116 Orat. Panegyr. de Victoria Turnhout. Leydæ 1597. 4.
117 Titus Livius, Franc. 1602. Caftigat. par Ian. Grut. 4.
118 Thefaurus Ling.Sanctæ.auth. Sante Pagnino. 4.edit. Leydæ, in 8.
119 Iof.Simlerus de Helvet. Rep. Parif. 1577. 8.
120 Thefaurus Ciceronianus ling. Lat. Argentorat. 1570. 8.
421 R.Bellarmini Grammatica Hebr.Lugdun.1596. 8.
122 Opera Auguftini 5.Volum. Bafil.1569. fol·
123 Bernardus, Bafil. 1552. fol.
124 Ambrofius, Parif 1529. fol.
125 Chryfoftomus, Volum. 5. Bafil. 1539. fol.
126 Theodoretus, Vol.2. Colon. 1569 fol.
127 Origenes, Vol. 2. Bafil. 1557. fol.
128 Summa Tho.Aquinat. Vol.4.cū comment. Caietan. Lugd. 1562. fol.
129 Oecumenius, Aretas in Acta, Epiftolas, Apocal. Antv.1545. fol.
130 Theophylactus, Colon. 1531. fol.
131 Raphael Vollaterranus, Bafil.1559. fol.
132 Bafilius, Antv. 1562. fol.
133 Iuftinus Martyr, Heydelb. 1594. fol. Græcolat.
    Item Theodoret. Græc.affect. curatio.Item Acta Synod.Ephef.Græci
134 Annales Baronij Volum.12. Antv. 1610.fol.
135 Annal. continuatio Abrah. Bzovij. Col. tom. 13.14.15. An. 1621.
136 Centur.Magdeburg. HiftoriaEcclef. tom. 13.Vol. 5. Bafileæ, fol·
137 Cyprianus, Genevæ, 1593. fol.
138 Athanafius Græcolat. Vol.2. Heydelb. 1601. fol.
139 Nazianzenus Lewenklaij, Bafil. 1571, fol.
140 Damafcenus Græcolat. Bafil. 1559. fol.
141 Hilarius, Bafileæ, 1570. fol.
142 Tertullianus Pamelij, B.Rhenan. Fr.Iunij, Franek. 1597. fol.
143 ·
144 Hiftoria Ecclefiaft. tripartit. Bafil. 1543. fol.
145 Threfoor der Zeevaert Lucas Ianfz. VVagenaer, Amft. 1609. in 4.
146 Deliciæ Italicæ & index Viatorius, Vrfellis 1603. 4.

147 P.Bertij

147 P.Bertij tabulæ geograph. contractæ,edit.3. Amft. 1606. 4.
148 P.Lombardi Sentent, lib.4. Lovanij An.1556. 4.
149 Iac. Arminij Difputat, 24. Leydæ 1609. in 8.
150 Den Bijbel Dordrecht 1612. in Folio.
151 Biblia Hebraica Eliæ Hutteri, Hamburgi, 1587 fol.
152 Biblia interlinearia Xant·Pagnini & A, Ar.Montani Antw.1594 fol.
153 Hiftoire de France de Haillan. Parif, 1615. fol. tom 2.
154 Polyanthea feu Florilegium Iof.Langij, Francof. 1613. fol.
155 Hiftorie Emanuels van Meteren, Haghe 1614. fol.
156 Hiftoire de Iaques Charron. Paris 1521. fol.
157 Plutarchi Parallela, Francof. 1580. fol.
158 Diodorus Siculus Græcolat. Hanov.1604. fol.
159 Anglica, Hybernica, Normann.Cambr.Camdeni, Franc.1602 fol.
160 Opera Pauli Iovij, Volum.2. Bafil. 1578. fol, cum Elogijs.
161 VVolfgangus Lazius, Franc. 1598. fol.
162 Ant·de Herrera novus Orbis, Amft. 1622. fol.
163 Io: de Laet Nieuwe Werelt / Leyden 1625.fol.
164 Exotica Car. Clufij, Leydæ 1605. fol.
165 Werelts Spieghel door D.T.V.H Amfterd. 1621.fol.
166 Io: Becani opera, Antw. 1580. fol.
167 Æneæ Syluij Opera,Bafileæ. fol.
168 Bibliotheca Iof.Simleri, Tiguri, 1574. fol.
169 Chronica Hartmanni Schedel, Auguftæ 1497. fol.
170 Acta Pacificationis Colonienf. Lugduni. 1580. 4·
171 Belegeringhe van Ooftende/Leyden 1614 in 4.
172 Vanden Doop Chrifti door Iac.Kimedoncium / Middelb.
    1589. in 4.   (1616. 4.
173 Iac.Wefenbeeck vanden ftaet der Religie in Nederlant.ibid.
174 Van.Heynfij Nederduytfe Poëmata/ Amfterd. 1618.in 4.
175 Effigies Theologorum, Hagæ, 1602. fol.
176 Annales Guil. Camdeni, Franc. 1616. in 8.
177 Defcriptio utriufque Germaniæ, Antverp. 1580.8.
178 Theod.Bezæ tractat.Theolog. tomis 3. volum. 1. Genevæ 1576. fol.
179 M.Bucerus in Pfal.Iudic. & Zophoniam, 1554 fol. Parif.
180 M. Bucerus in 4 Euangeliftas, ibidem, 1553. fol.
181 Io: Mercerus in Genefin & 5.minores Prophetas, Gen. 1598. fol.
182 Io.Simlerus in Exod, Mercer. in Iob.Prov.Ecclef.Cant. Tiguri, fol.
183 No.Tek.

FIGURE 1.1   The fourth and fifth pages of the Demetrius library catalogue. Here, folios, quartos and octavos are intermixed, unlike almost all other catalogues. *AC Daniel Demetrius 1628* (Dordrecht: Peeter Verhagen, 1628), USTC 1122269

IMAGE FROM BSCO. SCANNED COPY: COPENHAGEN, KB: 79II 39 2:18

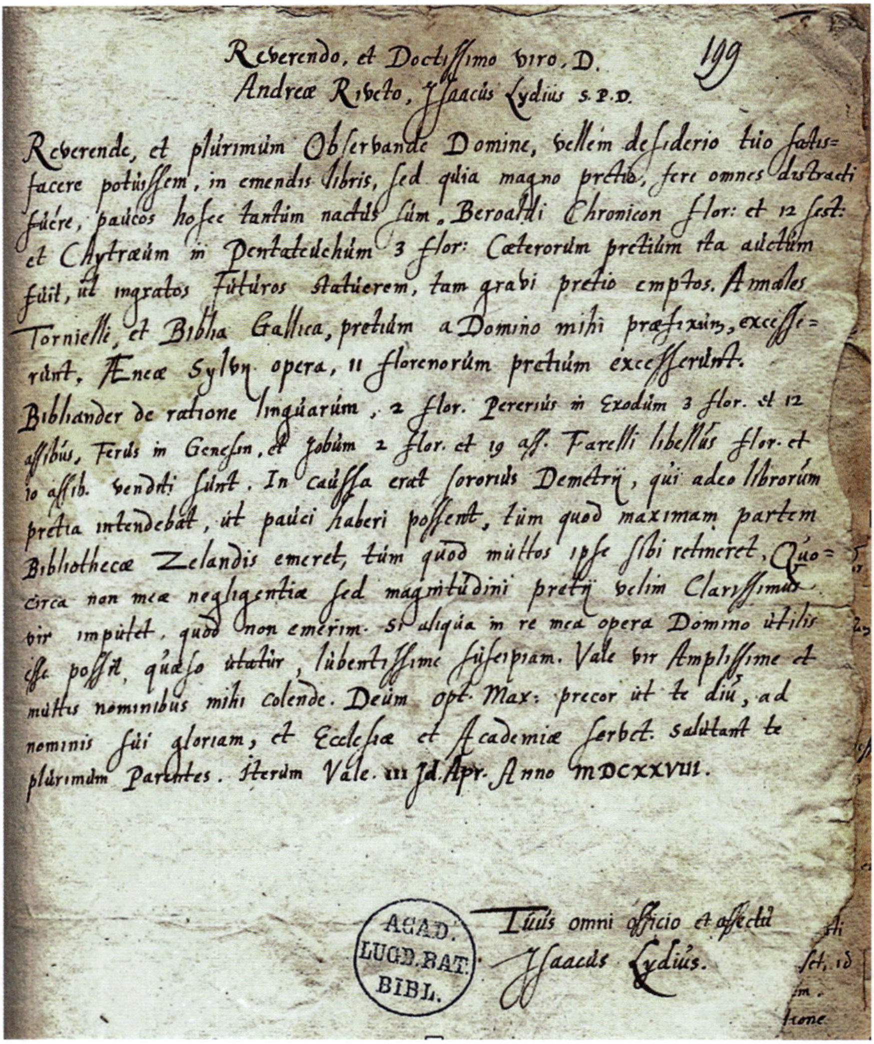

FIGURE 1.2 Isaac Lydius' letter to André Rivet, explaining how he was unable to procure books from the auction of fellow Dordrecht minister Daniel Demetrius' books in 1628. UB Leiden, ms. BPL 285 Bf199r
WITH PERMISSION FROM BIJZONDERE COLLECTIES-UNIVERSITEIT LEIDEN, AND WITH THANKS TO KASPER VAN OMMEN FOR PROCURING THE SCAN

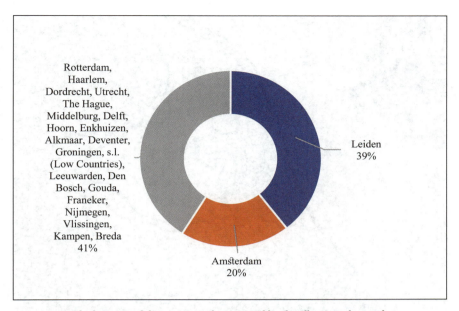

FIGURE 1.3 The location of the auctions of ministerial book collections during the seventeenth century. Leiden, given its geographical and cultural contexts, far surpasses all other places in the number of auctions that took place within its city walls

256 ILLUSTRATIONS

FIGURE 1.4 The cities in which the libraries of Dutch ministers were auctioned during the seventeenth century
ORIGINAL MAP IS REPRODUCED FROM JOHANNES JANSONNIUS, *BELGII FOEDERATI NOVA DESCRIPTIO* (AMSTERDAM: JOHANNES JANSONNIUS, 1658). AVAILABLE AT WIKIMEDIA.ORG

ILLUSTRATIONS 257

FIGURE 1.5 The cities, towns and villages where the ministers whose libraries were auctioned resided
ORIGINAL MAP IS REPRODUCED FROM JOHANNES JANSONNIUS, *BELGII FOEDERATI NOVA DESCRIPTIO* (AMSTERDAM: JOHANNES JANSONNIUS, 1658). AVAILABLE AT WIKIMEDIA.ORG

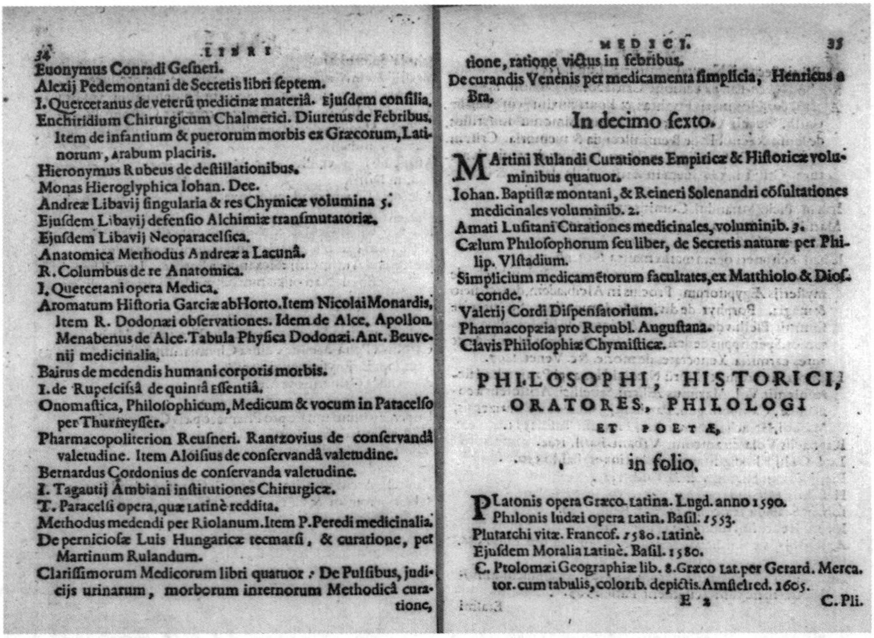

258 ILLUSTRATIONS

LIBRI

Euonymus Conradi Gesneri.
Alexij Pedemontani de Secretis libri septem.
I. Quercetanus de veterû medicinæ materiâ. Ejusdem consilia.
Enchiridium Chirurgicum Chalmerici. Diuretus de Febribus.
 Item de infantium & puerorum morbis ex Græcorum, Latinorum, Arabum placiris.
Hieronymus Rubeus de destillationibus.
Monas Hieroglyphica Iohan. Dee.
Andreæ Libavij singularia & res Chymicæ volumina 5.
Ejusdem Libavij defensio Alchimiæ transmutatoriæ.
Ejusdem Libavij Neoparacelsica.
Anatomica Methodus Andreæ a Lacunâ.
R. Columbus de re Anatomica.
I. Quercetani opera Medica.
Aromatum Historia Garciæ abHorto. Item NicolaiMonardis.
 Item R. Dodonæi observationes. Idem de Alce. Apollon.
 Menabenus de Alce. Tabula Physica Dodonæi. Ant. Beuvenij medicinalia.
Bairus de medendis humani corporis morbis.
I. de Rupescifsâ de quintâ essentiâ.
Onomastica, Philosophicum, Medicum & vocum in Paracelso per Thurneysser.
Pharmacopoliterion Reusneri. Rantzovius de conservandâ valetudine. Item Aloisius de conservandâ valetudine.
Bernardus Cordonius de conservanda valetudine.
I. Tagautij Ambiani institutiones Chirurgicæ.
T. Paracelsi opera, quæ latinè reddita.
Methodus medendi per Riolanum. Item P.Peredi medicinalia.
De perniciosæ Luis Hungaricæ tecmarsi, & curatione, per Martinum Rulandum.
Clarissimorum Medicorum libri quatuor : De Pulsibus, judicijs urinarum, morborum inremorum Methodicâ curatione,

MEDICI.

tione, ratione victus in febribus.
De curandis Venenis per medicamenta simplicia, Henricus a Bra.

In decimo sexto.

Martini Rulandi Curationes Empiricæ & Historicæ voluminibus quatuor.
Iohan. Baptistæ montani, & Reineri Solenandri cõsultationes medicinales voluminib. 2.
Amati Lusitani Curationes medicinales, voluminib. 3.
Cælum Philosophorum seu liber, de Secretis naturæ per Philip. Vlstadium.
Simplicium medicamêtorum facultates, ex Matthiolo & Diosc. coride.
Valerij Cordi Dispensatorium.
Pharmacopæia pro Republ. Augustana.
Clavis Philosophiæ Chymisticæ.

PHILOSOPHI, HISTORICI, ORATORES, PHILOLOGI
ET POETÆ,
in folio.

Platonis opera Græco.latina. Lugd. anno 1590.
 Philonis ludæi opera latin. Basil. 1553.
Plutatchi vitæ. Francof. 1580. latinè.
 Ejusdem Moralia latinè. Basil. 1580.
C. Ptolomæi Geographiæ lib. 8. Græco lat. per Gerard. Mercator. cum tabulis, colorib. depictis. Amstelred. 1605.

E 2   C.Pli.

FIGURE 1.6 The end of the medical section of Halsbergius' catalogue, and the start of the miscellaneous works. Elzevier separated the books into theology, jurisprudence, medical texts, a miscellaneous section called 'philosophy, history, oratory, and philology', music, another section of history, then vernacular texts, French, Italian and Spanish, German and Dutch, followed by unbound books, and an appendix. All of the books within these categories were then divided into size. AC *Johannes Halsbergius 1607* (Leiden: Louis Elzevier, 1607), USTC 1122231

IMAGE FROM BSCO. SCANNED FROM COPENHAGEN, KB: 79II 39 2:8

ILLUSTRATIONS 259

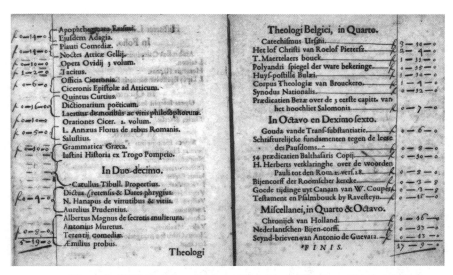

FIGURE 1.7   The end of Wilhelm Merwy's historical books, and the start of his Dutch books.
AC *Wilhelm Merwy 1636* (Leiden: Jan Pietersz. Waelpot, 1636), USTC 1027540
IMAGE FROM BSCO. SCANNED FROM THE HAGUE, KB: VERZ. CAT. 3463

FIGURE 2.1   Print was seen as a necessary tool for the combat of Roman Catholic error. Here, the printed Bible stands alone one the scales of truth. *De Bijbel op de weegschaal*, anonymous, 1677–1693 (Jochem Bormeester). Rijksmuseum RP-P-OB-78.823

FIGURE 2.2 In larger communities, godly reading was even central to taking communion. While reading, the believers wait patiently to take the supper. Frontispiece to *Het Rechte gebruyck van des Heeren H Avontmael* (Amsterdam: J. Spanseerder, [ca. 1730]). Universiteitsbibliotheek Utrecht – Bijzonder Collectie: EAG 21
WITH PERMISSION

60 Worstelende Kercke

komen het Koninkrijcke der Hemelen: dat
de mensche gebooren wort sonder erf-son-
de: dat de sonde maer door navolginge
overgaet van mensche tot mensche. Dat de
mensche door hem selven heeft krachten ge-
noegh om Godts Wetten te gehoorsamen.
-- Van de genade leerden sy datmen tot
de genade der wedergeboorte komen kan
door natuerlijcke krachten, eijschende,
soeckende, kloppende. Dat de genade gegeven wort na de verdiensten der menschen.
-- Van de Prædestinatie seyden sy/ dat
Godt maer de soodaanige heeft verkooren
dewelcke hij voorsagh dat waerdigh waren
de verkiesinge, en tot den eynde toe souden
den volharden. Dat het getal der uytverkoorne wordt vermindert en vermeerdert:
dat die kinderen verlooren gaen, jongh
stervende die Godt voorsagh dat qualijck leven souden, en dat die behouden worden,
die hy sagh dat wel leven souden, indien sy
bejaerdt wierden. Dat de uytverkoorne
konnen de genade of behouden of verliesen,
soo als sy willen.
-- Van de Rechtvaerdigmaeckinge leerden sy. Dat die geschiet ten allen tijde uyt
de goede wercken. Dat door natuerlijcke
krachten, sonder behulp der genade veele
niet alleen voor de komste Christi, maer
oock voor de Wet, sijn gekomen tot volle
reyne, en volmaeckte gerechtigheydt, en
verdient hebben kinderen Godts te worden.
-- Van den wech ten leven, datter zijn
drie wegen, door de Wet der nature, door
de Wet Mosis, en door de Wet Christi.
-- Van het geloove seyden sy. 'tGeloove
is in de macht der menschen. Voortijdts
wierden de menschen zaligh alleen door de
Wet: 't geloove is een werck der nature.
-- Van de goede wercken: dat die
vruchten zijn van de nature. Dat de mensche
kan volkomene goede wercken doen, ende
soo, tot volmaecktheydt komen, ensonder
sonde leven.
-- Van de Rijckdom, dat de Rijcke
moeten alle haer goederen afstaen, of datse
niet komen konnen in het Koninckrijcke der
Hemelen.
Dese ketterpen namen grooten voort-
gangh in Engelandt/ Vranckrijck/ en in
veel andere landen/ ende veel Leeraren en

Bisschoppen stemden deselvige toe.

Cælestinus. Anno 426.
Desen Roomschen Bisschop dede veel
dingen by de Misse, als de Introitus upt
Psalmen/ het Graduale, of offertorium. Crisp.

Nestorius Anno 429.
Desen man was geworden Bisschop
van Constantinopolen, zijnde seer wel
spreeckende. Desen Leeraer hoorde pre-
dicken Anastasium Ouderlingh/ die seyde
en sterck dreef/ dat Maria niet most ge-
naemt worden Theotokos, Godt-barende,
ende als dat veelen waer vreemt in de ooren
klonck/ soo nam Nestorius op dat te ver-
dedigen/ ende verviel soo tot dese dwae-
linge.
-- Dat in Christo zijn twee persoonen,
de eene, de Zoone Godts, ende de andere,
de Zoone van Maria, ende dat de Zoone
Godts sigh vereenight hadde met de Zoone
des menschen, niet in eenigheydt des persoons, maer (1) door inwoonende genade, Straet.
gelijck Godt met de geloovige vereenight Theo.
is, doch evenwel op een heerlijcker manie- p. 506
re. (2) Door de eenigheydt der affectie, gelijck tusschen man en vrouw. (3) Door eenigheydt of conjunctie der werckinge, voor
soo veel de Soone des menschen is een Instrument, waer door de Zoone Godts
werckt. (4) Door mede deylinge van excel-
lentie, voor soo veel als de goddelijcke ee-
re, die de Soone Godts toekomt, oock
eenighsints den Zoone des menschen wort
gegeven.
Dese dwalinge wierdt seer wijdt en breet
verspreyt/ ende van veel Leeraren en Bisschoppen aengenomen.

Prosper. Anno 433.
Desen vermaerden Leeraer der Kercke
hadde oock zijn feylen/ ontrent de goede
wercken/ want dus schrijft hy. Nochte
de wercken sonder 't geloove; noch 't gelove alleen sonder de wercken, rechtvaerdight. l.1.de
ô Wat een korte offerhande is de Aelmis vita
die den mensche van binnen en van buyten Cont.
reynight! De Aelmis verlost van de doodt, c.19.
en

FIGURE 2.3 The Rotterdam minister, Franciscus Ridderus set himself the task of helping
the church struggle against error. Here, Ridderus includes a brief article on the
early church heretic. Franciscus Ridderus, *Worstelende Kercke, ofte Historische
Vertooninge van het bestreden geloove der ware Christenen* (Rotterdam: Weduwe
van Aernoud Leers, 1679), USTC 1815770 p. 60
FROM THE AUTHOR'S PRIVATE COLLECTION

FIGURE 3.1 *Jacobus Arminius Oudewaterae natus*. Rijksmuseum RP-P-OB-55.251

FIGURE 3.2 *Portret van Balthasar Lydius*. Rijksmuseum RP-P-1883-A-7068

FIGURE 3.3 *Portret van Guiljelmus Saldenus.* Rijksmuseum RP-P-OB-17.521

FIGURE 3.4 *Portret van Tobias Govertsz. van den Wyngaert op 80-jarige leeftijd.* Rijksmuseum RP-P-BI-1837

FIGURE 3.5 *Portret van Franciscus Ridderus.* Rijksmuseum RP-P-OB-23.811

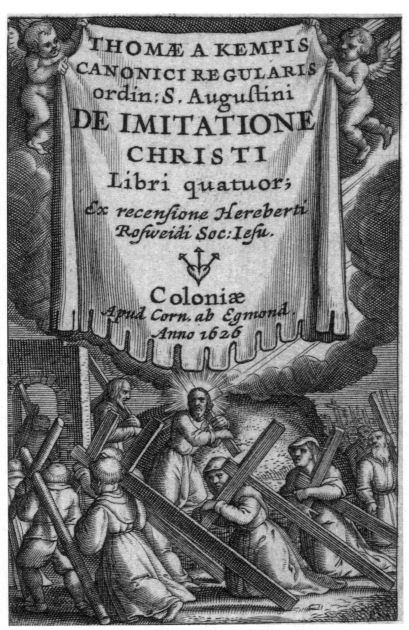

FIGURE 4.1 The title page for a 1626 edition of the *Imitation of Christ* likely printed in Amsterdam by Willem Jansz Blaeu, with a false Cologne imprint. A copy of this work was owned by the Remonstrant minister and medical doctor Justinus van Assche. *Christus en een gevolg kruisdragers Titelpagina voor T. à Kempis, De imitatione Christi,* Pieter Serwouters, 1626 Rijksmuseum RP-P-1886-A-10523

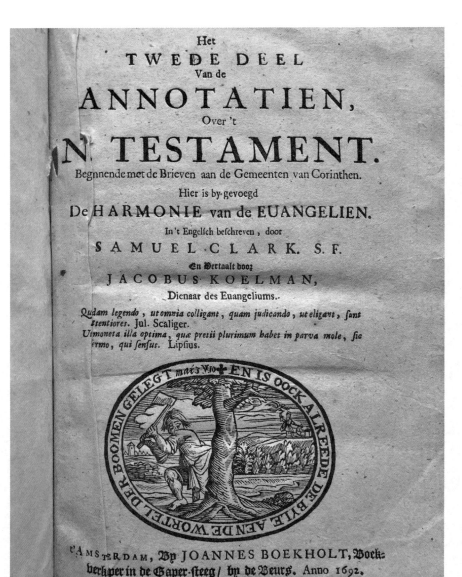

FIGURE 4.2 The title page from the Dutch translation of Samuel Clark's *Het tweede deel van de annotation, over 't N. Testament* (Amsterdam: Johannes Boekholt, 1692), USTC 1822720

FROM THE AUTHOR'S PERSONAL COLLECTION

ILLUSTRATIONS

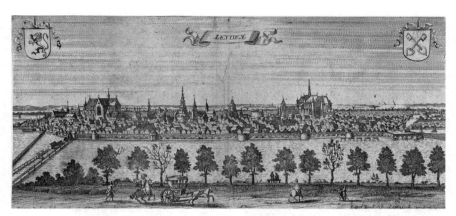

FIGURE 5.1 Leiden's two oldest churches, the Hooglandse Kerk and the Pieterskerk dominate the town's skyline. *Gezicht op Leiden*, Gaspar Bouttats, after Jan Peeters, 1675–1679. Rijksmuseum RP-P-BI-4251

FIGURE 5.2 Title-page by Pieter Holsteyn from Ridderus' *Historisch Sterf-huys*, 1665. Rijksmuseum RP-P-1893-A-18048

ILLUSTRATIONS

FIGURE 6.1   Title-page of the second edition of Johannes Lomeier, *De bibliothecis* (Utrecht: Johannes Ribbius, 1680), USTC 1816644. [Special Collections, University of Amsterdam, O 61-2850]

Index

Aarlanderveen 66
Abendana, Jacob 76
Abrahamsz, Galenus 120
Aemilius, Egbertus 94
Alkmaar
　City library 83
Alting, Heinrich 131
Amama, Sixtinus 77
Ambrosian library 195
Ames, William 15
Ampzing, Samuel 74
Amsterdam 183
　Bibles 114
Amyraut, Moïses 135
Anslaar, Guilielmus 76
Antwerp
　Bibles 114
Aquinas, Thomas 61, 110, 158
Aristotle 164–165, 181
Arlanderveen 148
Arminius, Jacob 15, 61, 68, 146, 199
　Astronomical books 186
　Controversy and books
　　Arminius 108–111
Assche, Justinus van 186
　Medical books 177
Assembly at Wesel 110
Auction Catalogues
　Historiography 4–8
　Leiden 18
　Methodology 8–11
　University of Leiden 19
Augustine 6
Aurelius, Marcus 167

Badius, Otto 164
Bahia, Brazil 51
Banbury 140
Banned books 47
Barentsz, Jan
　Medical books 176
Baronius, Caesar 66
Bartholinus, Thomas 176
Basel
　Bibles 114

Bastingius, Wilhelmus 61
Battus, Carolus 176
Bayle, Pierre
　The Lydius Family 67, 69
Bekker, Balthazar 46, 171
Belgic Confession 117
Bellarmine, Robert 110
Berdenis, Henricus 146
Bergen op Zoom 87
Bertius, Petrus 59, 109
Beukens, Wilhelmus 101
Beverwijck, Johan van 175, 178
Bibliothecae Zeelandia 2
Biesen, Jacob van 150
Binnenhof 11
Blaeus 54
Blaeu, Willem Jansz 126
Blanckhart, Roger 164
Boeken, Johannes 173
　Medical books 176
Bois, Jacob du 134
　Astronomy 186
Bontekoe, Cornelis 175
Bontekoe, Willem Ysbrantsz 170
Booth, Cornelis 85
　Franciscus Junius II 85
Borardus, Johannes 20
Borre, Adrianus van den 139, 167
Bouma, Gellius de 37
Brakel, Wilhelmus à 35, 39, 74
　Catholic books 126
Brandt, Marten Jansz 53
Breda 51
Brès, Guy de 117
Brown, Thomas 84
Bruyn, Gualtherus de 25, 193
Bucer, Martin 133
Buchelius, Arnoldus 100
Buchell, Huybert van 85
Bullinger, Heinrich 133, 158

Calendrini, Cesar 25
Calvin, John 133, 134, 158
Cameron, John 138
Cardinal Borromeo 195

INDEX

Carleton, Dudley   45–46, 93–94, 151, 174
Case, John   181
Cassiodorus   158
Chrysostom, John   2, 93–94, 158, 178
Church and Education   38–41
Church discipline   47
Classical books
    Printing locations   165
Classical works   163
Classis of Leiden   184
Classis of Utrecht   40
Cleaver, Jacob   88
Cloppenburg, Johannes   88, 183–184
Cocceius, Johannes   54, 76, 105, 133–134, 142
Colvius, Andreas   84, 98
Comet of 1664   185
Commelin, Hieronymus   110
Corput, Abraham vander   75
Corputius, Henricus   75
Corvinus, Johannes Arnoldus   59, 193
Courcelles, Etienne de   60, 73
Couwenhoven, Theodorus van   199
Crellius, Johannes   152
Cuijk   176
Cuilemann, Jacob   105, 114–115, 139
Cunaeus, Petrus   193
Curcellaeus, Stephanus   73

Danish ministers   7
Dapper, Olfert   170, 172, 174
Dathenus, Petrus   118
Delft   176
Delft Bible   114
Demetrius, Daniel   1–3, 11, 84, 146
    Medical books   176
Den Briel   28
Descartes   25, 56, 64, 77–78, 160, 191–192
Deux Aes Bible   115
Deventer   19, 23, 42, 109, 117
Diest, Heinrich von   38, 71, 159
Dijk, Johannes van   115
Diodati, Giovanni   115
Doctors and their libraries   101–103
Dokkum
    City library   196
Dordrecht   2, 19, 20, 21, 25, 32, 42, 66, 75, 84,
        88, 91, 97, 98, 145, 154, 175–176, 178, 182
Dousa, Janus   110
Dutch stranger church   141

Education   17–18
Eliot, T. S.   151
Elzeviers   54
Emden   34
Emmerich   88
Emmius, Ubbo   111
English to Dutch translation   142–143
Enkhuizen   44, 70
    City library   84
Episcopius, Simon   168
Erasmus   17, 113, 134
Eton College   93

Fabius, Guilielmus   74, 113, 115
Fernel, Jean François   175
Format   92
Foxe, John   34
Frankfurt Book Fair   13
Frederick of Norway   42
Fredrick Henry   160
Froben   94

Gaillard, Jacobus   94, 97
Galileo   186
Gelliers, Carel de   17
Geneva
    Bibles   114
Göllnitz, Abraham   174
Gomarus, Franciscus   20, 71, 108, 115
    Catholic books   111
    Disputations   60
    Division of catalogue   23
Gorinchem   87
Gouda
    City library   86
Graaf, Christopher de   84
Grevinchovius, Nicolaus   42
Gribius, Petrus   9, 146
Groningen
    Ministers   40
Gronovius, Johannes Friedrich   181
Grotius, Hugo   58, 60, 134–138, 161, 184, 200
    André Rivet   135
Gruterus, Samuel   61, 173
Guicciardini, Lodovico   15

Haarlem   176
    magistrates of   74
Hales, John   139

INDEX

Halsbergius, Johannes 22
  Medical books 177
Hamel, Theodorus 104
Harderwijk, 38
Harmelen 197
Heidanus, Abraham 91–93, 113
  Astronomical books 186
Heidelberg Catechism 117
Heinsius, Daniel 58
Herrera, Antonio de 174
Heurnius, Johannes 179
Heurnius, Justus 75, 174
Hildersham, Arthur 150
Hilten, Caspar van 50
Hobbes, Thomas 47
Hommius, Festus 59, 73
Hooft, Cornelis Pieterszoon 14
Hoornbeeck, Johannes 94, 173
  Classical books 166
Hulsius, Antonius
  Jacob Abendana 78
Hyperius, Andreas 158

Illustrious School at Deventer 71
Illustrious School at Harderwijk 71
Il Pastor Fido 98
Ireneus Philalethius. *See* Teellinck,
  Ewout 50
Isenhagius, Guilielmus 88

Jacobsz, Laurens 83
Jansz, Broer 50
Jean François, Fernel 179
Junius, Franciscus 75, 105, 139

Kechel, Samuel Karl 186
Keckermann, Bartholomäus 189, 191
Kempis, Thomas à 125, 126
Kepler, Johannes 187
Klundert 32
Koelman, Jacob 49, 96, 150
Kuchlinus, Johannes 94

Laet, Johannes de 78, 172
Langle, Jean-Maximilian de 78, 127
Languages 96–99
Lansbergius, Philip 187
Laovicus, Aegidius F. 62

Lasco, John à 95
Laud, William 141
Laurentius, Thomas 32, 88, 161
  Medical books 177
Lawyers and their libraries 100–101
Leffen, Pieter 24
Leiden
  Bibles 114
Leipzig Book Fair 13
Leupenius, Petrus 73
Leur 20
liefhebbers 153
Linschoten, Jan Huygen van 170
Literacy Rates 15
Lomeier, Johannes 195
London Polyglot Bible 113
Lord's Supper
  Reading 43–44
Lubbertus, Sibrandus 25, 89–90, 129
  Copernicanism 189
Lutherans 3
Luther, Martin 33, 130, 132, 134, 178
Lydius, Balthazar 2, 25, 67, 121
  Dordrecht city library 83
  Medical books 177
Lydius, Jacob 67, 88, 105, 114, 131, 145, 182
  André Rivet 131
  Classical books 167
Lydius, Johannes 2, 66
Lydius, Martinus 76
  Amsterdam city library 83
  Sons 69, 97

Magnus, Albertus 110
Manilius, Marcus 187
Manutius, Aldus 13
Maps 173
Marchand, Prosper 80
Maresius, Samuel 120, 182
Marnix, Philips van 12
Mastricht, Petrus van 191
Maurius, Johannes 55
Mazarine library 195
Medemblik 117
Meer, Abraham van der 101
Meer, Dirck van der 87
Meer, Gerrit de 170
Melanchthon, Philip 6, 129, 131–132, 134

INDEX

Melekh, Shelemo ben 76
Mellinus, Abraham 33, 171
Mennonite ministers 3, 95
Merchants' Guild in Amsterdam 68
Merwy, Wilhelm 22, 74, 88–89, 91, 199
Meurs, Jacob van 174
Michiels, Jacob 34
Mijnsheerenland 32–33
Milletière, Théophile Brachet de la 127
Ministerial salaries 70
Ministers as public figures 3
Ministers' portraits 106
Minnertsga 89
Monastery of Gembloux
    Library 196
Montanus, Arnoldus 174
Muiden 23
Münster, Sebastian 187
Musculus, Wolfgang 129

Naeranus, Samuel 59
Nassau, Maurits of 51
New Netherland
    Education 41
Newspapers 49
Nicolson, William 86
Niel, Jacobus de 87
Nijmegen 70

Odoorn 32
Oosterbierum 89
Ortelius, Abraham 172
Oudaan, Joachim 75, 120
Oudewater 66
Ouwens, Nicolaas 87
Owen, John 46, 143

Paets, Jan 58
Paris
    Bibles 114
Pascal, Blaise 190
Pechlinus, Johannes 105, 171
    Astronomical books 186
    Medical books 177
Peenen, Marcus van 105
Picherel, Pierre 59
Piscator, Johannes 129
Pitatus, Petrus 191

Poitiers 140
Polyander, Johannes 97
Port, Gerardus van der 105, 173
Pours, Jeremie du 112, 168
Price
    John Chrysostom, Opera 14
Proclus 187
Ptolemy 187
Puttershoek 32, 88, 161

Quewellerius, Gerson 19

Rauwer, Johannes 197
Ravesteyn, Paulus Aertsz, van 115
Reformed Church of the Netherlands 3
Religion and Literacy 16, 17
Remonstrants 41–43
Remonstrant seminary in Amsterdam 60
Ridderus, Franciscus 28–30, 47–48, 69, 74,
    105
    Astronomy 189
    Catholic books 124
    Classical books 166
    English books 144
    Medical books 177
    Travel narratives 169–170
Rivet, André 2, 11, 20, 57, 59–60, 75, 94, 113,
    159
    Advertisement of catalogue 24
    Astronomical books 189
    Bibles 116
    Catholic books 127, 128, 167
    Descartes 77
    Libri miscellani 160
    Lutheran books 131
    Marin Mersenne 76, 190
    Pecherel 59
    Rivet 10
    Salary 71
    The Elzeviers 59, 80
    William II 9
Robbins, Lionel 181
Roman Catholics 3
Rosiere, Josephus van de 88
Rotterdam 15, 19, 28, 30, 39, 42, 48, 55,
    74–75
    City library 83
Rouen booksellers 78

Sacrobosco, Johannes de   186
Sagard, Gabriel   173
Saldenus, Guijelmus   44, 159
Salmasius, Claudius   181
Sammonicus, Serenus   176
Sarrau, Claude   10, 58, 135–138
Saumaise, Claude de   58
Scaliger, Joseph   15, 89
Sceperus, Jacobus   52
Schermerhorn   28
Schoock, Martinus   56–58
Schoonderoort, Daniel   87
Schoonhoven   174
Schulerus, Carolus   20
Schurman, Anna Maria van   75
Selden, John   190
's Gravenmoer   87
Sibelius, Caspar   109, 115
Sibema, Bouritius   67
Simonides, Simon   182
Sint Anthoniepolder   33, 171
Sir Henry Saville   93
Slade, Matthew   93, 151, 174
Sluis   150
Smout, Adrian   41, 99, 171
Sneek   31
Snellius, Willebrord   190
Socinian books   151
Solinus, Gaius Julius   187
Somer, Bernard   9, 88, 105, 115, 161, 171
Sozzini, Fausto   152
Statenbijbel   115
Statencollege   78, 109, 196
States of Holland   163
Stermont, Jacob   157
Streso, Caspar   120
Strijen   87
Study of English   143–144
Swartepaert, Adrian   119
Synod of Dordrecht 1578   31
Synod of Dort
    Education   40
Synopsis Purioris Theologiae   166
    Usury   182

Taffin, Jean   63, 126
Tallinn   7
Teellinck, Ewout   50
Teellinck, Willem   41, 52, 53, 140

Testard, Paul   138
The Council of Trent   33, 80
The Hague   70, 120, 157
Theological Education   37
The Reformed Church in the Netherlands
    Ministerial Candidates   31
the Remonstrant Controversy   118
The Republics   171
Thirty Years War   50, 183
Thysius, Anthonius   71, 114, 182
Tiberius, Thomas   104
Tocqueville, Alexis de   155
Trelcatius, Lucas   61, 134
Trigland, Jacob   53, 121, 183

Udemans, Godefridus   41, 76, 125, 134,
    153–154
    Astronomy   191
    Dancing   175
    Public intellectual   155
University libraries   84
University of Groningen   195
University of Leiden   2
    Library   12
    Senate   163
University of Utrecht   195
Updike, John   151
Urban and rural ministers   88
Ursinus, Zacharius   118, 129
Usury   181–182
Utrecht   38, 70
    City library   85
    Illustrious School   85

Verhagen, Peeter   1
Virmigli, Peter Martyr   61, 111
Visscher, Adolph   114
    Advertisement of catalogue   24
Voetius, Gisbertus   6, 25, 38, 46, 54, 56, 73,
    76, 94, 159
    Acquiring books   80–83
    Astronomy   185
    Bibles   122
    Catholic books   123
    Economic books   182
    English books   147
    Kempis, Thomas à   125
    Thomas Hobbes   47
    Usury   180

INDEX

Volkelius, Johannes 152
Voltelen, Salomon 162, 164
Voort, Martinus van Halewyn van der 84
Vorstius, Conrad 61, 70, 119, 199
Vossius, Gerardus 66, 77, 85
Vries, Meyerus van 32

Waesberge, Johannes van 56
Walaeus, Antonius 113, 129
   Seminarium Indicum 172
Walloon 19, 63, 72, 78, 87, 97, 112, 168
Wilhelmus, Wilhelm 196
William II
   André Rivet 160
Williams, Daniel 25

Witsius, Herman 44–45, 159
Witsius, Cornelius 44
Witte, Petrus de 36, 39
   Delft Thunderclap 185
Wittewrongel, Petrus 130
Woerden 154
Wtenbogaart, Johannes 48, 58, 97, 139

Yarmouth 144

Zeeland 2, 20, 41, 47, 53, 76, 101, 140–143, 153
Zoutelande 142
Zutphen 195
Zwingli, Ulrich 131–133